REDEFINING THE IMMIGRANT SOUTH

REDEFINING THE IMMIGRANT SOUTH

. . . .

INDIAN AND PAKISTANI IMMIGRATION TO HOUSTON DURING THE COLD WAR

Uzma Quraishi

Published in association with The William P. Clements
Center for Southwest Studies, Southern Methodist University,
by The University of North Carolina Press, Chapel Hill

Designed by April Leidig
Set in Minion by Copperline Book Services, Inc.
Manufactured in the United States of America

The University of North Carolina Press has been a member
of the Green Press Initiative since 2003.

Cover illustrations: Sharpstown Design Concept (1965), courtesy of the Houston
Public Library, Houston Metropolitan Research Center; Reading Room in the USIS
Bombay Library (1954), courtesy of the National Archives at College Park, Maryland.

Library of Congress Cataloging-in-Publication Data
Names: Quraishi, Uzma, author.
Title: Redefining the immigrant South : Indian and Pakistani
immigration to Houston during the Cold War / Uzma Quraishi.
Other titles: New directions in southern studies.
Description: Chapel Hill : Published in association with The William P. Clements
Center for Southwest Studies, Southern Methodist University, by the University of
North Carolina Press, 2020. | Series: New directions in southern studies |
Includes bibliographical references and index.
Identifiers: LCCN 2019053524 | ISBN 9781469655185 (cloth) |
ISBN 9781469655192 (paperback) | ISBN 9781469655208 (ebook)
Subjects: LCSH: University of Houston—History—20th century. | South Asians—
Texas—Houston. | Houston (Tex.)—Emigration and immigration. | India—
Emigration and immigration. | Pakistan—Emigration and immigration.
Classification: LCC JV7100.H68 Q87 2020 | DDC 305.8914/110764141109045—dc23
LC record available at https://lccn.loc.gov/2019053524

For Houston's Desi community

CONTENTS

FIGURES, TABLES, AND MAPS

FIGURES

TABLES

MAPS

ACKNOWLEDGMENTS

. . . .

In completing this book as it has evolved over many years, I have collected far too many debts to acknowledge sufficiently here, but I will do my best. My apologies for inadvertently overlooking anyone not recognized here.

My first real foray into a sustained and scholarly consideration of history took place at the University of Houston. Joe Pratt inspired my love of history and teaching through a U.S. history survey many years before I embarked on a graduate career in history. He and Marty Melosi encouraged my interest in urban history, especially exploring the rich history of my city, Houston. Steven Mintz believed in my project from its inception, while Landon Storrs and Gerald Horne provided sound guidance throughout. Xiaoping Cong and Sarah Fishman held my writing and argumentation to the highest standard, pushing me to strengthen both. Mohsen Mobasher and Jose Martinez helped me connect immigration history to the sociology and theory of immigration, passing on knowledge that I continue to draw on today. Kairn Klieman immediately welcomed me, becoming both a mentor and a friend. Daphyne Pitre in the history office facilitated everything with a smile. Clarissa Hinojosa, Ann Maley Kapp, J. R. Wilson, and Jeff Womack all provided good friendship and support.

At Rice University, John Boles and Kerry Ward were careful, conscientious, and enthusiastic mentors, both providing an endless well of support and sage advice. I thank Michael Emerson for his intellectual generosity and invaluable insights. I owe a debt of gratitude to others who helped make my project whole: Carl Caldwell, Stephanie Camp, Ed Cox, Allen Matusow, Caleb McDaniel, Martin Wiener, and Jack Zammito. For their support, I am deeply grateful to Lisa Balabanlilar, Alex Byrd, Becky Goetz, Randal Hall, Bethany Johnson, Elora Shehabuddin, and Lora Wildenthal. Ed and Alex encouraged me from the onset, seeing value in my research. I am grateful for the help of Department of History staff members Bev Konzem, Paula Platt, Lisa Tate, and Rachel Zepeda. I appreciate the friendship of so many at Rice, especially Andrew Baker, David Getman, Mercy Harper, Symbol Lai, Terri Laws, Sarah Paulus, and Elizabeth Rodwell. Writing partners Allison Madar and Jim Wainwright made the process more enjoyable. I will always value their steadfast example, scholarly rigor, and steady companionship.

Beyond history, the Rice campus offered up its bounties in the form of friendship and collaboration. The Chao Center for Asian Studies became a second institutional home, made especially so because of the community it fostered. Through CCAS, I was privileged to have the mentorship of Ratheesh Radhakrishnan, whose warmth, brilliance, and critical faculties enhanced every idea with which I engaged. Anne Chao championed the Houston Asian American Archive, creating a space for the voices of often overlooked Americans, and I am glad to have played a small part in building it. I have found in Haejin Koh a constant friend, always ready to offer support and a clear perspective. Linda Ho Peche gave me feedback at critical junctures and friendship along the way. Sociologist Jenifer Bratter spearheaded the Program for the Study of Ethnicity, Race, and Culture, bringing together faculty and graduate students, including me, from across the disciplines to engage vital topics of mutual interest.

I am so grateful to my sister scholars Samhita Sunya and Shani Roper, who tirelessly cheered me on at every juncture with encouragement, love, and wise counsel. Their example as scholars and friends of the highest order continues to inspire me. Other friends nourished my soul with laughter and joy, shattering what is otherwise a writer's solitary existence. For this, I especially thank Heba Khan, Shazia Manzar, Paige Hellmann, and Lila Rakoczy. I owe an intellectual debt to South Asian Americanist scholars and activists whose work and spirit continues to inspire me from near and far, among them Deepa Iyer, Amitava Kumar, Vijay Prashad, Natasha Raheja, and Samip Mallick.

My work could not have been completed without the support of my colleagues at Sam Houston State University and, in particular, chairs Pınar Emiralioğlu and Brian Domitrovic. I am indebted to Dean Abbey Zink for facilitating my year's leave from the university. This book has benefited immensely from discussions with fellow historians of Texas George Diaz, Wesley Phelps, and Bernadette Pruitt. Nancy Baker, Rosanne Barker, and Kate Pierce extended much-needed camaraderie and lively conversation. When solitude threatened to overwhelm, Jadwiga Biskupska came to the rescue as my trusty writing partner. I could not have found someone with more wit, humor, or the love of a good mélange.

A yearlong fellowship at The Clements Center for Southwest Studies at Southern Methodist University proved instrumental in bringing this book to fruition. I thank The Summerlee Foundation for sponsoring my scholarship on the recent history of Texas. Clements Center codirectors Andy Graybill and Neil Foley became trusted mentors and friends. My work was buoyed by their unfailing support, intellect, and advocacy. Despite their official titles, however, it is widely understood that Ruth Ann Elmore is the real boss of things. Her graciousness and hospitality immediately fostered a sense of belonging at the Clements Center, allowing me to concentrate on the task of writing (and food trucks). Along with Ruth Ann, Andy, and Neil, my fellow fellows Eric Meeks, Maurice Crandall, and Farina King nourished rich breeding grounds for scholarly discussion and debate. Together, we created a warm community, which eased my sadness at leaving my family. Ariel Ron, Ed Countryman, and Kathleen Wellman, among other SMU faculty members, also welcomed me into the fold.

While at the Clements Center, several historians from near and far gathered around a conference table one morning in Dallas Hall and spent a few hours discussing my book manuscript. Through the workshop, my work received the widest and closest scholarly attention. I appreciate Neil's leadership at the workshop and Ruth Ann's organization of it. Kevin Kruse and Madeline Hsu generously served as the main guest scholars, each providing verbal critiques and detailed reader's reports. Their invaluable feedback helped me to carry out a major reorganization of the manuscript, strengthening it into its current form. For their detailed reading and commentary, I thank Rachel Ball-Phillips, Gregg Cantrell, Sarah Coleman, Jo Guldi, Annelise Heinz, and Paul Renfro, along with Clements Center affiliates Andy, Eric, and Farina. I found Eric's and Paul's closely proofread and marked copies of my manuscript extremely helpful.

Several others generously gave their time to read the manuscript, and I cannot thank them enough. Tim Borstelmann (who read it twice!) drew my attention to some oversights but, more significantly, put my mind at ease with his thorough, instructive appraisal. Allen Matusow and Paul Spickard suggested, among other insights, that I condense the narrative, for which readers will undoubtedly be grateful. Casting a Cold War gaze over the manuscript, Nicholas Cull made suggestions that helped me define my terms and concepts more clearly. I appreciate the critical and thought-provoking feedback from Moon-Ho Jung on a much earlier draft. Conference copanelists, commentators, and colleagues at annual meetings sharpened my analysis, and although they are too many to name here, I nonetheless have benefited enormously from their feedback. When I could no longer see the forest for trees, Hollianna Bryan's close attention to detail, both technical and conceptual, polished off the manuscript in ways that only such a talented editor could do.

Archivists, library specialists, university staff, and others shined a light on the path ahead. David Langbart and the staff in the research room helped me navigate the labyrinthian holdings of the National Archives at College Park, Maryland. I appreciate the assistance of archivists at the Truman and Eisenhower Presidential Libraries, Houston Metropolitan Research Center, Library of Congress, Bobby Marlin at the University of Houston Special Collections, and Dara Flinn and Amanda Focke at Rice's Woodson Research Center. I relied extensively on the technical savvy of Jean Aroom and student worker Jessica Kuzmin (née Crisp) at the Fondren Library GIS/Data Center. I thank Mario Lopez at UH for his skillful work on my maps. The resourceful Anna Shparberg handled my many requests with ease. Similarly, Erin Owens at SHSU patiently and efficiently conjured up solutions to my sometimes obscure requests. Anita Gaines at UH, Marilyn Square at TSU, and Adria Baker at Rice provided me with data and information on international students. City of Houston administrators Bala Balachandran and the late Patrick Walsh furnished me with municipal demographic data. Pat also spent hours discussing this project with me over the years, kindly and enthusiastically offering to read the Houston sections of the manuscript; sadly, he left us far too soon.

This book project has found financial support in many quarters. The Center for Public History at UH provided summer research funding for my earliest oral history interviews. Credit is due to transcribers Suzanne Mascola and Michelle Kokes for their hard work and meticulous attention to detail. The Center for Engaged Research and Collaborative Learning (under the direction of Anthony Pinn) in conjunction with the African American Library at the Gregory School awarded me a research fellowship. I thank the staff at the Gregory School, particularly Hellena Stokes, for facilitating my research there. My trips to the Truman and Eisenhower libraries were made possible by a William Appleman Williams grant from the Society for Historians of American Foreign Relations. The Clements Center and especially the History Department at SHSU funded research trips small and large but always critical to the completion of the book.

UNC Press editor Chuck Grench's continued interest in and support of my project from its nascent stages have meant much to me. I am indebted to Chuck for his kindness, patience, and expertise as I labored through the process of writing this book. Thanks are also due to Dylan White and the staff at UNC Press for their efficiency and professionalism. I am so pleased that Charles Reagan Wilson has included the book in the New Directions in Southern Studies series.

Almost last but never least, I am indebted to my family, who supported me, listened to and laughed with me, and, most of all, loved me through the long execution of this project. I thank my Ammi and Abbi for the many meals and always open door and my father- and mother-in-law for their unwavering, absolute belief in me. Mona and Haris dispensed humor and encouragement, always ready to lend an ear or a shoulder. Their children were a source of delight throughout. I appreciate the concern of extended family members and in-laws near and far, and especially that of Noreen and Zubair. My children have sustained me with their irreverent sense of humor and by just being their quirky selves. No matter where their lives carry them, I keep them closest to my heart, always. Most important, I am deeply grateful to my husband, who shared with me the many joys and trials inherent in writing a book.

Finally, this project would not exist without the contribution of so many Indian and Pakistani Houstonians. Their shared stories, generous spirits, warmth, and resilience have opened my eyes, heart, and mind. Their narratives never failed to captivate me, and I consider myself privileged to have heard their life stories. To them I sincerely dedicate this book.

REDEFINING THE IMMIGRANT SOUTH

INTRODUCTION

In the mid-1960s, Rohan Patil worked toward his bachelor's degree in chemical engineering at the prestigious Indian Institute of Technology (IIT) at Kanpur in northern India. Originally from the western state of Maharashtra, Patil's father was also a chemical engineer, and his mother was a homemaker, though the family had settled in Kanpur years earlier. Patil's grandfather had been a forest ranger in Dehradun under the British colonial government. While at IIT, Patil learned something of Texas's universities from his professors.[1] Many had completed doctorates at universities in the United States in the preceding decade, and several visiting faculty members were American. All spoke highly of American higher education. The home institution of some of the visiting faculty was the University of Houston (UH), prompting Patil to apply to the master's program at UH, along with a handful of other universities.

Patil eventually completed his doctorate at UH, and while in graduate school in 1973, he returned to India to get married. After joining him in Houston, Patil's wife, Urmila, pursued her master's and doctorate degrees at the University of Texas Graduate School of Biomedical Sciences in Houston. The Patils settled in Houston as permanent residents, finding gainful employment in the booming economy. Eventually, they applied for and were granted American citizenship. Other Indian and Pakistani immigrants who arrived in Houston in the 1960s and 1970s recall learning about American universities through U.S. libraries scattered across their home countries. Still others were acquainted with the United States generally, and higher education specifically, through American visitors to grade schools in major South Asian cities such as Karachi, Lahore, Bombay, and Dacca. Patil's story, like that of other Indian and Pakistani immigrants to the United States, is the story of a life—at turns simple and joy giving, complicated and contradictory. It is a life story of the struggle for identity and the reconstruction of culture, as well as the accumulation of wealth and, with it, some degree of privilege.

Redefining the Immigrant South posits a central thesis: the privileges of selectivity on which Indians and Pakistanis migrated to the United States reverberated throughout their lives, placing in tension immigrants' own racial experiences with validation of the model minority myth. In addition to being a history of immigrants' lives, this book is an exegesis of power hierarchies in everyday life in the American South. The construction of South Asian immigrants' identities can be traced from before migration to well after, unfolding at multiple intersections of individual agency, state policy, and class and race prerogative. Using the experiences of educationally elite and professionalized immigrants who arrived in the United States from the 1950s to the 1970s, this transnational study examines hierarchies of privilege and barriers to success in the process of immigration and the making of a South Asian American middle class.

The book is an excavation of the migration process from its inception as an idea in the mind of a potential emigrant to its culmination at the end of an immigrant's life. For Indians and Pakistanis in the postwar era, the idea of migration to the United States emerged as an unintended consequence of U.S. State programs abroad.[2] The movement of educated South Asians to and from the United States starting in the 1950s was a Cold War imperative. Thus, this work addresses three central questions: What were the migration-related repercussions of massive U.S. public diplomacy campaigns in India and Pakistan during the Cold War? How did selective immigration into the United States, based on Cold War priorities, reinforce existing and enduring hierarchies of privilege in the recent South? In what ways were elite South Asian immigrants' class positions delimited by their own racialized status in the United States and the South?

In the 1950s, a small number of immigrants and college students from India and Pakistan began arriving in the United States for employment either via the McCarran-Walter Act (1952) or to pursue higher education at American universities.[3] Later, with passage of the Immigration and Nationality Act of 1965, a relatively select group of Indians and Pakistanis applied for U.S. admission under the act's third or sixth preferences: those with exceptional ability or professionals and skilled laborers in short supply (see Appendix, table 7). The spouses and children of resident aliens entered the country under family reunification, the second preference of the act. Thus, the confluence of South Asians' technological preparedness and the loosening of U.S. immigration restrictions, as well as the South Asian and American need for skilled labor, were crucial in accelerating rates of immigration to the United States. A lesser known source of this migration stream was the explicit pro-American public diplomacy conducted in India and Pakistan beginning in the early Cold War years. As Indians and Pakistanis completed their education at American universities, they searched for receptive labor markets in major U.S. cities, including New York, Chicago, Los Angeles, and Houston. By the 1970s, they found Houston to be an employment magnet, especially in engineering, and many settled in the city, laying the foundations for growing Indian and Pakistani communities. Many students remained in or soon returned to the United States to fill the demands of the labor market.

Their success after migration, however, was contingent on factors more complex than educational pedigree. Through their neighborhood residential patterns, public school selection, appeals to class conformity, and racial calculations, South Asian immigrants used their material wealth to position themselves strategically to gain the maximum privileges associated with whiteness. They also sought to create social and physical distance between themselves and other racialized, marginalized groups: African Americans and Latino/as.[4] Simultaneously, they negotiated thick Indian or Pakistani identities and, perhaps more interestingly, a pan–South Asian identity. I call this narrower form of panethnicity "interethnicity," wherein immigrants willingly overlooked premigration national antagonisms, religious differences, and language barriers in order to create community in diaspora. The benefits of the selective nature of immigration policy and South Asians' entry as skilled professionals and university students both materialized quickly and accrued over time. The economic and social wages enjoyed by South Asian immigrants, unlike whites, however, were complicated by immigrants' own racialization in southern American society.

The narrative arc of this post–World War II Indian and Pakistani immigration history to the United States begins with the formation of migration linkages among the South Asian middle classes, follows with the immigration of education-oriented South Asians, and ends with their incorporation into class and race hierarchies in a transitional Jim Crow city. The origins of this migration stream can be located in prewar, middle-class British India and a changing postwar world, in which the American and Soviet governments sought to broaden their spheres of influence and power in the Third World. Extensive Cold War public diplomacy programs in India and Pakistan targeted the middle classes, generating fresh interest in visiting and studying in the United States. Domestically, Cold War priorities recast long-reviled and excluded Asian Americans and immigrants as a new model minority.

The United States also underwent a period of significant political and social transition. In the two decades following World War II, civil rights legislation began to alter the social and political opportunities available to Americans of color. In Houston, as Jim Crow was finally abolished, old and new people-of-color communities—Latino/as, Asian Americans, and African Americans—continued to negotiate their positions, including access to housing (tied to zoned neighborhood schools) and employment. In this context of considerable flux and in response to U.S. public diplomacy and other overtures, Indians and Pakistanis began migrating to Houston. The history proposed here grapples with these transitions.

With regard to India and Pakistan, the actual origin of what is commonly termed "post-1965 immigration" was the creation of ideological linkages between the United States and South Asia during the early Cold War years. Although immigration from Asia remained mostly closed until 1965, thousands of South Asians pursued American higher education before this year, and many remained in the country long after completing their studies.[5] This student stream did not abate, increasing after 1968 with the implementation of the 1965 Immigration and Nationality Act. The profile of students and immigrants who visited, studied, and/or migrated to the United States during these decades conformed to Cold War priorities at the time. The United States sought to bolster its egalitarian image abroad by appealing to other countries' middle classes, based on the assumption that the most widely influential and accessible—and perhaps receptive—members of society were middle class. In addition, after the successful Soviet launch of *Sputnik 1* in 1957, the perception of a technological gap motivated U.S. lawmakers to encourage the immigration of highly skilled professionals. Thus, if advanced degrees can be construed as cultural capital that produce financial capital, then South Asian migration was marked by class advantage.

Indeed, as much as the decision to permit Asian immigration after 1965 was meant to demonstrate the superiority of American democracy, the entry of highly skilled immigrants from, for example, Taiwan, the Philippines, India, and Pakistan from the 1950s through the mid-1980s transformed our very understanding of immigration itself. Successful model minority Asian immigrants represented a newly idealized immigrant. No more would the United States be a haven for the "poor," the "huddled masses," or the "wretched refuse" of distant shores.[6] Those immigrants belonged to a romanticized past. After the onset of the Cold War, so-called good immigrants were those who possessed the skills needed to advance the American nation economically.[7] Indian and Pakistani immigrants were emblematic of this shift.

The Scope of This Study

This study is topically, chronologically, and geographically bounded within South Asian American history. It addresses neither post-1980 immigration from South Asia nor the children and grandchildren of Cold War era immigrants (the second and third generations). The chronological span of *Redefining the Immigrant South* stretches from the 1950s to about 2010, focusing on professionalized South Asians who entered the United States either temporarily or permanently before 1980. Many of the immigrants interviewed for this project arrived in the 1960s and 1970s to pursue higher education. Initially, they were granted admission into the country as temporary nonimmigrants (classified under the F category of visas for foreign students). On securing employment and adjusting their visa status, they remained in the United States, joining other highly skilled South Asian immigrants. The focus on pre-1980 educated immigrants is not by design; I simply set out to learn about the experiences of the earliest South Asian immigrants in Houston that I could find. Through this process, I found that these immigrants' journeys were unlike the typical Ellis Island or Angel Island narratives in U.S. immigration history.[8]

The millions of immigrants in the nineteenth and early twentieth centuries from southern and eastern Europe, Guangzhou Province in China, the Punjab region of India, Mexico, and the central Ottoman Empire—to name but a few sending regions—were mostly working class or with an agricultural background.[9] The post-1960 wave of South Asian immigrants, on the other hand, were well-educated professionals, fluent in English. By the time South Asian immigrants migrated to the United States in the latter half of the twentieth century, the U.S. economy had matured into a service and knowledge-based economy that matched their particular skill set.[10] Therefore, the project does not account for the next wave of South Asian immigrants: siblings and other relatives arriving mainly after 1980 on the basis of family reunification.[11] Their profile differs substantially from the 1960–1980 wave, since their entry into the United States no longer depended on their educational or professional selectivity. Consequently, over time, the range of economic diversity among South Asian immigrants came to resemble that of other groups.[12]

Professionalized South Asians, often with advanced degrees, possessed the requisite qualifications and skills to capitalize on the postwar, postindustrial economic system. Arriving mainly in the 1960s and 1970s, by the mid-1980s, these skilled immigrants sponsored extended family members—chiefly parents and siblings—who did not necessarily possess the same level of professional qualifications. I designate 1980 as the endpoint for this study (in terms of immigrants' entry date to the United States) because of increasing numbers of working-class South Asian immigrants who entered based on family reunification visas after the early 1980s. In 1970, about 90 percent of all immigrants from India were professional laborers, but by 1977, just 73 percent were professionals.[13] In 1983, only 45 percent of Indian immigrants had a professional background.[14] Moreover, as more South Asian families entered the United States in the 1970s, by the end of that decade, only 27 percent entered under occupational preference categories.[15] A majority were extended family members or nonpreference entries.[16]

Even though Indians made up the highest proportion of professionalized immigrants among all Asians to the United States, the shift from professional to less professional emerged by the late 1970s, became apparent during the 1980s, and was entrenched by the 1990s. I use decadal census counts as measures of professionalization levels, which is another important reason that I focus on immigrants who arrived before 1980, as the proportion of South Asian professionals declined relative to that of immediate and extended family members.[17] From the 1980s, South Asian Americans became increasingly diverse from a class and occupational perspective, although, to be sure, Indians and Pakistanis still tended to be more highly educated and professionalized than most other immigrants to the United States.[18] Thus, this narrative examines Indian and Pakistani professionalized immigrants who arrived in Houston between 1960 and 1980 (and, contextually, immigrants and Cold War visitors to the United States in the 1950s) and traces their experiences into the very recent past.

Situating South Asian American History in the Sunbelt South

Houston had been a biracial city since Reconstruction, when thousands of former slaves migrated there. In the early 1900s a sizable Mexican population also made the city their home. Before full racial integration in the 1960s, the city had operated under a Jim Crow system of "black" or "not black," but because most Asians arrived after 1965, they entered a city where official desegregation had already occurred. Nevertheless, immigrants of all backgrounds continued to face varying degrees of racism. Embracing its growing diversity, Houston's population grew by nearly a million people between 1970 and 1982.[19] From all walks of life, newcomers established ethnic entrepreneurial enclaves, community groups, churches, mosques, temples, and weekend schools. They celebrated their festivals, holy days, and national holidays, adding to the "roux for the rich gumbo of Houston's many different racial, ethnic, and national groups."[20] Today Houston, like Los Angeles, is a "majority minority" city, meaning that the non-Anglo population outnumbers the white population.[21] Within the nonwhite population, approximately 429,689 Asian Americans resided in the Greater Houston area in the year 2010.[22]

Building on an existing historiography that focuses heavily on South Asians on the East and West Coasts, *Redefining the Immigrant South* interrogates how immigrants from India and Pakistan arriving in the 1960s and 1970s emerged as among the wealthiest ethnoracial groups in the Sunbelt South by the late twentieth century.[23] Immigrant strategizing occurred within a broader southern context of federally legislated school desegregation and the rise of new and recently integrated neighborhoods in Sunbelt cities. By using South Asian immigrant experiences as a lens through which to view urban and suburban Houston starting in the 1960s, I illustrate the ways in which race continued to function as a salient category of analysis and a lived reality in southern American society after the demise of legally sanctioned segregation.

Immigrant strategizing also occurred within the context of demographic and economic change in the large metropolitan areas of what is sometimes called the Sunbelt. Regionally, the book offers a comparison for other Sunbelt cities in the South and Southwest—metropolitan cities that enjoyed federally funded expansion during and after World War II. It also requires some explanation of the terms "South" and "Sunbelt," as well as my use of these terms. Houston has straddled the line between Sunbelt and American South (for reasons discussed further in the book). The South is routinely regarded as a distinct region both popularly and historiographically. Its historical hallmarks, as Matthew Lassiter points out, are a "public culture of white supremacy," an "underdeveloped economy" excessively tied to agriculture, and a "single-party political system."[24] Numan Bartley insists that even if the South has merged with other parts of the country, it nonetheless has a distinctive past and culture with "its own myths and symbols."[25] However, Lassiter concludes that the age of southern exceptionalism has passed. Laura Edwards also argues that while "slavery and racial inequality took particularly extreme forms in the South," the rest of the country was also deeply implicated in these issues.[26] After the Civil War, while racial inequality was often a de facto reality in the North, southern and western states codified racial discrimination into law. For many Native Americans, Latino/as, Asian Americans, and African Americans, this has translated into enduring wealth and income disparity. Within the South, Texas occupies a distinct position. The state's diverse past and varied geography easily places it in the fields of Native American history, Mexican history, the borderlands, and southwestern history. Houston's own boosters aimed to distance the city and the state from its southern roots in the postwar years. Houstonians' signaling of a western or southwestern past evoked a sensibility of individual ruggedness—federally authorized warfare and dispossession of Indian lands notwithstanding.

However, Randolph Campbell states unequivocally that Texas "is far more southern than western and has been so for nearly two hundred years."[27] He offers as proof Texas's solidly slave past, preponderance of native southerners, staunch support for the Confederacy, hostility to racial equality, and consistent political conservatism. For the purposes of this study and its examination of the persistence of racial segregation, I interpret Houston through a southern or even an American lens, as federal redlining practices reinforced local Jim Crow statutes. Campbell continues, "Thus, when modern Texans in cities such as Houston put on their boots and Stetsons and head for the rodeo or hearken back to the days of movie westerns that portrayed their state as a land of cowboys, rustlers, and gunfighters, they are drawing on a collective memory that, although it has a basis in fact, is not the essence of Texas. The cold history of being southern is not as pleasing as the warm memory of being western."[28] Similarly, Andrew Baker writes that this "cowboy symbolism and mythology . . . could cloak the area's southern historical roots, social structures, and power relations under a veil of western nostalgia."[29]

After World War II, federal funding and private investment vitalized key cities in the South and Southwest, a phenomenon that produced the category of the Sunbelt and drew associations between cities as far-flung as Los Angeles and Atlanta.[30] The most recognizable features of Sunbelt cities emerged out of the New Deal. They included low-interest capital for investment, union-free workplaces, and a regulation-free economic structure, all contributing to a progrowth business climate.[31] As a result of the population boom, the creation of new urban forms (for example, sprawling suburbs and raised highway networks), and white flight, Sunbelt cities also cultivated and exported a new suburban political conservativism. As in other Sunbelt cities (for example, Phoenix and Raleigh-Durham), Houston's business elite boosted the city's economic potential, attracting companies with promises of tax breaks and land deals for new headquarters.[32] In the postwar era, new Sunbelt cities such as Los Angeles, Phoenix, Charlotte, Atlanta, and Houston enjoyed an infusion of federal funding, high rates of in-migration, and similar urban-suburban forms.

Although as an analytical category the Sunbelt fell from use in the 1990s, many historians and political scientists have resurrected the notion of a distinct Sunbelt since the mid-2000s.[33] Meanwhile, the U.S. Census continues to designate Houston as part of the South, not the Southwest, although the census also includes Texas as part of a "Sunbelt" region.[34] I find the Sunbelt a particularly useful framing device that explains Houston's emergence as one of the most important commercial hubs in the nation after World War II. In my analysis, Houston is indeed a southern city, just as much as it is a Sunbelt and an American city. As part of the South, the city continued to reel from the living legacy of Jim Crow. As a Sunbelt city, it enjoyed an influx of capital and people during, after, and because of World War II. Finally, because race was an enduring "American dilemma," in the words of Gunnar Myrdal, we can extrapolate the example of South Asian immigrants in Houston to similar urban communities across the country.[35] Thus, this study holds relevance beyond the South's regional boundaries and the Sunbelt's economic and geographic limits. Where appropriate, I do pull from contemporaneous sources that seem to reflect similar histories or sentiments as Houston-based sources, whether from elsewhere in the South or anywhere in the United States.

The example of South Asian immigrants in Houston reflects the experiences of South Asian immigrants in many other large cities at the time, including Chicago, Philadelphia, Los Angeles, and, later, Raleigh and Atlanta. Each of these cities offered immigrants both institutions of higher education and, after graduation, jobs. In these cities, highly educated South Asians formed the nucleus of their newly established ethnic communities. While South Asian immigrant experiences in Houston diverged to an extent from other places because of the city's own historical particularities, to the extent that race and class hierarchies were American and not just southern, the ethnic experience of South Asian immigrants in Houston approximated that of other highly professionalized South Asian communities in the South and the United States.

Some Notes on Methodology, Sources, and Terminology

This book builds on oral history, archival research, demographic data, and GIS (Geographic Information Systems) mapping, among other sources. All have been crucial in creating this narrative history. Each, however, required a particular methodology.

ORAL HISTORY METHODOLOGY

In order to access immigrants' ideas about identity, this project relies heavily on oral history interviews. Relatively little information on South Asian Americans' own perspectives can be gleaned from conventional, brick-and-mortar archival sources; neither newspapers nor government documents offer extensive depth or breadth. I interviewed thirty-eight Indian and Pakistani women and men who arrived in Houston between 1960 and 1980.[36] The Asian Indian interviewees came mostly from west, central, and east India. Almost all the Pakistani interviewees were born in India before Partition but raised in Karachi, Pakistan. Most were of the Hindu or Muslim faith, although there was one Jain and one Parsi (Zoroastrian).

Interviews were conducted mostly at participants' homes or, as some preferred, in private offices at the Rice University library. I recorded all interviews, initially with a cassette tape and recorder and later with a digital recorder. Many of the interviews (twenty-four in total) were supported by two grants from the Center for Public History at the University of Houston. The center provided for the transcription of all interviews submitted to them, and the transcripts were later archived at Special Collections, University of Houston Libraries. I visited a few interviewees more than once and followed up with all of them after an original transcript was available. All had an opportunity to review and amend their interview transcript before its final submission to the archive. Participants granted full permission to record, archive, and use interviews.

Interviews lasted from one and a half to three hours. I asked questions from a basic list but usually deviated from that list according to each interviewee's life experiences. Throughout, I took notes, sometimes jotting down important information shared before and after the recorded interview, as is often the case with oral history interviews. Often, when reviewing the transcript, if I noticed a compelling but unexplored line of inquiry, I followed up with questions over the phone that were not recorded in the official transcript. Although most of the interviews are archived, a handful of the recorded interviews were not archived because of poor sound quality. After lengthy deliberation, out of a concern for the privacy of the people whom I interviewed—most of whom still live in the Houston area—I decided to use pseudonyms instead of real names. The pseudonyms closely reflect the regional, linguistic, religious, and, where applicable, caste identity of the original names.[37] The Appendix provides a complete list of interviewees and basic information about each.

I used a snowball sample methodology wherein each interviewee I met suggested other possible interviewees from among their earliest social circle after migration. I then called the potential interviewee and conducted a preliminary interview over the phone. Some, as it turned out, arrived after 1980, while others were not interested in being interviewed. About seven out of every ten individuals with whom I spoke agreed to be interviewed. I tended to seek out those who were not community leaders, public figures, or exceptionally wealthy, as my focus was on the everyday experiences and perspectives of middle-class South Asian immigrants. Some of the interviews nevertheless were with important figures of some sort, often because they emerged as leaders among the earliest wave of South Asians in Houston. Many respondents had never considered their experiences significant enough to be represented in history. Like women, who "have a tendency to downplay the significance of their experiences because these experiences don't conform to what is publicly imagined as significant in mainstream history," immigrants of color find few, if any, popular representations of their experiences.[38] History, they seem to have learned, is about presidents, politics, and war, not about ordinary people.

Noticeable absences in this study, possibly resulting from the snowball method, include Dalits, South Indians (from Kerala, Andhra, and Karnataka), Sikhs, and Indian Christians (also mostly from South India).[39] This was not intentional, nor is this study meant to be a representative sample with a complete data set, a complete description of cultural identity, or an ethnography.[40] The project foregrounds historical methodology and archival sources, placing the narratives of South Asian immigrants within local and national events and processes of historical significance; in so doing, it underscores my contention that, although relatively small in number, the experiences of this immigrant community can nonetheless be crucial in illuminating larger processes under way from the mid- to late twentieth century.

Although the roughly forty interviews and numerous archival sources used in this study do not represent the entire range of regional, linguistic, occupational, and religious identities of Pakistani and Indian immigrants, they do reflect the historical experiences of a sizable group of these immigrants during the 1960s and 1970s. The narratives contained within these pages suggest possibilities and patterns rather than a rigidly defined model with universal applicability. Still, I think it is reasonable to extrapolate from these interviews that at least some others shared similar experiences elsewhere in the United States during the same time period. Nevertheless, to fill in some of these gaps, I turned to interviews conducted and archived by others, in particular, the Houston Asian American Archive, the Indo-American Oral History Project at the Houston Public Library, and the South Asian American Digital Archive. I also used oral histories not included in archives—for example, some that were a part of other studies.

I have striven to incorporate the experiences of South Asian women, including those who visited under the auspices of U.S. Cold War programs, those who were newly married and joined their U.S.-based South Asian husbands, and those who were students. Fourteen of the thirty-eight individuals with whom I conducted interviews were women. A majority of Indian and Pakistani students and immigrants to the United States between 1950 and 1980 were men; a notable exception were women nurses from South India (especially from Kerala) late in this period.[41] The number of female students at American universities increased over time, but during these early years of the post-1960 migration stream, most South Asian women entered the United States on the basis of "family reunification."[42] Often, the latter two paths intersected as many women sought advanced degrees after having migrated as wives. In addition to interviews, I turned to published memoirs and university reports to find traces of these histories.

This book does not analyze women as a distinct category from immigrants generally, although this does not mean that I regard their experiences as ungendered. Race and class are the main analytical categories employed throughout. Although exceptions, of course, existed, South Asian men and women tended to marry from back home within the same social groupings, whether through class, caste, religion, language, or region.[43] As spouses and children mostly migrated in the 1960s and 1970s via the second preference category (family reunification) of the 1965 Immigration and Nationality Act, they reinforced rather than altered or disrupted class, race, and caste positions. Consequently, I analyze family-based immigration in the 1960s and 1970s within the same grouping as "professionalized South Asian immigrant."

As to how interviewees discussed race, class, and caste, I avoided steering conversations down a path, preferring that individuals express their own understanding of group hierarchies. Most never mentioned caste, and indeed, as noted by an Indian interviewee in another study, "We don't ask the caste or say the caste. . . . In our family nobody asks that. You are not supposed to say right out or ask."[44] Ethnic studies scholar Shaista Patel contends that "South Asians cannot bear to talk about caste and [their] complicity in casteist violence," their silence essentially "maintain[ing] an innocence" akin to white repudiation of "colonial and racial violence."[45] Although a caste analysis is not employed here, caste nonetheless carried great significance for immigrants.

The focus of this book is the place of South Asians in American society broadly, rather than their own internal politics, whether divided by caste, region, religion, language, and so on. Thus, other categories of analysis and hierarchies of privilege proved more salient—in particular, class and race. Many perceived of themselves as middle class, though most denied that class and, especially, race had played *any* role in their lives. Because learned racial behavior entailed that one not speak openly about race, it became challenging for me to ascertain racial ideas. I conducted interviews without specifically referencing the word "race," yet race emerged time and again. Throughout, I have tried to avoid overinterpreting quotations from the interviews or overstating the relevance of race or other analytical categories. I have attempted, rather, to allow individuals to speak for themselves, narrate their own experiences, and define their own terms. I hope that I have represented them accurately and with dignity.

Another complicating factor for oral historians exploring ethnic histories is that of insider privilege. I acknowledge that I inhabit and perform several subjectivities, only one of which is imagined as shared by all my interviewees: being "South Asian." Although I was in a position to understand some complexities of their experiences due to my fluency in Hindi and Urdu and my familiarity with general cultural practices concerning food, clothing, family structure, gender norms, and such, in so many other ways, depending on whom I interviewed, I was an outsider: as a Pakistani American; as the daughter of Muhajirs, who supposedly betrayed the nationalist project of India by migrating to Pakistan; as someone mostly raised in the United States and never in

South Asia; as a student of the liberal arts (as opposed to sciences); as a woman; as a Muslim; and as a visible Muslima who wears hijab.

Interviewees navigated varying degrees of openness with me; some felt on very familiar terms, but others were more guarded in their communications. A prime example of this uncertain sense of community with me occurred when I interviewed a Madrasi man who had lived in the Houston area since 1970.[46] He greeted me with palpable caution, but through the course of small talk and meeting his wife, the interview proceeded well, if a little shorter (one hour) than other interviews. As I walked out, I thanked him and expressed my appreciation. After a moment's pensive silence, he responded, "You know. . . you were actually nice." In saying so, he betrayed his initial assumptions, based on any number of factors—my name, lack of Indian authenticity, performance of religion, his past experience, and so on—that I was not a "nice" person and, more pressingly, that I was not of his community.

OTHER SOURCES

Although oral history interviews formed the foundation of this project at its inception, other primary sources proved integral. Locally, I extensively consulted the holdings of the Houston Metropolitan Research Center and the municipal and university records of the M. D. Anderson Library at the University of Houston. GIS work was completed with the help of specialists at the Rice University GIS/Data Center at Fondren Library. Custom GIS maps also proved illuminating. By overlaying census data for all major racial groups with the "Asian Indian" subgroup, I was able to track residential patterns by census tract over time. This method revealed not only where South Asian immigrants chose to live in Houston but also, along with information from oral history interviews, how those decisions intersected with race and class hierarchies. Some of these maps have been included in this book.

Other sources included national and municipal government records, newspapers (both mainstream and ethnic), published memoirs, censuses, and census-derived reports. While local archives and oral history yielded rich textual, primary material signaling to the Cold War, the official records of the U.S. State Department and the U.S. Information Agency (USIA) filled in those gaps. The U.S. National Archives at College Park, especially Record Groups 59 and 306, and the Eisenhower Presidential Library were instrumental. Along with international student newspapers at the Library of Congress, I was surprised to find some illuminating memoirs by Indian university students in the United States before 1965. I was, however, unable to obtain a visa to conduct research in India, likely owing to my Pakistani background.

With regard to secondary literature, the book draws on the histories of race and ethnicity in the United States, the Cold War, immigration, Houston and the South, and India and Pakistan, as well as urban history and Asian American history. It also relies on theorizations of race produced by scholars of ethnic studies and especially Asian American studies. Wherever relevant, I have incorporated non-Houston sources, both primary and secondary, to emphasize the wider applicability of the Houston case to the history of South Asian American immigration.

TERMINOLOGY

The term "South Asia" emerged as a Cold War designation, reflecting the concerns of the United States about an expanding and influential China.[47] By defining the Indian subcontinent as a region distinct from the rest of Asia, the United States aimed to form strategic Cold War alliances with India and Pakistan. Here, "South Asia" refers specifically to India and Pakistan after 1947 as well as to East Pakistan and West Pakistan before their civil war of 1971. India and Pakistan sent, by far, among the largest numbers of international students and immigrants to the United States starting in the early Cold War years, and in addition, the two nations were favored targets of U.S. public diplomacy efforts. Accordingly, in this book, "South Asia" indicates just these two countries.

When writing about incidents occurring before 1947, I use the historically accurate terms "British India" and "India" interchangeably to refer to the same geographical space before Partition that would become modern-day India and Pakistan. Since its inception, the term "South Asia" has since been used with some frequency by academic specialists when referring to immigrants from the countries that have come to be regarded as part of the South Asian region: Bangladesh, Burma, India, Maldives, Nepal, Pakistan, and Sri Lanka. Less often, Afghanistan and Iran are included, although more typically they are categorized with the Middle East. More recently, officials and journalists have increasingly categorized Pakistan as part of the Middle East.

"South Asian" is primarily a political and academic label, seldom found in common usage among immigrants. Occasionally it is used commercially in order to appeal to a broad South Asian customer base, though even then "Indo-Pakistani" is the preferred term. South Asians rarely refer to themselves as "South Asian," preferring instead, national (for example, Pakistani, Indian, Bangladeshi, American) and regional or language-bound identities (for example, Bihari, Tamil, Sindhi, Marathi), or religious affiliations (for example, Jain, Muslim). These individuals are thick with identities, constantly layering, discarding, exchanging, and resting them as needed and shifting in their understanding of each identity. Post-1960 immigrants from India and Pakistan constructed and reconstructed Asian, South Asian, Indian, and Pakistani, as well as more localized ethnic identities, all of which were gendered and classed and raced, and rich with complexity. Nevertheless, under scrutiny, certain patterns emerged. An examination of immigrants' processes of acculturation highlights patterns of socioeconomic mobility, educational attainment, and residential settlement; these patterns operated within class and race frameworks. Their history reveals how these frameworks intersected to support the accumulation of various forms of capital among members of the middle class.

It is important to explain the representation of Bangladesh and Bangladeshis in this study. Because today's Bangladesh was East Pakistan from 1947 to 1971 (and part of British India before 1947), the region's immigrants to the United States were officially subsumed under the category of "Pakistanis" before 1971. In the National Archives at College Park, records relating to East Pakistan are cataloged in the general Pakistan files. In both the U.S. Census and international student figures, immigrants were counted as Pakistanis. After the creation of Bangladesh in 1971, Bangladeshis obviously became a distinct category. They entered the United States under their new country's quotas but migrated in much smaller numbers than Indians and Pakistanis, early on. Whereas in 1980, only 5,880 Bangladeshis lived in the United States, by 2010, the census counted nearly 150,000.[48]

During my oral history interview research phase, I was unable to locate any East Pakistanis or Bangladeshis who had moved to Houston before 1980, although I have recently learned of some. The Indians and Pakistanis I interviewed recalled a few East Pakistani students in Houston's universities, but they also noted that these students returned to East Pakistan after completing their studies. Also, most East Pakistanis in Texas opted to study at Texas A&M, as part of a large exchange program there, rather than at Houston's local universities. This is complicated by the classification in university records before the 1971 civil war of today's Bangladeshis as Pakistanis, erasing their distinct histories. Although I have tried to include their experiences through other sources (the National Archives and the Houston Asian American Archive), much more work remains on this important topic.

My use of the word "immigrant" is less a legal designation than a practical one. I use it to refer to any South Asian who traveled to the United States with the intention of remaining for more than a short visit. This includes students, as well as those who arrived with work-based visas in hand, although I alternate between "student" and "immigrant" in the early part of the book, as needed. The point at which students secured employment-based visas and obtained Green Cards varied greatly. Similarly, the moment when immigrants committed to remaining in the United States permanently or obtained American citizenship differed among individuals. The transitions between these phases of self-understanding are difficult to pinpoint, not least because they overlap. In their early years, immigrants routinely vacillated between states of permanent and temporary residence, functioning as transnational subjects all the while.[49] Some studies use the term "South Asian American" rather than "South Asian" or "immigrant," whether to refer to the U.S.-born second generation or to challenge a perpetual outsider status. I agree with these and other rationales for the use of other labels, but for the purposes of this book, the distinction between immigrant and native or citizen is necessary in order to highlight the specific advantages gained and obstacles faced due to immigrant status.

Despite my use of "South Asian," the construction of a diasporic, pan–South Asian identity has fluctuated over time within immigrant and subsequent generations. In the 1960s, the early years of modern South Asian American communities, small group size lent itself to a collective interethnic identity (that is, South Asian), whereas by the 1980s, now sizable South Asian subgroups began splintering into some of the linguistic and regional categories noted above. Critical mass, however, goes only so far as a rationale for the emergence of subgroups in diaspora. By contrast, in other significant ways "South Asian" as a unifying identity was anything but unifying. Established premigration boundaries, nationalistic divisions, and social biases were evident foremost in marriage practices. Marriage-group boundaries were often drawn between, for example, Hindu and Muslim, Pakistani and Indian, Hyderabadi and non-Hyderabadi.[50] Within subgroups, community members continued to erect class and caste barriers. Much later, in the wake of the Persian Gulf War, the attacks of September 11, the subsequent U.S. invasion of Afghanistan, and the policing of American Muslims, some South Asian Indian immigrants not of the Islamic faith opted to distance themselves from Muslims of South Asian descent.[51] During the early decades of Cold War migration from Pakistan and India, however, a South Asian identity proved useful and even necessary.

Second-generation South Asian youth in the 1980s brought into popular parlance the term "Desi" [DAY-see], to denote anyone of broad South Asian descent. Beyond Indian and Pakistani descent, "Desi" includes Bangladeshis and Sri Lankans anywhere in the global South Asian diaspora. It literally refers to those of "the land" (*desh* or *des*) or "the country"—a recognition of some collective or shared imagined heritage rooted in geography (interethnicity, as discussed later in the book). The term "Desi" has gained extensive usage in the United States among South Asian immigrants and successive generations. Vinod Prakash, one of the interviewees for this project, stated emphatically, "It's the word that was coined literally to describe the fact that we really don't care about these political barriers between countries."[52] The extent to and ways in which political and other barriers were simultaneously erected and dismantled by South Asian immigrants form part of the subject of this study. They strategically employed and disrupted this interethnic identity based on existing (premigration) and new (postmigration) cleavages. In post-9/11 America and England, politically engaged ethnic South Asians speak of "brown power" and "brown solidarity," which extend far beyond an imagined cultural community. Brownness is a call to resistance that also illustrates the dynamic nature of identities and labels.

Terms specific to the Cold War require some explanation. I borrow Odd Arne Westad's definition of the Cold War as "the period in which the global conflict between the United States and the Soviet Union dominated international affairs, roughly between 1945 and 1991."[53] A more contentious Cold War term, "propaganda," can be read, at best, as loaded and, at worst, as a "debased term" (per Nicholas Cull).[54] Internally, before 1965, the USIA routinely referred to the agency's work as "psychological operations" and "propaganda" even as it publicly circulated such terms as "cultural activity," "public diplomacy," and "information work." In his book *Total Cold War*, Kenneth Osgood uses the term "propaganda" to underscore the government's desire to influence and persuade various audiences rather than to neutrally inform.[55] After 1965, public diplomacy emerges as the preferred official terminology. I generally use the term "public diplomacy," employing "propaganda" only occasionally when contextually appropriate.

Categories of Analysis: Class and Race

The narrative contained within these pages is primarily, though not exclusively, interpreted through the frameworks of class and race.

THE CENTRALITY OF CLASS TO SOUTH ASIAN EMIGRATION

South Asian migration to the United States from the 1950s was an urban-to-urban, middle-class migration stream, distinct from earlier streams: for example, the rural-to-rural migration of Punjabis to the Pacific Northwest territories at the turn of the twentieth century; the rural-to-urban stream of Bengalis to Harlem and New Orleans from the 1880s; or the working-class migration of Indians and Pakistanis to the factories of England after World War II.[56] Indian and Pakistani immigrants who migrated to the major cities of the United States from the 1950s hailed from mostly middle-class or upper-middle-class backgrounds in substantially urbanized areas of their home countries. They emigrated from places like Karachi, Bombay, and Kanpur, but they were not newly middle class. Rather, their roots—however recent—originated in the expanding middle class of late colonial British India. Distinct from the Indian aristocracy, the members of India's historically middle-class elite have been cast variously as intermediaries between the aristocracy and the colonial administration, as spokespeople for local populations, as powerless, or as autonomous and with increasing class consciousness.[57]

In any case, scholarship has mainly focused on the upper middle class—either intellectuals in their vernacular languages (for example, writers and sociopolitical commentators) or the subset of English-educated, upper-caste Indians—those intellectuals who were heavily involved in nationalist resistance in the late British colonial era.[58] This study directs attention away from the "few" of the middle class to the "many" of the middle class, which entails a shift of interest toward salaried employees who did not organize, agitate for, or engage in nationalist politicking in the first half of the twentieth century. They did not necessarily have access to formalized English-medium instruction, though most had at least a passing familiarity with the English language.

Nevertheless, they shared with that elite segment of the Indian middle class a common recourse to the behaviors of modernity with an emphasis on education as an entrée to material and social advancement, and a culture of consumption. Consumption had become an essential measure of status, even for the lower middle class, in the late colonial period, although technically this was not a necessary feature of middle-class identity.[59] The behaviors and values that they ascribed to being middle class were reinforced by U.S. Cold War training programs, supporting eventual migration to the United States from the 1950s, while the privileges of class-driven upward mobility resonated throughout immigrants' lives.

India's middle class locates its origins at least as early as the period of the Sepoy Uprising of 1857 and subsequent transition from East India Company management to Crown Colony rule in 1858.[60] The rate of industrialization in the Indian subcontinent under the British corresponded with the geographic location of cities—that is, whether they were located close to ports. Bombay, Calcutta, and Madras all developed class-based societies much earlier than inland regions, by some accounts, even as early as 1815.[61] The autocratic colonial system of governance after the uprising required the growth and participation of a new middle stratum schooled in the expanding British-modeled network of higher education. In addition to preparing administrators and clerks for the colonial civil service, these colleges produced bureaucrats, lawyers, doctors, journalists, engineers, teachers, and literary persons.[62]

Although colonial economies suffered from overdependence on an external (that is, metropolitan) economy, in India, a growing middle class supported the routine administration of the state apparatus. The British exercised significant dominion over India's economic governance, and the colonial government neglected to invest fully in domestic infrastructure by exacerbating the demise of indigenous cottage industries and extracting a large amount of raw materials for the success of the metropolis over that of the colonized periphery.[63] Despite this, in dependent or colonial territories, "states assume entrepreneurial functions, giving birth to technocratic, managerial, and technical groupings that do not owe their existence to private property."[64] Within an externally imposed colonial structure, Indians strategized for themselves, making decisions that brought local middle classes into being. They not only sought professional occupations but also ascribed notions of appropriate behavior (*shareef*, discussed below) to this emerging identity.

After Independence in 1947, the state of semi-industrialization, based largely on textile manufacturing and railroad construction and management, required and produced a middling class that vacillated between growth and stagnation in the postcolonial era.[65] In either state, it never disappeared.[66] Between 85 and 99 percent of professional employees after Independence remained in the professional classes.[67] It was the children of this urbanized, literate, and professionalized segment of Indian and Pakistani society who availed themselves of postbaccalaureate education and/or American immigration opportunities.[68] Future emigrants to the United States descended from parents and grandparents who had already navigated their way into high and low professional occupations, straddling the spectrum from clerks to lawyers and everything in between.

The global middle class of the late nineteenth and twentieth centuries commonly articulated values that signified and aimed to preserve their middle-class status. A global middle class in the twentieth century existed across time and space, bearing its own ever-evolving but unique marks of locality and geography.[69] Being middle class often had little to do with occupation and much to do with prescribed values. For example, middle-class Muslims in Lucknow and Delhi during the late nineteenth century recast meanings of the descriptor *shareef* (or ashraf), newly defining it by behavior and accomplishment, as opposed exclusively to one's station of high birth or high caste position.[70] Loosely translated, *shareef* referred to "good" or "respectable" families, those with whom one shared both the practices and performance of middle-classness—a term that continues to resonate in South Asia, as well as in the immigrant diaspora, especially among middle-class Muslim immigrants from South Asia.

The meanings of the word *shareef* signify behaviors widely embraced by South Asians as representative of the middle class. A sociological survey conducted in 1966 in metropolitan Madras found that self-defined members of the middle class viewed their class as being "economically adequate or comfortable; residing in a house, which is often rented; [and] regularly employed."[71]

They marked themselves as "educated" and "well-mannered" (corresponding to *shareef*).[72] In the late twentieth century, the use of the word *shareef* continued to demarcate immigrant families who subscribed to conservative behavioral conventions and heavily prioritized education; thus, middle class is both an "idea" and a "practice of modernity."[73]

The boundaries of what is termed "middle class" in this project remain contested, fluid, and dynamic. India's and Pakistan's middle class in the decades bounding Indian Independence are better termed "middle classes," as they signify a wide and varied range of occupations, income levels, and public and private discourses. Nevertheless, both before and after migration, members of India's and Pakistan's middle classes defined the terms of their class affiliation by combining old and new modes of "appropriate social conduct" that they believed endowed them with class legitimacy.[74] This conduct continued to include educational attainment; aspirations for and a sense of entitlement to upward occupational mobility and correspondingly higher income; and appropriate social affiliations with *shareef* or respectable families and individuals.

In reality, this set of conducts often overlapped with discourses embraced by other classes as well. Whether elite, working class, or middle class, by the 1960s certain occupations in Pakistan and India signified middle-classness—in particular, engineering, medicine, and, for women, teaching. Although class as a hierarchy existed only in the intersection with other hierarchies, including religion, gender, and caste, these practices evolved over time and in relation to local histories, and they endured, forming a bridge for immigrants after they emigrated. As students and, even later, as immigrant parents, middle-class Pakistani and Indian Americans concentrated on the same middle-class occupations as before migration. Articulations of *shareef*, middle-class behavior enabled Indians and Pakistanis to form a common basis for ethnic identity formation across national and religious lines after migration.

THE SIGNIFICANCE OF RACE AND THE MODEL MINORITY MYTH FOR SOUTH ASIAN IMMIGRATION

I have found Claire Jean Kim's theory of racial triangulation to be useful in understanding South Asian immigrants' racial identities.[75] Kim posits that while marginalized groups within the American populace (for example, Native Americans, blacks, Mexicans, and Asians) have been racialized and ranked, these processes have been "profoundly interrelated." The term "Asian"—an aggregation of disparate groups of Asian immigrants and Asian Americans into one conveniently uniform grouping—can only be fully understood as relative to other racialized groups within what Kim refers to as a "field of racial positions." Although Asian immigrants were originally perceived as undesirable and thus barred from entry into the United States, those arriving in the postwar era were suddenly regarded as members of a model minority of Asian Americans.[76] In the press, the material success of these elite immigrants was juxtaposed against other minorities' supposed failure to succeed, disregarding various structural barriers historically faced by all minority groups in the country but especially African Americans. The model minority myth thus served to triangulate and divide people of color while fortifying white privilege.[77]

The narrative offered in this book refutes the model minority myth, which posits that Americans of Asian descent have found educational and material success because of race-based virtues of hard work and good behavior, unlike other minority groups, who purportedly have a weak work ethic and/or are combative. *Redefining the Immigrant South* shows, rather, that hierarchies of class (and, by extension, caste) and racial privilege were reinforced and maintained throughout the immigration process from South Asia to the United States in the mid- to late twentieth century, albeit in historically specific contexts.

Throughout the roughly seventy-year period under consideration herein, class, race, and caste hierarchies were used to great effect by both the American government and the South Asian middle classes. These processes were not unrelated. As the Cold War unfolded, the Dwight D. Eisenhower and John F. Kennedy administrations courted the educated middle classes in the Third World nations of Asia, Africa, and Latin America by establishing extensive public diplomacy programs that promoted a racially democratic image and by offering training, scholarships, and exchange programs in the United States.[78] In response, middle-class, upper-caste Indians and Pakistanis calculated the usefulness of such U.S. programs and opportunities abroad. By 1965, thousands of Indian and Pakistani students were pursuing advanced degrees in American universities, and thousands more had already visited and/or engaged with the United States in myriad other ways in India and Pakistan.

South Asian immigrants' rapid upward mobility and middle-class aspirations after migration to Houston built on existing historical formations of modernity, cosmopolitanism, and middle-classness in South Asia. Immigrants had already developed a sense of class consciousness before migration, one that loosely corresponded with American interpretations of class in the postwar period. Within this identity, immigrants possessed both a knowledge of class strategizing as well as the basic building blocks for social mobility—specifically higher education, but also a system of values and behaviors. Taken comprehensively, these characteristics, as conceived by immigrants themselves, created fairly clear boundaries of inclusivity and, thus, exclusivity. In a southern, American context, transnational class conceptions intersected with particular racial constructs; the ways in which immigrants performed class and understood the meanings of being middle class provides insight into the intersection between race and class. Constructions of class and modernity formed the backbone of a firmly rooted identity that facilitated South Asian immigrants' material success after migration, even as it came to mesh with a southern ideology of racial inequality and exclusion.

A SPECIAL NOTE ON CASTE

Despite the parallels between caste and race as systems of oppressive hierarchy, I limit this book to an examination of class and race, while remaining fully aware that caste continues to operate in this diasporic context. For the Hindu communities under consideration in this book, it is fairly safe to assume that the vast majority of Indian immigrants were upper caste.[79] While I have not found any large-scale studies specifically on Indians and caste in the United States, smaller studies, such as that of Hemalatha Ganapathy-Coleman, indicate that Indian immigrants, though with regionally and linguistically diverse origins, "had membership in the upper layers of the caste system."[80] Anthropologist Johanna Lessinger, in her landmark ethnography of post-1965 Indian immigrants in New York, explains that although Asian Indians in the United States come from a range of caste backgrounds, most are middle and upper caste, purportedly due to their educational and professional training.[81] Prema Kurien concurs, stating that despite India's small percentage of upper-caste members (only 25 percent), "given the elite nature" of post-1965 immigration from India, "most American Indians" are "upper caste."[82]

This caste status has, in part, positioned professionalized Indian immigrants somewhat laterally with other middle-class Americans, although in other significant ways, they remain marginalized in spite of class standing.[83] Thus, in the context of Indian Hindu immigration in the 1970s and especially the 1960s, class can be read, if cautiously, as a proxy for caste. Public diplomacy and exchange efforts in the subcontinent, along with U.S. immigration law, targeted the educated, middle-class strata of Indians (and Pakistanis). Since caste prohibitions have long prevented equal educational and occupational access to Dalits and other Scheduled Castes, opportunities to visit the United States via official programs or to migrate through the newly erected skilled-occupational preference or family reunification categories of the 1965 Immigration and Nationality Act were limited, at best, for them.

Although this book also assumes upper-caste membership for post–World War II visitors and immigrants, it is impossible to conclude definitively that every Indian immigrant occupied this position. Some may very likely have been Dalits or other oppressed castes, and in any case, a broader range of caste origins can now be found throughout the United States. The centering of middle-class, presumably upper-caste South Asians is not meant to privilege their histories over those of other castes.[84] If anything, it is to emphasize that the same foreign policies and immigration policies that have reinforced class privilege in the United States have simultaneously replicated caste privileges found in India.

In addition, caste in the Indian context and race in the American context share much in common. Historically they have both been social hierarchies, specifically, labor-based systems of oppression. Equally, they were and remain structures based on the perpetuation of power and privilege. As Gyanendra Pandey writes in his comparative history, and as others—including W. E. B. Du Bois, Mohandas Gandhi, B. R. Ambedkar, and Martin Luther King Jr.—have also noted, the two systems share "connection and parallels."[85] Nevertheless, Pandey and others warn of drawing too broad or even false a comparison between caste and race by overlooking local context and historical specificity.[86] Finally, caste operates *within* Asian Indian immigrant communities, creating fissures and fractures that emerge as yet another axis of privilege. Middle-class or wealthy upper-caste men have often occupied leadership positions, shaping the narratives of their communities and serving as gatekeepers.[87] I recognize that, although there is overlap, caste is not a replacement for class or race, for it continues to function distinctively from either, as an organizing structure within Indian immigrant communities. Marriage norms, in particular, are markedly determined by caste well after immigration to the United States. Nevertheless, the frameworks that I have found most useful in understanding Indian and Pakistani immigration itself, and the wages of selectivity long after, are race and class.

South Asian communities in major American cities in the 1960s and 1970s were composed largely of middle-class, urban-to-urban, professional, and highly educated immigrants who spearheaded community-building efforts, similar to the pattern found in Houston.[88] South Asian immigrants' class ascendance in those decades corresponded with caste ascendance, as well. In addition to being middle class and urban, Houston's South Asian Hindus were uncoincidentally upper caste, although a full consideration of caste is beyond the purview of this book.[89] As additional family members entered under the family preference categories, they maintained caste ascendance. That is, the wives, husbands, and children of skilled workers had similar caste backgrounds as the initial immigrant family member. However, as increasing numbers of Indians entered the United States as nonpreference immigrants who did not require stringent educational or professional qualifications, caste diversity likely expanded. Nonetheless, without hard data to support this, one can only speculate.

South Asian Demographic Data

Indian immigration to the United States before passage of the 1965 Immigration and Nationality Act totaled roughly 13,000, but from 1965 to 1970, 35,000 new Indians migrated, along with an equal number of Chinese and slightly fewer Koreans. Between 1958 and 1965, the number of Pakistanis who entered the United States was 1,224, but from 1966 to 1972, Pakistani immigration rose to nearly 8,000.[90] In the years just after passage of the legislation, from 1966 to 1975, professionals made up approximately 80 percent to 93 percent of all Indian and Pakistani arrivals, although that number has since steadily declined because of their sponsoring of nonprofessional relatives.[91] In 1980, the Indian population in the United States was 361,531, and by 1990, it had risen to 815,447.[92] The 2010 census lists 3.183 million Asian Indians in the United States, and the number has steadily increased since then. By comparison, the census reports 409,163 Pakistanis residing in the United States in 2010.[93]

South Asian immigrants' settlement patterns reflected the regional and national postwar migration trend toward large urban metropolises. Bound by their professional orientation, Indians and Pakistanis settled in areas of the United States that demanded their skills. This included "large, economically diversified [metropolitan areas], where building activity or manufacturing was strong."[94] Across the American South, South Asians—including Asian Indians, Pakistanis, and Bangladeshis—numbered 1.117 million in 2010, of which about 135,500 lived in the Greater Houston area.[95] Other southern metropolitan areas with substantial South Asian populations include Arlington, Virginia; Dallas–Fort Worth; Atlanta; and Raleigh-Durham. In 2010, Asian Indians were, by far, the largest Asian American ethnic group in the South, with a population of more than 930,000, followed distantly by Chinese, Vietnamese, Filipinos, and Koreans. Some 150,500 Pakistanis and 33,500 Bangladeshis resided in the South and were the fastest growing Asian American groups in the region. Texas was home to the most Asian Americans in the South, with nearly double the Asian American population of other such states as Florida or Virginia.

Currently, Houston is the second most populous Asian American metropolitan area in the South, surpassed only by Washington, D.C. Asian Indians and Pakistanis have flocked to Houston to take advantage of its booming oil-led economy, advanced medical complex, and steady growth of jobs for engineering professionals, as well as for working-class immigrants. Others are drawn to the comparatively low cost of living in Houston. The Houston area has among the largest Asian Indian and Pakistani populations nationwide, evidenced by the proliferation of Indian and Pakistani restaurants, groceries, salons, and other small businesses. Today, estimates range widely regarding the

Indian and Pakistani population in the Greater Houston metropolitan area. Census 2010 data indicate Pakistani and Indian populations in Houston of 32,331 and 100,125, respectively.[96] Community self-reported estimates suggest higher numbers, but anthropologist Ahmad Afzal suggests that ethnic minority populations tend to overestimate their size, probably to create a stronger political presence.[97] Most likely, actual populations fall between undercounted census data and inflated self-reported numbers. Large groups of immigrants may remain unaccounted in census data, including undocumented Pakistani and Indian immigrants. In addition, community sources such as the Indian and Pakistani embassies, religious organizations, and cultural associations use head counts at large-pan-Indian and Pakistani programs to arrange events for concrete numbers of people. Even a cursory totaling of these numbers reveals larger populations than the census reflects. For the purposes of this study, however, I rely on official census data and immigration statistics.

Organization

The book is arranged chronologically, examining the entire migration process from the formation of migration linkages in the 1950s, to immigrant community formation in the 1970s and 1980s, to immigrants' lives after retirement in the 2000s. The entire process is bound by hierarchies and barriers of privilege, specifically those of race and class. After a prologue that provides context on the histories of anti-Asian immigration law in the United States and Indian immigration, the narrative takes as its starting point expansive U.S. public diplomacy programs in the developing world during the early Cold War years, when the American State reached out to the Indian and Pakistani middle class. The subsequent chapters place South Asian immigrant history within the specific contexts of Houston's urban, social, and economic history, as well as within the regional patterns of suburbanization, white flight, and school segregation. With the exception of the first chapter, every chapter examines this history through the lenses of class, race, and ethnicity.

Chapter 1 is an examination of the major public diplomacy programs of the USIA and foreign policy initiatives of the State Department in the 1950s and 1960s. In the early years of the Cold War, the United States implemented a wide range of programs in India and Pakistan, inadvertently laying the foundation for migration networks between South Asia and the United States. Concerned about the appeal of communism in the Third World, State and USIA used economic and military aid, exchange programs, and public diplomacy to strengthen the American image abroad.[98] American public diplomacy operations in these two countries were respectively the second and fourth largest in the world by the early 1960s. In particular, State and USIA focused their efforts on the middle classes, reasoning that they were the most sympathetic to the U.S. diplomatic mission. Through a series of meticulously planned programs, the American State prioritized South Asian college and university students as major targets within the middle classes. Over two decades, this cultural intervention resulted in South Asians pursuing higher education in the United States, rather than in their historical preference for the United Kingdom.

Chapter 2, "Getting Acquainted with the University and the City," concerns the arrival of South Asian students and immigrants in Houston during the 1960s. Along with college towns and major cities across the United States, Houston was an ideal host city for would-be immigrants. As South Asians attended local universities, the University of Houston became the hub for all cultural activities in the city and a key site for identity formation. South Asians constructed ethnic, national, class, and racial identities through the university and the city. The segregated neighborhoods in which they resided as students, along with the city's Jim Crow structure, provided a counterpoint to their university experiences. In addition, their own paradoxical subject positions (financially constrained but on the cusp of upward mobility; racialized foreigners but valuable Cold War assets; and temporary students but potentially permanent immigrants) reinforced flawed southern conceptions of race and class.

South Asian immigrants reconciled notions of class and race from India and Pakistan with those of a changing American South, as shown in Chapter 3, "The Formation of Interethnic Community." Tolerated but socially marginalized as too foreign, Indian and Pakistani students collapsed their own national identities to form what I call interethnic community identity, mainly through the university. In addition, through the American Host Family program, a Cold War initiative, students built an off-campus support network. South Asian women participated in other off-campus initiatives as well. As a strategy for belonging, however, ethnic identity provided students with welcoming spaces where they could reconstruct and celebrate Indian and Pakistani culture and a new South Asian interethnic identity. Students established the city's first Pakistani and Indian ethnic organizations, arranging Hindi-language film screenings and large-scale variety shows that included skits, song performances, and fashion shows on campus. Still, ethnonational and religious identities formed the limits of interethnicity.

Chapter 4, "Inhabiting the Internationalizing City," and Chapter 5, "Riding Up the Oil Boom, Sliding Down the Oil Bust," analyze Houston's economic boom and bust years placing immigrants' residential settlement patterns in those contexts. During the 1970s alone, Houston's overall population soared and its foreign-born population doubled, from 9 percent to 18 percent of the total, altering the profile of Houston's residents but also attitudes toward foreigners. As new middle-class residents embraced a pattern of suburban flight, South Asian immigrants took their first steps toward permanent residence in the Greater Houston area, reinforcing existing residential trends. Whether in the older wards of the central city or in newly developing southwesterly suburbs, Houston's neighborhoods maintained a racial and class architecture before and after the civil rights era. Then, in response to the oil bust of the early 1980s and especially the much-delayed desegregation of Houston schools, neighborhood boundaries and demographics in the 1980s underwent reorganization, nonetheless reinforcing an entrenched culture of residential racial segregation.

Chapter 6, "Finding Whiter and Browner Pastures in the Ethnoburbs," sheds light on the ways Houstonians navigated their city in response to changing schools and neighborhoods, again reinforcing existing class- and race-based segregation. Chapter 6 continues the spatial history laid out in Chapters 4 and 5, following the movement of Indian and Pakistani immigrants from southwest suburban Houston to present locations in suburban Sugar Land. The terms that characterized residential decisions or mini-migrations across the city— "suburbs," "good neighborhoods," "poor people"—were loaded with meaning. To be sure, neither all nor most South Asian immigrants adhered to this specific pattern, nor does this chapter trace all South Asian movement through the metropolis. But Sugar Land has the highest concentration of South Asian Americans in the Greater Houston area, and this bears some explanation. By focusing the study on a target group of class-cohesive immigrants and a few areas of significant settlement, my research interrogates the actions of this group as a window into Houstonians' views of race, the city, and its environs in the aftermath of de jure racial segregation to the present.

PROLOGUE

The history of postwar South Asian immigration to the United States converges at the intersection of race, class, and geopolitics. Simply stated, Cold War priorities dictated that the U.S. government engage middle-class Indian and Pakistani publics abroad while simultaneously reassessing the racial scripting of Asian Americans at home. The two processes—engagement and reassessment—had in common the American State's strategic uses of Asians at home and abroad in the context of the Cold War. The resulting recasting of resident Asian Americans and new Asian immigrants was delimited by class. That is, the very middle-classness of newly successful Asian Americans in the postwar years and the new immigrant stream existed in tension with and served to displace a historical legacy of state-sanctioned racial discrimination against people of color in the United States. Thus, class emerged as a crucial analytical lens.

The formation of the Indian middle class around the mid-nineteenth century and of race-based U.S. immigration exclusion in the same time period bears some explanation, since these spatially distinct but temporally overlapping processes merged during the Cold War. This convergence refashioned immigration from South Asia to the United States as primarily skilled, rather than working class or agricultural, as in the past. The new Asian immigrants were hailed as exemplars of minority success against the purported failings of other, less materially successful American minority groups.

The historical development of these eventually entwining, transnational narrative strands forms the substance of this prologue. Concentrating on the nineteenth and early twentieth centuries, the prologue provides the foundational context on which to build a history of postwar South Asian immigration to the United States. It demonstrates, first, the role of immigration policy in shaping race relations toward Asians in the United States. Next, it illuminates how class (and caste) privilege—especially through language and education—predated and facilitated migration. Eventual migration to and material success in the United States were rooted in these colonial hierarchies and class/caste order. Understanding these particular histories is essential to understanding the history that follows.

Nineteenth-Century to Early Twentieth-Century
Asian Indian Immigration

In the United States, the popular perception of Asian Indian immigrants as reviled foreigners at the turn of the twentieth century was transformed into that of a purported model minority in the Cold War era. This reversal was both reflected in and reinforced by the tightening and eventual loosening of exclusionary, discriminatory immigration law. Before the Cold War, white attitudes toward Asians of any ethnic background were forged through a broad framework of historically anti-Asian laws.[1] Starting in the 1870s, lower courts and the Supreme Court handed down rulings while Congress enacted laws, all pertaining to immigration, naturalization, marriage, property, employment, residence, and schooling. Together, these rulings and laws systematically aimed to prevent Asians from equal access to American society writ large.

Asian Indians began settling in the United States in numbers ranging from a few hundred starting in the mid- to late nineteenth century to a few thousand, prompting a nativist reaction. Where nativists had more easily overlooked the much smaller streams of Indian migration from Bengal in the 1880s, they did not ignore the few thousand Punjabis who began to replace barred Japanese agricultural labor in the early twentieth century in the Pacific Northwest.[2] Bengali immigrants had "cycled through" commercial and maritime networks spanning industrialized East Coast cities down through Texas.[3] In high-tourist areas, street peddlers sold tablecloths, handkerchiefs, and other textiles embroidered by women in Hooghly, Bengal. Patronizingly described in the American press as both "handsome" and "ridiculous," many settled on the outskirts of Storyville, New Orleans's red-light district, and entered into intimate relationships with local African American and Creole women.[4] From New Orleans, these peddlers ventured across the South, as far as Houston and Atlanta, to sell their goods but also to reside in Galveston, Memphis, and Charleston. A second group—Indian maritime workers in the engine rooms of British merchant steamships—began deserting their ships in port, hoping to find less grueling work in the United States. World War I, especially, brought larger numbers of Indian ex-seamen to provide labor in American munitions, shipbuilding, and steel factories. Later, they expanded their occupational pursuits to include Detroit's automobile plants, as well as the service and hospitality industry throughout the Northeast. As in New Orleans, they frequently married into communities of color (especially African American and Puerto Rican), sometimes opening restaurants and other small businesses in these segregated neighborhoods.[5] While precise numbers are difficult to obtain, between 20,000 and 25,000 Indian steamship workers passed through New York harbors, while a few hundred docked in Galveston.

A separate stream of British Indian immigrants—lumber and railroad workers from Punjab—first began settling in the Pacific Northwest after being violently driven from British Columbia, Canada, in 1907. That same year, white lumber workers in Bellingham, Washington formed a mob that rioted against and overran the living quarters of Indian workers, assaulting and expelling them from that town. The exiled Indians headed south to California, where they settled. In 1908, Canadian authorities passed legislation limiting the entry of any "immigrant of Asiatic origin"; intended specifically to target Asian Indians, this law drastically reduced immigration after 1909 and effectively diverted it to the United States.[6] The Indian population resided in many of the major American cities of the East and Midwest, as well as the South, but it was heavily concentrated in central California. In 1920, the U.S. Census reported 2,544 "East Indians" in residence nationally. Of these, 1,723 lived in the central California agricultural valleys of San Joaquin, Sacramento, and Imperial.[7] They hailed mostly from Punjab but also from Bengal, the western state of Gujarat, and the United Provinces, and they either owned, labored on, or leased farmland.[8] They married into local Mexican-descent communities.

Anti-Asian nativist groups, having successfully curtailed Chinese and Japanese labor migrations in 1882 and 1907–8, respectively, turned their renewed scrutiny onto what they described as the "Hindoo invasion," "tide of turbans," "and "horde of fanatics."[9] Throughout the Pacific Northwest, Indian laborers met with mob rioting, looting, and burning of possessions, as well as organized efforts on the part of local whites to drive them away.[10] Anti-Asian groups, especially the Asiatic Exclusion League, established in 1905, quickly organized against what they described as a looming Indian "menace" in the western territories.[11] By cultivating a strong circle of influence, first among immigration officials and then with U.S. congressional representatives, the league successfully pressured officials to deny admission to over a thousand Indians between 1908 and 1910.[12] The league's momentum capitalized on decades of militant nativist maneuvering that had previously resulted in passage of the Chinese Exclusion Act (1882).[13] Their actions would further give rise to state passage of Alien Land Laws (enacted in 1913 and renewed in 1920) and, finally, to immigration restriction at the federal level in 1917.

In 1917, in the midst of war, the U.S. Congress passed an immigration act creating an "Asiatic barred zone... [that] covered South Asia from Arabia to Indochina."[14] It effectively excluded all Asians from entry into the United States, but it was intended specifically to exclude Asian Indians, since both

Chinese and Japanese had already been excluded or restricted by law. The exclusion of all inhabitants from a wide expanse of what Congress designated as "Asia" ensured that Asians would remain perpetual foreigners in the United States for the next fifty years, until 1965. Rooted in an entire architecture of racially discriminatory laws, such as a foreign miners' tax, the Chinese Exclusion Act, the "Gentleman's Agreement," and Alien Land Laws, this new legislation attempted to maintain the "racial purity" of a white American population against what was cast as a "polluted" Asian race. This system of structural and social racism led to a drastic reduction in the population of Asians in the United States. As a result of immigration exclusion and the comprehensive spate of complementary legislation, fewer Indians opted to enter the United States, and many left the country in search of more equitable conditions. Meanwhile, American immigration agents denied entry to nearly 3,500 Indians between 1908 and 1920.[15] At its height, in 1910, the national population of Indians numbered almost 5,500, but by 1940, only 2,400 remained—an almost uniformly male population.[16]

U.S. Law and Asian Racialization

Asian Indians' racial classifications in American society and the legal system—as well as the rights associated with different classifications—were ambiguous, with official records documenting them variously as black, mulatto, white, or even Oriental, Turkish, or Malaysian. Socially, they assumed tenuous, vacillating identities. They were, at turns, granted citizenship based on a fleeting whiteness; tolerated as exotic outsiders, as purveyors of exotic goods, and as mediators between a consuming public and its desired products; or stripped of citizenship on the basis of an irredeemable foreignness. The framework of structural racism erected to bar the entry and advancement of Asian immigrants was experienced on the ground as open violence and hostility at the hands of whites. At the same time, Asian immigrants resisted these attacks by finding ways to circumvent them. They used the court system, found white Americans willing to help them strategically navigate the law, and employed a host of other strategies.

The legally sanctioned political exclusion of Asians, generally, was rooted in Reconstruction era debates that aimed simultaneously at expanding civil rights for some while curtailing them for others. At the historical juncture during which Congress extended citizenship rights to African Americans through the Fourteenth Amendment in the wake of the Civil War, it explicitly denied Native Americans and Asians the same right. The Naturalization Act of 1870 specifically and intentionally excluded foreign-born Chinese, with congressional debates entertaining the idea that the "Asiatic population" was incapable of "either understanding or carrying" out a republican form of government.[17] The act established the first official precedent for barring Asians from the American polity, heralding further state and federal legislation in subsequent decades. In 1872, the California Civil Code stipulated that "all marriages of white persons with Negroes, Mongolians, members of the Malay race, or mulattoes are illegal and void."[18] Similar antimiscegenation laws—pertaining most often to white-black unions but also and specifically to Native Americans and the aforementioned groups—were passed in most western and southern states in the nineteenth century and remained in effect until the mid-twentieth century.[19] Congress renewed the Chinese Exclusion Act in 1892 for another ten years and later for an indefinite period, barring the immigration of all Chinese and setting another precedent for the ultimate exclusion of all Asians from the United States.

Like Washington Territory and Oregon State in the mid-1800s, the state of California passed its first Alien Land Law in 1913, prohibiting "aliens ineligible for citizenship" from leasing and owning land. The law was aimed at curtailing Japanese agricultural success but, after the Supreme Court ruling in *U.S. v. Thind* in 1923, affected Asian Indians as well. In response, Indians mostly partnered with white American farmers, bankers, lawyers, and others, forming corporations in order to purchase land for Indians (a common practice of resistance among Korean and Japanese farmers in the American West).[20] Some Asian Indians moved to other states, and a few transferred ownership of their landholdings to their Mexican wives.[21] After a 1933 court case jeopardized the Indian-white corporations, many transferred land ownership to their U.S.-born children.[22] Punjabi immigrants, despite successfully leasing over 160,000 acres of land in central California by 1919, were nevertheless occupationally confined mainly to farming.[23] Berkeley doctoral student-turned-farmer (and later congressman) Dalip Singh Saund explained that, because of racism, "few opportunities existed for me or people of my nationality."[24]

Segregationist policies based on a doctrine of "no Negroes–no Hindoos," "no Asians," or "no non-whites" in the American West and South meant that Indian immigrants suffered the indignities of racism in a white supremacist culture.[25] For example, although Bengalis in New Orleans could pass through transitory spaces like hotels and restaurants, they remained barred from residence in white neighborhoods and from marriage with whites—sites of relative permanence. Because of this fluid racial scripting, some African Americans even found it advantageous to "pass" as "Hindoo" peddlers and entertainers.[26] Ultimately, the biracial children of Bengali immigrants were subject to the rule of black hypodescent, consequently identifying as African American or with the other minority communities in which they were raised.

The comparatively high population of Asian Indians in California, though never very populous, nonetheless faced a host of race-based obstacles. In urban areas, Indian Punjabis resided with other Asians (Japanese and Chinese) in segregated Chinatowns or in "foreign sections," often alongside Mexicans.[27] Statewide, they were routinely denied service in restaurants, hotels, movie theaters, and barber shops.[28] Hospitals sometimes refused them urgently needed care.[29] In agricultural areas where Punjabi men married Mexican-descent women, the children of Punjabi and Mexican or Mexican American intermarriage were categorized as people of color and usually, "regardless of what school district they actually lived in, were directed to the 'nonwhite' schools," along with local Mexican and African American schoolchildren.[30] Punjabi fathers sometimes successfully fought to place their mixed-race children in white schools.[31] In everyday exchanges, they were reviled as "slaves," "niggers," "black," and "Hindoos," even as anthropologists labeled them "Aryan" or "Caucasian."[32] Thus, in the realms of education, housing, marriage, land ownership, employment, and citizenship, Asian Indians faced a front line of race-based obstacles; they repeatedly fought these strictures through the legal system.

American courts inconsistently granted Asian Indians citizenship, determined by whether they met a racial prerequisite for whiteness based on rationales of either scientific evidence (per the German anthropologist Johann Friedrich Blumenbach) or what they described as common knowledge.[33] Naturalized citizenship cases—such as those of Asian immigrants Ah Yup in 1878, Bhicaji Balsara in 1910, Ajkoy Kumar Mazumdar in 1913, Takao Ozawa in 1922, and Bhagat Singh Thind in 1923, among others—both constituted and reinforced the privileges and conflicting meanings of whiteness. The *Balsara* and *Mazumdar* federal court cases authorized naturalized citizenship for Asian Indians on account of their being scientifically "Caucasian." A decade later, in the *Thind* case, the Supreme Court reversed position, stating that Asian Indians were "not white," whether according to the "numerous scientific authorities" cited in the *Ozawa* case or per the "understanding of the common man."[34] The *Ah Yup* and *Ozawa* cases had already barred Chinese and Japanese immigrants, respectively, from naturalization. The *U.S. v. Thind* ruling retroactively stripped Indian Americans of their citizenship and, in states where alien land laws applied, revoked ownership of land.[35] The status of Asians as "aliens ineligible for citizenship" was once again reinforced through the law.[36] Until 1946, Indian immigrants were denied naturalized citizenship and Indians prevented from permanent entry into the United States. Access to the American nation, both literally and politically, was subject to a racial prerequisite.

The proverbial nail in the Asian immigration coffin was secured in 1924 with passage of the National Origins Act, also called the Johnson-Reed Act. Under continuing pressure from nativists during the surge of nationalistic fervor in the wake of World War I, Congress passed the act, which numerically limited immigration into the nation, based on a system of global racial hierarchy.[37] The act aimed at reducing entry from what were deemed the racially inferior regions of southern and eastern Europe (relative to allegedly racially superior Anglo-Saxons), targeting Jews, Italians, Slavs, and Greeks.[38] Although Asians were already generally excluded via the 1917 act, the 1924 act went a step further by removing the remaining entry categories for Asians—students, merchants, and teachers—on the basis of their ineligibility to naturalized citizenship.[39]

Race- and nationality-based quotas would remain the normative framework for immigration into the United States for the next several decades. Consequently, although a small stream of Asian students entered despite exclusion laws, Asians continued to embody a racialized, permanent foreignness in the American imagination and law.[40] The exclusion of Asian immigrants from the American polity and the legal codification of racial discrimination against all people of color upheld the dynamic of white supremacy, casting those of Asian descent as perpetual outsiders.[41]

Immigration Law during and after World War II

Despite their civic exclusion, Indian residents of the United States capitalized on the juncture of World War II to secure their right to citizenship.[42] Indians in the United States built support among prominent Americans and members of Congress to urge President Franklin D. Roosevelt to promote India's independence from Great Britain and to obtain U.S. citizenship. Toward this end, they held press briefings, invited nationalist leaders from India to deliver lectures, and published anticolonial pieces in major American newspapers.[43] In the mid-1940s, members of Congress—including John Lesinski, William Langer, and Clare Boothe Luce and Emanuel Celler—introduced three separate bills in favor of American citizenship for Indians.[44] Two of the bills were supported by two increasingly divergent U.S.-based organizations: Mubarak Ali Khan's India Welfare League and J. J. Singh's India League of America.[45] In 1944, the Senate considered the India Welfare League's Langer bill, which granted citizenship only to those Indians resident in the United States before 1924.[46] Although the Langer and Lesinski bills were ultimately tabled, Congress continued to weigh the Luce-Celler bill.[47]

In addition to establishing organizations and print publications, the crowning achievement of this small but politically active community of Indians in the United States was that of generating support for the Luce-Celler bill. After many years of cultivating ties with influential American journalists, academicians, and politicians, they found champions for Indian citizenship rights in Republican congresswoman Luce and Democratic congressman Celler. First introduced in 1943 and supported by the India League of America, the Luce-Celler bill offered citizenship to those of Indian nativity regardless of entry date into the country. In hopes of "strengthening ties with India" and its (soon-to-be victorious) independence movement, Congress passed the Luce-Celler Act in July 1946, granting Indians U.S. citizenship rights before India had even been granted independence.[48] The Luce-Celler Act, which also applied to those of Filipino descent, "authorized admission into the United States of persons of races indigenous to India" and "ma[d]e them racially eligible for naturalization."[49] The act thus repealed the exclusion of Indian and Filipino nationals (but not all Asians), allowing a total quota of one hundred nationals per country to enter the United States annually. Although this number was a mere trickle, the decades-long battle for citizenship rights affecting thousands of American residents of Indian and Filipino descent finally met with success. Coupled with passage of the Magnuson Act in 1943, which repealed Chinese exclusion, the Luce-Celler Act symbolized a modest liberalization of American immigration policy, which had just undergone the most restrictive period in its existence.

Although Congress slightly amended immigration policy with regard to specific Asian nations during World War II, Cold War foreign relations precipitated a turning point in the official attitude toward Asians. However, given the persistence of Asian American Othering, the turning point should be considered limited at best. At least among liberal white Americans, diplomatic circles, and government officials, there was a growing consensus that "treating Asians more equally at home would strengthen America's appeal abroad."[50] The election of Californian Dalip Singh Saund to the U.S. House of Representatives in 1956 from a state that only recently had supported the wartime internment of its Japanese American citizens indicated a shift in perceptions. In the not-so-distant past, Californians had championed Asian exclusion, discriminatory land-ownership laws, antimiscegenation statutes, and racially segregated public education. In the decade after passage of Luce-Celler, Saund repeatedly campaigned for elected office. That the Democratic candidate Saund was elected in a Republican district illustrated not only that international relations had demanded more equitable relations with Asian nations and, consequently, official acceptance of more equitable Asian American rights, but that there was also a growing tolerance of Asians in the American midst.[51]

Following nearly eighty years of vehemently anti-Asian legislation, even nominal changes were important. In the context of the Cold War, perceptions of Asian Americans began to soften. Various postwar refugee acts of the 1950s included Asians, although the main concerns were for displaced Europeans and for the American image abroad. The McCarran-Walter Act, passed in 1952 in the thick of the Second Red Scare and the nascent Cold War, allowed for the detention and deportation of suspected communists and leftists while also establishing a new preference system for immigrants that prioritized the entry of the world's skilled immigrants above others.[52] This idea of preferring occupational skills was a significant departure from and a lasting transformation in immigration policy, and one that would prove especially useful to immigrants from India and Pakistan.

The 1952 act, however, was racialized and discriminatory against Asians. Though appearing to be more egalitarian than existing immigration law pertaining to Asians, the act created an "Asia-Pacific Triangle" that approximated the Asiatic Barred Zone created in 1917. On the one hand, unlike the 1917 stipulations, Asian inhabitants of the newly named triangle were now admitted to the United States, and the 1952 act permitted naturalized citizenship in spite of Asian birth. Each Asian country within the triangle, however, was allotted a roughly one-hundred-person immigration quota for a sum total of two thousand for the entire triangle.[53] That is, the quotas continued to reinforce the idea that Asians were a race apart, requiring their own dedicated immigration policy and quota ceiling, unlike for European immigrants. With regard to Asians, U.S. immigration policy shifted from exclusion before World War II to extreme restriction in the decade after the war.

The changes were admittedly minimal and meant to symbolize a more welcoming, tolerant America; however, the blatant racial discrimination borne out by the designated Asia-Pacific Triangle raised concern within the Harry Truman administration. "These restrictions would announce to the peoples of Asia 'the United States still considers you undesirable,'" wrote one official to the president.[54] Senator Hubert Humphrey voiced concern that the bill's racial stipulations "would bring about the worst kind of international relations."[55] Increasingly, domestic policy, (including on immigration) conformed to foreign policy. Painfully aware of the potential for international consequences, Truman appealed to Congress "to enact legislation removing racial barriers against Asians from our laws. Failure to take this step profits us nothing and can only have serious consequences for our relations with the peoples of the Far East."[56]

Just two years earlier, in 1950, during congressional debates on passage of a refugee act concerning the immigration of Jewish Holocaust survivors, Senator James Eastland, a longtime opponent of immigration, cautioned that a possible consequence of admitting Holocaust survivors would be the admission of other undesirable immigrants—namely, Asians. He stated, "No one can deny the compelling humanitarian reasons which will be advanced to obtain special consideration for millions of unfortunate displaced victims of the war in China, or approximately 10,000,000 Pakistanian [sic] displaced persons in the partition with India."[57] Eastland was a Democratic senator from Mississippi and a staunch nativist. His position on the issue reflected the racial conservatism of the McCarran-Walter Act, but Eastland also meant that by making an exception for Jewish refugees, others—even Chinese or Pakistanis—could make a legitimate moral case for immigration into a historically white-dominated nation.

Eastland's imagery of the Asian masses at the gates emblematized American lawmakers' resistance to racial equality in immigration law. Even though Congress passed the McCarran-Walter Act over President Truman's veto, expressing its willingness to include resident Asians in the body politic of the United States of America, the inclusion of the Asia-Pacific Triangle demonstrated that the act was a fundamentally conservative piece of legislation. Changes in immigration law in the 1940s and 1950s, especially with regard to Asians, were rooted in the demands of U.S. foreign relations and strategic national interest.[58] The warming of relations between the United States and Asian countries—for example, China, the Philippines, India, and Pakistan—presented a paradox, since at the same time, restrictive American immigration laws were firmly in place. In the wake of World War II, although the United States rescinded the absolute exclusion of immigrants from Asian countries, these were largely symbolic adjustments, significant mainly for the legal entry of Chinese war brides, and not intended to open America's doors to all Asians. Similarly, the 1946 act regarding citizenship and entry of Filipino and Indian immigrants permitted a token one hundred immigrants—in no way a substantive change. The McCarran-Walter Act remained in effect until passage of the Immigration and Nationality Act of 1965, a major immigration policy overhaul. The 1965 act removed national origins and racial quotas and expanded family reunification while preserving occupation-based categories, with an emphasis on the highly skilled and highly educated. Also, as with McCarran-Walter, American congressional leaders had no intention in 1965 of altering the nation's ethnic composition.[59] The retention of occupation-based immigration and family reunification, however, would defy congressional motives of selectivity.

Education as a Pathway for Upward Mobility

During the exclusion and restriction years, a separate but parallel process evolved in the Indian subcontinent that would ultimately intersect with changing U.S. immigration law. It was no accident that English-speaking, highly educated Indians and Pakistanis made up almost the entirety of South Asian migration to the United States from the 1950s through the 1970s. Their training, qualifications, and language fluency—a core foundation built on the Western colonial system of education in British India—greatly expedited their collective economic success as immigrants. Other immigrant groups lacking educational credentials on entry into the United States struggled for far longer and for much lower compensation over time.[60] Indeed, it was the centrality of higher education in the subcontinent as it evolved in the nineteenth and twentieth centuries, along with fluency in English, that enabled South Asian immigrants in the United States to achieve upward mobility in the 1960s and 1970s.

English-language fluency among Indians was officially encouraged in the early 1800s and quickly became a tenet of government policy toward education in the subcontinent. The British colonial government resolved in 1835 that it "would impart to the native population a knowledge of English literature and science through the medium of the English language."[61] Henceforth, government funding for indigenous education ceased.[62] Soon after, the Resolution of 1844 specified that graduates of English education schools (that is, those schools founded and funded as a result of the 1835 resolution) would be given priority in civil employment positions.[63] After 1844, English became a ticket to employment within the ranks of the British government.[64] By learning the English language and adopting the British system of education, middle-class Hindus stood to gain a foothold that would challenge British hegemony over India and, just as importantly, the Muslim and Hindu aristocracy.[65] Thus, the "Englishing of India" was a response to the commercial and administrative needs of the British government and subsequent demands by Indians desirous of gainful employment.[66] By the mid-twentieth century, demand for English education continually surpassed available resources, and between 1885 and 1947, the number of large colleges increased from 21 to 496.[67]

Offering employment as an incentive for completing education at English schools set a precedent for creating a culture of higher Western education. In less than one hundred years, a growing class of English-speaking, Western-educated Indians had emerged. Some adopted, as well, the English manner of dress, speech, taste, and habit.[68] For most, Western education meant gains in opportunities as well as social and economic status.[69] Although overwhelmingly Hindu, this elite slowly included Muslims of the old aristocracy under Mughal rule. The sons of farmers who would otherwise have remained on the family farm were afforded the opportunity to attend grammar schools, learn English, and vie for positions in local colleges and universities. They became the new middle class, and though very small at first, they also married into the more established, elite class. In this way, the number of educated Hindu and Muslim Indians increased.

After Independence in 1947, the leaders of postcolonial India and Pakistan envisioned technologically modern nations—the prime path toward which was higher education. Bringing this vision to fruition would prove daunting.

As early as 1947, future prime minister Jawaharlal Nehru "noted that the 'new India' was to be closely linked to the world of science."[70] Both nations embarked on a path of industrialization, but India formulated a clearer vision and committed greater resources to the task. Ultimately, it fell far short of its goals, but part of this project of modernization was the expansion of the university system, a post–World War II phenomenon transpiring around the world, as well as in India and Pakistan. The development of higher education in India and Pakistan coincided with the United States' own unprecedented expansion of higher education in the postwar years.[71]

Sharing a "common origin" in the British education system, the university systems in independent India and Pakistan prevailed as the path to upward mobility for a growing middle class, building on existing educational infrastructures and with abundant foreign aid.[72] Rapid industrialization depended largely on an educated and technologically skilled labor force largely consisting of engineers and technicians, as well as skilled and semiskilled workers.[73] Problematically, in the immediate post-Independence years, a majority of Indians and Pakistanis in higher education continued to favor liberal arts degrees as had been encouraged during colonial rule; the aristocracy in Pakistan and India was well versed in Western classics but lacked expertise in the applied sciences and technology.[74] The technological fields, however, quickly gained a foothold. Some eighty thousand Indians opted for degrees in science and engineering by the early 1950s. Where the colonial government had built four engineering colleges (in 1794, 1847, 1854, and 1856), as well as medical and legal colleges, with fresh commitment in the Independence era, India, in particular, invested its own resources and was successful in securing external support for the establishment of several institutes of technology and management.[75] In collaboration with various other Western countries, the Indian federal government founded the elite Indian Institutes of Technology.[76]

Despite this vision and interest, institutions of higher education in both Pakistan and India faced considerable challenges. At Independence, between twenty and thirty universities existed in India along with 636 smaller colleges and thousands of two-year specialized training centers.[77] These colleges and polytechnics offered specialized basic training in medicine, engineering, law, commerce, and so on, serving as a transition between high school and university, where students studied another two years for a bachelor's degree. In 1947, some 240,000 students were enrolled in higher education in India and Pakistan.[78] In 1948, the Indian government appointed a commission to periodically assess the state of higher education in the country, plan appropriate changes, and commit to the state expansion of higher education.[79] Older universities expanded tremendously in size and scale.[80] By 1962, 4,555 students were enrolled in doctoral programs in India, another 66,000 studied at the master's level, and 4.5 million Indians worked toward their bachelor's degrees.[81] Although the raw numbers seem impressive, the total number of educated Indians accounted for less than 2 percent of the population. In the effort to "democratize" education, the Indian government actively sought to "open up the universities to all sections of society"—that is, to include minoritized groups such as Dalits, women, and Muslims. Their efforts were successful inasmuch as the number of these groups attending university increased. Still, university students continued to hail largely from the middle and upper classes, and upper castes, especially before the educational reforms of 1977.[82] These students would form the backbone of the new South Asian migration stream to the United States.

At formation, Pakistan had only two major universities. Before 1947, most professors were Hindu, and in the immense cross-migration that occurred at Partition, these Hindu educators largely migrated to India, "stripping the faculties of much of their academic strength."[83] Muslim academics filled some of the open positions. Soon after its founding, Pakistan had thirty-one liberal arts colleges but only one agricultural college and one engineering college for all of East and West Pakistan.[84] In addition to the large universities, numerous smaller, subject-specific institutes or colleges operated under the administration of the universities. By 1950, four technical universities had been launched. In 1952, the Ford Foundation opened three polytechnic institutes to "fill the gap" between vocational schools and engineering universities, thereby widening the scope of opportunity to more Pakistanis.[85]

As the new industrial-capitalist class of elites pressed for regional autonomy, securing their grip on economic and, consequently, political power, the small but growing middle class sent their sons and daughters to these newly created universities in hopes of upward mobility.[86] In addition, private entities funded several secondary educational institutions that prepared the middle class for universities both within and outside Pakistan. The cost of privatized education was well beyond the reach of most Pakistanis.[87] By 1955, the Pakistani government had opened four more universities, bringing the total to six, and through public and private funding, 191 colleges and 46 professional schools had been launched. Even as student enrollment increased, however, the universities faced a shortage of qualified teachers.[88] The rapid expansion of higher education in Pakistan, as well as in India, led to wider access by students but did so by sacrificing quality of instruction, at least in these early days of nation building. In part because of this emergent state of higher education, many middle-class students, like the elite before them, contemplated studying abroad, especially in the United States.

Regardless of a student's course of study, English continued to be the language of instruction after Independence at the postsecondary and especially graduate level in India and Pakistan, thus ensuring that South Asians seeking postgraduate degrees at American institutions would have a working fluency in English. As the rapid expansion of South Asian higher education produced an increasing supply of technically skilled, English-speaking, middle-class South Asians, their number outpaced the availability of jobs. Further, as evidenced by the national rate of literacy, "education remained a distant dream for the vast majority."[89] At Independence in 1947, the literacy rate in India stood at only 15 percent, increasing to 28 percent by 1960 and 34 percent in 1970.[90] All in all, those seeking entry into the United States, whether directly as immigrants or via the student migration route, were subject to relatively stringent admissions criteria, either as skilled professionals or on the path to higher education. Together, the qualified professionals and student migrants represented a fraction of the overall South Asian population, a credentialed elite composed mainly of the middle class and, for Indians, the upper caste. They were primed to succeed both before and after migration to the United States.

The Cold War and Changing Foreign Relations

Migration pathways between South Asia and the United States were forged in the arena of the Cold War. The Cold War became the blueprint for U.S. foreign policy, guiding major and minor decisions, from 1948 (the year the Marshall Plan was implemented) through the fall of the Berlin Wall. Even countries of modest global standing were drawn into the orbit of U.S.-Soviet hostilities. At the outset of the Cold War, American involvement in the Indian subcontinent occurred within the context of continuing U.S. immigration restriction of Asians. That is, even though the American State began to regard Asian nations as potentially valuable allies, Asians had been officially regarded as unfit for U.S. entry and naturalized citizenship since 1870. In particular, the United States sought to influence the South Asian middle classes—the same middle classes that had emerged largely in the late colonial era and expanded through the twentieth century through the avenues of formalized training and education discussed in this chapter. Ultimately, they provided the core group from which students, engineers, scientists, and physicians migrated to the United States in the 1960s and 1970s. How the United States established ideological linkages in the 1950s that would unintentionally encourage migration is the subject of the next chapter.

. . . .

CHAPTER ONE

U.S. IDEOLOGICAL LINKAGES

WITH INDIANS AND PAKISTANIS,

1950S–MID-1960S

"I came to America in . . ." So begin the stories that people often convey about their journey as immigrants. In their telling, the narrative commences at the point of arrival in the United States. In my understanding, however, the journey originated well before immigrants set foot in this country. With regard to postwar immigration from India and Pakistan to the United States, the process of migration originated with the building of a relationship between the two regions. The expansive programming activities of the American State during the first twenty years of the Cold War inadvertently created migration linkages between the United States and South Asia. Thus, even before passage of the Immigration and Nationality Act of 1965, South Asians had already visited and begun imagining the United States as a destination for migration or higher education. American public diplomacy programs frequently targeted middle-class South Asians, prefiguring the idealized, highly educated "immigrant type" embodied in the 1965 immigration act.[1] From its inception, the development of modern migration linkages with South Asia (and East Asia) relied on class as a privileged point of entry and as a means of strategically reenvisioning the long-excluded, much-maligned "Asian."[2]

In the wake of World War II, the newly empowered United States sought to contain the spread of communism both covertly and more openly in Pakistan and India—Asian countries initially on the periphery of American foreign relations and the Cold War but ultimately not overlooked.[3] Together, the State Department and United States Information Agency built a complex web of economic assistance, educational exchange, and information dissemination, coordinating their efforts with American universities, industry leaders, and private organizations and targeting their work primarily at the South Asian middle classes. Formed by President Dwight D. Eisenhower in 1953, USIA battled communist, anti-American propaganda overseas through its own propaganda campaigns. Indian and Pakistani responses to these programs indicated both a healthy skepticism of the received official narrative and individual strategizing for opportunity and upward mobility at home and in the United States.

Robert McMahon, in his landmark work, *The Cold War on the Periphery*, writes that the massive dollars in aid given to India and Pakistan "produced amazingly little support or understanding for the United States in either country."[4] A closer look at public, rather than government, diplomacy, however, shows that by the time new American immigration policy came into existence, American public diplomacy operations in effect in the region since World War II had established deep migration linkages. Although the overhaul of immigration legislation would have heralded this migratory shift anyway, it is important to note the role of American public diplomacy efforts in transforming middle-class attitudes toward the United States before 1965. The 1965 immigration act, in particular, was less an awakening to the possibility of the United States as a host country than a tool through which to implement a desire already widespread among the South Asian middle classes—and one cultivated by the American public diplomacy machine.

Indeed, the decades-long effort yielded far-reaching consequences that would, in part, help reshape American cities through immigration from the subcontinent from the late twentieth century and into the twenty-first century. Rooted in the later years of World War II but especially active in the early Cold War, American State–sponsored public diplomacy and exchange programs in Pakistan and India were so sweeping and so expansive that it would have been surprising if they had not made an impact. Where McMahon focuses on U.S.–South Asia government relations to conclude that there resulted scant sympathy for the United States, I counter that public diplomacy efforts and educational exchange produced fruitful support and an earnest attempt to understand the United States, at least among the substantial middle classes of South Asia. Public diplomacy programs served as the starting point for the migration process because the programs created an ideological foundation among the South Asian middle class for imagining a life in the United States. When paired with U.S. immigration policy favoring skilled, educated, middle-class migrants (specifically, the McCarran-Walter Act, passed in 1952), public diplomacy during the 1950s was a key agent in precipitating immigration from targeted Third World nations. As much as immigrants' own narratives routinely begin at the point of migration, often the first step in the migration process between two places is the formation of an ideological connection between them.[5] Obviously, several factors contribute to emigration from any given place. Local economic malaise, wartime upheaval, and quality of life are all significant, but as Saskia Sassen notes, "while the nature and extent of these linkages vary from country to country, a common pattern of expanding U.S. political and economic involvement with emigrant-sending countries emerges."[6] The United States entered into future emigrants' spheres of knowledge in many ways, one of which was through public diplomacy. As a result of these programs, the notion of emigration to the United States—albeit temporary migration in the minds of most students—was rendered increasingly plausible.[7]

To be sure, other factors may have contributed to the formation of migration linkages between the two regions. Along with U.S. public diplomacy programs, American nonprofit organizations and institutions had a strong presence in Pakistan and India, including development projects, aid, technical assistance, and educational outreach. Even though many of these programs ran concurrently, they nevertheless diverged in significant ways, and for the purposes of this narrative, they only minimally (if at all) bolstered migratory linkages with the United States. American modernization and development efforts must undoubtedly have bred some sense of familiarity. Also, the impact of American military, economic, and food aid to Pakistan and India in the 1950s and 1960s, along with the work of the Ford Foundation and other philanthropic groups, may have generated positive public opinion overseas, at least initially.[8]

One key difference was that cultural diplomacy efforts directly engaged the educated middle classes as well as mass audiences, whereas philanthropic organizations usually addressed the rural masses, often through local Indian and Pakistani agents. However, the nonprofit organizations did not seek out publicity to the extent that USIA did, nor was their success incumbent on positive public opinion. Through USIA and educational exchange, the State Department explicitly demanded that Pakistanis and Indians turn their attention toward the United States, consider it as an educational destination for students and professionals alike, and regard it as the global paragon of democracy. They did not anticipate that South Asians would envision permanent migration to the United States—only that some foreigners would visit the United States briefly, become convinced of American cultural superiority, circulate this knowledge, and, finally, reject communism while supporting U.S. foreign policy objectives in the region and elsewhere.

The State Department, White House, and Joint Chiefs of Staff did not initially envisage Pakistan or India as relevant to the emerging Cold War, though this would quickly change. In the earliest years of the Cold War, fears of the Soviet Union expanding into Eastern Europe guided American foreign policy, with concern that the Soviets could secure control over unstable postwar nations and their economies and thus pose a direct threat first to Western Europe and then to the United States.[9] Within this framework, the United States and Soviet Union mostly dismissed as insignificant the new nations of Pakistan and India following Independence in 1947. By 1948, increasingly certain that Soviet designs involved nothing less than global conquest, the U.S. military promoted greater involvement and investment in Asia and other parts of the Third World in support of the nascent Cold War.[10]

By 1950, the United States expressed a more serious interest in South Asia, particularly toward Pakistan as a key ally.[11] American engagement in the Third World, however, must be framed within the central guiding concern of the time: the containment of not only Soviet communist expansion and influence but also, by the early 1960s, China. By his second term in office (1957–61), President Eisenhower had largely shifted his focus from rebuilding Europe to influencing the sovereign nations of the Third World, including Pakistan and India.

Thus, when Eisenhower toured South Asia in 1959, he visited India, Pakistan, and Afghanistan. Soon thereafter, Chester Bowles, undersecretary of state in the Kennedy administration, envisioned a coalition of India, Pakistan, and Japan as a counterbalance to Asian communist heavyweight China.[12] Strategically, the United States viewed India and Pakistan as a regional "South Asia"—a valuable frontline against "Asia," with its dominant China and the perceived threat of Chinese communist overreach.[13]

India and Pakistan pursued their own interests, complicating American commitments in each country. With regard to the young nation of Pakistan, Washington anticipated that with extensive military and economic support, the country could serve both as a defensive outpost to protect valuable Middle Eastern oil reserves against any future Soviet threat and as an intelligence outpost for covert surveillance of communist foes. Pakistan quickly and eagerly donned the role of American ally and was deemed by U.S. officials as particularly "friendly" to the United States.[14] President of Pakistan Mohammed Ayub Khan referred to the country as "America's most allied ally in Asia."[15] With respect to India, the United States sought the open support and alignment of Asia's most populous and prestigious noncommunist country—one that might then voice support for American foreign policy aims both at the United Nations and through mutual cooperation.[16] The United States worked to "maintain a significant presence in India and Pakistan through economic aid and loans, technical assistance, and cultural exchange programs by heaping a massive $12 billion in total aid to India and Pakistan between 1947 and 1965."[17] By 1965, American aid to India and Pakistan far surpassed that to most other countries.

India's importance to the United States increased in response to Soviet advances toward the new nation. India became a focal point for the Cold War after Nikita Khrushchev assumed control of the Soviet Union in 1953; he subsequently conveyed heightened commitment to India by visiting and offering aid. Indian prime minister Jawaharlal Nehru, however, continued to espouse a policy of nonalignment and refused to allow the affairs of powerful Western nations (that is, the United States and the Soviet Union) to dictate the terms of India's foreign relations, thereby stirring up much concern within the Eisenhower administration (particularly with Secretary of State John Foster Dulles) and in Congress.[18] Idealistically and ideally, Nehru would have India meet other nations on its own terms.[19] Because Nehru forcefully advocated a position of nonalignment and took a leading position on the issue among Third World nations, the United States paid particular attention to swaying this influential South Asian nation.

Building the Public Diplomacy Apparatus in South Asia

Information and exchange activities in South Asia were expanded in the early 1950s, reflecting Pakistan's and India's increasing importance to American officials.[20] Operating in Europe, Asia, Latin America, and Africa during World War II, and serving as a bridge between the wartime information offices and postwar information work, United States Information Service (USIS) posts were USIA's branch offices overseas. Working under the direct supervision of U.S. foreign embassies and the State Department, small USIS posts remained in key cities around the world after the war.[21] In the postwar era, the Department of State expanded USIS operations in India and launched a new information program in the fledgling nation of Pakistan. Starting in 1948, commensurate with Cold War fears and more than a doubling of the congressional budget for information activities, the United States substantially increased the annual budget for USIS operations in India.[22]

In 1950, USIS India could report a consistent information program replete with library work, press and publications, film screenings, photo and art exhibits, and extensive networking activities.[23] USIS posts in India and Pakistan, as in the rest of the world, relied on staffs consisting of a managing core of U.S. nationals who supervised hundreds of local employees. The USIS program expanded through the decade to include the educational exchange of students and lecturers between the United States and South Asia, and more USIS branch centers and libraries opening in West and East Pakistan and India. Based on the number of personnel (as well as other criteria), by the late 1950s, USIA ranked the five most prioritized countries for information campaigns as Germany, India, Japan, Pakistan, and France.[24] These nations were prioritized according to their strategic value or their susceptibility to communism.[25] A "Plan of Operations" for Pakistan summed up the goals clearly: "Rigorously

pursue effective information and education programs designed to broaden support for actions consistent with U.S. policies and to diminish susceptibility to
communist appeals."[26] Allotted annual budgets averaged one million dollars
to each country.[27] Educational exchange programs also flourished throughout
the 1950s.[28]

The public diplomacy work of USIA and its USIS offices around the world was
made possible through the U.S. Information and Educational Exchange Act.
Also known as the Smith-Mundt Act, it was signed by President Harry S. Truman in January 1948 and was crafted "to promote the better understanding of
the United States among the peoples of the world and to strengthen cooperative
international relations [through the] interchange of persons, knowledge, and
skills."[29] In essence, the Smith-Mundt Act extended wartime propaganda efforts into permanency, although, in theory, cultural exchange and propaganda
were to be conducted through separate government agencies because of the
taint associated with propaganda.[30] President Dwight D. Eisenhower proved an
even more committed proponent of what officials then termed "psychological
warfare," and this conviction fundamentally shaped his foreign policy.[31]

In the main, USIA targeted what it described as "the moulders of public
opinion" or the "key attitude forming groups," consisting of current and future
political leaders, teachers, journalists, military personnel, government officials,
and college and university students—essentially the middle class.[32] American
officials never aimed to reach the entire peoples of both nations or even the
entire middle classes of either nation: USIA determined that persuading the
entire South Asian populace of millions of "inhabitants of varying stages of
literacy, speaking diverse languages and with widely differing backgrounds"
was untenable.[33] After Partition, with India's immense population of 361 million and East and West Pakistan's combined population of 75 million—mostly
outside the reach of radio and television broadcast—the task would have proved
daunting, if not impossible.[34] Instead, even as USIA launched programs with
mass appeal, it courted the native, literate classes through a creative array of
print, radio, and visual media, as well as education and exchange activities.[35]
It expected this native leadership to fulfill the implicit task of promoting the
United States, thereby supporting American initiatives. In countries all over the
world, hundreds of USIS posts, centers, and libraries worked the ground operations for the USIA headquarters in Washington. As USIS offices in India and
Pakistan expanded their operations and overcame hurdles, they came to judge
their work as successful, formulating a multifaceted assessment apparatus that
included formal opinion surveys, follow-up polls, anecdotal evidence, and surveillance. Although, as historian Jason Parker observes, actual persuasion is

challenging to gauge, if measured by South Asian participation in USIS events, inquiries regarding study at American universities, and attendance at USIS libraries, the educated classes were *very* interested in the United States.[36] The shared interest between them and the U.S. government was mutual.

American agencies attempted to sway mass opinion but endeavored especially to influence the South Asian middle classes through an array of tools, which resulted in fostering long-term migration linkages between the United States and these countries. Using various forms of media communication and marketing, these tools included, but were not limited to, establishing libraries, distributing a vast print catalog, arranging traveling exhibits and films, providing a steady stream of American lecturers and entertainers, promoting higher education, and issuing special U.S. visas. The State Department and USIA regarded this last category, Indian and Pakistani visitors to the United States, as a valuable asset in their propaganda war against the Soviet Union. Returnees were enlisted as spokespeople—mouthpieces to disseminate accounts of a rosy America. Taken comprehensively, USIS programs consisted of a plethora of information activities and the robust exchange of people; the programs precipitated a shift in perceptions as middle-class Pakistanis and Indians shared information and experiences with each other. They constructed and engaged in new narratives about an America that might figure into their own lives.

USIS offices operated under the direction of the U.S. ambassador, underscoring the alignment of USIS with foreign policy objectives. For example, in Karachi—home of USIS headquarters for West Pakistan—the headquarters were housed *in* the American embassy. Likewise, USIS India headquarters were housed *in* the American Embassy at New Delhi.[37] Additional posts were scattered in major cities—Bombay, Madras, and Calcutta in India; Lahore in West Pakistan; Dacca in East Pakistan. They worked closely with U.S. consular offices and with several libraries and smaller reading rooms dotted throughout the countries. Based on their wartime propaganda experience along with new information updated continually, USIA and the State Department created the following sections of large USIS foreign offices: Cultural Affairs, Information, Educational Exchange, Library, Press, Publications, Film, and Radio Broadcasts.[38] Beyond the work obviously indicated by the section titles, local USIS offices organized American art exhibits and handicraft shows, hosted afternoon teas, and meticulously documented each and every event, small and large.

In order to do this effectively, they evaluated and reevaluated, reported on, and adjusted every program, endeavoring to address weaknesses, close gaps, and measure success. They constantly sought to expand their audiences, pressing existing Indian and Pakistani target audience members for additional

FIGURE 1. Reading Room in the USIS Bombay Library, 1954. According to the NACP description, "The library maintains a collection of 9,000 books and more than 200 of the latest magazines, newspapers, and periodicals. An average of 500 persons uses the library each day." (306-PS-56–7314; NACP Still Pictures Division)

names. The breadth of information gathered by the embassies and USIS posts in this surveillance effort was comprehensive—from maps denoting every college and university to detailed lists of communist and noncommunist newspapers to in-depth Indian and Pakistani opinion polls. At their height in the early 1960s, USIS branch offices in East and West Pakistan had expanded to hundreds of staff members.[39] Exhibits frequently pulled in anywhere from several thousand to tens of thousands of viewers over time. Taking as an example the year 1961, in the smaller cities and towns of East Pakistan outside Dacca, the five USIS branch centers screened 281 shows in 1961, pulling in a total of 115,000 people. An additional 165,000 saw smaller shows hosted privately. About 26,000 East Pakistanis visited USIS branch libraries, borrowing nearly 9,000 books. Thousands enrolled in library memberships.[40] These numbers give some indication of the potential reach of U.S. public diplomacy programs in South Asia.

South Asians' Engagement with Public Diplomacy

As a result of these widespread efforts, some South Asians began to envision a place for themselves in the United States, even if just as visitors. With the United States openly inviting "useful" and qualified foreigners to visit, train, and study in the United States—to come and see American superiority firsthand—Indians and Pakistanis began to apply for the several types of visiting opportunities available to them. High- and mid-level foreign leaders were encouraged to visit the United States through the International Visitor Program, founded in 1941, and through the educational exchange provision of the 1948 Smith-Mundt Act. Although the Smith-Mundt Act permitted travel and training, it did not categorically stipulate funding. Thus, when the State Department agreed to arrange the placement of one Mushir Hasan, an employee of Pakistan's central government, for training with an American newspaper, it clearly noted that the U.S. government would cover none of the associated costs, but this did not deter South Asian visitors.[41]

The Foreign Leader Program established under the Smith-Mundt Act awarded South Asians with access to the broader public (Pakistani and Indian intellectuals, politicians, editors, journalists, school principals, and librarians) the opportunity to travel throughout the United States with itineraries carefully tailored both to their specific occupations and interests and to U.S. interests.[42] The program fostered the development of skills and technical expertise for the hundreds of Indians and Pakistanis who visited the United States. Applicants' files were reviewed with an eye toward disqualifying those with, in the words of one U.S. official, anything "derogatory" in their records.[43] Grantees were invited to submit a list of their preferred sites of interest, which included a mix of specific universities (ranging, for example, from Stanford University to Texas A&M University), newspaper and radio headquarters, USIA offices, laboratories, and tourist attractions. After their arrival, they embarked on curated tours, visiting institutions that reflected their areas of specialization.[44]

In 1959, the State Department established the Exchange Visitor Program, through which foreign specialists could visit the United States to enhance or share their expertise. Visitors were placed in small and large universities from Jarvis Christian College in Texas to more prominent institutions across the country. On his return to India, one such grantee, C. Subramaniam, the minister of finance for Madras state, wrote to Secretary of State Dean Rusk that he found his six-week American tour in 1961 "of great educative value." His guided tour, led by a State Department escort, not only introduced Subramaniam to "many leading personalities" but included visits to educational and other institutions. He returned to Madras with a far greater understanding of what he called "the American way of life."[45]

Grantees were expected to be established and experienced in their fields and, on their return, to serve as informal ambassadors of the United States. One such grantee, Begum Shams Ehsun Qadir, school principal of Municipal Girls College in Sargodha, Punjab, after visiting the United States, gave the inaugural speech at an American photography and art exhibit featuring the work of Ansel Adams and Walt Whitman, jointly sponsored by USIS and the Pakistan Arts Council. Speaking to an audience of approximately 1,700 Pakistanis, she found favorable comparisons between American ideals of "democracy, mutual help, and understanding" and the "Islamic concept of universal brotherhood."[46] Occasionally, grantees received permission for a spouse to accompany them to the United States, if the spouse was socially well placed. One such husband, referred to only as Mr. Hamidullah, self-funded his trip with his wife, Zeb-Un-Nissa Hamidullah, a grantee under the Foreign Leader Program. It was noted that Mr. Hamidullah's "political and social connections are very wide."[47] In this way, the United States essentially got two leaders for the price of one, widening the network of influence in Pakistani social circles, especially among that class of Pakistanis most likely to send their grown children to the United States for higher education.

Although the total number of Indian and Pakistani grantees was never high, USIS's strategic use of grantees' corroborative experiences in and impressions of the United States expanded the reach of the Foreign Leader Program. Indeed, their selection for such grants was heavily swayed by the potential degree of influence they could later exercise. According to an embassy official recommending a Pakistani woman named Sarwat Qureshi, she was selected over another because "she will be in a position to make a greater contribution upon her return to Pakistan." After their return, grantees received regular mailings apprising them of U.S. foreign policy developments as they pertained to India or Pakistan.[48] As they circulated information about their experiences in the United States, the foreign leader grantees became an important strand in the creation of migration linkages between the South Asian middle classes and the United States.

Pakistanis and Indians who had visited the United States served as potentially invaluable witnesses to American habits, attitudes, policies, and thoughts. Because they were fellow nationals, their experiences abroad lent their narratives an air of authenticity that rested on America passing muster through the eyes of a skeptical foreigner.[49] Representing a geographic cross section of their home countries, grantees returned home and were later called on to formally speak about their experiences in the United States in events organized by local

USIS posts. Often, returnees spoke in glowing terms about their stay in the United States and about the country itself. Pakistani M. A. Azam returned to Dacca after studying and living in the American Midwest for five years. Speaking at the USIS Dacca auditorium in 1954 before one hundred East Pakistani educators, students, government officials, and other guests, Azam cited the "human character" of the American nation—one that was "inspired by patriotism, fraternity, charity, and other laudable human traits, [more] than any other country."[50]

An Indian alumnus of Wayne State University, P. T. Joseph strongly believed that "the Indian student who returns after higher studies in America is perhaps the best advocate of the American system of university education."[51] USIS officers considered these favorable reviews as "just and true pictures," ideally suited to challenge communist, anti-American representations.[52] American-educated Indians were sought out by other elite Indians as reliable sources of information on the United States—regarded perhaps as more genuine than the six thousand Americans in India. USIS officials viewed Indian graduates of American universities as "play[ing] a vital interlocking role between local Indians and Americans" in the effort to increase Indian familiarity with the process of democracy—never mind that India was already a democratic nation.[53]

Outside the confines of formal USIS events and State programs, middle-class South Asians disseminated information about the United States through the complex channels of everyday knowledge circulation. Yasmin Iqbal's recollections provide an example of how "America" entered the South Asian imagination in the early Cold War years. Iqbal, a woman from Pakistan but born in the Indian village of Nowgong in the early 1940s, recalled her earliest perceptions of the United States, long before migrating to Houston. At Partition, she had migrated as a five-year-old with her family to Karachi. As with nearly all Partition migrants heading east or west, Iqbal's family brought with them few belongings. They built their material circumstances virtually from the ground up, having no employment, basic furniture, or home goods. Toys were a luxury, she admitted.[54] Nevertheless, as part of an emerging middle-class family, Iqbal attended all-girls' schools through college. Before ever thinking about migration, she had an impression of the United States, which she characterized as a place of "richness and freedom." Iqbal believed that it was "a very rich country. . . a democratic country." She had heard stories of the United States being so rich that "even the postmen, [when] they come and deliver the mail, they have a car. At that time, [this] was not imaginable in Pakistan."[55] She had heard firsthand accounts of the United States from "people talking. Sometimes when we were in college, somebody came for education over here [to the United States]. [Also] the professors they [came] back and they told us that [American] people are helpful."

Iqbal had access to networks of knowledge, the kinds of social networks that, to varying extents, enabled access to privilege.[56] Several other interviewees also alluded to having access to this kind of social capital. Iqbal continued, "Sometimes, you read articles or listen to the radio. [The] TV station was not there when I left Pakistan. It opened after a couple of months so I cannot say that I watched any TV programs." The professors and friends who had traveled to the United States, as well as American visitors to Pakistani grade schools, were vital nodes in the networks of knowledge circulation in newly forming migration flows. In 1968, Yasmin Iqbal and her husband, Jamal, moved to Houston after Jamal received admission to the University of Houston to complete his training in power engineering.

By the late 1950s, news of the American government's overtures to educated Indians and Pakistanis was spreading. Individual educators often sought information on participating in some sort of teaching exchange or lecture series in the United States. The president of the Madras Bar Association, for example, wrote to U.S. senator John Sherman Cooper, inquiring about a possible lecture tour.[57] Officially, local USIS offices helped to vet the applications of potential South Asian visitors to the United States, while the State Department organized the itineraries for their stays. Unofficially, even when visits were independently funded, they might nevertheless prove useful to USIS, such as when a group of ten Pakistani businessmen, civil servants, and landowners privately arranged a group tour in order to build ties between American and Pakistani Muslims. Learning of the imminent group tour, Chargé d'Affaires ad Interim John K. Emerson at the American embassy in Karachi promptly wrote to the Department of State. He proposed that the department and USIA use their available media resources to promote the visit, as it "could do much along the lines of USIS program objectives."[58]

On top of these efforts by USIA and the State Department, other governmental and semigovernmental initiatives encouraged a veritable flurry of exchange activity between the United States and South Asia. The work of American educators, philanthropists, and other foundations directly and indirectly lent support to U.S. foreign policy goals of containment. Through the Fulbright Act (Public Law 584, signed in 1946), American educators sought opportunities to teach and research in India and Pakistan.[59] By 1952, the United States had sent several American scholars to conduct research projects in India and Pakistan. In those first years, grantees included professors of art, Sanskrit, and linguistics.[60] Some were specifically selected to promote American education through workshops with local teachers, as referenced by Garrett Soulen of USIS Karachi: "Among the teachers of the Punjab and the NWFP [North-West Frontier Province], there is increasing enthusiasm for American education and training methods, thanks to the successful workshops carried out by two Ful-brighters."[61] Similarly, other education specialists on Fulbright awards achieved distinction when students at the Karachi colleges where they were stationed earned highest marks on university examinations.[62] Under the International Educational Exchange Program (established through the Smith-Mundt Act of 1948), for example, American high school teachers and principals lived in one of roughly twenty-five countries for up to a full academic year. Teacher George McKelvie of Long Beach, California, was awarded such a grant to teach in India from 1961 to 1962.[63] These educators were expected to teach their content areas but equally to serve as representatives of the American system of education.

American efforts in India did not go unnoticed among Indians already res-ident in the United States. Dalip Singh Saund, a Democrat from California and the first U.S. congressional representative of Indian descent, endeavored throughout the 1950s and 1960s to foster stronger ties between the peoples of India and the United States. He met with Indian trainees who visited on U.S. exchange programs. He wrote to other members of Congress, with a mission to cross-promote understanding and knowledge between Indians and Ameri-cans through privately funded travel and study grants to both countries. The Friends of India Committee, cofounded by Saund, wrote to Undersecretary of State Chester Bowles and stated that they were "well aware of the excellent work being done in the 'exchange of persons' field of agencies by the Indian and the United States governments."[64] Encouraged further by the U.S. ambassador to India and the Indian ambassador to the United States (Ellsworth Bunker and Mahomed A. C. Chalga, respectively), Saund hoped to increase the limited gov-ernment resources presently available. Replying on behalf of Bowles, Secretary of State Dean Rusk stated that he was "completely in sympathy with" Saund's and the others' efforts and offered "tangible assistance."[65]

Separately, in 1961, the Indian Students Association (ISA) of Iowa State Uni-versity wrote to President Kennedy, inquiring as to how they could privately assist government exchange programs. They proposed raising funds sufficient to send American students to India. In addition, ISA members gave talks when visiting India and wrote letters to their fellow nationals in praise of American universities. In his reply, Assistant Secretary of State Brooks Hays suggested that ISA also serve as hosts in Ames, Iowa, to Indians who visited the United States under government or other private grants. Such personal commitments, Hayes offered, were "one of the best ways of increasing mutual understanding and the hope for peace."[66]

The sum effect of these wide-ranging public and semiprivate endeavors ex-tended beyond recasting America's image in the eyes of Pakistani and Indian visitors. These individuals returned home full of stories about their experiences in the United States. Indians and Pakistanis who traveled to the United States in any of these capacities usually proved to be optimally useful Cold Warriors after their return. USIS Karachi officer Garrett Soulen summed up the work and perceived successes of the public diplomacy program in Pakistan:

> The combined use of Specialists sent by the Department with FOA [Foreign Operations Administration] technicians and other American talent, together with returned Pakistanis who have studied in the U.S., has provided a tremendous impact on audiences at the Karachi USIC [USIS Center] through a program of lectures and round tables on American Higher Education and Training for the Professions. These series have received wide acclaim from professors, teachers and students alike as well as from professional men, writers and other members of the local intelligentsia.[67]

For the purposes of this project, however, they were also a crucial part of the shifting, middle-class attitude toward the United States and higher education in American, as opposed to British, universities. As the preferred target of wide-ranging public diplomacy programs, educated South Asians became consumers of American-produced literature, art, information, and education. As empowered agents in their own lives, they weighed these cultural forms and determined how their very consumption could be construed as opportunity. Whether reading U.S.-produced literature on offer at USIS libraries and reading rooms, attending lectures by American university professors, or participating in exchange programs, Pakistanis and Indians strategized about what these actions could mean for them, not what they meant for the United States. Public diplomacy programs and the full range of state-sponsored interventions in India and Pakistan during the early Cold War decades were indeed a catalyst for changing perceptions of the United States. At the decidedly limited invitation of the American State, Indians and Pakistanis established the foundations for migration flows.

Higher Education and the Promotion of the American State

Between the dawn and dusk of the twentieth century, South Asians fundamentally altered their preferred destination for higher education abroad. Whereas elite British Indians had once pursued higher education mostly in the colonial metropole of England, by the end of the century, middle- and upper-class Indians and Pakistanis opted for the universities in the United States. This transformation was most obviously the result of the Immigration and Nationality Act of 1965, which encouraged high-skills immigration, along with British passage of restrictive immigration laws in the early 1960s. By way of explanation, some might also cite a certain inevitability that the United States, empowered in the postwar era as a global political and economic leader, would also emerge as the preeminent educational leader. Well before passage of the 1965 act, however, the. Department of State and USIA, through careful planning and concerted effort, deliberately put American higher education on the radar of South Asian students.

The United States actively promoted American higher education among South Asians as a symbol of American intellectual superiority over communism. In addition to sending South Asians to the United States through passage of the Fulbright Act (1946) and Smith-Mundt Act (1948), the State Department and USIA exhausted every opportunity to send American lecturers, exchange professors, performers, and athletes to hundreds of schools, colleges, and universities throughout India and Pakistan. In 1949, the American Council on Education, working closely with the State Department, stated that "it is now a policy of the United States Government to encourage and facilitate [educational] exchanges, written into various acts of Congress and implemented by several governmental agencies."[68] American outposts in India and Pakistan held education workshops, arranged for consultations with American educators, hosted lectures on the merits of U.S. education, and even facilitated the college application process. As a result, the United States emerged as the prime destination for higher education for South Asians. While some South Asians experienced the United States personally, others learned about American education secondhand, but both groups spread word in their own family and social circles.

Pakistanis and Indians with access to formal education comprised those nations' middle-class elites. Most were neither landed gentry nor industrialists (as with the wealthiest families in India and Pakistan), but by virtue of their education, they nevertheless stood apart from their countries' majority populations. The State Department and USIA focused the bulk of public diplomacy work on this educated stratum in South Asia—the group from which future emigrants to the United States would hail. By the time these Indian and Pakistani middle-class elites became immigrants in the United States in the 1960s and 1970s, they had at least a basic familiarity if not a functional fluency in English, as well as training in Western educational approaches. That is, their class ascendance, while built on structures established up to two centuries earlier by the British, was facilitated by U.S. information circulation in the early Cold War years.

In competition with the Soviet Union for Indian and Pakistani support, both the U.S. and Soviet governments heavily concentrated their efforts on the literate classes (faculty and students). While their aims were less philanthropic than calculated to bolster U.S. policy goals, the inadvertent consequence of targeting colleges and universities in South Asia was, in fact, to win over more than a few admirers. Many professors, students, parents, and community members began to regard the United States as a desirable educational destination. The combination of education-related and cultural diplomacy cast the United States as a land of technological superiority and economic abundance. The result of the U.S. cultural mission and economic and military aid was a palpable climate of "optimism" toward the United States, in the words of an American embassy official in Karachi.[69] India-U.S. relations remained tense through the mid-1950s but shifted favorably by the end of the decade and into the 1960s under the Kennedy administration.[70] No longer were South Asians seeking educational advancement limited to Great Britain and a few other places. Now, the United States and Soviet Union offered appealing opportunities. Ultimately, however, the United States proved the bigger draw, as comparatively fewer South Asians expressed interest in Soviet education.[71] Where appealing to the South Asian middle classes was the first strand in the migration process, targeting higher education was a critical second strand.

By 1954, students formed the backbone of the target groups to which USIA tailored its objectives. In a report prepared for the Jackson Committee (officially the President's Committee on International Information Activities), the USIS India office explained, "Realizing that the frustrated young intellectual is the major target of communist propaganda and yet at the same time the major potential strength of the future, USIS has tried to help fill the ideological, intellectual, and emotional vacuum."[72] Pakistani and Indian students were regarded as the most vulnerable and sympathetic segment of South Asian society toward communism. With 50,000 students in Pakistan's colleges and universities, and more than 240,000 in India by the early 1950s, they represented the "primary target group" for U.S. public diplomacy efforts.[73] Surveys conducted by USIS revealed that South Asian students often regarded communist viewpoints as objective but American statements as propagandistic.[74] In 1953, working closely with the American embassy, USIS India inaugurated a new project, the College Contact Program.[75] This robust and "systematic university contact program" aimed to connect with 250,000 Indian students. The program would establish USIS reading rooms on key college campuses in India within two years and, soon after, in Pakistan.[76] These students were enrolled in the roughly eight hundred colleges associated with India's thirty universities.

Supplementing USIS's existing information-dissemination efforts, the College Contact Program included a comprehensive schedule of American faculty visits, lectures, conferences, and workshops for student groups; separately, for the faculty, the program provided question-and-answer sessions with speakers. Less directly, USIS distributed millions of informational pamphlets, some

FIGURE 2. Kamala Bhoota, Indian student at the University of Michigan,
speaks at a panel discussion titled "The Indian Student in America"
during America Week, a USIS Bombay event in October 1948.
(306-PS-49-1549; NACP Still Pictures Division)

through USIS centers and libraries but primarily at universities and colleges.[77]
The agency kept extensive records of all institutions of higher education in
India (and Pakistan as well, although with far fewer universities, this was a less
daunting enterprise), including such information as student population, area
industries, the significance of particular towns, cities, and universities, and the
number of previous grant awards.[78]

USIS posts in India and Pakistan viewed the disaffected South Asian student
intellectual as simultaneously highly susceptible to communism but, if aggressively targeted by the United States, an ideal champion of American interests.
They estimated that 10 percent of Indian students were committed communists, while another 40 percent were potentially susceptible. "Stated in general
terms," according to a USIS report, "our objective has been to stop the spread
of Communism in Indian colleges; to spread knowledge of democratic ideals,
in an attempt to win allegiance to these ideals and processes; and to build confidence in America and in America's leadership of the free world."[79] Certainly,
communist propaganda efforts with students influenced both the degree and
types of propaganda-based undertakings by the United States. A confidential

country report in 1954 reported, "The Communists have long been active with student groups, recognizing their importance. USIS must not only counteract this influence but offer something positive and concrete in its place. This is the job of "selling" democracy. . . . The Communists have gone to great lengths to provide in India large quantities of communist publications of all kinds at extremely low prices. USIS is countering these inroads."[80] In line with the goals of the State Department, foreign missions believed that the College Contact Program encouraged pro-American attitudes. An American embassy official in New Delhi, writing to the State Department, reflected, "We are building confidence in America and American leadership."[81] The program served multiple aims: undermining communism, promoting democracy, advancing "America," and countering Soviet propaganda.

By the early 1950s, specific targets of USIS and embassy efforts included educational institutions, youth groups, and students who were invited to lectures, seminars, and student conferences. In India, U.S. information offices reached their goal of contacting eight hundred colleges in one year alone. Together with the American embassy, USIS connected with hundreds of thousands of college and university students annually from the 1950s onward. In East Pakistan, USIS branch centers made over 320 contacts with colleges in their first five years of operation (1956–61), as well as 1,250 contacts with schools and 300 contacts with cultural organizations.[82] This massive effort resulted in a "marked increase" in the demand for USIS materials and supporting services, whether library use, film requests, or circulation of their own periodicals.[83]

Harun Farid, who would eventually migrate to Houston, was one such beneficiary of USIS educational diplomacy efforts. Born in Rampur, Uttar Pradesh, India, Farid attended high school and intermediate school in the city of his birth.[84] When Farid faced a decision regarding college, his father—who owned a *jagir*, or small territory gifted to military leaders and others in pre-Partition India—insisted that he attend Aligarh Muslim University.[85] Instead, Farid felt more inclined to join his cousins and other distant relatives who had migrated to Pakistan in 1947. Without his father's blessing, Farid traveled to Karachi in 1955. At the University of Karachi, he completed his bachelor's and then master's degrees in physics. During this time, he came to know of the libraries at the American embassy and the British consulate, both in Karachi, and "so [he] used to frequent it quite much." There, he found "all kinds of books about America." Setting his sights on pursuing his doctorate in the United States, Farid "got this information about the schools, where to apply, and what to do" at the USIS library in Karachi. Because funding was a matter of some concern for Farid, a professor at the University of Karachi suggested that he apply for a Fulbright, which he was awarded.

Under the Cold War aim of containing communism, hundreds of thousands of Indian and Pakistani students were introduced to American higher education, regardless of their attentiveness to communist ideology or lack thereof.[86] In reality, most Indian and Pakistani students had no direct interest in communism, although they weighed carefully the communist critique of American capitalism and of the United States against its self-promoted American narrative. P. T. Joseph, who wrote a memoir of his experiences as an international student at Wayne State University in Detroit, recalled the various means the United States used to reach South Asian student audiences:

> Almost in the wake of the destruction of World War II came reconstruction, and in the Allies' program of reconstruction education had its due share. The Fulbright Program, for instance, enabled a free exchange of American students with those of various countries like India. This project raised a rich crop of goodwill ambassadors on both sides, many of whom brought back fascinating stories of hospitality and friendliness. The publications of the United States Information Service in India revived my interest. . . . Their bulletins advertised the plentiful opportunities offered by American Universities for higher studies and research.[87]

As Joseph mentions, the United States offered information on American education in India starting even before the Cold War. Through their public affairs branch, libraries responded to queries from Indians about university admissions. In a 1946 report, the American Library in Bombay reported that "higher education in the United States continues to be one of the major interests in both mail queries and requests at the Information Desk."[88] Confidential reports such as "Stereotyped Concepts about the United States Presented in Selected Foreign Countries" (1947) demonstrate that the State Department was well aware of Indian impressions of the United States as "materialistic" and "racially discriminat[ory]" but that, increasingly, promotion of U.S. higher education could be an effective countermeasure.[89] The examples of Harun Farid from Karachi and P. T. Joseph from Trivandrum, South India, epitomize the argument suggested here. Without any intention of developing thick migratory ties between the nations, the United States' Cold War schemes did precisely that. Obviously, with immigration restriction very much in place and the doorway effectively shut (the one-hundred-person annual quota for Indian immigrants under Luce-Celler can hardly be understood as a reversal of exclusion), the State Department had little practical reason for concern. Government officials had no way of knowing that in 1965 that door would open, albeit only selectively.

In the meantime, the accessibility of USIS and American embassy events to the Indian and Pakistani student population was always of paramount concern, and for this reason, USIS strove to offer events free of cost or at least affordable to students. Routinely, USIS made "a special effort . . . to obtain the participation of large groups from the Universities and colleges of Pakistan."[90] American specialists lectured at universities across India and Pakistan, including, for example, Islamia College, University of Sind, University of Karachi, Government Teachers Training College, Urdu College, and Dacca University. Specialists met with youth groups both formally through scheduled meetings at the American embassy (or consulate) in various cities or informally at follow-up discussions immediately after scheduled lectures or at lecturers' hotel rooms, adding an air of accessibility.

Even when events were generally regarded as a "complete and resounding success," student reception weighed most heavily on the scale, as when the American consul general's office at Dacca stated that "it was especially noteworthy that the student group so ardently supported the performances."[91] USIS Karachi officer Garrett Soulen quoted the Dacca office in a glowing report back to Washington: "The students who met [the Americans] here, and there were hundreds, still treasure the experience. Most of them have become members of the USIS Library, many now attend cultural functions . . . and generally are seeking to maintain their newfound contact with America."[92] Although the United States had no interest in opening up avenues for permanent migration to the United States, overseas officers certainly desired students' tacit support and even a sense of commonality with America. Still, what the United States understood as a growing preference for democracy may just as likely have been students' strategizing on how attendance at U.S.-sponsored events might work in their own favor.

USIS always made certain that universities and other educational institutions were part of the targeted audiences for visitors through the Specialists Program, scheduling both formal meetings with faculty members and special visits to local colleges. One American specialist, Abraham J. Moses, was invited on a lecture tour of Karachi schools to speak exclusively with high school students and teachers about college life in the United States, sharing sixty slides of Amherst College and a film on Dartmouth College. In addition, the American Women's Club in Karachi arranged for Moses to meet with small groups of Pakistani students in the homes of American expatriate families—an effort lauded as "winning considerable goodwill for the United States among the students."[93] American university-themed lectures included "Who Should Study in the U.S.?" and "American Education as a Pakistani Educator Saw It." Such lectures often pulled in several hundred attendees in one sitting. An exhibit at Dacca University—officially "unattributed" to USIS but covertly a USIS-produced exhibit—on the American contribution to the expansion of the university, was viewed by at least 90 percent of the students and faculty during its two-week run.[94]

Even those specialists whose areas of expertise lay in the performing arts and athletics, not lectures, visited postgraduate institutions to give special performances. For instance, in addition to their main scheduled performances in the mid-1950s, members of the Martha Graham Dance Troupe gave talks and dance demonstrations at Karachi colleges.[95] When American Olympian and practicing physician Major Sammy Lee toured Asia in 1954 under the College Contact Program, planners decided that his background and training warranted military and medical professionals as his prime audience. Even so, in many cities, including Madras, Bombay, and Karachi, planners made certain to invite students to Lee's swimming and diving demonstrations. In Madras, two separate diving demonstrations by Lee at the YMCA College Pool were arranged exclusively for area high schools and colleges. When American specialists' tours did not include the delivery of numerous lectures at institutions of higher education, they nevertheless often included meetings, lunches, or brief interviews with school and college principals and school inspectors. Underscoring the centrality of higher education for the American public information mission abroad, the State Department, foreign embassies, and USIS posts well understood that this key audience must be included in some form or another.

Other educators beyond the target audience of university students were invited to attend U.S.-sponsored programs. Local teachers, students, and college faculty attended events that were organized variously by major Pakistani and Indian universities, the United States Educational Foundation (USEF), the ministries of education, and USIS offices. A major educational workshop held in 1955 in Karachi, for example, was attended by more than sixty Pakistani teachers and was composed of lectures, consultations, and school tours in which American educators toured Karachi-area schools, observing and advising on classroom practices.[96] Yasmin Iqbal, who would migrate to Houston with her husband, described the school as having a basketball court and baseball field—both singularly American sports. She attended an Urdu-medium school (in which the language of instruction was Urdu), Fatima Jinnah Girls Secondary School in Karachi, and gained some familiarity with American cultural forms.[97] Another woman who migrated from Karachi distinctly remembers American women educators visiting her Urdu-medium grade school, speaking to the student body as a group.[98]

These education-themed events were never solely that. As one embassy official reported, the American embassy and USIS post worked closely in planning events. USIS books and films traveled with many events.[99] These educators, in turn, returned to their institutions with firsthand encounters with Americans and shared their experiences with other teachers, faculty, and students. Thus, the U.S. government reached the masses of students strategically through such in-person events. Beyond even these audiences, USIS and the American embassies often recorded lectures for later broadcast over the radio. Political science professor Jan Karski spoke on the subject of "American and European College Education—a Comparison" during his visit to Karachi in August 1955. This lecture, unlike Karski's many others, was recorded for later distribution and broadcast through Radio Pakistan.[100]

Already by the mid-1950s, USIS India felt that educational specialists invited to the country had exhausted the topic of general American education, and so, from that point onward, visitors increasingly spoke on programs like Fulbright Fellowships or Smith-Mundt grants, private scholarships, specific college admission requirements, part-time employment, and estimated expenses. Although relatively few South Asians were qualified for the stringent educational and financial requirements of most of these opportunities, USIS enthusiastically publicized them anyway. In response to passage of the Fulbright and Smith-Mundt Acts, the United States organized a massive effort to provide international students a place in American universities. Under the Fulbright Act, a limited number of grantees received one full year of tuition and a stipend, but most received only round-trip travel to the United States.

Referring specifically to Pakistan, the Department of State expressed "the belief that through their experience in the United States, they will be able to contribute to the friendship and understanding between the peoples of Pakistan and the United States."[101] In the 1954–55 academic year alone, more than eighty Pakistani nationals, including ten women, were studying in the United States through grants authorized under the acts. They studied fields as diverse as philosophy, criminology, physical education, history, and engineering. In addition, several other students were placed in teaching hospitals to complete postgraduate medical training. The forty receiving universities ranged from agricultural colleges in Utah to Ivy League universities on the East Coast, but only two southern universities.

Two years earlier, 80 Indian students plus 13 faculty and teachers had received Fulbright grants, some of whom were also supported by Smith-Mundt monies. An additional 140 Indian specialists traveled to the United States on technical training programs under a separate grant.[102] Between 1951 and 1961, 67 East Pakistani leaders and specialists, along with 86 East Pakistani scholars, secured Fulbright grants to study in the United States.[103] On completion of their degrees or training, many of these students—just one of many groups— would return to their various hometowns in Pakistan and share their experiences, many of which presumably would have been positive.

These word-of-mouth networks were crucial in creating the robust migration streams that would follow after passage of the 1965 immigration legislation, though Fulbright scholarships continued to figure prominently for Indians and Pakistanis in creating pathways into the United States. Harun Farid, the Indian-born Pakistani student mentioned earlier, secured a Fulbright scholarship and admission to the University of Cincinnati in 1966. Farid—who ultimately chose to complete his PhD in physics at Texas Technological College (later renamed Texas Tech University) in Lubbock instead of Cincinnati—remained in the United States after graduation, never to permanently reside in Pakistan again. He settled in Houston in 1974. Fulbright scholarships were available to foreign students through application at local branches of USEF. These offices provided information about Fulbrights, counseled students about study in the United States and nongovernmental aid, and offered general information about American universities and contact information for specific institutions.[104] USIS posts and centers also counseled students; USIS Dacca advised some 17,400 students between 1951 and 1961.[105] Many Fulbright recipients eventually applied for permanent residence in the United States.

The Ford Foundation, along with other nonprofit organizations, developed programs for higher education in American universities, as well.[106] By the mid-1960s, the Ford Foundation helped fund colleges in East and West Pakistan. Selina Ahmed, a Bengali woman who pursued her graduate degree in Texas in 1971, had attended the College of Home Economics at Dacca—the only home economics college in East Pakistan in the 1960s—established by the Ford Foundation.[107] In addition, the foundation facilitated partnerships between East Pakistani and American universities, including one between East Pakistan Agricultural University in Mymensingh and Texas A&M University. As Jamal Iqbal, a West Pakistani student at A&M in the late 1960s, recalled,

> In those days, there was a program between Mymensingh University in East Pakistan, it being an agriculture university, and A&M, which in those days was basically mechanical or agriculture. So, there were a lot of people who were coming through the Ford Foundation. They didn't come on their own. They came here for two years or three years, got their degrees, and they went back home. But they were mostly from East Pakistan. So, we had a lot of Bengalis there.[108]

In addition, the International Educational Exchange Program (under the Smith-Mundt Act) offered financial aid to a limited number of qualified international students seeking advanced degrees. Recipients were required to be between the ages of twenty-four and thirty-five and to hold a master's degree and have two years of work experience.[109] Foreign students could apply only from their home countries, not as international students already enrolled in American universities.[110] Separately, the Institute of International Education (IIE), a private nonprofit organization founded in 1919 by funding from the Carnegie Foundation and based in New York, worked closely with the State Department on the International Educational Exchange Program and ran the preliminary review of Fulbright applications. The institute administered hundreds of private scholarships, fellowships, and other study opportunities to international students both before and after enrollment in American universities. The IIE's comprehensive "Handbook on International Study" listed American universities, courses of study, job opportunities, and scholarship aid.[111] The State Department routinely advised foreign students to contact the institute for securing funding beyond that covered by Fulbright grants or the department's International Educational Exchange Program.[112]

American Universities in Pakistan

At the institutional level, American universities established a presence in India and Pakistan by sending faculty members for extended teaching opportunities, arranging tours for American students, and offering advisement to Indian and Pakistani universities. For example, Texas A&M University sent a group of professors to Dacca in 1955 for one-year assignments. The American consul general in Dacca found a year's duration too short to be of lasting impact and envisioned an extended four-year stay with the long-term goal of permanent, locally taught courses in American literature, drama, history, and government.[113] Southern Methodist University professor of education B. G. Woods secured a year-long teaching position in Karachi, while Louisiana State University (LSU) and Dacca University formed an arrangement whereby LSU professors of geography would teach at Dacca University.[114] Of student-centered activities, University of California, Santa Barbara, founded its own "Project India" in 1951 in which American students would visit India on guided educational outreach tours, jointly coordinated with USIA and local USIS posts.

On the ten-year anniversary of Project India, Phillips Talbot of the State Department sent a letter of recognition and encouragement to the university's chancellor, Samuel B. Gould.[115] Offering praise, Talbot wrote that even the short-term presence of American college students in India made "a significant contribution to the over-all objectives of United States foreign policy." He added that their presence was "particularly valuable in correcting misconceptions about American life and creating a feeling of camaraderie with their Indian counterparts."[116] Although the State Department neither funded nor administered Project India, it nevertheless gave its implicit sponsorship, based

on the understanding that recognition of such nongovernment initiatives fur-
thered foreign policy goals. Even after the waning of U.S.–South Asia relations
resulting from the 1965 Indo-Pakistani War, State Department executive secretary Benjamin Read, urging President Lyndon B. Johnson in 1966 to meet
with fourteen Project India students as they embarked on a two-month tour
of India, wrote, "While the group has no official status, members are regarded
as representatives and spokesmen for the students of America."[117] From its inception, USIA endeavored to "serve the purpose of American policy" in India,
Pakistan, and other countries.[118] In due time, University of California students
with the new "Project Pakistan" embarked on an educational mission in West
Pakistan in 1964, meeting with hundreds of Pakistani students.[119]

Assisted by the State Department and USIA, American educators visited
Pakistan and India with the aim of fostering both formal and informal interest
in the new Cold War discipline of American studies. As defined in a joint statement from the State Department and USIA in 1959 to all USIS posts, American studies could include any related discipline, for example, American literature, history, or political science. The statement clarified further, "In a broad
sense, American studies include not only separate courses solely or mainly
concerned with the United States, but also treatment of civilization in such
courses as modern history, English language, English literature, comparative
constitutional government, [or] history of philosophy."[120] Wherever the study
of America could be incorporated, posts were encouraged to make every effort
to facilitate its inclusion. This emphasis was reinforced by the many American
specialists and Fulbright scholars whose expertise was in one of these subjects
and who visited Pakistan and India. In July 1964, USIS Pakistan and USEF
held a ten-day seminar on American literature in scenic north Pakistan. Led
by American specialist and University of Oregon professor of literature James
B. Hall, twenty-six mostly Pakistani attendees engaged in ten days of discussion and debate, parting with promises of developing new American literature
courses at Pakistani universities.[121]

Pakistani and Indian International Students
in American Universities

Both before and after South Asian students' enrollment to American universities, the United States envisioned these students as unofficial representatives
of American Cold War concerns. Before South Asian students embarked on
their journey abroad, the American embassies and USEF centers hosted one- or
two-day orientation sessions with dinners at embassy officers' homes in order
to prepare students for problems they might face and to ease their transition.

Most importantly, embassy officials hoped that "the ready rapport established" through these orientations would eventually "enhance the Mission's ability to contact these people after they return," for the purposes of public diplomacy.[122] For the same reason, once students were in attendance at their respective universities, the U.S. government monitored their activities. In regard to a gathering of students in 1954, a representative for the USIA Press Service wrote, "We covered the recent national convention of Pakistani students in Chicago. Three of four good stories were developed."[123] Students were thought to be useful as role models back in their hometowns.

A memorandum from USIA informed USIS Karachi in 1955 that "the Agency feels additional benefits could be obtained from more extensive coverage of the hundreds of foreign students now enrolled at U.S. colleges and universities."[124] Specifically, USIA suggested that USIS posts should showcase students in their local hometown newspapers. The memo suggested that an "illustrated account" might accompany an interview in which students elaborated on their reasons for going to the United States and selecting a particular university. Sharing their daily routine, leisure activities, and plans after returning home would "be of considerable reader interest in [the student's] home area." Though the number of students in American universities was limited, the impact of their experiences could be magnified if handled for maximum effect by USIS and local media sources. The agency continued this practice of producing exhibits on Indian and Pakistani students in the United States well into the 1960s.

Once students had settled in at American universities, USIA's Press and Publication Service, which provided USIS posts with the source material for many of their publications, conducted interviews with students, asking pointedly about the communist threat and other policy-related issues. Several Pakistani students at American universities offered their perspectives. One student responded that poor economic conditions would give rise to communism and that, therefore, developing nations needed to continue their investment in nation building and mass education. Kazi Enamul Haq, a doctoral student at MIT, concurred, stating that robust economies were "an essential weapon against communism." Speaking on the topic of nonalignment (though avoiding that term while obviously directing the comment at India), University of Michigan doctoral student M. Sulaiman Kakli suggested, "I do not think that it is possible to be neutral at this stage. Things have so developed that the world is in two camps and you must choose a side." Kakli also encouraged U.S. military aid to Pakistan.

When he sent the text of these interviews to the USIA directorship, Mike Giuffrida of the Press and Publication Service noted that he believed such interviews "to be a good example of what can be done with loaded questions to

FIGURE 3. (*Above*) Officers of the newly established Indian Students Association of Kansas State University with faculty sponsor, 1960. Approximately 130 Indian students attended the university that fall, by far the largest group from any foreign country. (306-PS-61-1920; NACP Still Pictures Division)

FIGURE 4. (*Left*) Pakistani students from Lahore at Columbia University Teachers College in New York, 1952. (306-PS-52-6901; NACP Still Pictures Division)

put over policy points."[125] First, it is striking that USIA found students who so keenly championed American policy. Second, although there likely were students who expressed contrary opinions, USIA, of course, featured the more sympathetic students in its publications. Giuffrida noted that although students were opinionated, they avoided "a subversive tone."[126] Third, the interviewed students had gathered in Chicago at a national convention of Pakistani students in American universities; these types of student conventions became

FIGURE 5. Begum Haya-Ud-Din moderates a panel discussion at the fourth annual convention of the Pakistan Students Association (PSA) in Louisville, Kentucky, 1957. The PSA was composed of students in American colleges and universities. (306-PS-57-16526; NACP Still Pictures Division)

prime recruiting grounds for students who might become spokespersons for the United States in the Third World.

Meeting in 1954, the first national convention of Pakistani students (the precursor to nationwide campus branches of the Pakistan Students Association) convened in Chicago. Indian students had already established a national organization and branch chapters. The keynote speaker and guest of honor was the Pakistani ambassador to the United States, Syed Amjad Ali. [127] Staffers for USIA conducted interviews with attendees and took photographs, less for the purposes of surveillance (although that is possible) and more as visual media to promote policy imperatives. One such photo, of student Begum Haya-Ud-Din speaking at the 1957 annual meeting, features a large American flag as a prominent backdrop (fig. 5).[128] The students placed a small tabletop Pakistan flag at front center. The photo, meant to circulate through USIS posts in Pakistan, would have signified the availability of educational equality for all nationalities and both genders in American universities, and with great emphasis on equality, generally.

Photos such as these buttressed American claims to egalitarianism against Soviet charges of racial discrimination. In 1955, students met in Madison,

Wisconsin. Chief officer Allan L. Swim at USIS Karachi telegrammed them the following message:

GREETINGS FROM AMERICAN UNIVERSITIES ALUMNI IN PAKISTAN ON EVE OF YOUR SECOND CONVENTION PAKISTANI STUDENTS IN THE UNITED STATES. "ROLE STUDENTS IN PROGRESS PAKISTAN" IS MOST APT THEME YOU HAVE CHOSEN FOR CONVENTION. AS STUDENTS IN UNITED STATES, YOU HAVE WONDERFUL OPPORTUNITY LEARNING NOT ONLY MOST RECENT ADVANCES YOUR RESPECTIVE FIELDS, BUT ALSO CERTAIN LASTING VALUES YOU CAN OBSERVE IN AMERICAN WAY LIFE. TREMENDOUS RESPONSIBILITY LIES ON YOUR SHOULDERS.[129]

The agency left no opportunity to chance. Something as seemingly innocuous as a gathering of foreign students was gauged for its usefulness. By placing a burden of "tremendous responsibility" on the students, USIA, through the Pakistani alumni, reinforced a state policy position. It was no secret that the "lasting values" referred to in the telegram indicated a commitment to democracy and the free market, as well as a repudiation of communism. Yet representing the students as a special, chosen few also imbued the act of study in the United States with a certain gravity, as though students must never fail the nation that privileged them with the gift of education. Select international students even met with the president, as when students from India and Pakistan met with Lyndon Johnson in 1965.[130]

By the mid-1960s, U.S. government officials had refashioned "international" students—a Cold War neologism that replaced the previous term, "foreign" students—into Cold Warriors. Before the Cold War, according to a contemporaneous researcher, "foreign students appeared to most college administrators as a marginal luxury. They brought to the campus a touch of exotic color."[131] By contrast, in 1964 President Lyndon Johnson addressed a group of international students at the White House: "I hope that what you have learned here will help you advance the progress of your own people, for this is no time for men of knowledge and learning to be above the battle, to stand aloof from the fight for a better world." He continued, "Your education is a solemn trust. It carries the responsibility of a lifetime of service to your own country and to the world."[132] The pursuit of knowledge for the sake of knowledge was no longer sufficient. Students carried back to their own societies the message of "America . . . as an unfinished society" striving and struggling toward progress.[133]

Just before they returned to India or Pakistan, some students were invited to attend international student forums at universities around the country, including at Rice University in 1962. Organized by IIE, the forums, stated an editorial in the *Houston Chronicle*, "seek to interpret their views and to sort out their impressions on American life." The editorial lauded "what the Institute of International Education attempts in the good name of our country for foreign students."[134] The events also gave international students one final opportunity to enjoy "a taste of American hospitality and home life," but the editorial stressed that "these students have not been 'indoctrinated' in the American way of life. For, as a free society, we need to do no more than offer them what we are and what we have. Whatever these students take with them is enough."[135] And yet, these exit events suggested that leaving students to their own ideas, without "sort[ing] out their impressions," could not be left to chance.[136]

After students returned to their home countries, they joined the ranks of other returnees, often serving as unofficial ambassadors for the American State. Some student returnees secured faculty positions, just as USIA and the State Department anticipated. Joining the faculties of major universities in India and East and West Pakistan, they served as informal advisers to students on American higher education.[137] Others, such as Indian international student P. T. Joseph, wrote memoirs. Reiterating the standard Cold War mantra, Joseph wrote, "The American concept of education is based on America's firm faith in democracy."[138] In a more official capacity, returnees were screened by USIS to ascertain their favorable views of the United States. If they were judged suitable, USIS invited them to participate in events and lecture about their impressions and experiences. Meanwhile, USIS used the students' examples in their materials. For example, Pakistanis who pursued master's and doctorate degrees in the natural sciences were showcased at an exhibit titled "U.S. Science Serves Mankind."[139] American education was thus cast as a service rendered to the developing world. Although there may have been some truth to this (on the part of American educators in South Asia, for example), the promotion of higher education in the United States was more a Cold War strategy consistent with American geopolitical aims than the American State's attempt to uplift an emerging Global South.

Even when Pakistan-U.S. relations soured after the Indo-Pakistani War of 1965 and the United States came to gradually withdraw intense involvement in these two struggling nations, foreign missions hoped for a "more liberal policy toward research grants in [American] universities."[140] Also, despite the official impasse between the United States and the subcontinent, USIA continued its efforts after 1965, although at a contracted pace. In some instances, USIA expanded operations by establishing new programs and, for example, a new American University Center in Calcutta's college district. Meanwhile, several USIS posts in India directed up to 70 percent of their efforts toward youth programming, geared especially at high school and university students. In their thirty-seven programs held at major universities in India in 1965, some 326,555 Indian students and faculty attended.[141]

Leadership at USIS continued to maintain that young South Asians represented the agency's most interested, accessible, and valuable audience. Continuing to target universities, USIS staffers organized debates, quiz competitions, and seminars that modeled participatory democracy, "alerting [Indian youth leaders] to their special responsibility in the democratic, social, and economic development of India."[142] Film screenings continued to be wildly successful in drawing packed audiences, while the American Specialists Program hosted several lecturers and performers (including, for example, the Yale Glee Club). Writing to the State Department in July 1965 on the subject of "Emphasis on Youth," the American embassy in Karachi stated that it had "undertaken a number of activities to increase the American influence among the potential leaders of Pakistan."[143] Working with USIS Karachi, staffers had built a large program of activities specifically geared to appeal to the various "segments of the younger leadership group."[144]

Certainly, USIA and State Department public diplomacy efforts were not the sole drivers of South Asian student interest in American higher education. By the late 1960s and 1970s, unstable conditions in the colleges and universities of East and West Pakistan included frequent student protests, rioting, and school closures. Students demanded, among other things, lower tuition rates and book fees and a greater administrative voice. By that time, however, the loosening of immigration restrictions in the United States, particularly pertaining to those seeking higher education, provided a normalized category for entry into the country. Before this pathway opened, the United States had actively engaged with Indian and Pakistani students from grammar school through all levels of postsecondary study since the early 1950s. Out of an exaggerated concern for communist sympathies among the student populations, USIA and the State Department heavily promoted American culture and values. American universities worked in tandem with the state to reform Indian and Pakistani higher education. Furthermore, the broad exchange of faculty members between the subcontinent and the United States expanded familiarity with American universities.

The Turn to Selective Immigration

The Hart-Celler Act, officially the Immigration and Nationality Act of 1965, abolished the national origins quota system and eliminated race or ancestry as grounds for immigration; its passage would supplant the need for extensive educational outreach overseas. By this time, however, the network of education-based linkages from the Indian subcontinent to the United States, as developed for the previous two decades, was firmly in place. In fact, Hart-Celler formalized the now well-established precedent of encouraging the entry of highly qualified South Asians. Where President Kennedy had envisioned a system that "meant both an increase in fairness to applicants and in benefits to the United States," in the final version, it allowed mostly for family reunification immigration and, to a lesser extent, skill-based entry.[145]

Supporters of the bill assumed that few Asians would qualify for entry under the preference for family reunification. A revision to the original bill increased the allotment for family members of lawful American residents, not out of concern for long-separated family members but in order to maintain the majority white ethnic composition of the United States. Fewer non-Europeans were expected to immigrate as a result of this change. On the one hand, the 1965 act reflected the United States' recognition that its previous race-based immigration policies were discriminatory, although as Madeline Hsu notes in regard to the 1965 immigration act, "the push for immigration reform had been a protracted, deeply contested, and long-delayed" struggle by ethnic Americans, a few sympathetic congressional representatives, and other concerned citizens.[146]

On the other hand, passage of the act also reflected a crucial need for skilled foreign labor by expanding opportunities for highly trained or skilled persons to immigrate and creating preferences for professionals, scientists, and engineers. Although proponents of the law emphasized its corrective nature, many also anticipated the boost to the American economy and technological competitiveness that skilled immigrants would provide—a serious national concern since the 1957 launch of *Sputnik*. The United States responded to this perceived crisis by expanding advanced education in the natural sciences and by tapping into international sources of skilled immigrant labor. Congress founded the National Aeronautics and Space Administration (NASA) and passed the National Defense Education Act, both in 1958, while the National Science Foundation arranged for thousands of graduate scholarships in the sciences.

Still, many felt that additional sources of skilled labor and scientific scholarship were needed. With the American economy experiencing "unprecedented expansion and transformation," the United States scrambled to fulfill the demand for engineers, scientists, and doctors.[147] President Kennedy's vision of new immigration legislation in 1963 emphasized immigrants' occupations in the context of U.S. labor needs. Those Asians possessing the skills most needed in the technological competition of the Cold War had greater chance of admittance into the country. Although Congress revised the act (eventually passed in 1965 and enacted in 1968) to reflect family reunification more than skill set, Kennedy's version more accurately reflected Cold War priorities.

Not everyone was sanguine about the repercussions of the act. In an attempt to quell concerns, Attorney General Robert Kennedy confidently informed the House subcommittee on immigration in 1964 that with regard to "the Asia-Pacific Triangle, it [immigration] would be approximately 5,000, Mr. Chairman, after which immigration from that source would virtually disappear; 5,000 immigrants would come in the first year, but we do not expect that there would be any great influx after that."[148] Echoing the same sentiment, the bill's cosponsor Emanuel Celler assured Congress in regard to the bill's family reunification emphasis: "There will not be, comparatively, many Asians or Africans entering this country. . . . Since the people of Africa and Asia have very few relatives here, comparatively few could immigrate from those countries because they have no family ties in the U.S."[149] As legal scholar Gabriel Chin carefully argues, many members of Congress clearly understood and anticipated *some rise* in Asian immigration.[150] However legislators did not believe that the composition of the United States would be *substantially* transformed. By the time the bill was passed, after Kennedy's assassination, President Johnson explained to the American public that the bill was not "revolutionary," suggesting that it was simply never intended to significantly alter American demographics, least of all by the unanticipated millions of Asians and Latino/as who would actually comprise the bulk of newcomers after the 1960s.[151]

Where the McCarran-Walter Act of 1952 set up a preference system that favored "highly skilled immigrants" (this First Preference category was allotted 50 percent of all immigrants from a country's quota), the 1965 Immigration and Nationality Act reduced that allotment to just 10 percent (the Sixth or possibly the Third Preference in 1965) of a country's quota.[152] No matter the exact number, Indians and Pakistanis used the skills and family preferences as a means of immigrating to the United States, so much so that they underused other preference categories.[153]

The American perception of a technological gap coincided with India's and Pakistan's need to industrialize and South Asians' increasing preference for American higher education. Within the larger migration of "worldwide professional cultures" in the 1960s and 1970s (also known as brain drain and defined as the migration of high-skilled knowledge workers from less economically developed countries to more economically powerful nations), thousands of South Asian students seeking advanced training in technical fields were increasingly drawn toward American universities and away from British ones.[154]

Since the colonial encounter, students from the Indian subcontinent had traveled to the United Kingdom for advanced degrees, mirroring the educational patterns in many colonized places with their respective metropoles.[155] Both Nehru and Gandhi obtained degrees in England and later formed the core of the new Indian nationalist leadership. Similarly, Muhammad Ali Jinnah, Pakistan's founder and first governor-general, studied law in London before returning to India. Some had also pursued advanced education in the United States in the early twentieth century, most notably the Indian anticolonialist leaders who spearheaded the revolutionary but ill-fated Ghadar Party from the Pacific Coast.[156] U.S.-bound Indian students, however, were the exception rather than the norm. After the completion of higher education in Britain, most Indians returned to India, with many determined to apply their knowledge toward the self-determination of their nation. After Independence, even as elite South Asians disparaged American ideals of materialism and individualism, and other civic leaders (led by Nehru) criticized the escalating Cold War, they understood the necessity of scientific and technological knowledge for their own nation-building project.

Although more and more South Asian students began seeking degrees in American universities, they continued to regard British higher education as superior in the humanities. This opinion correlated with the South Asian contention that as the United States was heavily industrialized and technologically advanced, its academic strengths lay in technological fields (engineering, scientific research, and so on).[157] While many Pakistanis and Indians pursued the liberal arts, education, journalism, and social sciences at American universities, the overwhelming majority inclined toward the sciences. As Indian student P. T. Joseph observed in his memoir, "American Universities have developed into the foremost centers in the world for scientific research and technological progress."[158] He mentioned that this was not limited to his opinion but that other Indians were quickly embracing the idea of an American college education.[159] As early as 1949, a majority of Indian students in the United States pursued engineering or agriculture, both necessary to strengthen their young nation's infrastructure.[160]

South Asians' transition from universities in the United Kingdom to the United States occurred over the 1950s and 1960s. Pakistani student and immigrant Jamal Ahmed Iqbal, who pursued his bachelor's and master's degrees at universities in Texas in the mid-1960s, recalled, "Ninety-nine percent of the people in those days who came to America, mostly came for the higher education. There were not that many educated people who came to America. Most of them went to Europe, mostly to England and Germany."[161] By the time he applied for admission in 1965, several of his friends had either already left or were about to depart for American universities.

In addition to the easing of immigration requirements for students and the highly educated in the United States, three other factors help explain the significant shift in South Asian immigration trends from the United Kingdom to the United States (table 1). First, migration to the United States appealed to Indians and Pakistanis due to increasing anti-Asian sentiment in Britain. The "rivers of blood" speech in 1968 by Conservative Party member of Parliament Enoch Powell, gave voice to this popular racist sentiment, while Parliament's passage of restrictive immigration acts in 1962 and 1965 had already codified popular fears.[162] In contrast, Indian and Pakistani students found comparatively open reception in the major cities of the United States, particularly on college campuses. Second, some South Asians refused to migrate to England, homeland of their former colonizers. A long, complicated, and antagonistic history with England made some Indians and Pakistanis wary of any future connection with the British Empire.[163] When asked if he had considered higher education in England, U.S. immigrant Jamal Ahmed Iqbal replied, "Never thought of that. With our background . . . our experience with all those colonialists, we never thought of that."[164] Finally, possibly more than in any other nation at the time, American universities offered financial assistance to international students. As a result of the National Defense Education Act of 1958 and funding through the National Science Foundation, assistance became available in the form of scholarships, fellowships, graduate assistantships, loans, and part-time employment.[165] A few South Asians did attend universities in the Soviet Union and Yugoslavia, but these remained very few.[166] By 1968, nearly 30 percent of all foreign students in the world attended American universities, far outpacing those enrolled at universities in any other industrialized country.[167]

Although professionals and the highly educated emigrated for any number of reasons, economist Walter Adams suggests that additional reasons were relevant to Indian and Pakistani immigration: higher salaries, better opportunities for professional research, and high unemployment in their home countries.[168] Because of the transitioning economies of India and Pakistan in the 1960s and 1970s, jobs in engineering and the sciences were more abundant in the United States, particularly in the expanding Sunbelt cities of the American South and Southwest. Immigrants themselves have indicated that the income difference was significant. Even educated European immigrants (whose premigration baseline salaries were much higher than those for similar positions in South Asia) doubled their salaries after gaining employment in the United States.[169] Other observers at the time maintained that service economies, such as that found in the United States after 1965, have had greater need for and more employment opportunities for the highly educated.[170]

In 1950, India had 188,000 qualified physicians, engineers, technicians, and scientists. In addition, in 1961, 13,820 students graduated from Indian institutes of higher education in 1961.[171] By 1968, the numbers had increased to include 332,000 qualified engineers and 122,000 physicians.[172] The Indian economy, however, lacked a sufficient supply of jobs to employ qualified college graduates, and thus graduates faced high rates of unemployment in India.[173] Between 1965 and 1968, unemployment among engineers rose from 16,500 to 56,700.[174] Economists estimated that this rate would increase to 100,000 by 1974.[175] Employment opportunities, especially for the highly educated, were limited. Over the subsequent decades, the economy expanded, but even as late as 1980, the number of highly educated graduates in India significantly outnumbered available jobs, resulting in the "overproduction of educated persons."[176]

It is commonly known that the number of Asian immigrants and students in the United States increased steadily after passage of the Immigration and Nationality Act of 1965, but in fact, these numbers began their rise well before 1965. Although permanent immigration was extremely limited for Asian Indians (and, after 1947, Pakistanis), student migrants were granted temporary entry, providing a gateway into the country (see tables 1 and 2). Between 1950 and 1970—from about the beginning of the Cold War to just after *enactment* of the landmark immigration act in 1968—the resident population of South Asians in the United States rose from under 2,500 to about 15,000.[177] In addition, in the 1969–70 academic year, roughly 13,000 international students from India and Pakistan attended American institutions of higher education, up from just 1,500 in the 1949–50 academic year. Many either stayed on or returned to the United States as immigrants. Indians, in particular, made up a substantial portion of international students at American universities since the 1950s (see table 2). By the early 1960s, approximately 10 percent of all international students in the United States were Indian.[178]

Although these numbers are not extraordinary relative to the total U.S. population, they nevertheless reveal an extraordinary story. The several thousand students and U.S. residents from India and Pakistan by the late 1960s were not just the tip of an iceberg: they were the result of two decades of massive American public diplomacy and exchange.

The governments of developing nations initially supported their citizens' pursuit of American higher education with the understanding that returnees would strengthen their home nations with their expertise, but many officials quickly realized the problem of brain drain. During the 1960s, some 300,000

TABLE 1. South Asian population decadal totals in the United States, 1900–2010.

Year	Indians	Pakistanis (after 1947)*	Bangladeshis (after 1971)*
1900	2,050	N/A	N/A
1910	2,546	N/A	N/A
1920	2,495	N/A	N/A
1930	3,130	N/A	N/A
1940	2,405	N/A	N/A
1950	2,398	N/A	N/A
1960	8,746	N/A	N/A
1970	13,149	1,708	N/A
1980	361,531	6,182	**1,015
1990	815,447	81,371	11,838
2000	1,899,599	204,309	57,412
2010	3,183,063	409,163	147,300

Notes: N/A = Information not applicable.

* U.S. data not available for postwar decades.

** This figure, on Bangladeshis, is not census based; rather, it reflects the number of immigrants entering the United States from Bangladesh. Rahman, *Bangladeshi Diaspora in the United States After 9/11*, 36.

Data aggregated from multiple sources: U.S. Census Bureau data and reports; Pew Research Center reports; Xenos et al., *Asian Indians in the United States*, 24–26; Melendy, *Asians in America*; Rahman, *Bangladeshi Diaspora in the United States after 9/11*.

highly skilled professionals left developing nations and permanently migrated to Western countries. The main sending region was Asia, with the highest number of professionals hailing from India.[179]

Officials had linked the problem of brain drain to the immigration of highly skilled professionals, but university admission was another key strategy for brain drain immigrants. After traveling to the United States on study grants and student visas, many students simply never returned home permanently.[180] Investigations carried out by immigration subcommittees in Congress in the late 1960s found that of the 7,913 scientists, engineers, and physicians who "immigrated" in 1967, half had entered the United States on international student

TABLE 2. International students in the United States by selected places of origin with emphasis on Asia, 1949–2000.

Place of Origin	1949/50	1954/55	1959/60	1964/65	1969/70	1974/75	1979/80	1984/85	1989/90	1994/95	1999/00
Asia (Total)	6,806	10,175	17,808	30,640	51,035	58,460	81,730	143,680	208,110	261,789	280,149
South and Central Asia (Totals)	1,522	2,048	4,520	8,235	13,442	13,890	13,350	23,334	38,852	47,836	58,150
India	1,359	1,673	3,780	6,814	11,329	9,660	8,760	14,620	26,240	33,537	42,337
Pakistan	102	255	534	1,081	1,576	3,140	2,660	4,750	7,070	6,989	6,107
Bangladesh	—	—	—	—	—	480	980	2,010	2,470	3,371	3,845
Bhutan	—	—	—	1	1	3	6	8	29	21	57
Nepal	—	4	34	84	109	58	180	320	610	1,264	2,411
Sri Lanka	13	34	73	96	159	230	490	1,480	2,210	2,097	1,968
Afghanistan	48	82	99	159	268	290	270	138	220	111	110
East Asia (Totals)	4,160	5,423	9,268	16,222	27,589	30,720	45,710	72,630	127,320	168,190	180,147
China, People's Republic of	—	—	—	5	19	22	1,000	10,100	33,390	39,403	54,466
Taiwan	3,637	2,553	4,546	4,620	8,566	10,250	17,560	22,590	30,960	36,407	29,234
Hong Kong	—	—	—	3,279	7,202	11,060	9,900	10,130	11,230	12,935	7,545
Japan	265	1,673	2,248	3,534	4,311	5,930	12,260	13,160	29,840	45,276	46,872
South Korea	258	1,197	2,474	2,604	3,991	3,390	4,890	16,430	21,710	33,599	41,191
Europe	6,105	5,648	7,290	11,323	20,022	15,361	25,200	38,190	51,190	73,489	90,661
Africa	901	1,234	1,959	6,855	7,607	18,400	36,180	39,520	24,570	20,724	30,296
Latin America	6,044	8,446	9,428	13,657	24,991	26,271	42,280	48,560	48,090	47,239	62,097
Middle East	1,724	3,636	5,579	8,762	11,761	22,290	81,070	51,740	32,180	21,568	22,725
North America	4,362	4,714	5,761	9,338	13,415	8,630	15,570	15,960	18,590	23,394	24,128
Oceania	198	337	568	1,265	2,077	2,650	4,140	4,190	4,010	4,327	4,677
World Total	26,433	34,232	48,486	82,045	134,959	154,580	286,340	342,110	386,850	452,635	514,723

Source: Data extrapolated from Institute of International Education, "All Places of Origin of International Students, Selected Years: 1949/50–1999/00,"
Open Doors Report on International Educational Exchange.

visas (F visas). When isolating Indian professionals from the data, nearly 80 percent had entered the United States on F visas, regularized their visa status, and remained in the country. The process of adjusting a student F visa to an immigrant visa or to permanent resident status was not cumbersome.[181] As noted by another researcher, "In actual fact, the F visa can rather easily be turned in for an immigrant visa once a student has earned a baccalaureate degree, provided that an immigration quota number is available."[182] The researcher mentioned the belief, widespread in the late 1960s and early 1970s, that "many would-be immigrants have used the F visa as a device for *immigration* more than as a passport to an American *education*."[183] Senator Walter Mondale testified before Congress in 1967 that approximately 30 percent of Asians who had entered the United States on F student visas changed their visa status, despite their initial declaration of intent to return to their country of origin.[184] By the mid-1960s, Indian university administrators expressed growing concern about the permanent loss of Indian students to the United States. In order to keep Indians from leaving the country, one Indian vice-chancellor proposed that the U.S. government should extend grants to Indian nationals to pursue studies in India instead of offering them grants to study in the United States.[185]

Oral history interviews with South Asian immigrants show that many students had only a passing notion to remain in the United States after graduation and, even then, only for a short time in order to gain practical work experience. Most immigrants expected to return to India or Pakistan, even though finding employment back home may have posed challenges. Although jobs could be found in their home countries, opportunities were limited. Finally, some immigrants who already had secure employment in India and Pakistan simply desired the excitement of opportunity that migration to the United States might offer.[186] As some immigrants stated in interviews, they left India and Pakistan in search of "adventure." At the same time, the United States structured entry into the country specifically on the basis of scientific and technological education and skills, facilitating permanent residence for mainly highly qualified South Asians. So, for a variety of reasons and due, in part, to historical, Cold War–generated linkages between the United States and South Asia, Indian and Pakistani engineers, physicians, and researchers made up the bulk of that immigrant stream—part of an Asian American subgroup eventually championed as a model minority.[187]

The machinations of the American State resulted in increased enrollments of international university students from India and Pakistan. In the 1965 academic year alone, nearly twice the number of Indian students attended universities in the United States (2,018) as in the United Kingdom (1,180). That gap would only widen with changes in American immigration laws. In 1970, those figures were 3,549 and 571, respectively. Some increase in South Asian immigration was expected after 1965; it was, after all, part of the rationale for passage of the law.[188] The increase throughout the 1950s, however, was neither as obvious nor as expected. It occurred not because of dramatic changes in the law but because, as the Cold War raged, a quiet battle for hearts and minds was waged in the schools and universities of India and Pakistan. By the time the new immigration law took effect, South Asian students were "primed"—that is, fully cognizant of, experienced in, and open to expanding entry into American universities specifically and the United States in general. Although the United States encouraged the formation of higher education linkages with India and Pakistan—precisely because such affiliations were temporary—it did not desire anything so permanent as Asian immigration to the United States.[189]

Conclusion

Just as the 1965 act would become a law of unintended consequences, so too did public diplomacy activities have unintended consequences. The Department of State and USIA intended for Pakistanis and Indians to support U.S. policies and embrace American-style democracy from afar. American officials did not view their public diplomacy work as an invitation to South Asians to actually move to the United States, as evidenced by the closed-door immigration policy before 1965 and the fact that the 1965 act was not an open-door policy but more a door-ajar policy, meant to usher in family members of U.S. residents, along with primarily highly skilled individuals and their families.

Through sweeping public diplomacy efforts, the United States created a front line of expatriate Americans, South Asian exchange returnees, U.S.-educated students, and scores of admirers who, in turn, "won friends for America all along the way."[190] These included the emissaries who either had firsthand experience in the United States or gained a measure of familiarity with the country directly from American representatives at USIS facilities, college campuses, schools, or small meetings. The overall consequence of American public diplomacy in South Asia from the early 1950s through the mid-1960s was that the Indian and Pakistani middle classes began to view the United States more favorably, although not uncritically. Keenly aware of racial inequalities, they nevertheless believed that higher education in the United States would be equitable enough for them. They came to regard it as a golden opportunity. Many genuinely came to view the United States in positive terms, highlighting the success of American public diplomacy efforts. Even for those who remained skeptical about the American government's potential for good, this public diplomacy front line, at the very least, ensured that the South Asian middle classes kept the United States freshly in mind. This flawed, imagined America was simultaneously democratic and racist; generous and self-promoting; open and disingenuous. It was also precisely where many middle-class Indians and Pakistanis envisioned themselves or their college-age children.

· ·

CHAPTER TWO

GETTING ACQUAINTED WITH

THE UNIVERSITY AND THE CITY,

1960S—EARLY 1970S

Pakistani and Indian immigrants—ambitious students, eager spouses, and hopeful families—left behind loved ones and familiar communities for the United States beginning in the 1950s but especially in the 1960s and 1970s. Over a decade of aggressive public diplomacy coupled with the easing of immigration laws forged a new high-skills labor migration pathway between South Asia and the United States. Unlike many other immigrant streams to the United States, South Asian immigrants from the 1950s to 1980s were overwhelmingly middle class, whether already credentialed or seeking educational credentials. Indian and Pakistani physicians and engineers arrived under visa categories specifically created to attract professionals, as stipulated in the Immigration and Nationality Act of 1965. However, this group alone overlooks the many thousands of South Asians who entered the United States temporarily via Cold War programs and through what historian Madeline Hsu calls "the side door" of student migration.[1] Where formalized, quota immigration from India in the postwar era slightly increased as a result of the Luce-Celler Act, international student enrollment at American universities accounted for an ample stream of immigrants in the long run, as students converted their visas to remain in the United States. South Asians entering on such programs were classified as nonquota or exempt—as nonimmigrant aliens.[2] Although often categorized too hastily as "temporary" movements, in reality, many migrations are neither linear nor permanent at their inception.[3] The decision to settle permanently often unfolds over years. In addition, even those who stayed only temporarily for technical training or state-sponsored visits were incorporated into the new migratory flows as they provided yet another link between the countries.

Whether as immigrants or students, Indians and Pakistanis in the 1950s and 1960s sought new opportunities that would eventually enhance their success back home or help situate them in the United States. As students, they pursued degrees at moderately priced universities across the United States. Among the many cities where South Asians attended university and found employment, Houston emerged as one of many desired destinations from the 1960s, after which the South Asian population in the United States began its sustained growth. During these decades, Houston's institutes of higher education and the availability of economic opportunities made graduates into white-collar workers. Indian and Pakistani engineers, scientists, and business majors found an abundance of employment options in midcentury Houston, with its booming, oil-dependent economy, high rate of migration, and construction frenzy (which, in turn, created more jobs). This chapter explores how Pakistani and Indian students familiarized themselves with the social landscape of the city, its residents, and the university while learning to navigate the racial and class hierarchies of a transitional Jim Crow, Sunbelt city. This examination of students' foundational experiences illustrates the intersectional processes of ethnic, racial, and class identity formation.

Houston's Historical Landscape and Increasing Diversification

South Asians flying into Houston International Airport from Karachi or Bombay in the early 1960s might have glimpsed over the horizon a cluster of downtown buildings surrounded by the city's paper-flat landscape.[4] Emanating outward from a centrally located downtown, grid-patterned neighborhoods dotted with live oak were situated between ten major bayous winding through the city.[5] They may have noticed, viewed from above, the giant chemical industrial complex at the Port of Houston due directly east of the city. Beyond the city's fringes to the north and west stretched seemingly endless piney woods or prairie grassland, while the Gulf of Mexico's shores lay some forty miles from Houston's southeastern edge. Since its founding in 1836, Houston had undergone near-constant transformation. From its original, carefully planned 147-acre plat on the banks of Buffalo Bayou at the center of today's downtown, the city of Houston, located in Harris County, expanded first southward and eastward in a somewhat haphazard pattern, not conforming to the uniform, neatly ordered streets that made up its core.

The city's rate of growth ebbed and flowed relative to larger events: the emancipation of enslaved African Americans that brought rural folk into the city; the construction of railroads in the late nineteenth century that made Houston a regional financial center; and the discovery of oil at Spindletop in 1901, after which oil companies looking for a base from which to conduct business settled on Houston. By the turn of the century, Houston was still a small city, although its boundaries encompassed an area of nine square miles and extended well beyond today's downtown district.[6] Even before the completion of the fifty-two-mile long Houston Ship Channel in 1914, Houston served the region as an inland trading hub for cotton, corn, and hides.[7] True to the vision of its founders, the Allen brothers, Houston received international cargoes of cloth, flour, gunpowder, and other goods, and its participation in global trade networks through the Houston Ship Channel would only expand in the interwar period. Houston's prominence as the oil service capital of the country grew over the twentieth century.

In the interwar years, the city began to diversify beyond its mostly white and black populations, although little changed in the way of its racial status quo.[8] Because of Asian exclusion in immigration law, Houston's Asian-born and Asian-descent populations had remained consistently small, numbering only several hundred between 1870 and 1940.[9] Asian groups in Houston included mostly Chinese and Japanese, with a few Filipinos, Koreans, and East Indians in the Greater Houston area.[10] They were concentrated mainly in agriculture, small business, and restaurants selling mainly to whites and Mexicans. Through the mid-twentieth century, individuals of Asian descent in Texas had faced various barriers to inclusion, from alien land laws preventing the ownership and long-term rental of property to Jim Crow laws prohibiting the use of public swimming pools.[11] In Houston, they attended both white and black schools.[12] A surge of new Mexican immigration across the Southwest in the wake of the Mexican Revolution increased Houston's Mexican-descent population from 6,000 in 1920 to 15,000 a decade later.[13] Texas's substantial Mexican-descent population (albeit much larger than Houston in such cities as El Paso and San Antonio and in the borderlands along the Rio Grande Valley) distinguished it from the rest of the South. Still, despite the presence of these communities, as a former Confederate state with well-established institutions of slavery and Jim Crow, Houston and Texas could hardly be extricated from a southern identity.

The foundations established during and after the postwar years would prime the city for its explosive growth and international turn during 1960s and 1970s. Houston's key industries transitioned from agriculture and oil before World War II to oil, petrochemicals, and natural gas during and after the war.[14] The growing national demand for oil-based products propelled a burgeoning chemical production industry in the vicinity of the Houston Ship Channel, making Houston the largest petrochemical manufacturing center in the world.[15] Starting with the New Deal but especially as a result of World War II, the federal government directed major infrastructure and, later, defense projects to the American South and West. As new military bases were established across the South, nationally Houston was the sixth largest recipient of federal funding for war-related factories, including steel plants, shipyards, and facilities for manufacturing airplane parts.[16] During the war years, the University of Houston established an industrial education program that trained service members; the program also facilitated the growth of an engineering technology program at the university, which would draw prospective South Asian students in subsequent decades.[17] Large companies, followed by new residents from near and far, began a long trend of relocating to the Sunbelt cities of the South, lured by these cities' probusiness environments.[18]

In the postwar era, Sunbelt cities such as Los Angeles, Phoenix, Charlotte, Atlanta, and Houston enjoyed an infusion of federal funding, high rates of in-migration, and similar urban-suburban forms. Over a forty-year period starting with World War II, a flurry of building, investment, and migratory activity reshaped these regionally significant Sunbelt cities such as Houston into globally important, cosmopolitan urban centers with extensive international connections.

Houston's thriving economy began attracting newcomers from across the country and, ultimately, from around the world. The global, skills-based economy into which Houston was rapidly integrating would create an employment haven by the late 1960s for professionalized workers, including those from India and Pakistan. By the 1970s, white-collar professionals made up half of the metropolitan workforce.[19] Increasing numbers of immigrants began settling in Houston in the postwar years, and in 1960, about 9 percent of Houstonians were foreign born. Houston, like Los Angeles and Atlanta, for example, enjoyed above-average population growth—much of it international.[20] That year, the census counted over 4,000 Asian-born residents in Houston, although it did not specify from which countries in Asia. In addition, in 1970, over 35,000 Houston residents listed their birthplace as Mexico—by far the largest origin point for immigrants. Germans, English, Italians, Eastern Europeans, Canadians, and Asians were other large groupings.[21]

South Asian Students in American Universities

Within the national context of South Asians pursuing higher education in the United States, Houston's universities were not the largest recipients of international students. Most students attended institutions on the East and West Coasts, especially in New York and California, as well as in the Midwest. India, however, was among the top-four sending countries of foreign students to the United States from the early 1950s onward, with more than 1,800 Indian students nationwide in 1955.[22] In 1960, some 3,780 Indian and 534 Pakistani foreign students were enrolled at American universities.[23] In the South, the only university to attract a large number of foreign students was the University of

Texas, with 487 such students as compared to the nearly 1,600 at New York University in 1960.

In Houston, only a fraction of these larger totals attended UH and Texas Southern University (TSU) (and, to a lesser extent, Rice University). However, it is notable that UH and TSU nevertheless collectively attracted hundreds of foreign students through the 1970s, even though the universities served an almost exclusively local resident population, were virtually unknown outside the state, received lower funding than other public institutions of higher education (for example, the University of Texas and Texas A&M), and lacked the name recognition and prestige of Ivy League schools. Former South Asian students— UH alumni from the 1960s—state that low tuition, financial aid, and relatively strong science, technology, and engineering programs put UH on their radar, although some mentioned that they knew someone who had already been admitted to the university. Other reasons include former undergraduate professors in Pakistan or India who recommended UH as a good choice. By the mid-1970s, about 175 Indian students and 80 Pakistani students attended the University of Houston (table 3).

The experiences of South Asian newcomers to Houston in the early 1960s— mostly university students at UH—reflected the changes transforming the city during the postwar decades. Indians and Pakistanis arrived in Houston during a period of renewed investment and expansion. Total enrollment at UH swelled in the postwar decade, rising from approximately 2,500 to 13,500 in the 1940s alone.[24] Although there was a slight drop in 1950s, UH nevertheless continued to expand and develop its programs to meet the needs of the city's labor market. Almost from its inception, the University of Houston envisioned its role as educating the public and, in doing so, to "assist modern industry in obtaining intelligent leaders and workers."[25] The university's growth and stability served a vital support role in the city's economic turn and its need for a highly skilled labor source.

Through various means, the University of Houston formed linkages with South Asian, particularly, Indian students overseas. In oral history interviews, Indian and Pakistani student alumni recall that they learned about UH from their professors and other word-of-mouth networks.[26] They also discovered UH through U.S. State promotion of higher education in India and Pakistan via the placement of American university catalogs in USIS cultural centers and libraries. Engineering and related programs at UH were of particular interest. The university formed deep linkages with Indian institutes of higher education, especially with programs of engineering technology. After expanding its own College of Technology in 1962, UH partnered with the U.S. Agency for International Development (USAID), the State Department, and the government

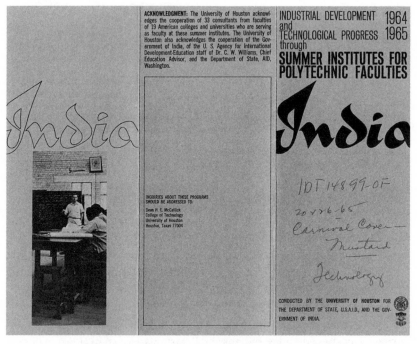

FIGURE 6. Brochure for a polytechnic program cosponsored by the University
of Houston, U.S. Department of State, USAID, and the government of India, 1964.
(UH College of Technology Records, 1940–2009, Box 1, Folder 4,
Special Collections, UH Libraries)

of India to conduct a series of summer educational exchange programs. In
reality, the "exchange" was unidirectional, as UH coordinated the appoint-
ment of American faculty members from nineteen universities nationwide to
polytechnic colleges in eight Indian cities.[27] The goal of these Summer Institutes for Polytechnic Faculties programs was "to advance the qualifications of
Indian polytechnic faculty and increase technological achievements" in India
(fig. 6).[28] A less expected outcome was Indian students' new familiarity with the
university itself via faculty trained through these programs.

As word spread among students in India and Pakistan, South Asian student
migration to Houston's institutions of higher education steadily increased, and
it has yet to ebb. A few had enrolled at UH by the late 1950s. The earliest available
university records indicate that by the mid-1960s, some 35 South Asians attended UH and 43 had enrolled at Texas Southern University.[29] Within five
years, 135 Indians and Pakistanis attended the University of Houston, while
an additional 45 South Asian students enrolled at TSU and 20 more attended

TABLE 3. Raw numbers of selected University of Houston international students by nationality, 1964–1980.

Year	India	Pakistan	China*	Vietnam	Mexico	Saudi Arabia	Iran	Philippines
1964	29	6	68	1	32	5	28	4
1965	31	9	71	1	38	5	32	4
1966	36	10	88	0	31	4	32	4
1967	39	9	109	0	35	2	34	9
1968	65	9	137	2	45	2	37	5
1969	123	10	149	2	56	N/A	33	N/A
1970	132	12	188	2	66	N/A	39	N/A
1971	117	18	185	6	68	N/A	43	N/A
1972	115	25	188	9	80	N/A	63	N/A
1973	126	39	188	16	97	N/A	103	N/A
1974	143	75	178	32	149	N/A	181	N/A
1975	173	N/A	196	35	N/A	N/A	N/A	N/A
1976	207	88	214	49	198	6	223	6
1977	198	85	206	51	190	9	258	8
1978	201	87	317	131	190	10	259	12
1979	167	67	265	156	139	7	218	13
1980	136	73	306	190	135	9	217	22

Notes: N/A: Data not available

* The Chinese population included students almost exclusively from Taiwan, rather than mainland China.

Sources: UH: Annual Enrollment Reports, 1969–80; Office of International Student Admissions; Directory of International Students, 1969–70, 1974–75, and 1977–78, International Student Office.

Rice University.[30] A majority of these students were men, although South Asian women's attendance showed a slow and steady increase from 1967. At the national level, 97 percent of Indian students at American universities were men in 1950s and 1960s, but by the late 1970s, some 30 percent were women.[31] While women generally made up a far lower percentage of foreign students at any American university, India (and, by extension, Pakistan) sent among the fewest women students of all countries.[32] Regardless of gender, many more Indians enrolled at American universities than did Pakistanis.

The disparity between the numbers of Indian versus Pakistani students reflected India's vastly larger population size overall but also its greater number of universities and, consequently, more college graduates. Although both nations invested in higher education after Independence, many more universities existed at Partition in India than in Pakistan, and thus, Pakistanis had fewer options for higher education than did Indians. Conversely, given India's vastly larger population size, one could interpret the numbers of Pakistani students in American universities as disproportionately *high*; by 1974, only twice as many Indians than Pakistanis attended UH, whereas India's and West Pakistan's populations in 1971 were 548 million versus 65 million, respectively.[33] Another possible explanation for the number of Pakistani students in American universities was the aggressive Cold War effort to promote American higher education in Pakistan. A combination of the emergent state of Pakistani universities, Pakistanis' English-language fluency, and Pakistan's strategic value to the United States worked together to produce a sizable outflow of Pakistanis seeking higher education in the United States.

The profiles of Indian and Pakistani students differed significantly in another way: while the overwhelming majority of Indians entered UH as graduate students, most Pakistanis were admitted as undergraduates. This was consistent with national trends, as India produced the highest number of students seeking graduate study abroad by 1960.[34] Nationally, about 60 percent of all foreign students from any country were undergraduates, while 40 percent were graduate students.[35] Between 1966 and 1978, the proportion of Indian graduate students at UH increased from 70 to 90 percent, while the opposite was true for Pakistanis. Starting in 1966, the split between undergraduate and graduate Pakistani students was about half, and this swung in favor of undergraduates by 1978. Increasing numbers of Pakistani students pursued bachelor's degrees at UH, while fewer sought graduate degrees. Because Pakistan's educational situation was in a more formative state than India's, Pakistani students often fulfilled all of their university training overseas. Pakistan had less to offer in the way of fully or even partially trained labor but much in trainable labor, with a solid foundation in and a commitment to higher education, as well as a keen interest in American universities. Where most Indians were graduate students in American universities, many more Pakistanis were admitted as undergraduates before moving on to complete graduate degrees, usually at the same institutions.

Mirroring the urban-to-urban demographic profile that characterized South Asian immigration in the 1960s and 1970s, South Asian international students in the United States hailed mostly from India's and Pakistan's urban, literate centers. In India, the highest-sending states from 1965 to 1975 were Maharashtra, West Bengal, Gujarat, and Tamil Nadu.[36] In West Pakistan, parallel sending cities would presumably have been Karachi, Lahore, and Islamabad, and for East Pakistan, Dacca and Chittagong.

During the 1960s, UH offered a range of engineering majors, and South Asians made engineering their major of choice (see fig. 3). South Asian students' pursuit of engineering and the natural sciences corresponded with features often, though not always, ascribed to the middle classes in India and Pakistan.[37] High school students with the highest nationalized test scores were tracked into these occupational fields, establishing pathways to stable employment and income. In 1966, half of all Indian and Pakistani students at UH majored in engineering. Pakistani students pursued engineering at a rate of approximately 40 percent throughout the 1970s. Within three years, Indians continued to choose engineering at a rate of nearly 70 percent, decreasing to 50 percent by 1978. When asked, "Why engineering?" Suman Parikh, who had enrolled at Kansas State University in 1961, responded, "Back in those days, there were only two fields where you could readily find jobs in India: engineering and medicine."[38] Parikh's statement affirms South Asian students' preference for engineering, but the matter was more complex than simple job prospects. The two career paths of engineering and medicine represented among the best compensated and highest status professions in South Asia and the United States—both crucial factors in the selection of college majors. From the 1950s through 1960s, more international students chose engineering above other fields, including 22 percent of Indians.[39] In the early 1960s, roughly 2,000 Indian students in the United States pursued engineering majors, while relatively few studied education or agriculture.[40]

Beyond engineering, nearly 20 percent of Indians and 10 percent of Pakistanis chose science majors between 1965 and 1978. Hardly any students pursued business majors during the 1960s, but by 1978, 30 percent of both Indian and Pakistani students opted for business degrees.[41] Among the early immigrants in my interview group, 70 percent selected engineering, while the remainder chose the natural sciences. They almost entirely excluded education, the humanities, and mathematics. This particular group of immigrants selected the University of Houston precisely for its strength in engineering, and so that concentration was disproportionally high. Nationwide, however, South Asian students in the United States exhibited a wider range of preferences at other universities, especially those that excelled in the liberal arts and thus attracted more of those students. Still, the preponderance of engineering and science majors among South Asian students reflected middle-class educational norms in India and Pakistan. As one Indian engineer observed, "India is different than the States in that our best prefer engineering over medicine. Thus, it was a shock and disappointment to have engineering as my field and come to the States to learn that it is ranked below doctors, who in India are second to us."[42] Science and technology, rather than liberal arts subjects, were also regarded as vital to India's and Pakistan's still nascent nation-building projects and, coincidentally, to the American middle class.

Middle-Class International Students and Middle-Class White America

After they arrived in the United States, one of the ways South Asian international students in Houston (and other cities) familiarized themselves with "mainstream," middle-class, white American society was through participation in the Host Family program, a government-supported effort organized by the nonprofit Institute of International Education. Thus, the Cold War continued to exert influence in the form of a government-university initiative to connect international students with American families. Participation in the program allowed international students of color to use their foreignness as an entry point into middle-class, white America. Although I have not found solid evidence on the racial makeup of host families, it is safe to assume that they were mostly, if not almost exclusively, white. I am not at all suggesting that international students sought participation *because* host families were white, because I have not found any evidence to indicate this. Rather, because the program was operated and supported largely by white Americans, students of color encountered this segment of American society. Their host family relationships mirrored the same white, middle-class social structure they found on campus at UH, reinforcing class and race hierarchies in students' lives.

The Houston branch of IIE—housed in the World Trade Center in downtown Houston—was the regional center for ten surrounding states, serving more than six thousand students. Working through its own International Hospitality Committee of Houston, IIE described the families who agreed to greet, host, and entertain international students as "Main Street Diplomats."[43] Such hospitality committees existed in hundreds of U.S. cities. According to an article published in the *Houston Chronicle*, "The Family Program . . . provides each student from abroad with a Houston family which sees him at least once a month, takes him to concerts, the theatre, etc."[44] The Host Family program was a collaborative Cold War effort among the university, the state, and the city's middle- and upper-class residents to promote the Fulbright Act's goal of the "promotion of international good will," and IIE administered the nation's Fulbright scholarships.[45]

The Institute of International Education actively sought out American families (assuming that they were at least middle class) to host international students as a counterweight to Soviet appeals to students abroad. In 1960, the *Houston Chronicle* reprinted a *New York Times* article stating that five hundred students from sixty-five countries had enrolled at a new Soviet university built especially for students from the Third World; the article subtly emphasized the urgent need for American families to intensify their efforts with foreign students.[46] Especially active host families were recognized at an annual gala awards ceremony. Host families tended to be older couples, although IIE-Houston launched the World Affairs Discussion group initiative in 1959 to draw young adults in their twenties into hosting.[47] Host families also tended to be middle or upper middle class, even though funding was generated privately among the city's wealthiest elite, as in 1963, when IIE partnered with upscale Texas department store Neiman-Marcus to host a fund-raising designer fashion show.[48] Like USIS posts, IIE also hosted special events such as afternoon tea or holiday parties for select international students.[49] According to a university report on international students at UH, the program endeavored to give students "an opportunity to establish a lasting, ongoing relationship with an American family."[50] UH Pakistani student Jamal Iqbal stated that international students could opt into the Host Family program on admission to participating universities. Host families were then responsible for picking up students from the airport on arrival and taking them to IIE-sponsored orientation sessions.[51] Thus, in many cases, students' formative interaction with Americans in the United States was through a Cold War program.

Students like Zafar Waheed and Ramesh Lal were matched with host families who presumably were white and middle class.[52] Waheed, a Pakistani student who worked toward his master's degree in biology from 1963 to 1966, explained, "My host family, they were a middle-aged husband and wife, and two children. For every festivity, like Christmas or New Year's Day, they would invite me and I would spend the festivity with them. At other times, they also took me to different places," such as area attractions. His relationship with his host family was so earnest that, at their insistence, he called them "Mom" and "Dad." He added, "I was virtually like a son to them."[53] In 1966, Waheed moved back to Pakistan, married, and worked, returning to UH in 1969 to pursue his doctorate. When he returned, he had filed for and obtained an immigrant visa with the sponsorship of his host family. They vouched for his financial solvency, committing their own wealth as his financial security in his visa application.[54] His wife, Sara, and infant son followed in 1970 after the processing of their visas, and they were met at the airport by Zafar and his host family. Sara Waheed recalled that they "welcomed us very well."[55] The two families remained close and in regular contact for nearly twenty years.

Through the University of Houston, Ramesh Lal also participated in the

Host Family program, which he described as "very nice."[56] He found that while most other white Americans refrained from forming meaningful relationships with him, he was able to "get to know" his host family. Many South Asian students found it difficult to connect with Americans outside of their academic departments, but not for lack of trying. Lal remembers that initially "when I went to the campus, I was a little bit disappointed in the sense that I think the international community of students over there had very strong ways, in the sense that they had good interactions . . . but there was very little interaction between international students and other American kids in those days."[57] Lal found that if he "initiated conversations with them, [he] got good responses but they were courteous responses. [He] did not develop deep relationships with Americans until [he] went into the workforce," after which he was able to form those relationships "quite a bit."[58] While Lal felt disappointed in the lack of friendship potential with American students, he enjoyed the relationships fostered with his host family.[59] The program left him sufficiently inspired to eventually host an international student from China some years later. For Yasmin Iqbal and her husband, a student at UH, their interactions with their host family also formed the most developed relationship they had with an American nonimmigrant family. Yasmin noted that their host "mother," a "grandmother at the time [while] I was a young mother," worked at the university bookstore and that "they would visit each other's homes."[60] Along with the coethnic friend network that functioned as fictive kin, host families also assisted in the transition between home and host societies by fulfilling a familial support role.

Another means of breeding familiarity and acculturation for South Asian students was the UH Office of International Student Services' (ISS) collaboration with area churches and church outreach programs. The University of Houston encouraged international students "to learn about the people and customs of the United States," and through *International News*, the international student campus newsletter, local churches invited students to activities.[61] Church Women United, a group of women from various Houston churches, volunteered to host a weekly lunch event on campus, the International Coffee Hour, facilitated by the International Student Services organization at UH. The luncheon provided free sandwiches and gave "international students an opportunity to get together on a regular basis,"[62] fostering interaction and acculturation. Ramesh Lal Zafar Waheed, for example, attended the lunches on campus hosted by the church outreach programs.

In addition, the South Main Baptist Church arranged what it called a "mini-vacation" in the form of a Sunday afternoon of "fun-filled" activities at the church. Ads in the campus-run *International News* stated clearly that there was "no obligation to attend religious services" and that transportation, childcare, food, and sport activities would be provided.[63] The UH Baptist Student Center also invited international students to afternoon parties, although they were not required to attend services.[64] The ISS aimed to familiarize Americans, both on and off campus, with the new arrivals by encouraging international students to give "short talks" at organized community events.[65] For example, churches such as St. Paul's United Methodist, submitted a request to the ISS for a student to speak about his or her religion.[66] The office hoped to increase international student interest by providing a small fee to willing speakers.

Off campus, area churches set up programs to accommodate immigrant women. Varuni Gil found a friend in her upstairs neighbor, Wilma Curry, whom she described as a "lonely old woman."[67] Gil explained that, like herself, the neighbor was also "bored," and since Gil was a young woman trying to learn about American society—something she believed this neighbor could teach her—"we were good company for each other, actually. It worked out very, very nice." The neighbor directed Gil to a Methodist church in their neighborhood, where she began to improve her English. The church outreach group provided her with an additional support system that eased her adjustment to life in Houston.

Informed by a Spanish-speaking neighbor about a church support group for immigrant women, Sara Waheed attended a program hosted by a Baptist church near a Sears store in downtown Houston.[68] The church hired a yellow school bus for transportation; the buses "pick[ed] up different ladies from their houses or apartment and they used to take them to the church."[69] The church provided for free childcare on the premises. There, Waheed found "ladies [who] were from Mexico, from India, Pakistan, China, and American ladies," from whom she "learned a lot also, because people were coming from different places and I had a chance to learn their recipes, their cooking. We would share our cooking and recipes, too." Through the church, immigrant women met weekly for two to three hours. In addition to sharing international foods, the women worked together on handicrafts. Church members did not aggressively proselytize, but immigrant women were encouraged to ask faith-related questions during meals and activities.[70]

Another Cold War–driven social trend similarly promoted an open, welcoming, tolerant American society with the aim of familiarizing foreigners with American families. According to a *New York Times* article in 1962, "Having a foreign visitor to dinner has become the fashionable thing to do," especially for Thanksgiving.[71] Houston families joined a Cold War tradition growing in nationwide popularity, as American families sought out international students in their midst. Advertising in UH's *International News* newsletter, Houstonians wanted to "show gratitude for the blessings... and share with guests" their Thanksgiving dinner.[72] These Thanksgiving invitations were immensely popular, optimally pairing displaced internationals with patriotic Americans during a holiday that celebrated the American family and nation. Soon after Thanksgiving, *International News* happily reported that several UH international students had responded to Thanksgiving dinner invitations facilitated by the Office of International Student Services.[73]

Americans in other cities also favored the trend, as other newly arrived international students recalled. Tahira Lakhani related that at her university in North Carolina in the early 1970s, an American classmate whom she did not know invited Tahira and her husband, Idris, to Thanksgiving dinner. The classmate had said, "My parents want somebody that is away from home to come and have Thanksgiving dinner with us." Hesitant to visit a stranger, Tahira intended to decline the invitation, but Idris thought otherwise. The gracious hosts turned out to be no less than the governor of North Carolina and his family.[74] Najma Rizvi, an East Pakistani student at Cornell University in the early 1960s, spoke of a professor inviting her and her husband for a formal Thanksgiving meal.[75] Efforts such as the Host Family program and Thanksgiving dinner were government sanctioned but implemented at the grass-roots level.

These initiatives had the tacit support of the federal government, middle-class Americans, and international students, which partly explains their success and longevity. The presence of international students was particularly convenient in the context of the government's efforts to transform the country's global image. International students were assumed to be studious and hard-working. They hailed from mostly middle-class to upper-middle-class backgrounds. Invited into middle- and upper-middle-class homes, they were fluent in a fluid global language of middle-class sensibility. In short, they were the right kind of foreigner at a time when the Cold War demanded increasing internationalism to deflect attention away from long-standing structural racial inequalities.

Middle-Class Permutations for South Asian Students

Even though Indian and Pakistani international students in Houston were mostly middle class—and, in the case of Hindu students, upper caste—"middle class" did not necessarily mean financially independent.[76] Rather, the conversion and devaluation of their rupees to dollars made finances a major concern. For many, even the journey from India to the United States entailed taking out interest-based loans from Indian moneylenders. Suman Parikh tells the story of how his uncle and guardian advised him to pursue an American university education. When Parikh inquired from friends about the cost, he found that the amount needed—fifteen thousand rupees—equaled five years of his uncle's salary. Instead, he said, "I got a loan for nine thousand rupees at 4.5 percent interest, and told my uncle that the cost of studying in America was only ten thousand rupees."[77] In his memoir, P. T. Joseph wrote of vouching for his financial solvency in Trivandrum and, only after a lengthy process, departing for the United States with fifty dollars in hand.[78]

The generous amount of financial support available at American universities—unlike at other Western universities—was an important part of the calculus by which middle-class South Asian students opted to pursue higher education in the United States. In 1963, American universities and the U.S. government paid for one third of education-related costs for international students, regardless of major.[79] Approximately half of all foreign students were supported by scholarships and grants in the 1960s.[80] By the 1970s, British universities began drastic reductions to international student support, further contributing to the rise in international student enrollment in the United States.[81] Pakistani student Zafar Waheed commented that "the only reason I chose the U.S.A. was that in the 1960s, the United States was the only country which was giving financial aid to those students who were trying to get their Ph.D. In England or Australia or Canada, we had to pay for our education, but in the United States, we were offered teaching or research fellowships. . . . [We] came to the United States by getting some kind of financial grant from the university."[82] Waheed embarked on a master's degree in biology at UH in 1963.

Indeed, although UH did not expressly designate scholarships for international students, graduate departments offered teaching and research assistantships, tuition-waiver scholarships, and monies from its International Student Emergency Loan Fund.[83] The university granted admission to international students "on the basis of a letter of financial backing" that confirmed the student's financial independence, whether through a bank or some other institution in their home country. Waheed secured a letter backing his financial solvency from his home academic institution in Karachi, where he was a junior instructor. Additionally, he secured a partial scholarship from UH.

The university admissions office placed no quotas on the number of international students from any single country; although students were admitted based on academic merit, financial solvency was also a prerequisite. Students who produced the required letters struggled, nevertheless, to make ends meet. Some sought additional income after their arrival in the United States.[84] Because international students entered the United States mostly on F visas during the 1950s and early 1960s, students were not permitted to work during their first year of study out of concern for new students' adjustment to American life and academic demands.[85] To meet all expenses, less affluent students worked off-campus at low-paying service jobs even though they were not always authorized to do so. Some did so at the risk of having their student visas revoked.

In order to work, students had to apply for permission with the Immigration and Naturalization Service by demonstrating financial need. Pakistani student Jamal Iqbal applied in September 1965 and received a work permit in January 1966.[86] Zafar Waheed worked as a busboy, earning seventy cents an hour. Later, he was promoted to waiter. Working only on weekends, he put in six-hour shifts, totaling six dollars per day plus tips. By his calculations, "at that time, it was good money."[87] Jamal Iqbal and his wife, Yasmin, moved to Houston in the mid-1960s. Jamal worked on his bachelor's degree in power engineering while Yasmin remained at home, caring for their young daughter. When they first settled in Houston, Yasmin stated that "there were financial hurdles."[88] At first, they could not afford a car and used public transit instead. While working on his bachelor's degree, Jamal worked part-time. Yasmin explained, "You had to watch your budget." Although Indian and Pakistani students who graduated from American universities would quickly rise through the ranks of the middle class wherever they settled, many experienced lean years during college. They often describe their student phase as financially challenging and thus regard themselves as "self-made."

Racial Calculations in Houston's Public and Private Spaces

Although class was a defining factor in South Asian international students' lives, neither their class status nor their educational pedigree could shield them from the racial order of the university and surrounding city. While they witnessed and contributed to the city's favorable economic fortunes and evolving social climate, as represented by increased globalization in commerce and subsequent internationalization of residents, their history reveals the stubborn intransigence of a white supremacy that placed those perceived as nonwhite outside the range of social desirability. Indeed, post-1965 South Asian immigrants were, in vital ways, the antithesis of turn-of-the-century Indian immigrants to the United States—those factory workers, farmers, and peddlers who were subject to immigration exclusion and barred from naturalized citizenship.[89] Where the earlier wave of Indian immigrant men assimilated by marrying into other nonwhite communities, including African Americans in New Orleans, Mexican Americans in rural California, and Puerto Ricans in Harlem, post-1965 immigrants to Houston moved into mostly white, middle-class suburbs. Nonetheless, their residence among white neighbors would be more accurately characterized as residence *alongside* white neighbors, rather than cultural assimilation *into* white communities. Like other groups of color in the United States during these decades, immigrants' strengthening of identities occurred against the backdrop of legal and economic inclusion but social marginalization. As international students—many at the graduate level—South Asians enjoyed open passage in many university spaces. As international Asian students during the Cold War, they enjoyed the rewards of favorable U.S.–South Asia foreign relations. At the same time, their experiences were mediated through local racial constructs made explicit in their interactions on campus, in the neighborhood surrounding the university, and in the wider city itself.

The University of Houston in the early 1960s was a space carved out by an overwhelmingly white populace and a nearly exclusively white faculty and staff. Until 1962—the year that UH desegregated and just before it became state funded—the hundreds of African American students who inquired about admission or applied to UH (they were required to stipulate their "race" and "color" on admissions applications) were firmly steered down the road toward Texas Southern University (formerly Houston Colored Junior College).[90] Both UH and TSU—blocks away from each other—were located in Third Ward, which by 1960 was a heavily African American neighborhood.[91] Only in June 1962 did UH conditionally and quietly enroll its first African American student, Charles P. Rhinehart.[92] Once the university decided to change course, the number of African American students quickly increased. By March 1963, 20 African American students had enrolled at UH; their population would balloon over the next decade.[93] By 1966, 200 black undergraduate and 200 graduate students had enrolled at UH.[94] By 1970, well over 1,000 African American students attended UH, while a decade later, that number had jumped to 3,000.[95]

Public institutions of higher education in Texas sometimes granted admission to Mexican Americans, who faced systematic discrimination in this sphere to a lesser degree than did African American college applicants.[96] By 1969, even though the city's Hispanic population was estimated at over 14 percent, less than 4 percent of UH students identified as Hispanic.[97] By fall 1971, some 1,218 Hispanic students and 1,244 African Americans were enrolled, representing a combined 9 percent out of a student population of 26,475.[98] This was still a relatively small percentage. More than 90 percent of UH students were white.

Houston's three major universities catered to three distinct groups, divided largely along lines of race and class, though all accepted international Asian students of color. The University of Houston was easily the city's largest university by 1950, joining the Texas state system of higher education in 1963. The institution had historically served white Houstonians. Texas Southern University continued to educate the city's African American residents. The city's best elite white students, along with a few rural white students and international students, meanwhile, attended the tuition-free Rice University, which had opened in 1912.[99] Rice University achieved legal desegregation in 1965, among the last of southern universities to do so.[100]

International students at these Houston universities and other southern universities straddled the line between belonging and unbelonging. East Pakistani student Najma Rizvi recalled that when she was a master's student at the University of Florida in the early 1960s, "there were some professors who had very liberal outlooks. Some were very nice to foreign students." [101] They did not seem to extend the same courtesy to African American students, who, in the Jim Crow South, Rizvi continued, "wouldn't be sending their children to the same school. But otherwise, [the professors were] very gracious to foreign students." During and after the Jim Crow era, South Asian international students arguably experienced less racism on university campuses (whether in Houston or elsewhere in the South) than off campus. Even though South Asian students considered themselves temporary migrants, they lived and learned among other Houstonians. Their temporary status did not divorce them from the social worlds around them.

Off campus, a majority of UH and TSU students from India and Pakistan shared inexpensive apartments within one or two miles of the universities in the surrounding neighborhoods of Third Ward and University Oaks. A rare few could afford lodging in campus dormitories. UH was situated in the northeast corner of Third Ward, with TSU just blocks away. Third Ward thus served as a "gateway" neighborhood.[102] Since the late nineteenth century but particularly following World War II, Third Ward became home to one of the largest concentrations of African Americans in Houston.[103] Although the neighborhood had maintained segregated white and black populations throughout the early twentieth century, by the 1940s, the area boasted an even higher concentration of African Americans than Houston's historically black Freedman's Town, also known as Fourth Ward, which lost much of its African American community before and after the war.[104] White residents largely abandoned Third Ward, perhaps because of the Great Depression, so that by 1940, census data indicate a 98 percent African American population.[105] In the late 1940s, the construction of two major highways, Interstate 10 through Fifth Ward and Interstate 45 through Fourth Ward, destroyed local black economies and the sense of community in these areas as the African American population of both areas rapidly declined.[106] During the 1960s, the population of Third Ward expanded to incorporate displaced African Americans residents from Fourth and Fifth Wards.[107] By the late 1970s, Third Ward had become one of the most densely populated areas of the city.[108] Thus, Third Ward replaced Fourth Ward as "the hub of black social, cultural, and economic life in Houston."[109] By 1980, over 90 percent of Third Ward's population identified as African American, while roughly 6 percent were white and 2.5 percent were Mexican American.[110]

Residing in a majority African American neighborhood but attending a majority white university, South Asian international students interpreted southern racial and class scripts and their own place within them; that is, they constructed their lifeworlds through interaction in these particular social and material landscapes.[111] During the 1960s, they tended to live in apartments near the university, some in units so small that they were described as "cabins" by their student occupants.[112] Many lived at Cullen Field Apartments, Cougar Apartments, King Apartments, or other multiperson accommodations in the immediate vicinity of UH.[113] Students usually economized by sharing bedrooms with roommates, and because of the preponderance of two-bedroom units, each apartment unit often housed three or four students who divided the cost of rent. Suresh Bhatt, an engineering graduate student who arrived in 1974, described his "huge" complex as "crowded," "rat-infested," "run-down," and "not very well kept."[114] He recalled that this large complex was perhaps 70 to 80 percent student occupied, mostly by international students. Although some shared cars with other, more senior coethnics, many students walked or rode bicycles to the university, taking them through the greater Third Ward neighborhood. Some lived in these apartments for as little as a year, as in the case of Jamal Iqbal, who moved into his own apartment after his wife arrived in Houston from Pakistan in 1967.[115] Others remained there for the duration of their studies.

The neighborhood and university served as gateway sites, providing South Asian students with their formative racial and class perceptions of African Americans. Rohan Patil, an Indian student who lived off Wheeler Street, within two or three blocks of campus, "found that [Third Ward] was a very unique and different culture of its own."[116] Suresh Bhatt recalled what he perceived to be innocuous distinctions, such as an audible African American "accent" and "phrasing," as he put it, cultural markers not commonly encountered by him on campus.[117] Indian and Pakistani students, many pursuing graduate degrees, noticed that, in large part, their African American neighbors did not attend the same university as they did. As an engineering graduate student in the early 1970s, Bhatt stated that "there was no African American graduate student in the chemical engineering program that I can recall at the time that I was there."[118]

Soon after his arrival in Houston, friends warned Bhatt about the dangers of the neighborhood. Although they lived close enough to campus, friends let him know that students walking to and from their apartments had been robbed and assaulted. He observed that "the neighborhood around there was not very safe," subtly foreshadowing a flawed association between crime and African Americans that would only gain greater purchase with time.[119] Ramesh Lal began doctoral studies in engineering at UH in 1974. He briefly roomed with coethnics in nearby apartments before moving to the campus dormitory and later joined another friend in area apartments. Soon after arriving in Houston, he "started hearing some stories that were not very flattering" to African Americans, resulting in his having "a poor impression" of them. He heard the stories "from other students [and] from the media."[120] The stories generally linked African Americans with crime—the media, as Lal explained, being particularly "good at portraying crimes; they are very descriptive."[121] For these reasons, most Indian and Pakistani students felt that they "didn't have the opportunity to strike sort of a friendship with" African Americans either on or off campus.[122]

Other Indian visitors to the United States echoed very similar race and class constructs as those voiced by South Asian students in the American South. Visiting New York and a handful of American cities in 1959, Indian astrologer Bangalore Venkata Raman wrote in his memoir, *A Hindu in America*, that Harlem "represents the highest and the lowest status attained by the Negroes in North of the U.S.A."[123] He observed that there were "some successful Negroes who live with dignity" but that "lower-class Negroes" exhibit "vice, disease, [and] delinquency."[124] Indeed, he insisted that "our 'untouchables' lead [a] more contented and happy life."[125] For Raman, part of that alleged state of contentment and happiness among Indian "untouchables" was bound to fiercely nationalistic notions of India's timeless, "ancient civilization and culture" built on a "strong and stable cultural unity."[126] Throughout the memoir, Raman makes no association between "lower-class" whites and delinquency. The base assertion regarding poor blacks was not about their poverty but about their blackness being normatively delinquent, although Raman mentioned "some" exceptional black individuals. Jewish, Italian, and Chinese residents of Lower East Side slums, on the other hand, lived in "congested streets" and were described by Raman as "underprivileged"—both decidedly structural descriptors in opposition to embodied terms such as "disease" and "vice."[127] Nor was the affluent, white Upper East Side noted by any negative descriptors; it was a space inhabited by "fashion" and "wealth."[128]

South Asian perceptions of African Americans or other ethnoracial groups, however, were not singularly one-sided, characterized only by fear or emotional distance. Some dated and married outside of their national groups. Yasmin Iqbal recalled a Pakistani friend who married a German woman, two Pakistani brothers who married white Americans, and another Pakistani who married an

Afghani woman. She remembered a few other men who married white women but ended up divorcing them.[129] Varuni Gil and her husband regularly hosted small parties at their apartment where their Indian and Pakistani friends often brought their white American and African American girlfriends.[130] Several other interviewees confirmed that some of their Indian and Pakistani friends became romantically involved with white and African American women. Ramesh Lal met and married a Chinese student at UH, and after some initial hesitation, both his and his wife's families accepted their choice to marry outside of their ethnic groups. South Asian men generally married women from India and Pakistan, but this tendency did not represent the full range of relationships that occurred as immigrants sought ways of belonging and companionship after migration.

In 1974, Ramesh Lal moved into the campus dormitory at the University of Houston as a doctoral student in chemical engineering. In describing his relationship with the majority white student population, Lal found that white American students "were not very talkative to us." He observed that white students socially shunned him and other South Asians. During communal mealtimes on campus, he also noted that while white Americans would not join him in the cafeteria, an undergraduate African American football player "used to come and sit with me at lunch, dinners."[131] They established a friendship, and through this relationship, Lal realized the invalidity of the rumors he had heard about African Americans. As he phrased it, he finally "understood that five fingers are not equal anywhere," by which he meant that everyone is unique but integral to the larger fabric of humanity. Outcast separately, the two formed something akin to a collective minority consisting of students of color in the cafeteria, as suggested by the title of Beverly Tatum's book *Why Are All the Black Kids Sitting Together in the Cafeteria?*[132] In the context of the college cafeteria, Lal found himself similarly racialized as an African American student, forcing him to confront his position in the southern racial hierarchy. Lal and the football player could each have sat alone, but they recognized in each other a shared marginalization, one that exposed white supremacy's binary structure, not just as white/black, but as white/nonwhite.[133]

Expanding on his interactions with the white student majority, Lal haltingly recalled,

It was just . . . I really don't know but I mean, there were some international students that would go and venture into fraternities and things like that but not much. Graduate students of course, in a given department, they . . . they were very free, freely interacting, exchanging thoughts and ideas and other things but not so . . . I was . . . for a year, I was in the Quadrangle in the University of Houston. And even when I'd go out and sit for lunch or dinner or something like that most of the kids would not . . . were not very talkative to us so we would sit and . . . it just so happened that international students would sit in the same table and talk with each other but the other kids would not join them.[134]

Nevertheless, when pressed to expound further on South Asian students' relationship with the white majority students at the university, Lal refrained from a blanket condemnation of discriminatory white behavior. By saying "it just so happened," Lal removed responsibility and intention from the equation altogether, suggesting that the pattern of behavior was unintended and indiscriminate. In doing so, he erased the existence of race as a factor in his life.

Scholars Sunil Bhatia and Rosemary George write that by denying the existence of racism in their own lives, Indian immigrants (and, by extension, Pakistani immigrants) "overcome their sense of difference" while distancing themselves from marginalized, stigmatized people of color.[135] As university students, Indians and Pakistanis strategized to transcend the lowly forced status of southern blackness by emphasizing their own educational credentials and class standing, while some trivialized or completely dismissed the impact of race in their lives. As they constructed their identities as students and immigrants, South Asians increasingly found that an embrace of ethnicity might facilitate this attempted strategy of deracination. Within their own ethnic groups, at least, they faced no racial hostility, reinforcing the appeal of formulating an ethnic immigrant identity in the United States.

Other interviewees also sensed that white Americans were reluctant to socialize with them whether in the 1960s or after.[136] Jamal Iqbal explained that in the mid-1960s, when he and his family moved to Houston from Pakistan, "the Americans normally did not want to be friends with you." As noted by another researcher, on college campuses, "those [international students] whose appearance most closely resembles that of Americans (Europeans, for example) are least likely to encounter prejudicial rhetoric or behavior."[137]

Away from the relative racial safety of the university campus, however, South Asians were variously treated as black, white, or "foreign"—an ambiguous identity that sometimes permitted them to pass through normatively white spaces but sometimes resulted in racial discrimination.[138] Triangulated against African Americans and Mexican Americans, elite South Asians in post–civil rights era Houston provided a foil for historically disadvantaged populations. Standing inside a bank in Houston in 1962 with two bathroom doors before her, Mrudula Bavare was perplexed. One door stated, "Colored," and the other, "Whites." As a recent immigrant woman from the state of Maharashtra in western India, which one was she? Another bank customer, a southern white woman, noticed her hesitation, so the Indian woman relayed her dilemma. Steeped in their own class identities and racialized knowledge of a South Asian postcolonial past, Pakistani and Indian immigrants struggled to reconcile notions of caste, class, and race from South Asia with those of a changing American South. The southerner paused for a moment, looked over the very fair-skinned foreigner, and decided that she "should use the restroom for whites."

Bavare explained that it must have been her comparatively fair skin that decided the matter for the white woman. Another possibility was that Bavare's foreignness placed her outside the category of "local African American."[139] Skin color, nonetheless, became a crucial phenotypical marker of race for South Asian immigrants, easily if inconsistently and crudely read on the body. It was one of many racial ambiguities evoked by the presence of South Asians. "Foreignness," articulated by immigrants as Indian or Pakistani culture and by scholars as ethnicity, likewise emerged as potential tool by which immigrants attempted to bypass racial assignations altogether.[140]

Despite the potential for racial ambiguity, South Asians recognized themselves as distinct. In search of a haircut, Zafar Waheed rode his bicycle one day in 1963 to a barber shop near the university in a working-class area of Telephone Road. Waheed, a man of relatively dark complexion, had just stepped into the shop when the white shop owner stopped him and told him to get out. "He just kicked me out. He said, 'Don't enter my shop!'" Waheed recalled, shaking his head, "That was one of the bad experiences."[141] Waheed rationalized the incident in two ways. First, he linked poverty with racism by noting that he "could see that that area had some kind of poor shops and some kind of low-quality stores." Waheed quickly calculated which spaces were safe for him to enter. He never again returned to Telephone Road, but by avoiding poor white spaces, he underscored an association between race and class. Second, he understood that phenotype, as locally specific cultural capital, was either a gateway or a barrier, highlighting the intersection of race, skin color, and blackness. He offered that "in the 1960s, there were so many racial problems and I am a brown person, you see?" He did not clarify whether "brown" here meant the literal color of his skin or a foreign ethnicity, distinct from the more dominant white and black categories in the United States. In either case, for Waheed, brownness was neither white nor black, but it was, nonetheless, a problematically "racial" category. Identifying as brown also offered Waheed a way to resist the stigma of black status.[142]

It is also interesting that Waheed described himself as a "brown person" in a region deeply committed to anti-*black* racism, discrimination, and segregation; this is especially noteworthy because while the white barber might have recognized Waheed's foreignness, he just as likely read Waheed's body as that of a black man in a white shop. Indeed, just a few years earlier, in 1955, in a well-known incident, the Indian ambassador from Delhi, G. L. Mehta, was racialized as a black man. En route to Mexico City from his post in Washington, D.C., he stopped for a brief layover at Houston's International Airport.[143] Presuming that Mehta and his secretary (also Indian) were African American, the manager of the dining facility, May Alley, directed Mehta and his Indian secretary to the "Colored" section, separate from Mehta's all-white entourage. Several witnesses heard Alley say, "The law's the law."[144] Mehta and his secretary refused to be segregated, and so Alley denied them service. Because Mehta was a diplomat, the incident was widely publicized and rapidly escalated into a national embarrassment, prompting personal apologies from Houston mayor Roy Hofheinz and Secretary of State John Foster Dulles.[145]

Although American officials expressed regret in the aftermath, the incident demonstrates that for Mehta and other people of color in the South, class status was not a shield against racialization. The incident occurred a decade before the end of Jim Crow and roughly coincided with the arrival of the earliest Indian and Pakistani students at the University of Houston. Under Jim Crow, darker-skinned South Asians were routinely treated as black and thus subject to laws governing segregation. As with Bavare's experience at the segregated bathrooms mentioned previously, they were variously also tolerated as not black, indicating the fluid boundaries of racial construction. Whether before or after 1964, however, the change in law could not shield Indian and Pakistani students from their own racialization into nonwhite unbelonging. This process of racial formation was co-constitutive; South Asians confronted existing race and class ideologies, just as race and class ideologies were reconstructed through South Asian incorporation. And although in some ways, the growing, changing university setting provided a safe haven from the most egregious instances of racism, in other ways it reinforced the power hierarchies (including race and class) of the city beyond its boundaries.

A bustling commercial center that provided economic opportunity, Houston also had a long history of hostility toward perceived outsiders. In the somewhat distant past of the 1920s, Houstonians had actively supported the Ku Klux Klan.[146] In addition, Houstonians harbored strong anti-immigrant sentiment against Mexicans specifically, dating back to the Battle of San Jacinto in 1836.[147] In the early 1960s, reactionary, conservative, anticommunist groups—such as the John Birch Society, Christian Anti-Communist Crusade, Freedom-in-Action, Christian Crusade, and others—maintained active chapters in Houston.[148] Even after the demise of the Red Scare, committed ideologues would continue to gravitate toward the so-called Radical Right and, later, the Reagan Right and sociopolitical conservatism more generally.[149] Although each of these movements had its own particularities, all displayed a resistance to racial pluralism and the easing of immigration laws.

Within this racial dynamic, South Asian students arriving in the 1950s found their own racial position unclear, complicated by their middle-class status, high level of education, and white-collar employment but simultaneously their social marginalization. They could both empathize with and strategically distance themselves from other minority groups. Although Rohan Patil, for example, did not cultivate friendships with African American (or Mexican American) students, he became aware of their history as a group, which alerted him to the possibility of persistent discrimination. In the Third Ward neighborhood where he lived and in other places he frequented, though he "did not see any direct evidence" of the recently dissolved Jim Crow statutes separating the races, he "kept hearing about these things a lot." It struck him that segregated public spaces were only in the *recent* past. He reflected, "This was the early seventies we're talking about, and it was not too long before that, that there were things like separate water fountains and separate eating places and so on, for people who were not whites, even as late as in the sixties."[150] Furthermore, he noticed that in the neighborhood, police routinely stopped African Americans—whether for traffic violations or for other reasons he could not know. The police stops struck him as significant in light of recent allegations of racial profiling against the Houston Police Department.[151] It seemed to Patil that African Americans were being stopped less for what they had done than for "who the person was."[152] Heavy police scrutiny of his Third Ward neighborhood struck him as anomalous—as unlike what he had witnessed in white majority spaces, leading him to wonder if the police vigilance was inequitable and race based.

This complex, sometimes conflicted understanding of race echoed that of the rest of the country. Raj Bindal related that having moved directly from Punjab, India, to New York City in 1970, he "was walking down the street in New York. It was dusk. It was in the evening after hours between when the sun is setting so *the complexion is darker.* . . . I remember walking in Queens on a street to try to go to my house and I think I lost my way. . . . This is in my first twelve months, so now I'm trying to ask somebody, and they thought I'm going to go and *attack or mug* somebody."[153] Refusing to answer Bindal, the pedestrian hurried along, which in Bindal's view indicated that the pedestrian was concerned for his safety. This signaled to Bindal that men with dark complexions—men other than himself—could not be trusted. He decided then that he ought to seek a brightly lit area so that others might more easily distinguish between a dark-skinned Indian immigrant and other dangerous, "dark-skinned" pedestrians.

Bindal had offered the incident in response to my question, "Did anyone ever treat you badly on the basis of your being a foreigner?" The short answer to my

question was that he had been treated "not badly but differently."[154] He understood the pedestrian's fear because, to Bindal, the fear was legitimate. A lone
black man walking down the street constituted a threat. Philosopher George
Yancy has written about the experience of being that black man on the street.
He writes of being "unable to stop white women from tightening the hold of
their purses as I walk by, unable to stop white women from crossing to the other
side of the street once they have seen me walking in their direction, unable
to stop white men from looking several times over their shoulders as I walk
behind them minding my own business. . . . The depiction of the Black body
as the quintessence of *evil* has endured across historical time and space."[155]
Bindal wants it to be clear. He is not *that* black man. Like his experiences, he is
not "bad," just "different."

Conclusion

South Asians who came to Houston as college students in the 1960s and 1970s
regard these years as *the* crucial starting point in their immigrant narratives.[156]
However temporary, residence in these apartments alongside other individuals
of humble origins corroborates for immigrants the trajectory of their personal
American Dream narratives or rags-to-riches origin myths.[157] The majority of
these foreign students left South Asia with very little money and, like some of
their African American neighbors, struggled to live on meager means. Today,
they can laughingly compare stories about what little money they arrived
with in the United States. Their narratives of spatial mobility, commencing
in rented, multiunit domiciles or small homes in the American inner city and
culminating in ownership of spacious houses in the suburbs, demonstrate to
South Asian immigrants the possibilities available to all Americans who "work
hard," as they themselves have. However, initial residence among struggling
African Americans—whom immigrants understand as the most marginalized
of all American racial groups—imbues South Asian immigrants with a mis-
construed sense of shared origins. That is, residence in Houston's Third Ward
establishes a baseline from which immigrants measure their own material and
social progress over time against what they perceive as an African American
failure to achieve.

For many of the South Asian immigrants that I interviewed, the resulting
false binary, that of their own "success" versus black "failure," lends legitimacy
to their own championing of the model minority myth. The circumstances
permitting migration from Asia and American tolerance of their presence were
rooted in the Cold War. Many thousands more South Asians migrated during
the 1950s than had before 1950, and yet this time there was no anti-Asian nativist hue and cry, not even in the segregated South.

Arriving during the Cold War, Asian immigrants were recast from an excludable, undesirable, racial pariah group to a model minority.[158] Not only were they held up to other American minority groups as exemplars of racial respectability, but they exemplified to other nations the virtues of American democracy. Popularized since the mid-1960s by a liberal white American press, the model minority myth extoled Asian Americans and Asian immigrants' material success as resulting from good behavior, hard work, and family orientation. The myth juxtaposes "Asian success" against other minorities' "failure" at material success, erroneously finding explanations in racial values instead of structural racism and highly selective U.S. immigration policy.[159] Equally problematic, the purpose of the myth is not the inclusion of Asian immigrants and their descendants as Americans, since it reifies difference under the silken guise of false praise. Rather, it "reinforce[es] White dominance and privilege" by triangulating racialized groups against each other—all subject to an entrenched white power structure.[160]

Not only did the vast majority of Pakistani and Indian immigrants after the 1950s have the means necessary to strategize their advancement, but they were also aided by the Cold War–driven recasting of Asians (and, thus, Asian Americans) as assimilable, the loosening of immigration exclusion, and the lowering of anti-Asian racial barriers to education, housing, and employment. The transition of the status of America's Asian-descent populations from despised foreigners to exemplary minorities—"good immigrants," in Madeline Hsu's words—bears some explanation.[161] After all, South Asian immigrant success in the late postwar economy is better understood in light of state and federal limitations on Asian-descent communities before the war. The same national priorities engendered by the Cold War that recast immigration as a skilled-labor solution that subdued nativist objections also positioned educated Asian immigrants as exemplars of American democracy at work.

After enduring decades of legislative obstacles (such as racial restrictions in immigration, bars to naturalized citizenship, interdiction of land ownership, school segregation, residential segregation, and employment discrimination) and the ensuing racial Othering that arose from such statutory injunctions, many Asian Americans themselves embraced the model minority myth. As Ellen Wu demonstrates, Asian American positive "self-stereotyping" was a strategy employed to challenge derisive and long-standing stereotypes against the "yellow menace" and "Hindoo hordes."[162] While it is true that the Asian immigrant model minority was upheld as a foil to the African American black power movement, it is equally true that as a result of new wartime alliances (with China, in particular) a segment of the Asian American population helped perpetuate this image of a singularly and uniformly family-oriented, hardworking, studious community.[163] In other words, Asian-descent community leaders exercised their own agency in destroying a racist apparatus that had sought to circumscribe their opportunities since their earliest arrival in the nineteenth century. They ascribed to the model minority myth less because they recognized its divisive consequences than because the pairing of education and material success served as one of the only ways that they and their children could overcome racial marginalization.

Indian and Pakistani students learned the language of American race relations through their routine interactions. They quickly realized the price of blackness and wages of whiteness while they calculated their place within. In the American South in the 1960s and 1970s, newly arriving Asian immigrants navigated legalized black exclusion from private and public places during Jim Crow to a bounded social inclusion after the end of Jim Crow. Where white supremacist laws could no longer bar people of color from intermarriage, public education, or employment, widespread social perceptions nevertheless continued to cast South Asians generally as outsiders and specifically as foreigners. Although many endured varying degrees of racism, their embrace of middle-class values and their uncertain standing as guests in a host country undermined any formalized attempts at solidarity with other people of color communities.

Immigrants were unsure whether the government would authorize their permanent residence in the United States and unsure of their own commitment to remaining permanently in the country. These ambiguities thwarted Houston's South Asian immigrants' commitment to racial justice struggles or any outspoken political activism. Many intended to complete their graduate education and return home or to gain short-term work experience in the high-skills labor market before returning home. As they worked toward their goals, they nonetheless could not help but be forcibly triangulated in a white-dominated landscape.[164] South Asians in the 1960s and 1970s occupied a distinct position at the intersections of class belonging (ascendant middle class), racial unbelonging (not white), and exoticized Other (not American) that routinely merged, resulting in their social semiexclusion but economic inclusion. This ambiguity impeded their acceptance in American society insofar as they were normatively scripted as "not white" but, in some contexts, they were read as "not black" either, facilitating their access to education and employment. The conditional path of acceptance—of limited permission to participate in American society—led Indian and Pakistani immigrants to conclude that although their university education granted them access to the American economic system, the trade-off was a nonconfrontational existence at the social margins.[165]

. . . .

CHAPTER THREE

THE FORMATION OF

INTERETHNIC COMMUNITY,

1960S–1970S

Jamal Iqbal was born in India two years before Partition. His parents migrated to Karachi in 1949, and Iqbal attended elementary through high school there. After completing an associate degree in air conditioning technology and starting work in Karachi, Iqbal and his family decided that he needed to further his education. He explained, "We had a couple of friends who were trying to come to America. Since I was working, my major field was air conditioning. . . . So, that was one reason to start looking in the States and it wound up that the University of Houston had a program . . . and I came to Houston."[1] Iqbal worked toward his bachelor's degree in air conditioning technology at the University of Houston between 1966 and 1969. He lived in an apartment shared with other South Asians near campus for almost a year until his wife, Yasmin, joined him from Karachi. Then, Jamal and Yasmin lived in apartment residences that were centrally located in developed commercial districts in the museum area and Greenway Plaza but removed from the inner city.[2]

On graduating, Iqbal pursued his master's degree in industrial engineering at Texas A&M, after which the growing family of three returned to Karachi, as planned. With the civil war of 1971 between East and West Pakistan raging, Iqbal could not find work. After another cycle of going to the United States and returning to Pakistan, the family circled back to Houston, where Iqbal found employment in his field, designing air conditioning systems. By the time their two children were ready for elementary school, the Iqbals decided to purchase a home in northwest Houston's suburbs in the affluent Spring Branch area, and they have lived there since 1977.[3] Throughout these years, Jamal and Yasmin attended a variety of Indian and Pakistani cultural events—all at the University of Houston. As graduates residentially dispersed across Houston, they remained connected to the university as an ethnic hub.

When the earliest Indian and Pakistani students joined the city's universities in the late 1950s and 1960s—UH, TSU, and Rice—they found no South

Asian community infrastructure. They took it upon themselves to make one. Whether through official ethnic student organizations or the development of their own social bonds, the university functioned as the formal and informal locus of South Asian residents' and students' social lives. Until the late 1980s, the University of Houston served as the hub of Pakistani and Indian community institution building, around which both students and immigrants organized cultural activities and events, long after students had graduated from the university. Wherever they moved across Houston, South Asians who were interested in ethnic events were repeatedly pulled back to the university. International students, alumni, and newcomers collaborated to reconstruct Indian and Pakistani culture in diaspora, often blurring the political and religious lines between them, especially in the university's ethnic spaces. Immigrants' visa status (student or immigrant, "temporary" or "permanent") faded into the background as "South Asian," "Pakistani," and "Indian" identities shaped events and experiences. Blurring the lines further, students often became immigrants, and immigrants occasionally enrolled as students.

As South Asian students completed their courses of study, they chose various paths moving forward. Some students returned to their sending countries. Others moved out of state. Immigration statutes at the time permitted international student graduates on F student visas to remain in the United States while working for up to eighteen months. Over time, their companies or even host families sponsored their permanent visa applications, or graduates applied for a visa adjustment, enabling them to secure Green Cards (permanent residency). In Houston, these educated, qualified graduates met with ample job opportunities in a robust labor market. Because Houston's vigorous economic expansion during the 1970s generated plenty of engineering and other white-collar jobs, many Indian and Pakistani students stayed. They secured full-time employment, relocating away from Third Ward and the university area, and joining Houston's emergent, residential South Asian community.

Over the 1970s, the community of South Asian university students and middle-class professionals burgeoned in Houston. Although only a few hundred South Asians lived in Houston before 1970, the city's total population increased by over 30 percent between 1960 and 1970.[4] Migrants from across the nation and immigrants from other countries, including India and Pakistan, streamed into Houston to take advantage of its thriving labor market. The 1970 census does not list the exact number of foreign-born Pakistanis and Indians, but it does document 1,802 Chinese, 834 Japanese, and 1,166 "other Asians," even though this likely overlooked the international student population.[5] Based on oral history interviews, attendance at South Asian events would bear out the estimate of several hundred Indians and Pakistanis settling in the Houston area by the early 1970s. Only a decade later in 1980, more than 10,000 Asian Indians and Pakistanis would reside in Harris County, which largely contains the city limits.[6]

The thousands of new coethnic women and men moving to Houston spearheaded community institution-building efforts and opened new ethnic businesses, accommodating the swelling numbers and needs of a steady stream of newly arrived South Asians. Many immigrants envisioned resettling in India and Pakistan at some point. While there is no way of tracking this data, anecdotal evidence suggests that, in fact, many did return overseas at some point. Some then remained in their home countries, while others returned to the United States and to Houston. This chapter traces how Houston's South Asian mostly male students, educated professionals, and women immigrants established the foundations of ethnic and interethnic community in the 1960s and 1970s; in doing so, their representation of Indian and Pakistani cultural practices reflected a distinctly immigrant, middle-class subjectivity. South Asian immigrants acculturated to life in the United States in many ways, but particularly through ethnic and interethnic community formation.

Pakistani and Indian interviewees spoke of a shared culture, referring to traditional understandings of "culture" as the entire way of life of a people. Academically, this has given way to definitions that present culture as a system of meanings. As explained by Clifford Geertz in his groundbreaking work, culture is better understood as a system that "consists of such symbolic vehicles of meaning: cultural beliefs, ritual practices, art forms, and ceremonies, as well as informal cultural practices such as language, gossip, stories, and rituals of daily life."[7] Culture is constituted less by physical manifestations—such as clothing and food—than by the significance that ethnic group members assign to these tools. In reality, the native food, language, and clothing practices of the wide range of Indian and Pakistani immigrants contained as many differences as similarities. Still, they blurred the differences among them, identified South Asian cultural practices that could represent them collectively, and thus produced diasporic interethnicity.

The University as a Site for Building Ethnicity

Students from the subcontinent formed a close-knit group, building ethnic identity rooted in imagined communities and racial exclusion. As engineering majors, they often took the same classes, sitting together, studying together, and comparing notes. After class, they socialized mainly with each other, spending time at each other's apartments, especially because their residences were often clustered in the same apartment complexes. Many lived near campus together as roommates. They recall East Pakistanis, Indians, and West Pakistanis sharing the same accommodations, even if most remained closer with their own conationals. Many remain friends to the present day, despite their home countries' openly hostile relations. Since the partition of British India in 1947, strained relations between India and Pakistan have regularly erupted into military conflict, escalating into open warfare in 1947, 1965, and 1971. A majority of these students were in their early twenties by the mid-1960s and had little memory of Partition itself; some of the slightly older graduate students at UH were about ten years old in 1947.

Their South Asian ethnic identity evolved out of their recognition of a shared birthplace; almost all of the interviewees, including the Pakistani immigrants, were born in pre-Partition India. In addition, they spoke of a shared geographic ancestry. The Pakistani interviewees also all had at least a few family members remain in India after Partition. Language, to the extent that several but not all students spoke Hindi/Urdu, also bred a sense of familiarity. Finally, their shared ethnicity was partly informed by their particular foreignness in the context of being abroad. In other words, South Asian students were outsiders united in their relative similarity, unfamiliarity, and marginal racial inclusion. The more they felt ostracized by the white majority, the more they sought safe, welcoming spaces; usually, they found these in the company of other South Asians. As is well documented in studies on panethnicity, panethnic group members broadly seek out similarities with each other, blurring ethnic differences in order to mitigate external hostility.[8] That is, they see in each other a cohesive group facing similar opposition, motivating them to construct an expansive panethnic identity.

Because of the high concentration of South Asians at the University of Houston, the university formed the nucleus of the burgeoning Indo-Pak community's lifeworld. All three institutions (UH, TSU, and Rice) served a growing body of international students, but ethnic community building coalesced at the University of Houston. Before their arrival in Houston, future students in India and Pakistan usually sought out contact information for other fellow nationals at the university. If they did not already have a point person in Houston, they inquired with the university's Office of International Students. Interviewees spoke of coethnics picking them up at the airport, having already arranged for temporary lodging. In this way, much like earlier waves of Italian or Jewish immigrants, for example, the earliest Indian and Pakistani immigrants immediately forged close ties with each other.[9]

On campus, students established ethnocultural and religious organizations, the first of their kind, serving all South Asians in Houston. Through the Indian Students Association (ISA) and the Pakistan Students Association (PSA), students and immigrant families arranged national (either Indian or Pakistani) celebrations and religious observances at the university. Because the organizations were registered on campus, student leaders could reserve campus venues, where they hosted large- and small-scale events. Other international student groups did much the same. Thus, the university emerged as the first site in which students, and soon, immigrant families from India and Pakistan began to reshape their understanding of ethnicity. Having grown up and come of age in independent, adversarial nations, Indian and Pakistani students and immigrants could have constructed entirely distinct communities consonant with the politics of their home countries. Certainly, they could have simply coexisted neatly without overlap, emulating the political boundaries between India and Pakistan.

Instead, Indian, East Pakistani, and West Pakistani students and immigrants in the 1960s and 1970s coalesced around a "found" interethnic identity, which their children (second-generation South Asian Americans) would later term "Desi." Though they did not describe themselves as Desi at the time, they enacted the identity that their children would formally name a generation later. I define Desi as an interethnic South Asian identity borne out of the diasporic parallel experiences of social marginalization and real or fictively shared culture. Unlike very broad panethnic identities such as African American or Asian American, self-identifying Desis found shared ethnic meaning in their historical past overseas. On the one hand, ethnic identities are imagined communities bound by geography and ideas about shared culture and ancestry. On the other hand, panethnic identities subsume ethnic groups "previously unrelated in culture and dissent" and with "diverse national origins."[10] As Yen Le Espiritu states, panethnic identities arise when "linguistically, culturally, and geographically diverse groups come together in the interest of panethnic, or all-ethnic solidarity."[11] Like panethnic identities, interethnic identities form in response to external conditions and are "bound up with power relations.[12] With interethnicity, however, the focus is the identity that emerges *across ethnonational lines building on entangled pasts*. Unlike panethnic groups, South Asian immigrants were related in integral ways, sharing the same geographic and to an extent, linguistic origins, but were recently divided along national lines. After Partition, many South Asian lives nevertheless remained entangled both linguistically and through their families across new political boundaries between Pakistan and India.

South Asian immigrants elided identity shifts produced by the lapse between pre-Partition India—the imagined source of this new collective Desi identity— and the two ensuing decades of nation building during which these immigrants came of age. Following Independence, India and Pakistan each considered the other its greatest adversary, for reasons that only intensified over time. First, the very creation of a separate Muslim nation out of a unified independent India registered officially and on the ground as a virtually unforgivable act. Even Muhammad Ali Jinnah, the founder of Pakistan, grudgingly accepted an autonomous, separate nation only in 1947, the year of Partition itself.[13] Second, much of the animosity between the two nations found its origin and expression in conflict over the area of Kashmir, resulting in a near-perpetual state of dispute and two outright wars, in 1947 and 1965. Another point of contention for Pakistan was India's nuclear weapons test in 1974. With assistance from China, Pakistan soon expanded its own nuclear capabilities, the neighboring rivals now posing an even graver threat to each other than before.

Instead of replicating those fissures, in diaspora, Indian and Pakistani immigrants imbued the historical experiences of diverse geographies, languages, and cultural practices with a singular collectivity. In this way, they willingly overlooked national differences in order to create an interethnic Desi community on a set of shared practices that transcended the discreteness of political borders. Thus, while nation building itself is an ongoing political project— an uneasy contract between the state and its people—in the diaspora, discrete national identities simultaneously hardened and softened, as locally produced nationalism was reconstructed through ethnicity.[14]

This interethnic "Desi" identity revealed the inchoateness of national identity and political divisiveness as lived reality, as well as the essential contingency of an antagonistic India-Pakistan binary. That is, Desi-ness was in opposition to clearly demarcated national identities, as South Asians sought and reclaimed a shared history. And yet, national origins did not lose all meaning. Rather, being Desi in the United States functioned as an additional layer intersecting with already complex subjectivities. It did not replace national identity but pulled it into the service of a new (and simultaneously old) pre-Partition ethnic identity.[15] Still, the very act of community building on a college campus framed that process within exclusive class and race frameworks; even though UH attracted a sizable working-class population, the culture of a middle-class university permeated through its faculty, administration, graduate students, and academic milieu.

Establishing Student Organizations on Campus

Any South Asian immigrant arriving in Houston in the 1960s and 1970s, seeking ethnic community, would have ventured to the University of Houston, because the two campus ethnic organizations, Indian Students Association and Pakistan Students Association, formed the foundation for South Asian ethnic community activity in the city at that point. South Asian students established chapters of these patriotic national student organizations at UH in the early to mid-1960s. Of course, many South Asians fraternized with Americans and immigrants outside of their own ethnic groups, but every Pakistani and Indian immigrant whom I interviewed participated in university activities to some extent, whether or not they were ever UH students. In May 1971, Indian immigrant Uma Krishnan joined her husband, already employed as an engineer at Shell Oil Company in Houston. They had married in India just two months earlier, and she looked forward to beginning a new life with him in Texas. At UH, she found students and immigrants involved in the organizing ethnic activities through ISA. Along with other women—wives of UH students and wives like herself, with no UH affiliation—she became involved in ISA activities.

Meanwhile, the Pakistani couple whose vignette opened this chapter, Yasmin and Jamal Iqbal, adjusted to life in Houston, seeking out the culturally familiar and finding it at UH. Their yearning for familiarity brought them to the organized events of the university's international ethnic students' associations, which produced a collective, though selective, ethnic culture. The primary purpose of these associations was to provide a shared ethnic experience for national group members while promoting the culture of each nation. Students and immigrants used campus venues for organizing shows and events in which they produced and performed emergent, localized, diasporic cultures. By doing so, they united and created community around music, fashion, and film, especially in the 1970s. Many of the performative expressions of collective culture occurred at the university.

The building of ethnic community activity in public spaces and at a university campus was significant for several reasons. First, the selection of specific forms of visual and aural entertainment signaled to participants a set of culturally sanctioned practices, not only in terms of the tropes contained within skits or songs, but also within the genre of the skit, song, or fashion show itself. These entertainment genres came to represent Indian-ness or Pakistani-ness in ways that may not have been the case in India or Pakistan. While student organizations at universities in the subcontinent may have produced the same or similar genres of entertainment, the meanings of viewership (and of performance) were culturally mediated to produce localized experiences and meanings. The same dramatizations enacted in diaspora were complicated for participants by feelings of nostalgia and the production of diasporic memory.

Second, for South Asian immigrants, public performance became a claim to ethnicity—a claim to one's ethnic self. Simultaneously, by consciously inhabiting a physical space in "America," ethnic performance was a claim to

American-ness. This was the case even if participants insisted that they were preserving *their* culture. For example, South Asian immigrants organized and participated in International Day festivals in which ISA and PSA shared Indian and Pakistani food and displayed national artifacts and dress. Such uniquely diasporic displays of displaced culture did more than simply share a so-called foreign culture; they made it acceptable to exhibit that culture in an American space—a remarkable shift given the history of Asian exclusion and nativist opposition.

Next, the use of the university—a space that is perceived as having high cultural capital—as the venue conferred both high status and legitimacy to group members in attendance and to their ethnic claims. Finally, immigrants' embrace of ethnicity reinforced their place as distinct from other highly racialized minority groups. In their reckoning, being "Indian" or "Pakistani" or "Indian-Pakistani" was decidedly not black or Mexican; it was a "space apart."[16] By claiming an ethnic identity, they could bypass being racialized. In reality, as many South Asian immigrants came to understand, ethnicity did not remove them from either the process of racialization or from brute racism itself.[17]

For South Asians, the university ethnic organization experience in the 1960s fostered the development of future community leaders in the 1970s—that is, campus leaders soon settled in the Greater Houston area and continued their community-building efforts. Expanding beyond the university, the activities, interests, and vision of emerging off-campus community organizations, including the India Culture Center (ICC)—an umbrella group—and Pakistan Association of Greater Houston (PAGH), were led by many of the same highly educated professionals who had been active in ISA and PSA during college. After completing his master's degree at UH in 1966, Pakistani student Zafar Waheed eventually worked toward his doctorate at UH. Settling more permanently in Houston, Waheed played an active role in founding Pakistani ethnic activities and Muslim religious institutions.

These "pioneers," as many view themselves, remained in Houston and by the late 2000s had been instrumental in expanding the public presence and services available to Indians and Pakistanis, as well as others, throughout the city. Uma Krishnan has served on several boards of directors in Houston's fine arts scene and most recently spearheaded the effort to build a South Asia wing at the Museum of Fine Arts, Houston. Zafar Waheed and his wife, Sara, serve as unofficial family counselors for Muslims of all ethnic backgrounds in Houston. Zafar Waheed also played a role in establishing the first mosque and, subsequently, a centralized mosque system for the Greater Houston area.

The continuity of leadership between campus and community organizations reinforced a middle-class vision of ethnic culture that was safe and socially conservative, revolving around decidedly nonradical practices such as "traditional" dance and poetry and "mainstream" Hindi cinema.[18] On-campus events were targeted at Indian and Pakistani immigrants across the Houston area and at other Houston-area universities. Also, patriotic international student organizations in the United States not only supported U.S. Cold War aims but also lent tacit support to their home countries' governments. In 1974, when the PSA at the University of Houston hosted a regional conference of PSAs from colleges across the southwestern United States, they invited Sahabzada Yaqub Khan, Pakistani ambassador to the United States, as keynote speaker.[19]

The university-centric immigrant experience of Houston's Indians and Pakistani was similar to that of South Asians in many other major American cities from the 1950s through 1970s. Jyoti Patel moved from Gujarat to Philadelphia in 1969 before settling in Houston in the 1980s. Comparing her experiences in these two major American cities, she found that many Indian families in Philadelphia socialized with each other casually by meeting in each other's homes, "but when we all got together, they used to have some program or something at university—Drexler University or University of Pennsylvania."[20] As in Houston, university students and faculty at Philadelphia universities were among the earliest South Asian immigrants. As with Houston, the earliest ethnic organizations and worship services were established on campus; it stands to reason that educated South Asian immigrants in other American cities during the 1950s, 1960s, and 1970s replicated this pattern, whether in Chicago, Raleigh, Atlanta, or other cities with major universities. The India Association of Kalamazoo, for example, began renting an auditorium at Western Michigan University in 1970 for the screening of Hindi films.[21]

The earliest and most important large-scale events planned by ISA and PSA were Independence Day festivities. Indians and Pakistanis across the diaspora celebrated these events separately. Since their national Independence days fell one day apart—August 14 for Pakistan and August 15 for India—PSA and ISA at the University of Houston agreed to space festivities a week apart so that both communities could enjoy the occasion on a convenient Saturday.[22] Community members held flag ceremonies, complete with the colors of India or Pakistan. They organized ticketed entertainment and variety shows that routinely commenced with singing the Indian or Pakistani national anthem, followed by music, dance, fashion shows, and drama skits. They also prepared Indian or Pakistani food to serve and, in later years, as crowd size swelled, to sell at the events. Reflecting the biases within national identity formation in the home countries, specific regions and language groups were privileged above regional and dialectical variations—mainly north and west India (as opposed to South India, for example) for Indians, and Urdu for Pakistanis (instead of Punjabi, for example).

An article in the *Houston Post* in 1977 announced the celebrations surrounding India's thirtieth anniversary of Independence. Sponsored by the ISA, the cultural show at UH's Cullen Auditorium would cater to some of Houston's estimated four thousand–person-strong Indian community.[23] Within one week of her arrival in Houston in 1975, Bhanu Shekhar, a professionally trained classical Indian dancer, performed a dance sequence at an ISA-planned event in "celebration of India's independence."[24] Like ISA's cultural show, PSA's Independence-related events drew both students and immigrants. By the late 1970s, PSA's shows drew several hundred audience members. Regarding the PSA and its earlier shows, Pakistani immigrant Nadia Hasan explained,

> There was a Pakistan organization but it was, of course, a very small group and it was basically run by students at University of Houston. . . . When I came to America, they had a function [event] and I think it was Independence, fourteenth of August function. And I had just been married a few months. They came up to me and they said, "Oh, you know, we are having a modeling show and we want to show our clothes." They knew I had the original wedding dresses and the saris and all, and they said, "Can you please come and display those?"[25]

In these displays of patriotism, cultural expression coalesced around music, comedy, drama, dance, fashion, and food. Language, of course—mainly but not exclusively Hindi, Urdu, and Gujarati—was also a crucial ethnic boundary marker. English immediately emerged as a bridge among various language speakers.

Throughout the rest of the year, ISA arranged small-scale "variety entertainment show[s]" for Indian audiences of fifty to one hundred people through the 1970s.[26] In addition, prominent Indian singers and actors, such as Mukesh and Asha Parekh, also traveled to the United States on tour, including Houston as a stop.[27] According to Anita Sharma, who helped organize several Indian stage events in the mid-1970s, she and other Indian immigrants sold 180 to 200 tickets and cooked food for as many attendees. Sharma claimed that the show featuring Parekh drew in an audience of over one thousand. In addition, Indian and Pakistani students performed and participated alongside students from dozens of other countries in the University of Houston's International Night Show.[28]

Organizing Hindi film screenings—one of the most popular ISA-sponsored campus events among South Asians—ISA members ordered sixteen-millimeter films from an Indian supplier in Chicago.[29] These films were scripted in Urdu or Hindi (mutually intelligible sister languages) without the benefit of translation into English or any other language. They were part of a supply chain of films ordered from India and circulated throughout universities and major cities in the United States.[30] The films were initially screened at smaller rooms at the University Center, but by 1969, they were held at the much-larger-capacity Liberal Arts Auditorium at UH (later renamed Agnes Arnold Hall). Paying a dollar admission, Indians and Pakistanis gathered to watch Hindi films on occasional Saturday evenings.[31] By 1970, attendance at the movie screening ranged from 250 to 300 people and included both students and members of the broader Indo-Pak community.[32]

Almost every Indian and Pakistani interviewee with whom I spoke recalled attending these film screenings. Pakistani couple Yasmin and Jamal Iqbal often attended the screenings in the mid-1960s, as did Pakistani UH-Downtown student Javed Malhotra in the 1970s. One weekend a month, Malhotra and his undergraduate Pakistani and Indian friends headed to UH to watch international releases of big blockbuster Indian films. Yasmin Iqbal recalls that even though most of the audience was Indian, she and her husband nevertheless felt enough sense of community belonging to return time and again. The films functioned as an identity-building device that fostered interethnicity, partly through language, even if attendees' first language was not Hindi or Urdu.[33] Part of the impetus for seeking out this broad interethnic identity was a sense of isolation. Indian immigrant Tahira Lakhani revealed that, despite having attended convent schools in Gujarat, India, being fluent in English, and knowing American literature, this familiarity only nominally mitigated the transition of immigrant life in the United States. "You know, you are getting over a culture shock," she reflected.[34] Immigrants thus reconstructed the meanings of "community" broadly in these early years, in order to ease their transition.

Although ISA and PSA remain active at the University of Houston today, since the 1990s, their activities have no longer attracted the entirety or even the majority of Houston's South Asians. Decades later, ISA's and PSA's broad appeal has dwindled as the vast majority of Desi students on campus are of the second, third, and fourth generations. South Asian Americans might attend events and routinely embrace hyphenated identities (for example, Pakistani Americans or Indian Americans), but they are mostly not international students. Thus, the 1960s and 1970s represent a unique time in these communities' histories, when ethnic community making on campus merged with that occurring off campus to form a cohesive unit that operated within a particular middle-class focus on cultural "tradition," family-centeredness, and socially conformist attitudes.

Indian and Pakistani Immigrant Women's Lives

Approximately 40 percent of Indian immigrants to the United States in 1970 were women.[35] Most South Asian women entered the country on the basis of family reunification, but many eventually found employment. The women whom I interviewed entered the United States as wives, on the basis of their husbands' visa status, and although I was unable to locate any women students from India or Pakistan, anecdotal evidence suggests that several did attend UH in the 1970s. By 1980, the gender distribution among Asian Indian immigrants evened out, and many more Indian women applied for occupational visas rather than immigrating as spouses.[36] Women's contributions were central to notions of culture, family-centeredness, financial solvency, and the building of ethnic identity. The women with whom I spoke discussed their initial sense of isolation, attempts at acculturation, enrollment at local universities, involvement in ethnic communities, and devotion to their families.[37]

South Asian women created social networks with coethnics both within and outside of their neighborhoods, with neighbors to a limited extent, and with ladies' groups hosted by area churches.[38] Still, prohibited from working, unable to drive, and bound to the home, many of these women initially suffered from relative isolation, depression, and frustration. They experienced the newness of immigration in very dissimilar ways from their husbands, interacting with totally different people.

While they made attempts to acculturate, immigrants also maintained regular, if infrequent, correspondence with family members in their home countries. As wives joined their husbands in Houston, the responsibility of communication "back home" often fell to the women. Sara Waheed reflected, "It was not a very advanced system of communication [because] we did not have any email or computer. Naturally so, we used to write letters and we used to wait each day, minutes and hours—like, you used to count, if I wrote a letter . . . then I would count how many days have gone or passed by."[39] Yasmin Iqbal explained, "We didn't have this email that you send something to somebody and you can get the answer back within one hour or within a few minutes."[40] Women tended to write more frequently than did men. Because long-distance phone calls were far more expensive, contact was maintained more often through letters. Nadia Hasan spoke of calling her parents: "At that time, it wasn't easy to get them because we had to call the operator and the operator would tell us, 'We will call you and connect the line in two hours,' so we had to sit near the phone [waiting for] the operator [to] call. It used to be such a hassle." She found it more convenient to write letters to her parents, especially since her "father always preferred me writing letters because he could read it over and over again. So, he would not really want to talk to me over the phone. He would just collect my letters."[41] Tahira Lakhani, from Baroda, India, reflected, "You are in a different country. You are away from home. My parents didn't have a phone when I left India. Then, the phone came later on. And then, calling was very expensive. You wrote letters. Things are very different now. It is hard for somebody to imagine, it took ten days, twelve days, to get a letter."[42]

Usually immigrants mailed letters via the postal service, but certainly, if a community member or coethnic planned on traveling to or from major cities in India or Pakistan, Houston's immigrants sent and received letters and goods through visitors. They also received "paper clippings and some magazines of our language" from their families in India and Pakistan, recalled Nagaraj Shekhar.[43] He continued, "Once in a month or something, there would be a little parcel that would come, book post as you would call it. It would take about six weeks to get here." Sara Waheed added that "if somebody comes, then [our families in Pakistan] send along with them some pictures, some things for us ... presents or items. We get from them [our families in Pakistan] or saying somebody [from Houston] is going back, so we send something to them. So, that is the way we were in touch."[44]

In part, the duty of writing to family alleviated South Asian women's initial sense of isolation. Many South Asian women shared in common a difficult period of adjustment after migrating to the United States.[45] Nadia Hasan states that Houston "was a very beautiful place but I was very homesick because I came from a large, wealthy family. Here, it was just me and my husband in a small, one-bedroom apartment which just [was the size of] my bathroom back home, so I was kind of very upset about it and I didn't know how to react. But, in due time, I realized this was the way life was over here."[46] Others echoed the same sentiment. When asked what hardships she faced after moving to Houston, Yasmin Iqbal immediately said, "First of all, I missed the family. Loneliness was there. Being all by yourself. Waiting for the letters to arrive."[47] Reading letters from home and knowing that visits would be infrequent, at best, "used to make me very emotional and I used to cry," remembered Sara Waheed.[48]

For many immigrant wives, the loneliness was compounded by F-2 visa restrictions that did not permit them to work, at least not until they received their Green Card. Yasmin Iqbal explained, "Well, I was with an F-2 visa, and we didn't have permission to work. My husband was a student and I was a dependent."[49] Unlike their husbands, who were either students or full-time employees, most South Asian women could not enter a professional career immediately on arrival, and although some eventually pursued higher education, initially they did not.[50] While many South Asian immigrant women eventually worked outside the home, at first, most did not. Varuni Gil spoke of getting "very bored sitting in the home [*laughs*]—very bored! I mean I got so bored I hit the wall of the apartment. And I had no clue that walls are so hollow here."[51] Underscoring the same deep sense of loneliness as Gil, Yasmin Iqbal also longed for many years to return to Pakistan permanently. She reflected,

> My mind changed really. . . . I was after my husband for a long time to go, not only the first five years but after that, too. But when my kids came in higher grade, like eighth grade, ninth grade, then I thought I don't know whether they can adjust to the schools over there or not. And then, by that time, there were a lot of people coming from Pakistan and the community grew. So, then you were not that lonely. And then, you have already settled here for ten years now. I gave up after that.[52]

Many of these middle-class South Asian women had college degrees— ranging in concentrations from home economics to business and biology—at rates that far surpassed the average level of education for other immigrants and native-born Americans. Of the young Asian Indian women (ages twenty-five to twenty-nine) who migrated before 1965, 64 percent had completed a college degree. Of those who migrated between 1965 and 1969, nearly 50 percent had college degrees—this at a time when the percentage of all Americans having completed four-year degrees was below 20 percent.[53] Presumably, these women were either student immigrants who entered the United States for the purposes of higher education (master's and doctorate degrees) or, for the most part, highly educated wives jointly migrating with or joining highly educated husbands.

Several eventually obtained full-time employment, and some began their own businesses. Others worked part-time. In Pakistan, Sara Waheed's father encouraged all his daughters to obtain advanced degrees. One of Waheed's sisters became a doctor, another a town planner, and the youngest a teacher. She herself became a medical technologist, proudly building a career in Texas Medical Center hospitals. Namrata Chandra, from Maharashtra state in India, also trained to be a medical technologist and met Waheed through her workplace.[54] Chandra had previously trained in the United States, gaining admission and completing her master's degree at the University of California, Berkeley. Accounting was Vera Khatri's calling, and she earned her M.B.A. from Loyola University after having completed a master's degree in English literature at Delhi University.[55] The list continues, but it is important to reiterate that during this period of nation building in both India and Pakistan, contrary to popular notions of South Asian women as uneducated or crippled under a system of so-called Eastern patriarchy, many middle-class parents encouraged their daughters to obtain advanced degrees, and young Pakistani and Indian women sought such degrees for themselves. Often, these women had professional careers before marriage, and although some stopped working to raise families after marrying, many more eventually continued working in some capacity. Some pursued higher education as a goal in and of itself.

Not all South Asian immigrant women, however, had the same levels of higher education. Pakistani immigrant Nadia Hasan—who described her family as "well-to-do" with "our maids, we had our servants, we had a gatekeeper"—insisted that "back home, we [girls/women] are not raised to have dreams. . . . We are never told, 'Oh, when you grow up, you have to become a doctor or a lawyer or a business woman.' You don't."[56] She continued, "Yes, for boys, the parents tell them become a doctor, become a lawyer, become an engineer. Those are the things that the boys are taught. But in those days, no, there was no such thing. I did not have a dream like that. I knew I was . . . going to be married and I am going to have kids and I am going to be a housewife. Basically, that is how I was raised. And I had no problem with it."

Hasan's upbringing, however, was the exception among South Asian women immigrants to the United States in the 1960s and 1970s. Varuni Gil, from the village of Shikarpur, Pakistan, recalled that her family encouraged her to pursue a medical degree, even after marriage.[57] Instead, she opened her own, very successful beauty salon in Houston. The overrepresentation of educated, professional women among the South Asian communities in the United States can be explained in several ways. First, families in the post-1965 era were admitted because of high educational qualifications, and although this wave of migration consisted largely of men, their wives were also often highly educated. Second, in the 1950s—the period of nation building for both Pakistan and India—middle-class women were increasingly encouraged to seek higher education and employment as a mark of national progress toward modernity.

Ties of Interethnic Fictive Kinship

Immigrants from India and Pakistan formed their deepest relationships with coethnic families in Houston. For many South Asians, "coethnic" meant "same nationality" as much as it meant interethnicity. The bonds formed among community members transcended the usual exchanges of friendship. Pakistani immigrant Yasmin Iqbal—whose husband, Jamal, studied engineering at UH—recalled that Jamal's coethnic Indian and Pakistani classmates felt close enough to the couple that when they stopped by for visits, "they would come and . . . they would just open the fridge door and find whatever is there."[58] They referred to Yasmin as "Bhabi," an Urdu/Hindi term of respect meaning "my

brother's wife." On an almost daily basis, Yasmin and Jamal visited other Indian and Pakistani families in the neighborhood. She recalled, "I knew one or
two families very well, so we used to see each other maybe every other day if not
every day for just half an hour, one hour. [We] had dinner at home, [and then]
you know, 'Let's go visit across the street.' And it was easier to just go over there
and have tea and then come back."

Again, these fictive kin relations were both Pakistani and Indian, Muslim
and Hindu, as well as South Asian Christians, Jains, Sikhs, Parsis, and others.
Namrata Chandra and Sara Waheed both recall weekly dinners, birthday parties, and road trips, all spent with the same group of Pakistani and Indian
friends, who embraced the role that extended family would otherwise have
fulfilled. Many of these immigrants still meet monthly as groups and celebrate
friendships that have endured for more than forty years.[59] Many Pakistani and
Indian students blurred national boundaries to construct collective interethnic
Desi community rooted in the university setting.

Not only did they room together in apartments near the University of Houston, as families, but they also frequently socialized together. Pakistani student
Jamal Iqbal explained, "Coming from the same background, you know, we
never felt that they were against us or we were against them. We all used to
meet. They used to come to our apartment, and we used to go to their apartment. Plus, you would meet them on the campus.... We all had the same
classes. That also made it easier."[60] Saumitra Kelkar, an Indian graduate student in business at UH, elaborated on the term by using the example of his
next-door neighbors: "The very next apartment [there] was a bunch of Indians
with a Pakistani roommate who is still a delightful friend of mine. He went
back to Karachi.... Indians and Pakistanis really didn't care where you were
from ... so you could say we were 'South Asians.' We really didn't look at our-
selves.... Desis—it's the word that was coined literally to describe the fact that
we really don't care about these political barriers between countries."[61]

Indians and Pakistanis sought to overlook regional, linguistic, and other differences in one another, defining what it meant to be Indian and Pakistani in
America, and forming friendships along the way. Javed Malhotra, a Pakistani
undergraduate at a branch campus of the University of Houston, socialized
informally with both Indian and fellow Pakistani students on the weekends.[62]
Pakistani couple Yasmin and Jamal Iqbal enjoyed joining other South Asians
for the Hindi film screenings at UH. They also met regularly with "a couple of
Indian friends. They were living close to our house, so we used to go and visit
them. Because they were so little in number, you know, Indians and Pakistanis,
we got along very well."[63] Pakistani immigrant Sara Waheed explained that
their common ground was "place. That is, India and Pakistan have the same

kind of cultural things and for that, we had all that togetherness without thinking about which religion you follow or what is your practice." She felt that together, they were "a very congenial group because people who come from India, Pakistan, their culture and practices are so similar and the dress is also kind of much similar. So, we never felt kind of strange to each other." [64] By "culture and practices," she meant, among other shared features, clothing, food, and language, even though these objects and practices become cultural through the act of assigning them value and meaning. In this case, Waheed was alluding to interethnic culture, built across Indian and Pakistani ethnonational boundaries.

Ethnic community formation also evolved in response to feelings of alienation from the broader society, whether Latino/a or African American, but especially the middle-class whites with whom South Asian immigrants mostly interacted. South Asian immigrants did not have the privilege of choosing an ethnic identity; they were racially marked (physically, culturally, and linguistically, because of their accents) as "ethnic" against the backdrops of a quintessential Americanness—that is, white invisibility and black/brown hypervisibility. The question they faced was not *if* but *how* they would interpret and perform their ethnicity. Ethnic immigrant identities were positioned within what Stuart Hall describes as "narratives of the past," as Indians and Pakistanis reached back to pre-Independence India to locate themselves as an interethnic community in the present.[65]

Despite the rising and waning political tensions between the governments of India and Pakistan, many South Asians in Houston found familiarity in each other's company. In response to their countries' adversarial relationship, UH student Zafar Waheed explained,

That was a time that we did not have any kind of political polarization between Indians and Pakistanis. I think at that time, I was the only full-time [Pakistani] student. There were three more Pakistani students, but they were only half-time students. As far as India is concerned, I think there were about three or four full-time students, and the rest were all part-time students. We used to have a very good relationship with Indians and Pakistanis. . . . In 1965, there was the war between India and Pakistan. At that time, one of my closest friends was an Indian, and somehow the local newspaper came to know that I was from Pakistan and I was very close friends with an Indian. So, they came to my house and took an interview, [asking] "How come India and Pakistan are fighting and you are friends to each other?" . . . I said in my interview that as human beings, Indians and Pakistanis have no problem with each other. The fighting which is going on is political, but we still maintain good relations.[66]

India and Pakistan fought wars in 1947–48 and 1965 over the disputed territory of Jammu and Kashmir, and in 1971 over East Pakistan, which led to the secession and creation of independent Bangladesh. In addition, both countries finally developed nuclear weapons capacity—India in 1974 and Pakistan in 1983—although they had been in competition to do so since the mid-1950s.[67] Meanwhile, the Kashmir issue simmered unresolved for decades.

Many Indian and Pakistani students willingly overlooked these tensions, constructing ethnic community even though both groups were educated in newly independent, fiercely nationalistic countries. Of course, there were limits to interethnic identity (discussed below) when ethnonational identities prevailed, but interethnic connections nonetheless reveal the porousness of national boundary making. Through ISA and PSA, Indians and Pakistanis both on and off campus came together to construct what it meant to be South Asian in America. Later, this participation was extended to nascent off-campus ethnic organizations and cultural activities—many, but not all, bounded by national divisions. Some activities—in particular, music, radio, and literature— lent themselves to the formation of interethnicity, while others reinforced national identity.

Constructing Culture off Campus

Indo-Pak radio programming also provided immigrants with links to familiar cultural forms, though the format for radio programming in the United States differed dramatically from some of the programming found in India and Pakistan in the mid-twentieth century. Broadcast media plays a role akin to print media in its commodification of culture and coopting of ethnic identities, though initially this was not the case with ethnic radio. Nagaraj Shekhar, an amateur music aficionado, hosted the first Indian radio program in Houston in 1970. Shekhar named his show, which aired on FM 90.1, the *Morning Ragas*.[68] He played classical and contemporary Indian music from his collection of ten LPs and a few pieces purchased from a local home entertainment store that carried "international music," although he says, "everything was Ravi Shankar in those days." Friends also contributed music from their collections. After hosting the show for a few years, Shekhar yielded responsibility to Meena Datt in 1976.

Renamed *Music of India*, Datt's show became the longest-running Indian music program in Houston. By 1984, three more radio programs aired—two Indian and one Pakistani—but Datt's program remained the most popular Indian music program in Houston for nearly twenty years. In the process, Datt became a local celebrity within the Desi community. [69] Listeners from India and Pakistan tuned in on Saturday mornings for her "sometimes nostalgic mix of classical music and Indian film songs, anchored by Datt's soothing Hindi patter about people's birthdays and upcoming community events."[70] Tuning in to the weekly airing of Indian music allowed Houston's Indians and Pakistanis to coalesce around music in a way that they may not have in India or Pakistan. Also, for the listeners of the show—members of that audio, ethnic, imagined community—having airtime on FM radio (even if it was community radio) legitimized their existence as an American ethnic group.[71]

Literary Activities

Just as Hindi-language radio served as a forum for articulating Indian and Pakistani interests and the formation of interethnic Desi community, Urdu-language activities served much the same purpose, albeit on a much smaller scale, under the banner of the Urdu Literature Group. Formed in 1969 by Pakistani student Zafar Waheed, the group allowed Pakistani and Indian immigrants to gather monthly to hear recitations of Urdu poetry (*mushaira*) and music (*ghazal*).[72] Roughly half of the attendees were Muslim (from Pakistan and India), while the other half were Hindu, Sikh, or Jain. The Urdu Literature Group (later, the Urdu Society) was one of the few large events hosted by Pakistanis in Houston, as Indians organized most of the large events; other, much larger events included Pakistan Independence Day celebrations in August and Eid dinners—events that would not necessarily be geared toward non-Pakistanis. The enthusiastic attendance of native Hindi and Punjabi speakers was noteworthy in light of recent Partition-related tensions and the historic politicization of Hindi and Urdu.

As linguist Rizwan Ahmad states, the "articulation of language ideologies can also be seen as a form of practice which shapes and is shaped by broader developments in society."[73] Thus, language is symbolic of social and political identities. As in India, before Partition, Urdu literary recitals had broad appeal beyond religious boundaries—a phenomenon that continued in the South Asian diaspora. Still, this appeal was limited due to the divisive history of the language in India. Ahmad describes Urdu as a language that shares the same "linguistic structure" as Hindi, while Andrew Dalby, author of the *Dictionary of Languages*, calls Urdu the "twin" of Hindi.[74] According to another linguist, Urdu and Hindi share origins in a fourteenth-century language known as Hindi or Hindvi or Dehlvi spoken in and around Delhi.[75] By the late eighteenth century, the term "Urdu" emerged as the nomenclature in the royal courts for spoken Hindi/Hindvi but was still called Hindvi—its colloquial form—in rural areas of the Delhi region.[76] The Urdu script adopted by the courts was Persian, and in the courtly domain, Urdu was developed as a high literary art form. In 1837, the British colonial government passed a decree designating Urdu the official language of the courts in northern and central India, sparking a nationalistic resistance movement advocating for "Hindi" written in the Devanagari script.[77] Urdu then began to be described as "defective" and "foreign" and increasingly identified as a Muslim, rather than Indo-Aryan, language.[78]

As a result of these "language ideological debates," Lieutenant Governor Antony MacDonnel ordered in 1900 that Hindi join Urdu as an official language of the British Indian lower courts "as a way to balance Hindus against Muslims."[79] Nevertheless, the debates had facilitated the polarization of emerging communal identities. In the early twentieth century, Hindu intellectuals who had previously written prolifically in Urdu switched to the Hindi Devanagari script and "found it socially inappropriate to transfer the Urdu language and script to their children."[80]

Attendees of the Urdu Literature Group in Houston gathered under the conviction, in Sara Waheed's words, that "we were all speaking the language which was Urdu and that made us one group." She explained that the group was "language based" and had "nothing to do with religion." [81] The stripping of all social and political meaning from Urdu to render it a neutral space or buffer zone was another attempt to create South Asian interethnic community. In 1975, the Urdu Literature Group invited and hosted the renowned classical Indian singer, Mohammed Rafi, and both Indians and Pakistanis attended Rafi's music concert. Not all Pakistanis voiced an interest in Urdu literature and poetry, and by the same token, neither did most Indians. Waheed, who attended Urdu Literature Group events, recalled that "the Indians speak Hindi but this literature, this part of the poetry, the songs, and music, we all enjoyed the same thing. We were all speaking that language which had made us one group."[82] This interviewee, an Indian-born Pakistani, recognized a shared linguistic history and, by doing so, constructed a shared identity. This also occurred in India, where Indians of all religious backgrounds regularly attended *mushaira* and *ghazal* recitals. It is possible that for precisely those reasons suggested by Hindu nationalist reformers of the late eighteenth century—that Urdu was "the handmaid of the old decadent *nawwabi* culture"—and by attending Urdu *ghazal* recitals, Urdu and Hindi speakers could engage with a high-status literary art form.[83]

But the act of attending *mushaira* and *ghazal* recitals took on new significance and meaning in the diaspora. Beyond art appreciation, it was an act of ethnic identity formation. Language served as the linchpin around which other aspects of ethnic identity merged. The Hindi films aired at the University of Houston, for example, served a similar function as the Urdu Literature Group, with one notable distinction: the Hindi films were not an appeal to high culture but to popular culture and, as such, carried different cultural capital. Regardless, language was critically employed in both forms of entertainment in the construction of a South Asian—not Indian or Pakistani—identity. It is important to note, however, that neither the films nor the literature group could have appealed to *all* South Asians, limiting the domain of panethnic identity, since many South Asian immigrants spoke neither Urdu nor Hindi. Both Urdu and Hindi were designated as national languages in newly created nations where numerous languages were spoken.

Thus, the formation of South Asian identity in the United States involved English as much as any indigenous languages. All but one or two of the interviewees with whom I spoke were fluent in English. Yasmin Iqbal, who had attended Urdu-medium schools in Pakistan, explained that she could "read and write [English] very well" but did not speak as fluently "because unless you speak it, you don't pick up speed."[84] She "picked up speed" fairly quickly, being already familiar with the structure and lexicon of English. No doubt, the ability to comprehend language in an otherwise foreign space created the immediate possibility of belonging, at least in some degree. It could simultaneously create distance. Nadia Hasan, who was fluent in English because of her training in English-medium schools in Pakistan, found that she too easily slipped into speaking English when conversing with other Pakistanis. "People do get offended," she said, "because they feel like you are trying to put them down" or "show off."[85] Even though listeners understood English, indigenous language marked their ethnic identity by signaling group membership.

Likewise, in seeking to convey their cultural heritage, some immigrant parents insisted on teaching their children their native language. Tahira Lakhani and her husband, both holding advanced degrees from American universities and educated in British convent schools in Gujarat, decided that, with their two children, "we are not replying back to them in English." [86] They taught them to speak and read Urdu with fluency and to speak Gujarati at an elementary level, although with advanced comprehension. Yasmin Iqbal's daughter (part of the second generation) had enough Urdu language fluency that, as a teenager in the 1980s, she voiced an interest in attending the *ghazal* recital of a renowned visiting Urdu singer, Munni Begum.[87]

Others found ethnic significance in a shared past, underscoring the formation of interethnic identity. Pakistani immigrant Yasmin Iqbal was born in 1942 and grew up in Nowgong, a small village near Allahabad in Uttar Pradesh, India. She recalled her childhood as "very peaceful." In Nowgong, "there were a couple of Muslim homes, but not very many." Most of the villagers were Hindu. "Muslims were not in majority. Mostly our own family, they had a couple of houses. Distant family members were close by. My uncle, my mother's brother, was there. My grandmother was there. And then, a few houses that I remember that Muslims were there. Mostly were Hindus." Iqbal's grandmother passed down family lore about interreligious solidarity between Hindu and Muslim villagers in Nowgong during the Sepoy Uprising in 1857.[88] After Partition, Iqbal returned to Nowgong with her mother to visit family members who had remained in India. When she turned twenty-two, she married and, after three years, moved to Houston with her husband, Jamal, and their young daughter. As a family, they befriended other Indian families and attended a few Indian events, such as the movie screenings. But their attendance at events excluded the celebration of Indian Independence Day or observance of major Hindu occasions, such as Diwali.[89]

After migrating from their respective homelands, Indians and Pakistanis in Houston constructed new meanings of religion in their lives. Although they may have interacted in other spheres, religion created an exclusive space in which to express one specific aspect of Indian and Pakistani identities. While many of these early immigrants continued to build relationships across national lines, as more Indians and Pakistanis moved to Houston, especially after 1980, many increasingly preferred socializing with coreligionist South Asians— Hindu with Hindu, Christian with Christian, Jain with Jain, Parsi with Parsi, Sikh with Sikh, and Muslim with Muslim.[90]

Building Immigrant Religions

Since their earliest arrival, South Asian immigrants observed religious traditions at home and congregationally. Religious affiliations help immigrants cope with the process of acculturation by maintaining a spiritual connection with their native belief systems.[91] Nevertheless, religious orthopraxy and even orthodoxy develop within specific, local social contexts, creating unique interpretations, expressions, and definitions. In turn, these sets of belief are mediated temporally and geographically, so that the "Islams" of Karachi or "Hinduisms" of Bombay are qualitatively distinct from the Islams and Hinduisms of Houston in 1970 or 2010. For many South Asian immigrants, the significance of religion in daily life increased over time, as others have noted: "Immigrants are religious—by all counts more religious than they were before they left home."[92] Before emigration, many Indian and Pakistani interviewees did not regularly attend a place of worship or consider themselves especially religious. It is through migration into differently religious-majority countries that immigrants were forced to explain and define the terms of their beliefs anew. Long-term settlement often pushed religion to the forefront of immigrant consciousness, as it became a vehicle to transmit their cultural heritage to their children.[93] For most, religion *eventually* became important to them as a strategy to build and preserve for themselves and their children an individual and community identity. The foundations for larger South Asian religious institutions were built in the 1970s, although this section focuses on Hindu and Muslim institution building.

While religion mattered to some immigrants, it is important not to overdetermine the significance of religion as a bridge or barrier in the establishment of friendships among South Asians, especially in the early decades of settlement in the United States. Varuni Gil, a Pakistani Hindu immigrant, stated that she was "was born there [Pakistan] and the majority of my friends [here] are Muslim. I cannot say anything bad about Muslims because they have supported us. In Pakistan and here. My best friends in Pakistan were all Muslims."[94] Gil considered herself firmly embedded in Houston's small Pakistani and almost exclusively-Muslim community of the 1970s, recalling that "when anybody came from Pakistan, we would have a party because very few people were here. So if anybody came from Pakistan, [we said,] 'Oh, we have to go meet them.' Anybody. Because we were the little group here." Gil and her husband have maintained active friendships with Indians and Pakistanis but have had no institutional affiliations with either Indian or Pakistani organizations. Gil explained that she was just not "into" them. She emphasized that religion did not play a prominent role in her life, since for her, religion was "within you. It doesn't make a difference if you are a Hindu or Muslim or Christian. It makes no difference."[95]

If anything, based on frequency and depth of social interaction, the ethnic bonds between Indians and Pakistanis of any religion in 1970s Houston seemed as strong as, if not stronger than, the bonds of sociality formed between Muslim Pakistanis with Muslims of other nationalities. Asked about Muslims in the Houston area with whom she was acquainted, Pakistani immigrant Yasmin Iqbal responded, "We knew some people but we were not very close, you know. Oh, we met them in the mosque. So they were from Syria, they were from Iran, they were from Turkey, Jordan, and mostly Middle Eastern countries." "Of course," she added, "they were also from India and Pakistan."[96] Frequently, Desis befriended Desis, no matter the religious affiliation, underscoring for them the importance of shared ethnicity at least as much as shared religion.

On and off campus, Houston-area Muslims established various services to facilitate congregational worship. At the University of Houston, Muslim students arranged for their obligatory Friday congregational mass, albeit in an unofficial capacity. Also outside the aegis of group sponsorship, they coordinated the first congregational Eid prayers in Houston at UH in the mid-1960s, though only a handful of people attended. Held twice yearly according to the lunar calendar, Eid celebrations commemorate the end of Ramadan fasting and the annual Hajj pilgrimage to Mecca. In 1974, students founded a branch of the national Muslim Students Association (MSA) on campus.[97] The *International News*, a newsletter published by the International Student Services office, made the announcement, stating that "internationals from various parts of the world can become part of" the organization.[98]

In addition to campus congregational services, Houston's Muslims of various ethnic, racial, national backgrounds established an informal faith study circle in 1968, spearheaded by Ebrahim Yazdi, a local physician and medical researcher at Baylor College of Medicine in the Texas Medical Center. Arabs, Iranians, Pakistanis, and Indians, as well as other Sunni and Shi'a Muslims, met weekly at Yazdi's home. Yazdi was also a critic of the U.S.-supported military coup in Iran that brought Mohammed Reza Pahlavi to power in 1953. Yazdi came to the United States in 1961, eventually settling in Houston to complete his postdoctoral studies at Baylor. Unable to return to Iran because of his opposition to the shah's regime, he remained in Houston until 1977, when he joined his friend and fellow dissident Ruhollah Khomeini in France. In exile, they helped organize the Iranian Revolution in 1979 (though he was later imprisoned in Iran for his staunch government criticism and call for moderation). While in Houston, Yazdi used his knowledge of the Qur'an (he would go on to write two exegeses on select Qur'anic verses) to lead the weekly study circle. When attendance outgrew the available space in Yazdi's living room, the group moved their study circle to the new Rothko Chapel, opened in 1971.[99] Former attendees describe the group as completely apolitical, possibly because they eschewed any interest in the political and religious affairs of Iran.[100]

This small multiethnic group of immigrants from throughout the Muslim world and local converts to Islam were unconcerned with the political affairs of Iran or in dogmatic divisions between Shi'ism and Sunni Islam. Rather, in order to create community among the very diverse attendees, they promoted an inclusive vision of Islam, one that circumvented orthodoxy and the particulars of doctrinal difference. As the first president of the newly established Islamic Society of Greater Houston (ISGH), Yazdi told an interviewer for the *Houston Chronicle* in 1972, "We are avoiding the politics as much as we can," although he may have been referring as much to the politics of the Middle East as to the potential for political bifurcation within the group. The Islamic Society attempted to purchase property starting in 1971, but after a few failed attempts, Muslim Houstonians privately bought a house in the 1900 block of Richmond Street at Woodhead in the Montrose area to serve as the city's first mosque.[101] The renovated house cost the community $25,000, which they pooled together among themselves.

The mosque was opened to the public in July 1972. By this time, Yazdi estimated that the Houston area was home to some three thousand Muslims, who had attended various worship services, although the number may have been somewhat inflated.[102] According to local newspapers, this was the first immigrant mosque in the American South, though it is important to note that this was neither the first sizable presence of Islam in the South nor the first congregational space of worship. Islam had arrived with enslaved peoples from West Africa hundreds of years earlier. Often forced to hide or accommodate their religious practices, they worshipped congregationally in "created spaces" although not in formally "built spaces" such as mosques.[103] By 1960, Houston had the largest population of Muslims in the South, with adherents of the Nation of Islam (NOI)—an African American variant of Islam—and a growing immigrant community.[104] The NOI had established its own temples of worship, in the Chicago area in the 1930s. In the 1950s, the NOI founded Temple #45 (later renamed Masjid of Al-Islam) in Houston.[105] With the opening of the first immigrant mosque in 1972, the leaders of the Islamic Society, with Yazdi at the helm, envisioned a broad mission that not only served its members but also provided cultural assistance to new immigrants, foreign students, and Muslim patients seeking treatment at the Texas Medical Center. The Islamic Society further laid the groundwork for a prison chaplaincy program and interfaith work with local churches and synagogues.[106] For about a decade, it remained the only Muslim immigrant mosque in Houston.

Indian Hindus had gathered at area residences to conduct small-group prayer services until the establishment of first religious organizations and construction of the earliest temples. In 1970, Houston's Hindu community founded the Hindu Worship Society (HWS), the city's first Hindu organization. Like the Islamic Society at the time, HWS held worship services (pujas) at the Rothko Chapel, although unlike Islam (and Christian doctrine), Hinduism does not dictate that worshippers attend weekly congregational services, instead encouraging worship at home altars.[107] Still, Hindu temples were not unfamiliar to the United States—the first temple having been founded in 1906 in San Francisco by the Vedanta Society.[108] Over the decade, HWS registered several hundred members. As more Hindus moved to Houston, they formed private groups, such as the India Family Circle, that would arrange spiritual rites such as house blessing and wedding ceremonies. Charging a fee for such services, the group eventually collected about twenty thousand dollars, used to purchase an old house on West Little York Road, in northwest Houston, which served as the city's first official, if not purpose-built, temple. Without such a facility, over the years, they had gathered in unlikely places to worship: the university, rented commercial spaces, and a defunct bank.[109] The society also drew up plans to build a temple in northwest Houston in late 1982, replacing the old house on West Little York. By this time, Houston Hindus had established several religious bodies.

Less than a decade later, a group of Indian immigrants from the southern region of India separated from HWS, which performed rituals in the North Indian tradition.[110] Frustrated with their perceived marginalization, South Indians established a separate organization, the Sri Meenakshi Temple Society, in 1977. After purchasing land in Pearland, far south of Houston, the group inaugurated a small shrine on the future site of their temple in August 1979.[111] They raised private funds through the early 1980s, and with a loan from the State Bank of India, they inaugurated the first purpose-built temple in Houston to a crowd of 2,000 people in 1982.[112] The temple founders hoped to serve a self-reported estimate of 16,000 Hindus—or 5,000 families—in the metropolitan area.[113] Through the temple, they sought "a way of making sure that [the children] remember the traditions and ways of the Hindu religion."[114] The temple's membership remains South Indian—mainly Tamilian, Telugu, and Malayali, in that order—but other Indians also attend. As in India, the liturgical language is Sanskrit. Meenakshi Temple was also the largest Hindu temple complex in the American South, with a traditional South Indian architectural style, intricately hand-carved from granite and marble by over a hundred artisans flown in from India.[115] The temple complex faces east, as stipulated in Vedic scriptures, which explains why its founders selected Pearland as its location rather than any centrally located property in Houston. They originally purchased five acres and eventually expanded the property to over twenty acres, housing a main temple, smaller temples, priests' quarters, a youth center, and a visitor's center.[116] Of the vision for the temple complex, one of its priests stated, "The purpose of the temple is to perform . . . rituals and worship the manifestations of the gods" and to transmit knowledge of Hinduism to the second generation.[117] The temple's leaders continued to raise funds in the 1980s through private donations, and events such as India bazaars and music concerts, such as that of Ravi Shankar in June 1983.[118] The temple leadership referred all decisions related to the original establishment of the temple as well as ritualistic practice to priests in South India, and all of the temple's priests were and continue to be hired from India, reinforcing transnational ties between India and the United States.

Whether Hindu or Muslim, Houston's South Asian worshippers felt a degree of animosity directed toward them from non-South Asians. Part of the calculus for locating the Sri Meenakshi Temple in Pearland, according one of the temple priests, was minimizing the chance for conflict between Hindu worshippers and the local population. The location and size of the temple property provided a buffer between Hindu worshippers and neighbors, diminishing the likelihood of confrontation.[119] Residents in the sparsely populated farming area expressed some opposition in the form of letters to a local newspaper, voicing concern that the temple was of the Hari Krishna persuasion and that the temple was receiving too much attention from Pearland officials, namely the mayor, Tom Reid. After the Meenakshi Temple was built, Reid observed, "It does sort of come up at you out of nowhere, doesn't it?" He continued, "But isn't it a beauty? We're proud to have it in our town."[120] Public opinion seemed to range from an appreciation of the temple's architecture and fascination with the novelty of a Hindu temple in Texas farm country, to a darker call to redirect the spotlight onto a more desirable mainstream representation of Pearland. Early on, the temple community faced one openly hostile incident, in which a local white resident entered the temple complex, yelling at worshippers that they "would all go to hell."[121]

Muslims in Houston faced their own challenges in establishing a physical building for worship. After outgrowing the Montrose mosque, the Islamic Society attempted to purchase property in Houston. At least twice, their offers were rejected without explanation, and the properties were suddenly "withdrawn from the market."[122] Community leaders came to understand that private owners would not sell to an Islamic organization. Consequently, they purchased their new mosque headquarters on Eastside Street in 1979 in the name of individual community members and later transferred ownership to the Islamic Society. At least some of the leadership of the Islamic Society believed that this difficulty was caused by anti-Muslim sentiment, and there may have been valid grounds for this feeling. In 1970, Yazdi responded to an article in the *Houston Chronicle* that cast Islam as "deeply conservative, [and] not well suited in coping with technological innovations in the modern world."[123] Yazdi insisted that this was a baseless assertion and one that was offensive to the "hundreds of Muslims residing in the Greater Houston area," many of whom worked in science and technology. The work of challenging stereotypically disparaging misrepresentations in the media began well before the immigrant Muslim community had grown deep roots in Houston. Also, because community members chose to remain in the heart of Houston, where land was at a premium, conflicts over space (such as parking on days of worship) had ensued, especially before the move to Eastside Street.

In Houston, both mosques and temples brought together a greater variety of people than in their home countries. At the two main Hindu mandirs in Houston, worshippers speaking an array of Indian dialects and language groups gathered for prayer. Worshippers from throughout the Muslim world (predominantly South Asia and the Middle East) assembled alongside African

Americans for prayer at the ISGH mosque, even as African American Muslims continued to support the Masjid Al-Islam. In addition, during these early years, both mosques and temples combined a range of spiritual traditions. During these early years, the mosque equally served both Sunnis and Shi'as from several countries (including India, Pakistan, Iran, Egypt, and Jordan), while the temple reflected North or South India's regional diversity of Hinduism.[124] The dissimilarity between various groups, however, generated tensions, and eventually, despite a degree of unity through major events and commemorations, both Hindus and Muslims established separate places of worship that more closely reflected adherents' particular religious beliefs and practices.

Diversifying Desis

Throughout the 1970s, as greater numbers of Indians and Pakistanis moved to Houston, the communities diversified linguistically and ethnically. Numerous South Asian subgroups including Gujaratis, Keralites, Punjabis, Sindhis, and Muhajirs (Indians who moved to Pakistan after Partition; literally, one who migrates), as well as Indian-descended individuals from throughout the global South Asian diaspora, were drawn to the city. Christians, Jains, and Sikhs joined a majority of Hindus and Muslims to form an Indo-Pak community, writ large. In 1970, the population of Indians in Houston was estimated at around 1,500 (including 275 students at area universities), while the total Pakistani population numbered approximately 200.[125] Over this decade alone, these numbers would soar.

In 1973, Indian immigrants formed the India Culture Center and officially registered it with the state of Texas. In addition to hosting events at UH, the group also used the facilities of the Jewish Community Center in the Meyerland area of Houston while fundraising to buy their own land. The ICC raised funds within the Indian community and broader Houston base through a series of public service slides on local television.[126] Echoing the internationalist initiatives of the early Cold War, but intending to increase donations, the ICC was described in a local newspaper as "an organization to promote Indo-American friendship and understanding."[127] The center brought together UH alumni and other resident Indians—mostly doctors and engineers— to provide "cultural, education, social, physical, and spiritual welfare to [its] members."[128] To this end, it published a newsletter, screened Indian films, supported radio music programming, and sponsored Hindi and Gujarati weekend language classes for children. By the early 1980s, the India Culture Center had become a consortium of Indian organizations, representing a range of language, regional, and religious groups.[129]

At around the same time, Pakistanis established the Pakistan Association of Greater Houston.[130] Over the next decade, ICC and PAGH would assume the broad citywide ethnic-event planning that ISA and PSA had spearheaded, even as they cosponsored events with the campus student groups and used UH's large-capacity auditoriums for their events. In addition, the increasingly bifurcated communities founded smaller organizations that launched their own initiatives, independent of ISA, PSA, and the university.

By the mid-1980s, several such Indian organizations were registered under the ICC banner. As an example, among the largest groups of Indians in Houston was the Gujarati Samaj. Gujaratis comprised the largest Indian subgroup in other cities as well, including Chicago.[131] Gujaratis were among the earliest presidents of ICC, and according to a local newspaper source, some 40 percent of Houston's ten thousand Indians in 1979 were Gujarati, although this statistic remains uncorroborated.[132] Like the broader Indian community, many Gujaratis held advanced degrees, but as in Gujarat, they also owned and operated small businesses, such as accounting firms, motels, and apartment complexes. Others worked independently as realtors or as rental property owners. Still, like those who migrated to Houston the 1960s, these Indians entered the United States to pursue higher education.

Gopal Rana, from Gujarat, completed his master's degree in chemical engineering at Texas A&M in 1967. He moved to Houston to work as a project manager at Panhandle Eastern Pipe Line Co. soon thereafter and became active in Gujarati community-building efforts, as well as in ICC.[133] Rana stated that while he held a salaried position, "I'm not in business, but my eyes are open and my ears perk up each time somebody talks about opening a business."[134] Ethnic entrepreneurship flourished among Indians in the 1970s, catering to an ever-diversifying Indo-Pak clientele. From restaurants to grocery stores, travel agencies, and sari shops, by 1980, several businesses—some owned by Gujaratis—opened up in Southwest Houston. Food, especially, became a key site around the construction of ethnicity.

Procuring, Producing, and Consuming Ethnic Foods

After migrating to Houston, immigrant women and men struggled to re-create the foods with which they were most familiar. Lacking the conventional range of ingredients, they sought other means of obtaining those ingredients, creatively substituted other ingredients, or cooked dishes that were similar but did not quite replicate the foods they aimed to prepare. Immigrants employed various strategies in order to procure Indian and Pakistani foodstuffs. Many newly married Indian and Pakistani women transported their own spices and cooking apparatus when they migrated to the United States.[135] For years, immigrants wrote letters to their home countries requesting that their families send spices with anyone traveling to the United States.[136] Still others ordered ingredients from established Indian grocery stores in Chicago and New York.[137] In the late 1960s, Indian immigrants approached Jalal Antone, the Syrian American owner of Antone's, a Middle Eastern import grocery and po'boy sandwich shop that opened in 1962, and requested that he order a few basic ingredients for them. He obliged, and soon, Indians and Pakistanis purchased lentils, gram flour, and *achar* (a salted, pickled condiment), albeit at a high price.[138] Antone might have ordered these dried or jarred food products from Canada, likely from stores in Toronto's more established ethnic enclave, where Indians had first arrived during the late nineteenth century.[139] Also, during the late 1960s, one Indian family began selling Indian spices by using their garage as a storefront. In 1971, Meena Datt opened Jay Store, the first Indian grocery store in Houston. Located in Rice Village, it catered to the growing Indian and Pakistani population that had begun settling in what were then Houston's Sharpstown and Westbury "suburbs" but now are neighborhoods in near-southwest Houston.[140] Jay Store also supplied ingredients to the only Indian restaurant in Houston, Maharajah.

In 1972, four Indian immigrants opened Maharajah.[141] They chose to locate the restaurant in Rice Village on Times Boulevard—in the exclusively white, upper-middle-class neighborhood surrounding Rice University. It remained open for four years to a mostly white American clientele. The restaurant also hosted any visiting Indian dignitaries or artists, such as Indian classical dancer turned vegetarianism spokesperson Rukmini Devi and Indian ambassadors traveling to Houston. Cofounder Nagaraj Shekhar recalled that "Indians didn't much care for our cooking but non-Indians loved it."[142] During its first two years of operation, the engineers-turned-restaurateurs enjoyed brisk business and long waiting lines but found the challenges of managing a restaurant unsustainable in the long run.[143]

To an extent, educated Indians projected a sense of racial and economic belonging in the space they created. This is indicated in Shekhar's comment regarding the restaurant's closing: "When it shut down, we had a big, black tie morning session and all that . . . lots of Americans. All the Montrose gang was there."[144] The use of the markers "American" and "the Montrose gang" signified whiteness to Shekhar. The "black tie" session reflected a class posturing, though perhaps less so than the actual celebration of the restaurant closing. Secure in their ability to acquire salaried employment, these middle-class, educated immigrants could engage in marking the "failure" of their entrepreneurial enterprise with some measure of gaiety. While in Shekhar's words, they "often gather and have a good laugh about it" and "can now talk about it in all fun and glory," it is not only in memorializing the event that they can happily reminisce.[145] At the time, they could literally afford to celebrate the loss.

By the late 1970s, there were at least five Indian grocery stores selling spices, as well as canned and packaged imported foods from India.[146] The stores served an Indian population of approximately six thousand in the metropolitan Houston area, according to an ICC leader (self-reported estimates ranged widely).[147] In addition, possibly another two thousand Indians from surrounding areas sought out ethnic foodstuffs from Houston retailers—a trend that would continue into the present, as Houston became an ethnic retail hub for the entire southern United States. Local Pakistani immigrants regularly patronized Indian shops, a reality reflected in signage advertising "Indo-Pak groceries." Thus, the ethnic grocery store emerged as another site through which to construct an interethnic South Asian identity.

The Limits of Interethnicity

Houston's Indians and Pakistanis formed a single community in many ways, through film, music, language, and food, yet they also remained nationally separate and distinct. Uma Krishnan offered that the interactions among South Asian groups were "seamless" but also not "extensive."[148] Interviews suggest that since Pakistanis were relatively few in number, they more keenly embraced socialization with Indians, while the much larger, more institutionally developed Indian community had less imperative to attend Pakistani-sponsored events. Pakistani immigrants Yasmin and Jamal Iqbal frequently socialized with Indian families in their neighborhood and occasionally attended larger Indian community events. Yasmin explained that "there was a larger community in Houston—Indian community—than compared to the Pakistani community. This, I found out sometimes when we went to the University of Houston and we saw the students over there, if they had some function over there. So definitely that was the largest community at that time."[149] Almost every Indian and Pakistani interviewee with whom I interacted recalled attending the ISA-sponsored movie screenings. These films served as a bridge between the two national groupings in that they revealed the porousness of national boundaries. Immigrants interpreted the damaged relations between Pakistan and India by separating the *politics* of nationalism from the *people* of these nations. But Indian and Pakistani immigrants also worked hard to maintain group boundaries, especially evident in the celebration of national independence days and some religious observances.

Despite acknowledging a shared history, immigrants located several disjunctures, especially at the organizational level. Sara Waheed spoke of "students at the University of Houston [who] used to arrange some programs and gatherings and they had India and Pakistan—two different nations—but their activities are kind of similar."[150] She suggested that their activities were "similar" but not the same and that the respective student groups, the Indian Students Association and the Pakistan Students Association, represented, perpetuated, and reified those dissimilarities. Nagaraj Shekhar struggled to clearly articulate what the relationship between Indian and Pakistani immigrants had meant to him. He said, "It is very, very nice actually. There is really not a whole lot of . . . of . . . I mean, there are definitely differences but when it comes to shows and this and that and everybody is . . . I don't know, I think it is some cultural thing or something like that."[151] Shekhar began by wishing to highlight the solidarity felt by all South Asians, and although he wanted to say that there was not much difference, he could not. He stopped himself and noted that, actually, he perceived definite "differences." He then attempted to neutralize the degree of difference by highlighting the solidarity, underscoring the attendance of ethnic shows. Finally, he admitted that he really did not know how to make sense of the differences or relationships between groups, and attributed it to "some cultural thing."[152]

Conclusion

Pakistani and Indian immigrants would build on prior conceptions of national identity to construct new South Asian interethnic identities that, in part, rested on old pre-Partition identities. On the threshold of becoming fully invested residents of the United States, they mapped out their lives in complex ways. By reconstructing community and cultural practices, immigrants were embedded in South Asian national spaces but also detached from them. For Nadia Hasan, for example, Karachi as home was less a physical space and more about the people who inhabited it. India and Pakistan, for all their particularities, are evoked in diaspora through long-established relationships and reconstructed cultural practices. If those relationships have been transferred to the United States, so too have cultural signifiers such as food, dress, and music, rendering the homeland a mobile entity.

Although these immigrants remained deeply connected to their homelands, the homeland as a physical space simultaneously becomes obsolete and the cultural practices associated with it deterritorialized. The very processes of community formation and the formation of cultural identity are rooted uniquely to the host country, even as they bear the outer markings of foreign-ness. As Avtar

Brah notes, "home" is both a "floating and rooted signifier."[153] The examination of South Asians' ethnic lifeworlds illustrates the significance of and reasons behind why certain cultural practices were reconstructed in diaspora. It shows how middle-class South Asian immigrants variously determined the terms of their own ethnic culture and identity.

. . . .

CHAPTER FOUR

INHABITING THE
INTERNATIONALIZING CITY,
1970S

With their young children in tow, Yasmin and Jamal Iqbal moved from Houston to College Station in 1970. Enrolled at Texas A&M University, Jamal would complete his master's degree in industrial engineering. They lived in university housing about which Yasmin recalls, "The rents were really low. It was very helpful, $48 utilities paid. No air-conditioning, of course. No carpeting. It was small. It was the cheapest one—where we were living. Two bedrooms, furnished, but you can imagine: a two-seater sofa (small one) and one chair (rocking chair, wood) and a small dining table with four chairs, and we were blessed with a bed. That is what we had." Eventually, they saved enough money to purchase a second-hand vehicle. "We had an old car which used to stop everywhere. It used to heat up. I don't know how many times we had to leave the car on the road!"[1]

Jamal completed his master's degree in 1972 and, after brief stays in Karachi and Canada, secured full-time employment in 1975 in the Houston company where he had previously worked. The family first lived in an apartment in one of Houston's centrally located financial hubs, Greenway Plaza, before moving to Spring Branch in suburban northwest Houston. Jamal established his own air conditioning systems consulting firm in 1980. Once their three children reached school age, Yasmin often worked as a record keeper at Jamal's company. After twenty years of running the company, Jamal entered into semiretirement. His educational foundation had provided a baseline of capital on which to establish and maintain his family's class standing after migration, while Houston's strong economy in the 1970s supported this rapid class ascendance.

Moving from relatively unprosperous nations, many Indian and Pakistani immigrants and students on arrival in the United States lacked economic capital comparable to the existing white American middle class. South Asian immigrants remain keen quick to point this out. Still, they possessed the tools necessary to obtain financial success fairly quickly, as they have acknowledged in interviews. Unlike other immigrants of lower socioeconomic standing and educational attainment, Indian and Pakistani immigrants' advanced degrees in technical fields, in combination with Houston's strong job market, launched them squarely into the American middle class.

One of the more illuminating ways of tracing this middle-class trajectory is through tracking the neighborhoods in which immigrants resided over time, within the comparative context of Houston's social and economic hierarchies. As Indian and Pakistani students graduated from Houston's universities, found employment, and reconstructed ethnic identity, they joined other South Asian residents in settling throughout the city in the late 1960s and 1970s. Their ethnic community building occurred within a specific local context—that of an internationalizing, rapidly developing urban area. During the 1970s, Houston underwent major changes in the size and origins of its population size and economy, as well as the building of new construction to support new residents and businesses. The ways in which South Asian immigrants interacted with, understood, and settled into this changing city tells us as much about the experiences of Asian immigrants as it does about Houston itself.

As the formal architecture of Jim Crow was dismantled in these very decades, South Asian immigrants' engagement with the city in the late 1960s and 1970s reveals the persistence of class segmentation and racial segregation. Immigrants and other Houstonians infused class and racial meanings into their residential movement through the city, reinforcing and in many ways expanding the city's unequal spatial configuration. Class and race positions largely dictated how residents moved through the city—their pathways, the businesses they supported, the places they frequented, and the neighborhoods in which they lived. All the immigrants I interviewed could afford to purchase their first homes fairly quickly in majority white neighborhoods, indicating that even the earliest migration experiences were mediated through positions of relative privilege. Indian and Pakistani immigrants were uniquely positioned to find success as a result of a confluence of historical circumstances, modern economies, and their own strategizing. This chapter addresses South Asian immigrants' class- and race-embedded calculations regarding neighborhood selection, within the context of an internationalizing, growing city.

South Asian immigrant women and men entering the United States in the 1960s and 1970s were poised for material success. Before migration, these professionals and advanced-degree-seeking students were already embedded in global systems of class ascendancy and investment in education. These investments, then, aided immigrants in their quests for upward mobility after migration. Although one of the immigrants I interviewed rose from a very modest background, most hailed from middle-class families, and a few emerged from wealthy origins. Within the middle class, they spanned a full range of backgrounds, from lower to upper middle class, which meant that some necessarily had to live in more circumscribed situations for longer than others, but this simply meant that the more privileged were their origins, the faster and greater was their success in the United States.

While they may have embodied the hard-work ethic of the model minority myth, Indian and Pakistani immigrants possessed a combination of economic, social, and cultural capital that facilitated their success. Before emigrating, they were familiar with immigration networks and were at least rudimentarily acquainted with Western culture. As members of an educationally committed middle class in their sending countries, they arrived with the cultural capital to rise up. Their technical skills, language ability, and access to American higher education aided the process after migration. Their own narratives highlight lean times in their early years as student immigrants, pinpointing these years as the starting point in their journey as immigrants. However, it is far more significant that before migrating they were active participants in modernizing economies and modern sectors of their societies and that after migrating they quickly secured upward economic mobility.

This is not to suggest a complete elision between conceptions or the performativity of middle-classness in South Asia and the United States. Social and economic structures in specific locales, whether urban spaces in southern Asia or the southern United States, produced distinct middle-class subjectivities.[2] But despite nuances both significant and subordinate, South Asian immigrants mobilized around a common fundamental fluency in the economic behaviors of modern capitalist societies. Class consciousness, albeit locally produced, traversed national boundaries, shaping the behaviors of middle-class subjects in the United States, regardless of their point of origin.[3] Members of the middle class constantly strategized to maintain and/or enhance their access to resources—both material and symbolic.[4]

Taking a Global Turn: Houston's Internationalization

A booster article in 1975—a five-page spread titled "Dizzying, Dazzling Houston" in *Reader's Digest*—described Houston as "big, bustling, booming."[5] Its author, having caught the booster bug, projected that in fifty years, "Houston will be the biggest city on earth."[6] The article gauged the city's success largely on its wealthiest residents, biggest buildings, newest construction projects, largest philanthropic endeavors, and a generally healthy economy. By 1965, Houston surpassed other Sunbelt cities in terms of "population, manufacturing payroll, value added, and as an industrial and consumer market."[7] Major oil companies moved their regional headquarters to Houston in the 1970s.

Throughout the decade, Houston's economy expanded at a rate over twice as fast as the national economy, far outstripping any other city in the state or region.[8] Employment rates increased by 18 percent, while per capita income rose faster than that of any other American city.[9] By mid-decade, Houston led the United States in new manufacturing, joining the ranks of the traditional industrial centers of Detroit and Chicago.[10] One full-page advertisement by a steel company in the *Houston Chronicle* proclaimed that Houston "is the amazing city that appeared out of nowhere" and may eventually become "the biggest, richest city in the U.S.A., if not the world."[11] Houston's rise "rocks anyone's imagination," it continued. Houstonians, old and new, perceived Houston as exceptional; for companies and corporations, the city's rise was perhaps one of the purest urban embodiments of the free market.[12] "Capitalism is not a dirty word around Houston," the steel company advertisement boasted.[13]

Although other major American cities grew during the 1970s, none surpassed Houston in population growth (table 4).[14] During the five decades following World War II, the city's growth rate averaged approximately 43 percent.[15] Between 1950 and 1960, when the overall U.S. population increased by 18.5 percent, Houston's population increase was 54 percent.[16] During the 1960s and 1970s, the population rose by well over 30 percent in each decade.[17] The *Houston Chronicle* in 1970 proudly boasted that Houston was the "first city in the South ever to reach a million population" and was now poised to become the nation's sixth most populous city.[18] Over the 1970s, as almost all major metropolitan areas in the United States lost population (including New York, Chicago, Philadelphia, Cleveland, and Detroit), only Houston, Los Angeles, and Dallas gained in population.[19] Well over 350,000 newcomers arrived in Houston during the 1970s, while less than half of that moved to Los Angeles and only a fraction moved to Dallas.[20] Houston's growth outpaced any other city in the country, with no foreseeable cessation in its rise. However, the recession of the 1980s would strip the city of its gains, marking the 1970s as the culmination of a multidecade bull run.[21]

Houston arose as a city of newcomers, whether migrating from the East Coast, West Coast, Midwest, or abroad.[22] In 1970, the metropolitan area population was 1.74 million. This included a white population at 70 percent, a black population at 20 percent, 9 percent Hispanics, and only 0.7 percent of any other race.[23] By 1970, less than half the population resided in the same place as five years earlier, suggesting both movement within the city and the influx of new residents.[24] When *Reader's Digest* published the booster story on Houston in

TABLE 4. Population of the Houston area, 1850–2010.

Year	Houston SMSA	Harris County	City of Houston
2010	5,920,416	4,092,459	2,099,451
2000	4,693,161	3,400,578	1,953,631
1990	3,750,411	2,818,199	1,630,553
1980	3,135,806	2,409,544	1,595,138
1970	2,195,146	1,741,912	1,233,505
1960	1,594,894	1,243,158	938,219
1950	1,083,100	806,701	596,163
1940	752,937	528,961	384,514
1930	545,547	359,328	292,352
1920	348,661	186,667	138,276
1910	252,066	115,693	78,800
1900	202,438	63,786	44,633
1890	137,800	37,249	27,557
1880	112,053	27,985	16,513
1870	80,866	17,375	9,332
1860	55,317	9,070	4,845
1850	27,984	4,668	2,396

Source: U.S. Census; City of Houston Planning Department.

1975, its author estimated the city's racial minorities as "28 percent black and 12 percent Latin" but overlooked the thousands of immigrants from China, India, Pakistan, and other Asian countries who were also making their way to Houston.[25]

They migrated not only due to the availability of jobs but because of the very internationalization under way in the city. Internationalization, both economic and demographic, engendered more internationalization. Although at the state level New York and California already had far greater percentages of immigrants than Texas in 1960 and 1970, Texas made major gains in its foreign-born population as a result of the Bracero Program, which increased Texas's Mexican-born population, and passage of the Immigration and Nationality Act of 1965 (Hart-Celler Act).[26] In 1970 Houston was 9 percent foreign-born, with the largest proportion of this group born in Mexico (17,787).[27] Other high-sending regions included East and South Asia (over 5,000), South America, the United Kingdom, Germany, and Canada.[28] Immigrants from Latin America and Asia, especially, helped internationalize the city and, as they did so, helped to reconfigure the composition of neighborhoods new and old. Within a decade, by 1980, 18 percent of Houston's population were immigrants.

South Asians and International Houston

Professionalized South Asian immigrants flocked to Houston in the 1970s because of the city's thriving economic growth. The city's flourishing economy provided them with ample opportunity for employment in the primary labor market, especially in oil services companies, engineering and construction companies, and health care.[29] Because of population growth, developers, builders, and officials worked to expand the residential options and infrastructure.[30] The heady pace of new construction in residential and commercial buildings, roads, and highways provided abundant job growth in the engineering sector, and since so many Indians and Pakistanis had trained as engineers, their labor skills meshed neatly with Houston's labor needs.

Despite the recession that gripped the nation in the 1970s, Houston companies continued to hire, especially in engineering.[31] In 1973, just months before the national recession, Brown & Root—the same general construction contracting firm that had secured the contract to build NASA in Clear Lake—had been recognized as the nation's largest engineering contractor.[32] Houston's economic strength in the years marred by national recession allowed Brown & Root and other Houston-area firms to hire many thousands of engineers.[33] Companies like Brown & Root placed advertisements in the newspapers of major cities like Chicago and recruited from local college campuses and from across the country. A handful of the people I interviewed had migrated to Houston from Chicago after responding to job ads in local newspapers.

Despite these changes, some South Asian immigrants sensed a degree of hostility on the part of native Houstonians. Immigrants arriving in Houston during the 1970s vividly recall their initial impressions, as the event symbolized a major juncture in their life. Where some immigrants found that Houston was something of an oasis of hospitality, others felt an unwelcoming reception. Indian immigrant Ashok Dani lived in Houston for seven months starting in 1976, returning permanently in 1980. Having lived in New York for almost a decade, Dani found Houstonians to be "uncosmopolitan" and "rough."[34] Speaking about his experience as an architect at Bechtel, an international engineering and construction company, he explained that "in New York, they're very cosmopolitan, they accept [outsiders]. Their attitude is to accept. And our office in

New York transferred me to Houston. So, in '76 and '77, Houstonians, Texans, they're very rough. They cannot accept outsiders. So once you stay in New York eight years, to come to Houston in '77, I didn't like it. . . . No kind of manners or anything and they would talk to you and treat you like something different."[35] Dani's wife, Lata, offered that perhaps this rough treatment occurred only in the workplace, but Dani vehemently insisted that anti-immigrant sentiment existed "Everywhere! Everywhere!" Dani felt so discouraged by the treatment he received in Houston that he opted for a transfer to Louisville, Kentucky, where he found people to be "very friendly."

By the time he returned to Houston three years later in 1980, Dani discerned a "noticeable change" that he attributed to the influx of large international companies and, hence, greater numbers of foreigners in labor and management. When asked to interpret why he thought such differences existed, Dani reflected that "every place has special qualities" and that Texas, perhaps because of its size, was isolated from the rest of the country. At work, he said, Houstonians wore "cowboy attire" complete with bolo ties and "gumshoes," which indicated to him that Texans "were not ready to accept the modern world." In Texans' eyes through the mid-1970s, Dani surmised, "Texas was the only place . . . in the world" and its natives were in a "hard shell" and "never came out." They were "rigid." Unsure of how this reflected on or connected to the rest of the South, Dani simply concluded that "Texas is a big place in [the] South and we experienced this roughness."[36] Others, too, perceived that Houston was uniquely hostile toward outsiders.

Lata Dani reasoned that her opposing view must have resulted from her not working outside the home at the time. Ashok agreed, stating that "ladies, they are not exposed to outside. Gents, they face this and to live this every time, you know this is very difficult," at which point Lata conceded.[37] Although Lata quickly qualified her positive narratives of early life in Houston, her own experiences were as legitimate as those of her husband, Ashok. All the women I interviewed came to Houston as a result of marriage or a husband's job transfer, often enrolling in English-language classes and joining campus cultural organizations but not working outside the home initially. Their first impressions of Houston often differed vastly from their husbands' experiences in the workplace. South Asian women generally reported friendlier interactions with white American neighbors, often forming friendships with at least one female neighbor. They found the women at the churches where they attended English-language classes to be warm and helpful.

In explaining their dislike for Houston in the 1970s, Ashok and Lata measured the city by its degree of "cosmopolitanism." They had moved from Bombay to New York in 1968 and felt very much at home there, explaining, "We were

Bombay people. We liked New York."[38] Other interviewees also commented on how distinct Bombay was among Indian cities and, notably, how similar it was to other large, diverse cities in the world—as well as how Houston compared. Former Bombayites often employed the word "cosmopolitan" to describe the city of their childhood, meaning that Bombay, like New York, was a "modern" city—a city that thrived on the heterogeneity of its inhabitants. Immigrants from the major cities of India and Pakistan found remarkably shared "cosmopolitanisms" between highly urbanized, immigrant-saturated places in the United States. These were spaces that were fueled by diversity. Ashok explained, "New York life is for everybody" in that the poor, rich, and middle class each found their own way. From his perspective, jobs and accommodations of all types existed, and this, in combination with open movement into any part of the city, expressed support for all "style[s] of life." Ashok and Lata's impression of a global web of cosmopolitan cities that shared particular modern forms was only affirmed by their move to a place that they initially perceived as somewhat antithetical to modernity: Houston. These modern "global cities" shared similarly capitalistic orientations, laying the foundations for a resurgent globalization.[39] Only by the end of the 1970s did the couple find that Houston more fully became a city evoking the "modern" ethos of Bombay or New York. It was at this point that they believed Houston rotated its gaze outward by economically and socially welcoming outsiders.

Although Houston made real forays into the global market in the late 1960s and 1970s, when Shell Oil relocated its headquarters there and major oil companies including Exxon and Texaco established major operations bases in the city, it is likely that Houstonians' attitudes were somewhat slower in reflecting these economic shifts.[40] The movement of major oil companies to Houston after the 1960s was likely a watershed in altering Houstonians' attitudes toward foreigners, in large part because "Houstonians" were themselves increasingly non-native to Houston. For many Indian and Pakistani immigrants, "real" cities—ones that were fulfilling their potential—were imagined as thriving on change, bursting with diverse people, and running on commerce. Those cities that lacked any of these features or possessed them in small measure could not compare to "great" cities such as London, New York, and Bombay.

Bombay, as Indian immigrant Vinod Prakash observed, was "a terrific city . . . more of a melting pot than any other city that I've ever been to. People who are from different parts of the country" inhabit Bombay.[41] Moving from Bombay to College Station, Texas, in 1964, Saumitra Kelkar, another student-immigrant, felt insulted by stereotypes of Bombay.[42] He recalled that "even the college professors asked me dumb questions, like when I'd say I came from Bombay—and I'd say the population at that time was three or four million people—they would still ask me dumb questions or something." For example, they asked him, "'Do you have elephants on the street?'" Kelkar said, "I mean this is coming from a college professor, you know, with a Ph.D.—a guy who has been around the world, asking that type of question!"[43] For Kelkar, the large population signified modernity, not the type of imagined traditional society wherein elephants paraded through the streets. At the very least, information about the high population of Bombay should have alerted the professor, in Kelkar's eyes, to the reality of this modernity.

Kelkar further emphasized the level of education, indicating that the lesser educated could be expected to harbor ignorance even in the face of new knowledge, whereas, to him, a professor—who epitomized the height of modern achievement through knowledge of the world—displaying such ignorance made no sense. The cosmopolitan orientation of South Asia's bustling cities also contrasted with the seemingly provincial outlook of Texans and Houstonians in the 1960s and early 1970s. Tariq Rahman suggested that Chicago, where he first arrived in 1971, was more "cultured" than Houston—referring to the wide availability of Indian cultural events (such as ethnic entertainment shows and communitywide socials) as compared to Houston, and perhaps also assessing citywide attitudes.[44]

Newcomers' perceptions of Houston and Texas often coincided with a casting of the American South as uniquely archaic in its ideas. After Rohan Patil moved to Houston in 1970 to begin his master's degree in chemical engineering, his classmates from other parts of the United States "felt it was—there was more a gun culture in Houston and the classmates found that to be quite alarming. They felt like it was more common in this area for people to own guns and they were not that used to it" in the North.[45] Other immigrants were forewarned about Texas and Houston before ever setting foot in the state. Texas's reputation as a lawless land spread far and wide. Indians (and others) regarded Texas warily, especially since the assassination of President John F. Kennedy.

In November 1963, Saumitra Kelkar received word of his admission to a graduate program in engineering at Texas A&M University. An only child, he was born, raised, and educated in the Parla area of Bombay. Kelkar had first considered applying to universities in London, but at his father's suggestion, he had redirected his search toward the United States. He chose the university because a family friend was enrolled there. En route to saying good-bye to his grandmother, who lived in southern Maharashtra state at some distance from Bombay, he learned something of Texas:

We stopped where my father had gone to college in Kolhapur and there we were staying with one of our friends for two days. Then we visited his old

professor, and as soon as my father said, "Yeah, he's going to go to U.S.,"
[the professor asked,] "Where are you going?" We said, "Texas," and that's
the day Kennedy was assassinated. I mean, so we heard the news from
him because when you're away you don't listen to the radio and all that.
So that's how we heard and so everybody was scared. Everybody thought
Texas was—everybody's carrying a gun and shoots anyone that doesn't
listen, so to speak. . . . It was a cultural shock.[46]

In the global imagination of the late civil rights era, the United States, Texas,
and Houston occupied somewhat dissonant spaces. For one, the assassination
of President Kennedy substantiated perceptions of Texas as a violent place—a
place unlike the modern United States. The deep commitment to segregation
in Texas and the South seemed anomalous in an otherwise welcoming, tolerant
country. Still, whether immigrants' lived reality in Houston fit neatly in the
imagined liberal America or premodern violent South varied from person to
person. As perceptions were born of local experience, immigrants compared
Houston to their points of departure or to their points of entry to the United
States. Nagaraj Shekhar, a Bombayite who lived in Norman, Oklahoma, for
six months between 1970 and 1971, regarded Houston as "the closest civilized
metropolis" and gladly made the shift.[47] Having also lived in London in the
late 1960s, Shekhar had experienced residential discrimination and a racially
hostile native population there. He was relieved to find Houstonians comparatively welcoming.

Spatial Distribution of Houston

The contours of the city came to be defined within the broad social, economic,
and demographic shifts occurring during this decade, but equally by the everyday choices of Houston's residents. Neighborhood selection ranked among
the major decisions that shaped the lives of Houstonians and the city's urban
development. As Houston's robust, internationalizing economy drew newcomers, real estate developers saw opportunity in population growth, shaping the
course of the city's expansion and the residential patterns of new migrants and
immigrants (map 1). The city was a canvas on which Houstonians charted the
course of their lives, making long-term plans for their future. Some of Houston's neighborhoods were rapidly transitioning to reflect greater diversity while
entirely new neighborhoods allowed for the possibility of greater integration.
South Asian immigrants, having no ethnic enclaves in which they could cluster, learned and expressed the language of race as understood in the southern
United States through the act of neighborhood selection. This section examines

MAP 1. City of Houston, 1970 and 2018.

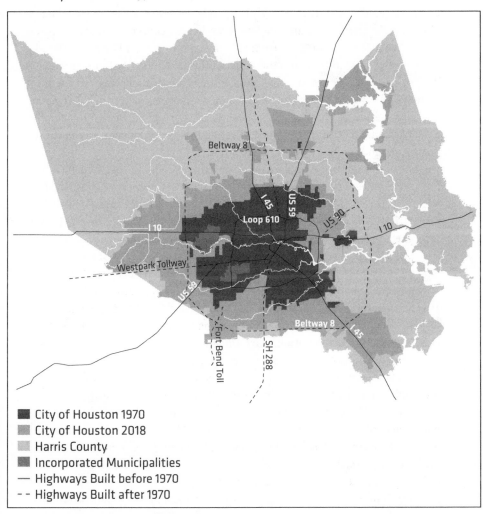

City of Houston 1970
City of Houston 2018
Harris County
Incorporated Municipalities
— Highways Built before 1970
- - Highways Built after 1970

Sources: City of Houston GIS; USGS.

the areas in which the wealthiest, poorest, and most underserved Houstonians lived, linking them to South Asian immigrants' settlement patterns. The racial and class mapping of Houston as it became an international city rooted in the legacy of Jim Crow lays bare the hierarchical structure in Houstonians' residential settlement patterns.

By 1970, the physical separation or residential segregation fostered by nearly a century of Jim Crow was only too apparent. As discussed previously, by 1950,

70 percent of Houston's African American population resided in Third, Fourth, and Fifth Wards in nearly exclusively black neighborhoods.[48] Two decades later, Houston's African American population was heavily concentrated in a narrow strip—"a black belt"—that ran from far northeast to central Houston around the University of Houston and then due southward to the city limits (see Appendix map 8). The second-most concentrated populations resided on the fringes of the city in far northwest Houston, with some smattering of African American residents interspersed between northwest and northeast Houston.[49] Last, African Americans continued to reside in large proportion in the rural areas surrounding the city of Houston, especially south of Missouri City. This was one of several such African American farming communities, which taken together formed a scattered ring around Harris County. What is especially striking is the virtual absence of this population in *any* other part of Houston. Few African Americans, for example, lived in Sharpstown or Southwest Houston—areas of recent growth. Similarly, Mexican Americans were concentrated in the barrios in the northwest and eastern portion of the city (see Appendix map 9). The segregated character of the city could not have been starker.[50]

Not coincidentally, the areas populated mainly by African Americans and Hispanics were also the ones with lower income levels and worse housing conditions. A report issued by the City Planning Department in 1973 indicated that houses of "poor condition" surrounded the downtown central business district, extending especially east of downtown. The northeast quadrant of the city had homes in overwhelmingly "fair condition," while homes throughout the southeast and parts of northwest Houston ranged from mostly "fair" to some in "good" condition. Houses in Southwest Houston, to where so many new Houstonians moved, were in "excellent condition," were newer than in other parts of city, and had working indoor plumbing systems, unlike those in the inner city stretch.[51] Because of the small government ethos, affluent Houston residents paid for what would elsewhere be publicly provided services (for example, indoor plumbing, modern sewer systems, and streetlights). Minority groups, nonetheless, organized to improve their living conditions. Between 1966 and 1969, because of grassroots activism generated (albeit inadvertently) by President Lyndon Johnson's federal antipoverty program, Houston's poorest residents successfully secured some gains in residential services; however, lacking the requisite purchasing power, most lower income residents simply did without.[52] Living conditions began to improve somewhat when the white population fled the city starting in the 1970s, leaving behind a majority minority city. As an unintentional consequence of white flight and the intentional consequence of enfranchisement, Houston's minority residents were finally empowered through sheer population numbers and continued activism to elect responsive political representation and demand substantial change.[53]

While Houston boosters boasted of the city's dazzling progress, clearly not all parts of the city and not all city residents enjoyed the fruits of this progress. By 1970, houses in the best condition were located in the southwest and western quadrants of Houston—areas where the most educated, professional, and employed Houstonians lived. Low-income housing, though in short supply, was dispersed across the city rather than just concentrated in a centralized, low-income area, as in the examples of Chicago or Detroit.[54] Unemployment in the Houston area, while much lower than the national average, was actually much higher in certain areas of the city—in particular, the central city. Nationally, in the late 1970s, the unemployment rate was about 7.5 percent, while Houston's was much lower, at 5.3 percent. In troubled areas of the city, however, the average was 8 percent, with unemployment in some census tracts soaring as high as 16 percent. As an official with the Texas Employment Commission commented, "Areas with high jobless rates need not be whole cities."[55]

The areas to which Houston's African Americans and Latino/as did not move during the 1970s—the silences in this narrative—reveal the intransigence of segregation, blurring the distinction between de jure and de facto categories. Areas including Bellaire, Meyerland, and West University, located close to the heart of the city and priced well out of the reach of most of an African American population so newly freed from the strictures of Jim Crow, remained almost exclusively white. From among the substantial black middle class, those who chose to live in lily-white areas did so at the cost of social isolation and increased discrimination.[56] Real estate developers also spoke a language that communicated the embedded racial value system (class segmentation was automatically reinforced through housing prices) without naming race as part of the system.

South Asian Immigrants' Adoption of Middle-Class Residential Patterns

South Asian international students heavily concentrated in engineering majors quickly secured gainful employment in the primary labor market on graduation. Former students left their roommates and campus-area apartments, although some had already left the vicinity of the university when they married. Now, paychecks in hand, recent graduates and, increasingly, newly arrived South Asian immigrants could afford higher-quality accommodations. As Indians and Pakistanis settled in Houston, they began to look at their city with fresh eyes—not as temporary students but as potentially permanent residents. For most, each passing year raised the likelihood of their remaining in the United States.

Houstonians engaged with space in ways that perhaps reveal more than they intended. Immigrants—and, by extension, many middle-class Houstonians— wound their way across the city with intention and purpose. Seemingly simple decisions about preferred neighborhoods transpired within several other contexts, so that upon interrogation, neighborhood choice illuminated socio- economic structures and discourses. In explaining why they chose to live in or move to one neighborhood over another, most of the immigrants whom I interviewed offered a standard array of reasons, ranging from school quality to new housing to affordability to coethnic clustering. Beyond these appar- ent reasons, immigrants also described eventual changes under way in their neighborhoods that they felt compelled them to move elsewhere. The patterns formed by their selection of neighborhoods illustrates the role of race and class hierarchy in Houston in the 1970s. Houstonians' pattern of suburbanization in this decade correlated with upwardly mobile South Asian immigrants' class privilege. Because they could afford housing in new subdivisions marketed for the middle class, they tended to move into majority white suburban neighbor- hoods southwest, north, and west of the city. More often than not, as shown above, Houstonians were tracked into neighborhoods on the basis of their in- come, which normatively corresponded with race.[57]

Overview of South Asian Residential Patterns

Typically, South Asian immigrants who moved to Houston in the 1960s and 1970s followed clear settlement patterns (maps 2 and 3). If they entered the United States for the purpose of higher education (as so many did during this period), they first lived in apartment residences in predominantly African American neighborhoods near the University of Houston. Soon after obtaining B.A., M.A., or Ph.D. degrees, often in engineering, they married and moved to apartments or homes in a large area of near-southwest Houston, encom- passing what is known today as the Greater Sharpstown District and Fondren Southwest. By the late 1970s and early 1980s, they sold their first homes in near- southwest Houston and purchased second homes in suburban Alief, in far- southwest Houston, or in northwest Houston's Spring Branch and Cypress areas. Those who opted to move to Alief often completed this suburb-bound journey with a final move in the late 1990s to early 2000s to affluent Sugar Land. Of course, not all South Asians followed this trajectory. Some remained in near- southwest Houston through the 1980s, though in areas that have maintained

MAP 2. Houston neighborhoods and suburbs, key locations, 2010.

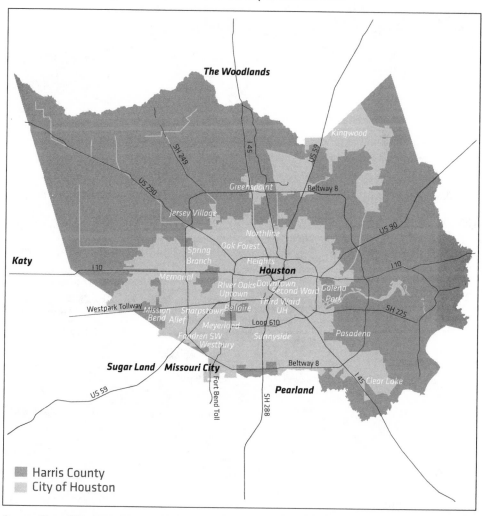

Source: City of Houston GIS.

at least a nominal white majority. Others moved to areas outside Houston, such Missouri City, Pasadena, or Clear Lake.[58] For the most part, the pattern of urban-to-suburban migration emerged as a preeminent model for pre-1980 arrivals of South Asian immigrants.

Even though by the mid-1970s, most South Asians in Houston moved to the city for the purpose of employment rather than education, for students, the university remained significant because of its discursive use as a narrative

MAP 3. South Asian ethnic clustering by neighborhood, 1960s–2000s.

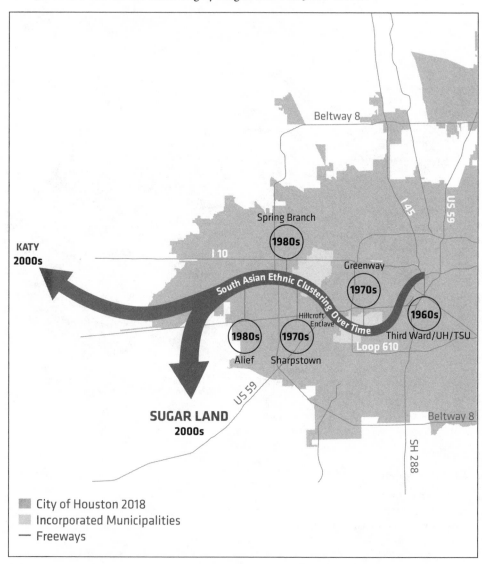

Source: City of Houston GIS.

starting point. Rohan Patil's description of his "pioneer days" as a graduate student at the University of Houston illustrates the point. Patil had obtained his bachelor's degree in chemical engineering at IIT Kanpur. In 1970, he joined the University of Houston's engineering MA program. After living in campus dormitories, he soon moved into a nearby apartment residence,

> Our "apartment" was a single-story, run-down house that three of us shared. You know we had three bedrooms so it was not a problem but it's— it was similar to what back home [were] servant's quarters.... There was no air conditioning, no central heat. We just had one big heater, a gas heater in the living room that used to give us the heat for everywhere. And in order to control the humidity we used to put a big pot of water on the top so that you still get some, otherwise it was too dry. So it was always fun![59]

Even if their accommodations lacked proper utilities or were in severe need of repair, because the students recognized this time as a transitional phase, they could endure the difficulties. These student immigrants anticipated that their temporary struggle would eventually lead to secure employment, perhaps in their sending countries but just as likely in Houston. In later years, they could even quip, "It was always fun!" Patil's concluding remark suggests that although immigrants narrated their experience as one that originated in hardship and struggle, they simultaneously understood the ephemerality of their "struggling time," in the words of another immigrant.[60] Stripped of all context, immigrants often pointed to this period of struggle as evidence of their own strong work ethic and as proof of the possible fruits of honest labor and commitment to education. More to the point, they suggested that the example of their own immigrant lives, beginning in the inner-city neighborhood of Third Ward, legitimates the American Dream. They erroneously conflated their short-lived tenure in unimproved, inner-city housing with the systemic municipal neglect experienced by their neighbors of color.

For Indian and Pakistani immigrants who never lived in the area around the University of Houston, the ways in which they navigated the pathways of the city drew on existing structures of privilege that simultaneously shaped immigrants' perceptions of the city. The spaces through which they moved and settled were a product of their own class position and the development of the city before and after Jim Crow. Arriving in 1971, Uma Krishnan, a young wife from Delhi and Madras, was particularly struck by "the newness of the whole city.... There were no buildings with age showing either in terms of the architecture or in terms of water that has stained the walls."[61] In the places that Krishnan and her husband chose to live, work, and socialize, they appreciated the fresh, untainted feel of the growing city. Her husband's employer, Shell Oil, had moved the family from California to Houston. With the income of a white-collar professional holding an advanced degree in engineering from Berkeley, Krishnan and her husband opted to reside in the Fondren Southwest area, an up-and-coming Southwest Houston subdivision.[62]

Contrary to Krishnan's impression of Houston, the city did have impoverished and declining areas even in the 1970s—for example, the predominantly African American neighborhoods of Settegast and Riceville. City reports indicate that homes in these areas lacked running water and had open sewage disposal systems and unpaved roads. Incidentally, Riceville was located just two miles south of the solidly middle-class neighborhoods of Fondren Southwest and Sharpstown. Roads and buildings were developed *around* the area.[63] South Asian immigrants at that time, however, held advanced degrees and thus economic capital, so they could afford to overlook the substandard living conditions in many areas of Houston, perceiving only a shiny, new city. As one historian notes, "Shell employees and their families, like many other immigrants to Houston, would never have to see much of the city anyway; they found themselves in suburban developments built specifically for the city's well-to-do newcomers."[64]

In the window between 1970 and 1980, South Asians formed a pattern of apartment rentals followed by the purchase of first homes in Southwest Houston, specifically in the subdivisions of Fondren Southwest and Sharpstown. Bhanu and Nagaraj Shekhar, a couple from India, first lived in Southwest Houston, and their experience exemplifies this pattern.[65] Trained as an electrical engineer, Nagaraj had already resided in Houston for five years, working in the information technology department at Rice University. He and Bhanu married in their home city of Chennai in 1975. She joined him a few months later, after her paperwork was processed and she received her visa. They selected Napoleon Square Apartments between Renwick and Rampart off of Bellaire Boulevard in near-southwest Houston.[66] Pushing farther southwest by just one or two miles, they later bought a condominium on Fondren and Bissonnet. Within a couple of years, they sold the condo and purchased their first house just a mile away, in the neighborhood across from Houston Baptist University, off of Fondren. Finally, remaining in Southwest Houston, they moved to a slightly larger house in the Westbury neighborhood by 1978, where they remained for about two decades and raised their children.

Southwest Houston appealed to immigrants for several reasons. Upward of 80 percent of all residents in the area owned their own homes in the early 1970s—among the highest such concentrations in the city.[67] For those not yet ready to buy a house, the area boasted some of the highest rates of new apartment construction, although it also averaged comparatively high monthly apartment rent. Along with west Houston, it housed among the most educated segments of the population.[68] Briefly living in Sharpstown in 1970, Saumitra Kelkar remarked, "That was a really nice area in those days! Most of the engineers used to live in Sharpstown."[69] The pet project of developer Frank Sharp in the late 1950s through the 1960s, Sharpstown stretched over four thousand acres of former prairie land and boasted upscale housing, apartments, condominiums, schools, a country club, a gigantic indoor shopping mall, and even a small Baptist university.

Sharp had purchased the prairie land for residential development in 1955.[70] Crucially, Sharp linked Sharpstown and Southwest Houston's development to Houston's downtown by negotiating the erection of a ten-mile stretch of highway, the Southwest Freeway (Highway 59), supporting a mere thirteen-minute commute to the central business district. Houston developers—Sharp included—would profit immensely from area real estate.[71] The Sharpstown development attracted middle- to upper-middle-class young families and singles through the 1960s and 1970s.[72] When Indians and Pakistanis began moving to Sharpstown and the area in the late 1960s, it was still new, with the new Sharpstown Mall having opened in 1962.[73] In the late 1960s, UH student Jamal Iqbal visited South Asian friends who had just purchased a home within walking distance of the mall. The development was so removed from the urban density of the university area that he teased his friends, "You couldn't find any other place . . . than coming out of town [to Sharpstown]?"[74] He explained, "There was nothing there. There were no high-rise buildings, [no] downtown. There was only one building in those days, probably twenty-five, thirty floors. That was it." Sharpstown, just within the city limits, embodied the suburban ideal of ranch-style homes, generous yard space, and a location convenient but not too close to the central business district.[75]

As depicted in a rendering of Sharpstown, Sharp's plans included at least ten skyscraper-like buildings and several more multistory office and residential buildings (fig. 7). Arranged on an organized grid, the tree-lined streets of garden apartments and shopping centers boast easy access to Sharp's freeway, Highway 59. Particularly striking in the sketched image, however, is the comparatively un-urbanized surrounding panorama. Sharpstown bursts out of an otherwise entirely agrarian landscape. Sharp's development of this part of Houston fundamentally influenced Southwest Houston, both near and far. In the immediate vicinity, developers built Fondren Southwest, while Sharp himself expedited the extension of Sharpstown several miles west by purchasing from oilman Robert E. Smith the 2,500-acre Smith ranch, thereby extending Houston's limits to the far western boundaries of Harris County.[76]

FIGURE 7. Sharpstown Design Concept, 1965. (Vertical Files, H-Subdivisions-Sharpstown, Houston Public Library, Houston Metropolitan Research Center)

"Most Indians seemed to live either in the southwest part of town or in the northwest," recalled Uma Krishnan, who moved to Houston from Madras in 1971 with her husband.[77] In describing Southwest Houston, longtime resident Namrata Chandra, a medical technologist who, with her engineer husband, purchased a home in the Glenshire subdivision of Southwest Houston in the early 1970s, recalled her neighbors as "mostly" or "all" professionals.[78] Another Southwest Houston resident characterized his neighbors as engineers and accountants.[79] In fact, residents living in the western half of the city, which included Sharpstown and Fondren Southwest, were highly professionalized and had an annual median income between $7,216 and $13,509.[80] With the exception of a few select pockets of affluence in the city, such as River Oaks, Southwest Houstonians outearned other residents of Houston (see Appendix map 12). By comparison, residents living in the vicinity of UH earned between $1,643 and $3,757 annually.[81] Namrata Chandra, who remained in Southwest Houston for over thirty years, found that her neighbors were "family oriented with young kids probably similar to my children's age."[82] Her neighbors were mostly

"Americans, white Americans as well as black" but "not too many [Hispanics]. At that time we did not know that many Hispanic people." Settling comfortably into young family life, Chandra reflected, "We were quite happy." Thus, Southwest Houston's new residential developments provided upwardly mobile, middle-class Houstonians—white, black, and South Asian immigrant (among others)—with the opportunity to purchase first homes.

South Asian immigrants found residence in the broad vicinity of Southwest Houston to be initially appealing, although, often in later years, problematic. On arriving in Houston as an engineering and an MBA student, respectively, Hemant Chokshi and his wife moved to Sharpstown because they had a friend who lived there. Residing in the Sharpstown area from 1979 to 1981, Chokshi offered that it used to be a "really nice place . . . but then there started a little down trend and then the apartment complexes, to keep their occupancy rates high, they drop their rates and that allows lower income folks, maybe, to move in."[83] Soon after moving to a Sharpstown apartment, Chokshi and his wife "had indications in 1980 that it was getting really bad out there" because of "a bad location." Within a decade, what Houstonians had once recognized as a prime neighborhood was transformed into an area to be avoided.

Some residents experienced crime themselves. One night a neighbor fired gunshots through Chokshi's bedroom closet. On another occasion, he recounted, someone tried to break down his front door with a sharp, heavy object, possibly an ax. Even those South Asians who lived in other parts of Houston—such as Montrose, inside the city, or further west, on Interstate 10 and Kirkwood—perceived that the Fondren Southwest area had "gone bad," meaning that as crime increased, "people started running further away."[84] Anita Sharma, from Bihar, India, explained that "there used to be huge houses, doctors all lived there. Then they built three or four apartments . . . and it deteriorated the entire South Fondren area completely. Good people moved out from there. So, it used to be a good area, close to town and everything. It has become . . . people are going farther and farther."[85]

"Moving farther" meant not moving east or back to the center of the city. While some South Asian immigrants and other middle-class Houstonians moved farther southwest, west, north, and southeast of the city, each of these directional thrusts was contingent on suburban development. During Houston's boom years, developers and home builders capitalized on the land far west of Houston, including more than nine thousand acres of prairie used formerly for cattle grazing and farming.[86] Aerial images of the Houston metropolitan area in 1975 reveal a heavily developed city core with remaining farmland to the far west and southwest of the city.[87] Because of increased prices near Houston's downtown and the cost of obtaining city permits, developers determined that building at least fifteen to twenty miles outside the central business district, on mainly farm and prairie land, would be less costly.[88] Neighborhoods like Memorial and Spring Branch, annexed in the 1960s on the former fringes of the city, had undergone development into suburban-style, low population density areas through the construction of single-family homes and multifamily dwellings. By 1975, the city limits extended well beyond these areas, and given their planned design and relative proximity to downtown, the highest prices by 1975 neared $100,000 per acre for developers. Attesting to the relative youth of modern Houston, only 14 percent of Houston's housing stock was over twenty-five years old in 1975. Existing home sales accounted for about 65 percent of all such sales in the Houston area, while new home sales made up 34 percent.[89] Leaving Fondren Southwest and Sharpstown, many Indian and Pakistani immigrants next chose to live in a wide band of west Houston, from Alief to Katy. The trend toward suburbanization continued.

Conclusion

Houston's economy, population, and physical size exploded in the postwar decades. The city's skyline, its aerial view, the composition of its inhabitants, and the lifeways characterizing this rising metropolis were dramatically altered; some of the more timeworn buildings and deep-rooted ideas, however, would endure. A city in the throes of transformation, Houston nevertheless retained a significant historical legacy, one rooted in racial hierarchy and class division. Houstonians, like other southerners, lived in a city long divided by Jim Crow segregation. Residential neighborhoods, occupational opportunities, and institutions of education were unequally accessed along a white/not-white binary, and while the civil rights movement shattered civic and institutional barriers, in the 1970s, the city's economic growth continued to provide opportunities unequally across racial and class axes.

In the Houston metropolitan area, suburbanization became the established residential pattern for much of the middle class; the net result of mass outmigration from the city was the permanent alteration of the city's demographic profile. Established white residents of Houston moved to the suburbs, as did a growing middle class and thousands of newcomers of all races. The selective basis upon which Indian and Pakistani immigrants had entered the United States in the 1960s and 1970s advanced their material success from their very point of arrival, enabling them to participate in this process of middle-class suburbanization. South Asian immigration to Houston in the 1970s was part of a larger internationalization trend in the city. These "pioneers"—students who arrived from the 1960s through mid-1970s, along with more recently arrived professionalized immigrant families, benefited from shifting Cold War priorities, advances in civil rights, and access to higher education. Each of these changes eased their entry into a growing American middle class. The increasing internationalization of the city drew more South Asians to the Houston area during and after the 1970s, but the ways in which this population spatially inhabited the city were firmly situated in local contexts of urban expansion, continued patterns of residential segregation, and, as discussed in the next chapter, school desegregation.

CHAPTER FIVE

. . . .

RIDING UP THE OIL BOOM,

SLIDING DOWN THE OIL BUST,

MID-1970S–1980S

The 1970s and 1980s were decades of marked economic and social change in Houston, characterized by public school desegregation amid frenzied annexation, population growth, and a construction boom, followed by a severe economic recession. Despite the tumult, a certain class- and race-based logic guided the evolution of the city. Although Houston had long been segregated, the movement of hundreds of thousands of middle-class Houstonians who newly took up residence in the suburbs in response to and against the backdrop of school desegregation greatly increased social distance between the city and its suburbs. The overlapping processes of suburbanization from the mid-1970s and economic fallout in Houston in the 1980s contributed to sweeping changes across the metropolis, and the intersection of these forces provides pivotal moments in which to examine social constructs such as class, race, and ethnicity.[1]

The experiences of Pakistani and Indian immigrants who participated in suburban flight illustrate how middle-class Houstonians defined and maintained socioeconomic hierarchies. The decisions made by old and new Houstonians and how they understood their choices show that residential patterns and school selection occurred and intersected within these constructs. Furthermore, the discourses surrounding neighborhood and school demographic shifts suggest that integration-oriented laws and policies enjoyed limited success in changing racial perceptions. Many middle-class Houstonians whose neighborhoods underwent the greatest demographic change due to the economic downturn quickly relocated to "whiter pastures" in the suburbs, affirming the endurance of entangled class and racial hierarchies in the post–Jim Crow South. That is, as more working-class African Americans and Latinos/as settled into neighborhoods with falling house values, established residents moved away. In addition, South Asian Houstonians redefined the suburbs for themselves through the establishment of ethnic enclaves.

Houston's Growth Economy and Suburbanization

Houston, the proud "Golden Buckle of the Sunbelt," had experienced only growth since World War II. Houston's boosters touted it as the fastest-growing city in the nation, with an unprecedented expansion of jobs, attracting 1,300 new migrants per week in the late 1970s.[2] Whereas the oil embargo in 1973 by OPEC (Organization of Petroleum Exporting Countries) precipitated a recession across the United States, as international oil prices rose, Houston's local oil-related machinery and metals firms expanded operations. In addition, high oil prices spurred oil exploration and drilling, stimulating Houston's overall economy, so that by the late 1970s, the city was heavily dependent on oil despite a slant toward economic diversification earlier that decade.[3] Oil imports flowed into the Port of Houston while oilfield machinery and petrochemicals were heavily exported.[4]

The increase in oil prices continued unabated from 1978 through 1981. Oil profits and speculation buoyed Houston's overall economy, creating white-collar jobs in a variety of sectors. Consequently, the housing market soared, both keeping pace with the needs of so many prospective new home buyers and also speculating on the future of unsustainably high oil prices. Home prices increased by nearly 20 percent between 1980 and 1982.[5] Houston's economy peaked in March 1982, at a time when over 55 percent of all jobs in the metropolitan area were linked either directly or indirectly to the production of oil, petrochemical refining, and related services and research based in the energy sector.[6] Major construction and engineering firms—M. W. Kellogg, Fluor Daniel, and Brown & Root—drew deeply on the city's technical expertise to support the petrochemical industry.[7] These companies eagerly sought out engineering graduates from the University of Houston; likewise, Indian and Pakistani international students and immigrants eagerly met the needs of this boomtown economy.

Unknowingly on the precipice of the worst recession in Houston's history, investors, developers, and residents radiated optimism and faith in Houston's continued potential for economic growth as they welcomed the 1980s. As compared to the national unemployment rate of 5.8 percent (the nation's lowest since 1974) or even that of the region's 4.1 percent, the health of Houston's economy seemed to surpass that of other cities with an unemployment rate of only 3.3 percent in 1979.[8] Speculation continued apace as oil companies projected oil prices of fifty dollars per barrel, or higher.[9] Led by the oil industries' overly optimistic expectations, Houston's many oil-linked and unrelated businesses forged ahead with plans commensurate with continued high rates of growth, including new residential and commercial construction. By 1979, real estate developers continued to build new subdivisions, especially outside the city limits.

Led to the suburbs by realtors and word-of-mouth networks at work and through social circles, South Asian immigrant suburbanites in the 1970s participated in a process of mass suburbanization that had occurred fairly recently in Houston. By 1980, although 57 percent of Houston's white population resided in the suburbs, when compared with other large metropolitan areas in the United States, this was almost the lowest proportion in the country. Over 90 percent of white residents already lived in the suburbs of Atlanta, Boston, and Miami by 1980.[10] Newspaper accounts and government reports in the mid-1970s lauded Houston's comparatively low rate of white flight and suburbanization when compared to such cities as Baltimore, Philadelphia, and Los Angeles, concluding that even though Texas's liberal land-annexation laws resulted in a sprawling city, they had simultaneously helped Houston to retain wealth inside the city limits. Making such comparisons in the 1970s, these reports noted that more of Houston's residents lived inside the city limits than outside them.[11] White flight, it appeared, was not a Houston problem.

However, although it was true that most Houstonians lived in the city rather than in suburbs outside of Houston, in reality, the city limits continually expanded to include what would have been suburbs without extensive annexation. During the decades of sustained massive population growth from 1950 through 1980, the city of Houston annexed over two hundred square miles.[12] Also, because school desegregation was a key factor in precipitating white flight, most flight in Houston occurred during the 1970s when desegregation measures were enforced in public schools, as the 1980 census makes apparent. Kevin Kruse defines white flight as "the mass migration of whites from cities to the suburbs [that] proved to be the most successful segregationist response to the moral demands of the civil rights movement."[13] Houston's white (and South Asian) residents largely participated in the suburbanization trend later than their national counterparts—that is, mainly after 1970. As census data, oral histories, and GIS mapping for subsequent decades show, Houston's newcomers and natives alike would indeed embrace the language and ideology of suburbia (safety versus crime, good versus bad, change versus stability), both of which were predicated on suburban exclusion and middle-class entitlement.[14]

Over time, as a subgroup, South Asian immigrant families overwhelmingly chose to settle in whiter, more affluent areas both in the city and especially in the suburbs of the city. Generally, their pattern of choices was informed by and reinforced existing national trends toward suburbanization and white flight from the city. The city of Houston had limited new housing stock by the late 1970s and comparatively high urban mortgage rates. House prices in some choice neighborhoods close in the city (for example, Memorial and West University Place) rose to the point that many prospective home buyers were priced out of the market. Affordable middle-class neighborhoods in Houston (such as Meyerland and Bellaire) were zoned to Houston Independent School District (HISD), a rapidly diversifying school district.

Furthermore, as developers invested in new subdivision growth, they enticed home buyers by offering slightly lower mortgage rates, at 2 or even 3 percent below conventional loans, Veterans Affairs loans, or Federal Housing Administration rates.[15] Such deals were available only in new construction, which, because of available space and low builder purchase prices, were located mainly in the suburbs. Also, because of Houston's lack of geographic barriers—rivers, mountains, or canyons—the city could ostensibly spread unchecked to the west and southwest. As a result of these kinds of lending discounts, it did precisely that. And although it could be argued that residential development and some territorial expansion of Houston was necessary to accommodate such massive numbers of new residents, the specific form of suburban sprawl embraced by city developers and officials exacerbated the urban-suburban divide by directing new investment and movement to the fringes of the city and beyond.

Searching for Suburbia, Finding an Ethnic Enclave: Alief

The pattern of well-educated, high-earning South Asians settling in affluent suburban areas, which I term "brown flight," illustrates the class and race stratification of Houston's neighborhoods. Brown flight and white flight share fundamental similarities as race-driven processes, but brown flight has the added dimension of the suburbs serving as ethnic enclaves. By the early 1980s, "the distribution of workers closely parallel[ed] the spatial distribution of income and education in the Houston area."[16] As immigrants just establishing their financial foundations in the early 1970s, the vast majority of these highly educated South Asians were usually priced out of the most expensive parts of the city, including River Oaks, Memorial, Briar Forest, and West University (although there were exceptions, particularly among much wealthier Indian and Pakistani physicians).

Middle- and upper-middle-income Houstonians in white-collar jobs resided chiefly in the west/southwest and northwest sections of the city, and, increasingly, in Clear Lake (a suburban area annexed in 1977 in far southeast Houston, and home of NASA), while working-class residents opted for more affordable housing in the east to northeast side (see Appendix map 12).[17] Residents employed in construction and manufacturing, for example, concentrated in small incorporated cities far east of downtown, including Pasadena and Galena

Park, which were nearer to the Port of Houston and related industries.[18] A small community of less affluent South Asians who arrived in the United States mainly on the basis of family reunification visas in the late 1970s and early 1980s also emerged in Pasadena by the mid-1980s. The two neighboring South Asian communities, in Clear Lake and Pasadena, differed from their inception, since education levels and median household incomes in the Clear Lake area were higher than in Pasadena.[19] South Asian immigrants, like other middle-class Houstonians, favored the brand-new residential subdivisions on offer from developers, first in the near-southwest and northwest Houston areas of Fondren, Sharpstown, and Spring Branch (discussed previously) from the early to mid-1970s, and in the far southwestern suburbs of Alief from the mid-1970s.[20] Alief, in far-southwest Houston, and Sharpstown or Fondren, in near-southwest Houston, formed a broad spatial swath in which numerous Pakistani and Indian families lived (see maps 4 and 5). The area serves as a useful case study for the rise of modern ethnic enclaves and the impact of the oil recession on Houston's middle and poorer classes. It also offers a compelling example of the social impact of economic change at the neighborhood level.

Alief, a highly sought-after area for new Asian immigrants in Houston, is located in the far western section of Harris County (although often regarded as far -southwest Houston). As its population expanded, the once-small farming town that had been founded in 1861 requested incorporation in 1974. Houston, in turn, annexed it in three stages between 1977 and 1982 in order to "protect" the city's western boundary from enclosure.[21] In 1970, Alief's population of 8,000 was almost entirely white and already fairly professionalized, with 33 percent in professional or technical occupations. Of the remaining individuals, roughly half worked in sales, management, and clerical positions.[22] Still, with a total number of 2,397 housing units in 1970, Alief was only minimally settled.[23] Within a decade, developers invested in 5,000 new housing units, and the population more than doubled to roughly 18,000 by 1980. Interestingly, after the white majority population, Asians comprised the largest racial group in Alief, at over 12 percent in 1980—well above Houston's Asian population of 2.1 percent.[24] In the Alief subdivision of Mission Bend, where so many Indian and Pakistani families purchased homes, almost 40 percent of all residents were Asian Indians, while in Alief broadly, Asian Indians made up more than 36 percent of all Asians.[25] Additionally, when factoring in the large proportion of Pakistani immigrants, Alief was a dense South Asian ethnic cluster.[26] Comparatively, only 20 percent of Houston's Asian population was Asian Indian. Also notable was the low percentage of African Americans and Hispanics in Alief, both less than 3 percent.[27]

South Asian immigrant interviewees reflected that Alief neighborhoods

MAP 4. Comparative spatial distribution of Asian Indian and white populations, 1980.

White Population
- <1,500
- 1,501–3,000
- 3,001–5,000
- 5,000–10,000
- >10,000

Asian Indian
- ● 5 People
- — Harris County
- — City of Houston

Sources: Census 1980; City of Houston GIS.

Note: In this and several of the following maps, the base map is composed of the Houston metropolitan area's census tracts. The depth of shade corresponds with density of the white population. The Asian Indian population is represented by dots transposed over the census tracts.

MAP 5. Inset of Asian Indian population concentration, 1980.

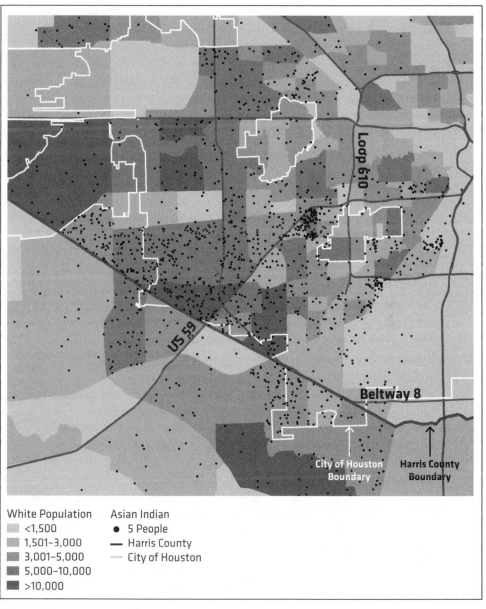

White Population
- <1,500
- 1,501–3,000
- 3,001–5,000
- 5,000–10,000
- >10,000

Asian Indian
- ● 5 People
- — Harris County
- — City of Houston

Sources: Census 1980; City of Houston GIS.

offered new housing—construction of most homes occurred between 1975 and 1978—open spaces, good schools, community, and, once again, white-collar neighbors.[28] According to a report developed by the Houston City Planning Department in 1975, the reasons that Americans chose suburbanization included "possible tax advantages, political power, more or less development controls and restrictions, racial and ethnic relationships, and to generally avoid being involved in the urban problems, of whatever nature, in the central city."[29] Real estate advertisements touted Alief schools as a strong selling point.[30] By 1980, an overwhelming 85 percent of Alief residents worked in professional, technical, or managerial jobs, outearning the average per capita income of other Houston residents by $8,000 per year.[31] Suresh Bhatt and his wife purchased their first home in Alief, explaining that "this was a new housing subdivision being built, so houses were new. We wanted a new house and we found a house that we liked and in our price range."[32] Bhatt continued, "We wanted to stay in the southwest part of town because most of our friends live in this neighborhood." Similarly, although Bina Parmar's husband worked in downtown Houston approximately twenty-four miles away, the couple purchased a home in the Mission Bend neighborhood of Alief. The Parmar family moved to Houston in 1976, and Bina observed that more and more of "our people were coming" to Alief.[33] During the 1970s and 1980s, immigrants from India and Pakistan began the process of ethnic residential clustering, wherein they structured their residential choices around ethnic community in suburban neighborhoods, including Alief, Pasadena, and Clear Lake. South Asian family after family moved into Alief. The lure of new houses, non-HISD schools, and, increasingly, ethnic clustering drove this stream of Indian and Pakistani homeowners.

Because of proximity, Indian and Pakistani immigrants could socialize more frequently in Alief. They routinely held large multifamily gatherings on the weekends, forging their own relationships and fostering their children's construction of cultural identity and friendship with young coethnics. As important as public community gatherings were in creating culture, weekend dinner parties served the same purpose on a much more frequent basis. Others have written about "ethnoburbs," where "Asian immigrants and American-born natives blend both contemporary and traditional elements of Asian culture with American culture to create a hybridized Asian American culture."[34] These small, social gatherings were spaces where the young and old defined ethnic identity through clothing, music, food, language, and behavioral norms (for example, *adab*, or manners with elders). Of course, the ethnic identities created by second-generation South Asian American youth in suburban Houston originated first and foremost in their *American* experience more than a mediated overseas culture in which they had never lived. Their interpretation of "culture" and "ethnicity" routinely diverged from that of their parents' in fundamental ways.[35] Nevertheless, regular social gatherings in ethnic enclaves reinforced a sense of belonging as ethnic Americans, whatever its particular meanings.

A similar process unfolded in other Houston suburbs, as well, although in the 1970s and 1980s, none held such a concentrated population of South Asians as Alief. Ethnic community building after the late 1970s was largely a suburban phenomenon, with the exception of the ethnic economy and the continuing but waning significance of the university.[36] Whether through the building of cultural schools (for the teaching of language, dance, music, and so on), religious institutions (such as temples and mosques), or, less formally, social gatherings, immigrants and their children actively constructed ethnic identity.

Wherever they resided in the Greater Houston area—Sharpstown, Alief, or Clear Lake—Pakistani and Indian Houstonians continued to drive into the city for ethnic purchases. By the mid-1980s, as a result of family chain migration, several Indian- and a few Pakistani-owned ethnic businesses had opened in in the city, especially on Hillcroft Street in near-southwest Houston.[37] Although small business owners established a handful of ethnic grocery stores and video shops in suburban neighborhoods to support growing South Asian populations, the main entrepreneurial hub emerged on Hillcroft. In time, Hillcroft would resemble Devon Street in Chicago and Gerrard Street in Toronto—both South Asian ethnic entrepreneurial enclaves. Hillcroft, however, also featured several Latino/a businesses, making it a multiethnic hub of sorts. Eventually, Pakistani businesses relocated to Hillcroft from another, much smaller hub on Bissonnet Street about four miles away.

The Hillcroft area developed a large South Asian ethnic economy featuring spatial clustering and a wide range of entrepreneurial enterprises that catered toward and employed coethnics but also served other ethnicities. Along with sari boutiques, small import grocers, and travel agencies, small business owners opened a handful of food-related enterprises.[38] Eventually, the ethnic economy provided another sphere in which to blur national identity boundaries, as ethnic grocery stores sold Indo-Pak groceries and restaurants served Indo-Pak cuisine. A well-known sweets shop on Hillcroft—Raja Sweets—touted in an advertisement in 1986 that it was "serving people of [the] Indian Subcontinent."[39] The owners invited readers to visit the shop and taste "our superb Indian and Pakistani sweets and cuisine." Travel agency ads promoted special deals to Bombay, Delhi, Karachi, and Lahore. Indian and Pakistani business owners routinely advertised in each community's newspapers and magazines,[40] such as *Indo-American News* and *Voice of Asia*, distributed free of charge at Indian and Pakistani grocery stores and restaurants on Hillcroft. Although the opening of small businesses on Hillcroft reflected the concentration of South

Asians in Southwest Houston neighborhoods, this budding ethnic entrepreneurial enclave was insufficient in and of itself to retain an ethnic residential population in the area. With Houston's urban layout supporting a sprawled city and Houstonians' willingness to drive vast distances, South Asians sought residence more remotely, with new construction, coethnics, and public schools in mind—namely, in the suburbs, and especially in Alief.

Desegregation and Public School Selection before the Recession

Perhaps even more than other parents, Asian immigrants carefully chose their neighborhood based on the quality of public schools.[41] Future emigrants structured their own life choices around heavy investment in higher education in their home countries and, later, in the United States. In the knowledge- and skills-based economy of the postwar United States, education was the most effective tool in achieving economic success, upward mobility, and some measure of social acceptance after migration. As South Asians completed advanced degrees, secured jobs, and bought houses, they factored in the quality of public education as a key consideration. They strove to ensure that, like themselves, their children would have fundamental educational advantages and learn to define success as linked to education.[42] South Asians who migrated to the United States in the 1960s and 1970s had used education as a strategy for upward mobility. Whether for themselves or, later, their children, educational attainment presented an accessible means to both greater economic capital and cultural capital—that is, a higher standard of living and higher social status.

Highly educated South Asian immigrants regarded the careful selection of public schools—in this case, in Alief—for the second generation as essential. During the 1970s and into the 1980s, Houston's public school system underwent major shifts related to desegregation and demographic change. Though the city of Houston annexed Alief, Alief's school district remained separate from the Houston Independent School District. Old and new Houstonians paid close attention to the changing demographics of area districts, because neighborhoods were zoned to specific schools within specific school districts. Alief's expanding Asian population was drawn to the area in large part because of the Alief Independent School District. The narratives South Asian immigrants shared about where they opted to school their children and why they made their decisions shed light on the discourses broadly circulated by Houstonians as they responded to the social upheaval in their midst.

South Asian immigrant choices and rationales about schools expose the ways in which southerners sought to preserve separate racial spaces for their children while also reinforcing the model minority myth. The white casting of

Asian Americans as a model minority—a group apart—in this racial landscape buttressed claims against other minority groups. Highly qualified foreigners of color who immigrated into the United States at the height of the country's desegregation battles provided the proponents of the myth with a foil to the nation's historically underprivileged minority groups. The model minority fiction worked in tandem with other cultural fictions about minority groups and thus was no less pernicious in its intent and effect. It was not tangential to perceptions about other minority groups; rather, the presence of high-performing Asian Americans was marshaled in the service of the racial scripting of African Americans and Mexican Americans.[43]

As in other southern cities, the desegregation of public schools in Houston unfolded turbulently over at least two decades.[44] Although a discussion of school desegregation originates in the 1954 case *Brown v. Board of Education of Topeka* and may seem out of place in a chapter on the 1970s and 1980s, the implementation and implications of the case did not fully manifest themselves until well after the ruling was handed down. What follows is a brief history of *Brown* and its impact on Houston area schools, in order to illustrate another principal reason for South Asian immigrant suburbanization. As numerous scholars have recounted, American (and especially southern) public schools were compelled by the Supreme Court's unanimous ruling in *Brown v. Board of Education* in 1954 to implement a process of desegregation. "Racial discrimination in public education," asserted Supreme Court Chief Justice Earl Warren, "is unconstitutional."[45] In the *Brown II* ruling a year later, the Court specified that the process should be undertaken "with all deliberate speed."[46]

By the time the Supreme Court ruled on the *Brown* case, Houston's African American community had waged successful battles for equal teachers' pay, employment as municipal police officers and firefighters, and the desegregation of city buses and golf courses.[47] Still, even as these victories chipped away at specific instances of discrimination, they did not attack the heart of segregation itself. That triumph would be achieved with *Brown*, which recognized the deleterious psychological effect of race-based segregation. Houstonians' repudiation of the ruling included the resurgence of a conservative school board, the refusal to implement real change, white flight, and eventually the resegregation of Houston's public schools. Although there was no widespread violence in response to school desegregation, both the Houston school board and the general white population expressed hostility in other ways. Their commitment to segregated schooling suggests the depth of their investment in and privileges accrued through Jim Crow, which were sustained by the circulation of cultural fictions regarding the city's African American and Mexican American populations.

In the Houston Independent School District, the school board initially responded to court-mandated desegregation with dismissiveness and delay.[48] In the fall of 1960, only under threat of court injunction and loss of federal and state funds did HISD grudgingly desegregate via a total of twelve African American students admitted to white schools in the entire district. The district was the largest public school district in the South by the late 1950s, schooling some 177,000 students, 22 percent of whom were African Americans in segregated schools.[49] By 1965, only eighteen elementary schools had even started desegregating, focusing mainly on admitting first graders.[50] The pace of desegregation continued sluggishly until 1970, when U.S. District Judge Ben Connally ordered HISD to propose a plan to speed up the process.

Implemented in 1970, the accelerated plan for desegregation relied on busing in students from across the district to integrate schools, as well as pairing students from white and black schools to achieve balanced populations. Houstonians responded in several ways. First, they began a mass exodus to the suburbs and other school districts, such as Alief, where they could effectively maintain de facto segregated public education for their children. The city of Houston lost white residents at an unprecedented rate: between 1970 and 1980, the white population of Houston declined by over 365,000, and HISD declined in total student enrollment. Astoundingly, the fastest-growing city in the United States lost roughly 40,000 students during one of its fastest-growing decades.[51] Conversely, the districts boasting the most growth were the newly developed suburban areas of Alief ISD and Katy ISD in west Houston, along with Klein ISD and Spring ISD in far north Houston. Each of these school districts was majority white.

Second, white parents enrolled their children in private schools. The evidence for this, however, is only correlative and speculative, because it is difficult to parse out the number of parents driven by racial motives versus the number of newcomers to Houston in a period of massive population growth. We can only surmise that, given the context of desegregating public schools, a substantial number of these parents were reacting to school integration by "protecting" their white children. Third, Houston's Mexican American residents actively protested the new plan because the paired schools were largely black and Hispanic. Hispanics were legally categorized as white, and this plan technically brought schools into compliance with desegregation orders without actually affecting white students and their schools. Mexican Americans boycotted HISD schools, keeping thousands of children at home and/or enrolling them at *huelga* or strike schools from 1970 to 1972.[52]

Fourth, west Houston residents undertook steps to secede from HISD by creating their own overwhelmingly white school district, naming it the

Westheimer Independent School District (WISD). As noted earlier, barring the single neighborhood of River Oaks and a few incorporated cities within Houston's city limits, such as Bellaire and West University, the most affluent region of Houston was its west side. Proponents of WISD spearheaded their effort for almost a decade, fighting HISD and repeatedly appealing court rulings that charged WISD with actively opposing existing desegregation efforts. The federal appeals court in New Orleans finally ruled against the formation of WISD in late 1978, questioning its intent and stating that its creation would only intensify white flight from the central city and from HISD schools.[53] In the 1970s, the percentage of white students in HISD dropped from 50 percent to 25 percent.[54]

Into this maelstrom came tens of thousands of new immigrants and migrants annually from across the country. Because the conventional historical record yields the accounts of historical actors more directly and publicly involved in desegregation battles, other agents of this history are overlooked. Certainly, immigrants' and migrants' roles can seem peripheral, considering their smaller population size as compared to the white majority and segregated African American minority. Still, the views of newcomers can illuminate existing social hierarchies. And when one considers the sheer numbers of newcomers arriving in the city, their impact on the direction of Houston's growth cannot be overlooked.

Immigrants learned about which schools were top performers through some of the same word-of-mouth networks that informed them about so-called good neighborhoods. Their coworkers provided them with information, but so did other friends, who, in turn, had learned from their friends and coworkers. This type of social capital—access to networks of information—aided access to high-quality neighborhoods and schools. Realtors, though legally prohibited from explicitly steering buyers to any specific neighborhood by sharing information about demographics or crime rates, could inform buyers generally that a particular area was zoned to a high-performing school district.[55] Some realtors may likely have overshared important neighborhood information in their zeal to sell houses. Builders, on the other hand, were under no such injunctions, and they could openly advertise "superior" school districts. Most houses in Alief were brand new and may have been purchased directly through builders. In addition to tapping into information networks, some immigrants said that they tracked school-related information in local newspapers. As Harsh Gil recalled, "Once a year in the newspaper . . . they mention about schools. They mention how many were National Honor students."[56] When asked about how he knew which school districts were good, Saumitra Kelkar stated that he "read about it" in the newspaper.[57] Similarly, Ashok Dani responded, "It's what you read in the paper."[58] Realtors also relied on newspapers and word-of-mouth networks to inform their buyers about school quality. Gil, an engineer turned realtor, argued that as long as the information was "open record" and a real estate "agent was knowledgeable" about general matters, she or he was free to share the information with clients.[59]

Lines of residential segregation in Houston aligned closely with schools and school districts in the city versus the suburbs. In 1977, developers advertised new homes in the new Fondren Southwest neighborhood as "the last new neighborhood in southwest Houston," close to the commercial centers of Sharpstown Mall, Westwood Mall, and Westbury Square and minutes from Houston's multinodal financial districts of the Texas Medical Center, Greenway Plaza, and downtown. Their ad taunted would-be suburban buyers, "Now that you've been to Timbuktu, come home to Fondren Southwest."[60] The reproduction of colonialist tropes aside (the casting Timbuktu as the periphery of civilization), other gaps in the advertisement are also revealing. There is no mention of "excellent school districts" or "family," as in ads for suburban developments, whereas a real estate ad for Quail Valley in Missouri City (a southwesterly suburb neighboring Houston) baldly stated that the neighborhood "is located in Ft. Bend County, where children attend academically superior schools."[61] Another suburban ad—this time for an Alief neighborhood— was sparse on details but was sure to feature prominently two simple words: "Alief Schools."[62] The unspoken binary alluded to in these ads, the antithesis of "superior schools," was Houston Independent School District versus suburban school districts. The "quality" of zoned public school districts became code for the racial demographics of a given neighborhood.

South Asian immigrant interviewees commonly cited "good schools" for their young children as a principal reason for where they chose to live. Bina Parmar lived briefly in Spring Branch, having heard from "so many friends" that the Spring Branch "school district was very good. . . . [Because our] kids were going to school, we were first looking at school districts."[63] As Indian immigrant Saumitra Kelkar emphatically stated, their children's school quality was of such central importance that if the neighborhood school "was bad we would have moved right then. Because, I mean there's no way I would have asked them to go to that school. Either we would have stayed there and [sent them] to private school or we would have moved out."[64] Interviewees spoke repeatedly of "good" and "bad" schools and neighborhoods. Their explanations of the meanings assigned to these simple labels reveal complex ideas on race, class, and identity reflected societal discourses at the time. Seemingly straightforward decisions regarding schools existed within these discourses.

Decisions assessing school quality, however, occurred and continue to occur within racial and class frameworks that used social, cultural, and symbolic capital. Indian immigrant Anita Sharma explained: "We moved to Katy in '73. . . . The school district was top. Now, Katy School District also has Katy [High School], right? But Katy High School's score and education is not that high, like us [at Katy Taylor High School]. Nobody liked to put our children in that school because it was all Mexican and black population."[65] In the passage above, Sharma alluded to the school district's high ranking, as did all other interviewees. In elaborating on what she specifically meant by "top" district, she noted that "scores" and "education" were of paramount importance. For Sharma, the low scores and poor quality of education at the other high school were embodied in its students: "Mexican and black" students. Sharma arrived in Houston in 1970. By the time her children were ready to attend high school in the mid-1980s, she had internalized the prevailing language and ideology of race in white, middle-class suburbs as they pertained to school selection. Although South Asian immigrants made the same choices that many other parents did (and, if given the option, the choice that many white, black, Latino/a, and Asian parents would make for their children), for all their normativity, these choices were no less embedded in racial discourses. Race was (and remains) at the heart of decisions regarding children's schooling. An exploration of the role of public school choice for immigrants reveals what dominant members of society thought about the marginalized, racialized groups of people in their midst.

The forced desegregation of schools in the Greater Houston area produced discourses that entangled categories of class and race with a range of negative behavior in a coded language that described school quality. Like white Houstonians and other Americans, South Asian immigrants collapsed features of poverty, oppression, and race so that blackness generally equated with poverty and criminality. As Lata Dani explained, the only way to discern between good and bad schools was to see if "all the kids were from a good family, [if] they are coming to school. Their habits, and everything. So that's how you say it's a good school."[66] When pressed to clarify what she meant by "good" schools, Lata Dani said that they sought educational excellence in the form of advanced placement classes, for example. Her husband, Ashok Dani, interjected that the price point of a neighborhood affected the quality of residents. Because theirs was a more expensive area, the residents were not "poor"—not "black" or "Mexican"—and *that* is what made area schools "good." In "bad" schools, Ashok pointed out, students' parents frequently changed out partners, were "rough," uneducated, drunkards, or of low character, as he understood it. Consequently, their children "dropped out" of school, left home, and joined gangs at a young age. He noted that these behaviors occurred among the "lower class."[67]

Parents with the material means choose to provide their children with the "best" education they can afford. It is therefore unsurprising that educated, professionalized South Asian immigrants uniformly structured their residential choices around school quality. What is interesting, however, is what they meant when, like Indian immigrant Saumitra Kelkar, they stated that "Alief school district was at top at that time."[68] South Asian immigrants defined good schools as ones whose students scored well on standardized tests, had students who valued education, hired well-qualified teachers, and provided their children with a challenging curriculum. They described good schools as being attended by students as studious as their own and from intact, stable families, as well as providing academic rigor for their children through advanced classes and offering a safe, relatively drug- and violence-free environment. These are the same reasons that many parents of any race or ethnicity still cite when selecting a school. They also identified good schools by their racial composition. Kelkar explained that the "Alief area was full of Indians and Chinese because everybody wanted their kids to go to the good school district." Both Alief ISD and Spring Branch ISD, according to Kelkar, fared much better than Houston ISD, which he described as "going down" in the 1970s.[69] Indeed, HISD superintendent Billy Reagan affirmed that test scores for the district had declined precipitously since 1970, the same year HISD desegregation began in earnest.[70] By 1976, elementary school children in two-thirds of HISD schools failed to show expected academic growth. A study administered by HISD found a "direct correlation between the number of students receiving free lunches and achievement."[71] The most rapidly declining racial group of the HISD student body was whites, while the fastest growing segment of Houston's population and HISD during the 1970s was Hispanics.

The Recession and Its Economic Impact

Houston's economy in the 1970s performed somewhat independently of the national economy. With a heavily oil-centric base, Houston's fortunes were deeply tied to the global oil market. In the 1970s, as oil prices remained high, the metropolitan economy soared even while the national economy suffered from a post–Vietnam War inflation-based recession.[72] Conversely, in the mid-1980s, as the national economy strengthened and unemployment declined between 1983 and 1990, Houston was hit hard by an oil bust.[73] The distant origins of the oil bust were located in the oil embargo implemented by OPEC in October 1973. From this point until the early 1980s, OPEC incrementally but consistently increased the price of oil. In 1978, oil was $15 per barrel of crude oil, $23 the following year, and $34 in 1980. It peaked in 1981 at $37 per barrel (OPEC had hoped to push it to $50).[74] As oil prices began their slow descent from $37 in late 1981 to $27 in 1985, Houston's economy correspondingly slowed. The impact was felt in other Texas cities, including Dallas, San Antonio, Austin, El Paso, and especially oil-centric cities like Midland–Odessa; however, despite being the largest city in the state, Houston's extensive dependence on energy made it extremely vulnerable to this downturn.[75] In 1986, following internal squabbling over pricing among OPEC members, oil prices again plunged, this time to below $15 per barrel. Reeling from this, Houston was unable to prop up an economy slumping since early 1982. The depression would endure until 1990—almost eight years.

During this time, Houstonians lost more than 225,000 jobs; that is, one in every eight jobs vanished. At its worst, thirty thousand homes were foreclosed in one year.[76] By 1986, Houston had at least a five-year surplus of residential and commercial space.[77] No longer able to make their mortgage payments and unable to sell in a shattered market, thousands of unemployed and underemployed homeowners walked away from their homes. The foreclosure crisis was compounded by the accelerated rate at which real estate—subdivisions, single-family homes, apartments, condominiums, retail, commercial, and industrial space— all had been overdeveloped in the years immediately preceding the bust.[78] The impact of the real estate market was also felt in banking: every major bank but one failed in Texas.[79] Bankruptcy rates continued to rise.[80]

In 1983, the first year of the oil bust, population growth for the Houston metropolitan area actually declined, and not just nominally. Population growth fell from a staggering 5.9 percent to 2.8 percent. It continued this downward trend, and in 1987, for the first time in recent memory, Texas's largest city showed a negative migration rate. The population for this erstwhile urban magnet declined 1.15 percent in 1987.[81] The Houston metropolitan area was converted from an influx metropolis between 1970 and 1982 to one of major outflux by 1989.[82]

While the oil boom and robust economy of the 1970s kept area housing prices inflated, the oil bust in the early 1980s toppled Houston's economy and housing market. Given the heights from which the city plunged—boosters had, after all, declared Houston a "miracle city"—its crash in the early 1980s was all the more catastrophic. The effect of the crash on Houston's housing and employment markets cannot be overemphasized. Houstonians, including immigrants from the Indian subcontinent, reeled from massive job loss, the inability to secure alternative employment, plummeting home values, and the subsequent failure to sell their homes. Not only did the economic devastation of the 1980s transform the city from one of migration to emigration, but also residentially, neighborhoods lost entire populations as Houstonians foreclosed on tens thousands of homes, further dropping home prices.

In Southwest Houston (including Alief), home values and rent prices plum-
meted, opening up Southwest Houston to a wider range of lower-income earners. Although the area did not suffer from a net population loss, it did undergo
population transfer. In order to protect themselves and their families from what
they perceived as higher crime rates, lower educational standards, and the lax
family values of lower-income earners, more South Asian immigrants looked
toward other suburbs and incorporated areas outside Houston. Middle-class
professionals began an exodus out of Alief. Saumitra Kelkar, who had lived in
Sharpstown in the early 1970s and later in Alief, explained the changes of the
1980s: once prices fell and lower-income earners moved into the neighborhood,
school district quality suffered.[83] Many of those South Asian immigrants who
remained in Houston eventually joined their coethnics in more distant suburbs
by the mid-2000s, although for reasons discussed later.

The depression both reinforced existing residential inaccessibility to affluent neighborhoods and granted lower-income residents access to moderately
middle-class areas. Indian and Pakistani residents of Alief in the 1980s noted
with alarm a wide-scale area transformation resulting from the devastating
regional economic recession. After continually rising for more than a decade
and peaking in 1982, home prices began a steep, rapid descent. The recession
disproportionately affected house values in Alief and other neighborhoods at
similarly moderate price points. Conversely, home prices in the highly affluent,
overwhelmingly white neighborhood of West University Place increased by
39 percent between 1980 and 1984, remained stable in the early years after the
recession, and declined only minimally thereafter.[84] The demographic composition of West University was largely unaltered. Affluent neighborhoods did
not racially diversify because of the recession since their nominally reduced
home prices remained out of reach for those struggling through the weak-
ened economy. Likewise, other less affluent but racially homogenous areas
near the city core, such as Meyerland and Bellaire, reflected a similarly stable
trend, although they lost more short-term value than West University Place.
On the other hand, by 1984, Alief homes, which had long sold at lower price
points than the aforementioned affluent areas, dropped to 1980 home prices
and continued falling. Neighborhoods with home prices comparable to Alief,
even those optimally located in the city, suffered price stagnation. For example,
just down the road from Meyerland, Fondren Southwest home prices in 1984
carried virtually the same price as they had four years earlier.[85] The surplus of
available, now-foreclosed housing drove down both home and rent prices in
Alief, allowing newcomers, once priced out of Alief, to afford residence.[86] As
Kelkar said, "After thirty years I didn't make any money on that house. . . . I
bought it for $90,000 back in 1980. I couldn't even sell it for that money. I just

gave it out to those Cheap Houses people so you don't have to worry about it. They just give you $20,000 less. Then you walk out."[87]

Alief homeowner Harun Farid shared a similar story. As he was driving around one afternoon in 1977, a well-groomed tree in front of a house for sale caught his eye. Stopping the car, he and his white American wife, Elizabeth, spoke with the owners and, impressed with their friendliness, looked at the inside of the house. Without any knowledge of square footage (it ended up being too small for their growing family) or repairs that may have been needed, they agreed to purchase the house in the Pompano Lane subdivision of Alief. Later, he judged his decision as "just stupidity." Harun said, "My wife still curses" that decision. "I was not very good with the real estate." Otherwise, he noted, they "could have bought a house in the central area" (such as Bellaire, Meyerland, or West University). The house never sold or appreciated much in value.[88] In 1981, Harun and Elizabeth placed the house for rent and moved to a "nicer," bigger house in another Alief subdivision. The new house cost them $200,000, and even though they considered it a strong investment, Harun lost his job during the recession, rendering the house payments a liability. In 1984, several house appraisals later, the couple was crestfallen to learn that appraisal estimates ranged between $110,000 and $120,000. They decided to sell the house themselves, rather than through a realtor, but this was a buyers' market. Eventually, a house-buying company bought it for even less than the appraisal price. Shaking his head, clearly still troubled by his experiences, Harun related that Houston went through a "devastation" that was "terrible." He repeated, "It was terrible."[89]

Aside from the financial losses sustained by Houstonians, Alief residents lamented other changes. Few interviewees employed the language of race when describing their decision-making process. Allusions to race surfaced only when immigrants reflected on how their Alief neighborhoods changed. After moving to Alief in 1970 because "Alief and Spring Branch were the two big school districts," Saumitra Kelkar lamented that both school districts had "gone bad" after the oil bust. He explained:

When all the companies went down, went from 2,000 people to 200 people ... those people were laid off so they left. ... So those apartment rates, apartments that [charged] $450 a month, went down. Within a year, they went down to $180. And with all these things, it's "one month free," and this and that. So all of a sudden, that thing, instead of being typical educated, white-collar workers, it became single parents or blue-collar workers and all that stuff. Then once that happened, then the school district went down, and then everything went down. So it's a vicious circle. [90]

But change in Alief was not just class-based, since, according to Kelkar, "most of the people that came in were either Hispanics or African American."[91] New neighbors, South Asians noted, seemed mostly to be African American and Hispanic, who were not white-collar workers. Kelkar observed that on their street alone, most of the original residents moved away. "Out of that twenty, there are only two people that are still there, everybody's gone." [92] Like Kelkar, Harun Farid noticed that the neighborhood slowly shifted from almost entirely white to majority "Hispanics." For him, this symbolized Alief's downturn.[93] "Older" residents, he said, kept "moving to the better places," and "the neighborhood went down a little bit." When asked to define "went down," Farid said, "it was almost 100 percent white" when they had moved there, though he quickly offered that the racial demographics were "not a question to me." Farid temporarily moved to other cities and even to Indonesia for two years when he found no employment in Houston, but he eventually returned. He estimated that by 2011, the population breakdown of his old neighborhood was roughly 70 percent Hispanic and 10 percent African American, with the rest white and Asian.

Because of the recession, Alief, once considered "hot" real estate, transitioned to "less desirable," at least for middle-income buyers. When realtor and former Alief resident Harsh Gil was asked about the current value of Alief as a buyers' market, he responded, "No, it's not a hot area."[94] The difference between desirable, attractive areas and others, according to Gil, hinged not only on property sales but also on race and ethnicity. Whereas during the 1980s "more whites" lived in Alief, by the 1990s, it had "become more [of a] mixed community. I see a lot of Chinese, Spanish, blacks, and whites." He added that in the 1980s, the "Mexican population was not so much as it is now." After the 1990s, he continued, the "percentage of whites may have gone down but otherwise, other communities are all there." In fact, Alief has been completely transformed within two decades from a professional, majority white and Asian American middle-class area to a working-class area composed of every major racial and ethnic group.[95] In addition, because of the chain migration of South Asian immigrants and the South Asian ethnic economy established in the early 1980s, that economy has flourished, as newer lower-middle-class and working-class South Asian immigrants replaced the former highly educated group. Today, a bustling, mature ethnic economy in Alief caters to the consumer needs of a more recent South Asian ethnic community, as well as to some original South Asian immigrant families who moved to Alief in the mid- to late-1970s.

The Recession and Racial Discourse regarding Public Schools

Although factors such as cost, location, and quality often affect desirability levels for a neighborhood, for many Americans, the perception of decreased value also aligns with the proportion of nonwhite residents and nonwhite students.[96] Neighborhoods and schools are among the most racialized spaces in American society, and because of school zoning, the two are entirely enmeshed. South Asian immigrants had prioritized their own education as a primary pathway to success, and consequently they emphasized public school quality in their neighborhood selection process. School quality maintained its importance for them as the recession changed the neighborhood demographics around them. Demographics in the metropolitan area and its school districts were undoubtedly affected by the effort to desegregate schools, but the role of immigration and the recession were also significant. The recession reinforced Houston's spatial distribution in some areas but triggered the wholesale transformation of others, strengthening assessments of the correlation between neighborhood and school quality. The influx of tens of thousands of immigrants from around the world in the 1970s but especially from Mexico and Asian countries diversified area school districts' racial profiles.

Recent sociological research shows that for white Americans, higher levels of parental education positively correspond with sending one's children to high-percentage-white schools.[97] Highly educated African Americans, on the other hand, choose schools that are diverse, with high academic standards and usually with a clear black majority.[98] Commensurate with their level of education, more highly educated white parents opt either to move to whiter neighborhoods with white-majority public schools or to privatize their children's schooling through private institutions or homeschooling.[99] Because the highly educated (regardless of racial background) already place a stronger emphasis on education, they use education both as a means to attain higher status and as a status marker in and of itself.

That is, education is cultural capital in two ways: it is both a vehicle for socioeconomic mobility and a claim to high status already. As a group, by the mid-1980s, South Asian immigrants had the highest level of education of any Asian immigrant group in the United States.[100] While 36 percent of South Asian immigrants held a Ph.D., by comparison, only 6.7 percent of white Americans, 13.9 percent of Chinese immigrants, and 13.1 percent of Korean immigrants had doctorate degrees. Indeed, fully 80 percent of South Asian immigrants had a college degree, versus 35 percent of whites, 45 percent of Chinese immigrants, and 64 percent of Korean immigrants who were college educated.[101]

By enrolling their children in majority white schools, South Asian immigrant parents aided them in maintaining class privilege based on perceived superiority in education. Creating distance from black students ensured that their children's status would remain untainted, in parents' eyes. For these parents, black-majority schools were not under consideration. Indian and Pakistani parents associated high-percentage-black schools with "bad" schools, which were those perceived to have discipline problems, a weak learning environment, and "black culture." In their perception, those schools could not have met their requirements. In transitioning from a "good" to "bad" school, the first indication to parents was that "first of all, the discipline became bad," meaning that there was an escalation in disciplinary infractions.[102] Saumitra Kelkar recounted the story of his college-aged daughter, who had recently visited her former high school teacher. The teacher discouraged her former student from visiting the school; instead they met at a restaurant. The teacher informed her that the Alief high school she had once attended had installed metal detectors to curb the presence of knives and guns in school. Fights and drug use had escalated among the student body. Still disturbed by memory of this transition, Kelkar said, "Just like that, it went from a top school to the bottom school. It's really very different. I mean there are still some good, smart students. I'm not saying that every student is bad, that's not what I'm saying, but as a group, it became . . . the emphasis was not on schooling and learning and all that stuff."[103] Alief resident Bina Parmar noted that although Alief schools used to be "very good," as she understood it, students in more recent years were heavily involved in "drugs and crimes and all these things."[104] Her main concerns were related to disciplinary infractions and providing a safe environment for children.[105]

One of the key characteristics assigned to blackness by both South Asian Americans and other Americans was a decided lack of commitment to education. Saumitra Kelkar suggested that African Americans "as a rule, they don't view education with as much importance as Asians do, whether it's Indian, Vietnamese, Chinese. . . . They [African Americans] just want athletics and entertainment."[106] Kelkar knew that not *all* African Americans ascribed to these aspirations. As he said (haltingly, as is often the case when interviewees attempted to speak about race), "They still are—there are some—and I have—one of my colleagues is African [American] and he's a very smart kid and his kids are very smart, so that's not the point." His point was that supposedly, the majority of African Americans were not invested in education, even though he knew that there were some exceptional individuals. Likewise, throughout his interview, Suresh Bhatt spoke with clarity and insight about South Asian perceptions. He was upfront about "all kinds of stereotyping that goes on" with regard to African Americans and Hispanics, expressing indignation that this was the case.[107] Others, as well, expressed the same indignation but struggled to extricate themselves fully from racialization processes. This paradox—the intersection of being implicated in a racial system as an economically privileged member but also as an outsider who in varying degrees sympathizes with other persons of color—characterizes the position of many South Asian immigrants.

Summing up the key reasons for what he saw as African Americans' failure to demonstrate a lifelong commitment to education, Indian immigrant Rohan Patil explained:

> Those problems that we hear people talk about, politicians talk about that. . . . Right from the start, their focus on education has not been there in the families, and this needs to happen right from when you are growing up. African American families, I also noticed a lot of times they would be single parent families and so from a . . . right from the family structure it seemed like, that there was not much of a focus on education. And hence, for that reason, you wouldn't . . . we didn't see any African Americans in the graduate student community."[108]

Patil reveals that his racial ideas were learned from "people" and "politicians." He linked blackness with broken families and educational disinvestment. Echoing ideas widespread in American society, Patil believed that a problematic black culture produces educational underperformance or failure. He seemed unaware of and unable to make the connection between the absence of African Americans in his graduate program and the repercussions of segregation on public and higher education.

By comparison, immigrants described the middle class as "better involved" in their children's education, giving them "good training," and residing in "good" neighborhoods. In their eyes, these behaviors resulted in having "good" kids who made schools "good."[109] In the 1980s most students at Alief's Elsik High School, by Ashok and Lata Dani's accounting, were white with some Indians and Chinese. In the Danis' view, African American social problems were linked to both race and class. Ashok explained that more problems "happen[ed] in [the] lower income group," whose "lifestyle is different, atmosphere is different" and among whom "gangsters" dominate. Ashok continued, if one belongs to the class of people who works, then you are "family people," and "you don't [experience] any bad things." There is a tension between the Danis' assigning blame to race or to class; on one hand, they believed that class disadvantages exacerbated aberrant behaviors, but on the other, they imagined that these problems were closely intertwined with blackness.

Saumitra Kelkar explained how the Alief school district changed for the worse since the recession: "Before . . . the kids' parents were college-educated people so naturally, they expected their kids to do well in school. Now all of the sudden you've got the people who are either high school [graduates] or high school drop-outs, so even though they may" say that they support their children's education, they "were not able to enforce" this commitment. Their "kids would say, 'Well, you didn't go to college.'"[110] In other words, they did not serve as positive role models for their children. Middle-class children, on the other hand, prioritized education because their "family concept was different, kids were different. They concentrated on studies. They were not dropouts or anything."[111] South Asian immigrants' children, interviewees stated, personified academic commitment.

The perception of a "gang problem" in public schools, generally, served as a rationale to enroll children in elite private schools or move to suburban school districts, buying the perceived protection that a middle or higher income could afford.[112] Hearing about "gang-related stuff" in public schools in the late 1970s, Hemant Chokshi enrolled his children in private schools from elementary school onward even though his children were zoned to Katy ISD, a majority white school district in the far western suburbs of Houston. He explained that "they have done extremely well and they have gone to Ivy League schools and all of that." When Suresh Bhatt moved to a racially diversifying neighborhood in southwest Houston in the mid-1980s, he and his wife quickly decided that "the schools in that neighborhood were not very good."[113] They enrolled their young daughter at St. Thomas Episcopal, an elite parochial private school, bypassing the local public schools that served a growing African American and Latino/a population. Their daughter remained at St. Thomas through eighth grade. Meanwhile, the family moved to Sugar Land (a suburb discussed in the next chapter), and for ninth grade, they enrolled their daughter at Kempner High School, a public school in Sugar Land. She enjoyed her first day there, and her parents withdrew her enrollment at St. Thomas. Saumitra Kelkar explained that suburban flight increased after the recession "because those who were white-collar workers, they were moving to Sugar Land or Katy. So that's what happened is all the white-collar workers were moving where the school districts were good, so they were going to Katy or Sugar Land on this side, or Clear Lake or wherever it was."[114]

Among racial groups in the United States, South Asian immigrants perceived other Asians to be the most academically competitive. For example, Kelkar continued, for "European Americans . . . even thirty years ago, education was not as dominant as it was in Asian communities and it is still not there." Nevertheless, Kelkar continued, European Americans exhibited greater educational focus, according to most South Asian immigrants, than "Africans or Hispanics." As a point of pride, Ashok Dani noted that Asians, while the children of foreigners, constituted the "top layer, academically" in schools. He continued, "so our students—outsiders—Indians and Chinese, they are continuing first, top. The Hispanic and other people, they are considered average." He considered Indians and Chinese as academically on par with each other. Simply put, "Asians especially" were "doing better" than others.[115] As echoed by other interviewees, Bina

Parmar pointed out that, in terms of educational accomplishments such as high school class rankings and test scores, "our people are first." This was possible because South Asian immigrants "are taking care of education" by "giv[ing] more time to kids for education."[116] Hemant Chokshi, who enrolled his children in private schools throughout their grade school years, explained: "Education is such an important part of the Asian culture, not only just in India but Pakistan, Bangladesh, China, it is very important, education is very important. Even as youngsters I would be telling them, 'Hey you've got to do at least your master's.' It's programmed in me. That's what [my wife] did, that's what I did, and education is what is going to make you successful."[117] For Chokshi, Parmar, and others, Asians seemed to value education in ways that other ethnoracial groups did not. In addition, they prioritized child-rearing and familism above other values. Parmar stated, "We were more family oriented" and "gave more time to [our] kids. [We spent more time] talking with the kids" about school, classes, their friends, and teachers. In addition, South Asian immigrant parents actively participated in school life by getting to know their children's teachers and going to their children's school "every week or two," according to Parmar. Parents like her wanted to "help [our] kids do something better."[118]

When Ashok Dani spoke above of racial group performance in schools, he referred to himself and others of Asian descent as "outsiders."[119] Dani's use of the term "outsider" conveys his own understanding of himself and his second-generation Asian American children as immigrants and as a defined, Asian American panethnic group. Regardless of how his South Asian American children identified, Dani nevertheless perceived a difference. From his perspective, not only were immigrants outsiders, but their children were also outsiders, supporting the notion of Asian Americans as "forever foreigners." This status was confirmed by an externally imposed marking of difference as well as an internally informed sense of similar values. While Dani found this outsider status problematic, like other Asian immigrants, he expressed pride in the educational accomplishments of Asian American youth, precisely *because* of their outsider status; they had excelled in a system in which they were a minority.

South Asian parents regarded other racialized groups as distinctly unlike them academically and culturally. Other children, in Bina Parmar's assessment, grew up "differently."[120] Their "parents were very busy and they didn't take care of their kids. That was also a big problem because most of these kids were staying home, and they were watching TV and all these things. They didn't get enough education and enough love in their house." Parmar interpreted South Asian parents' educational support as a powerful expression of love. Saumitra Kelkar clarified in regard to African Americans specifically that, rather than invest efforts in education and achieve material success that way, they risk lesser odds of success through athletics and entertainment: "With athletics and all of that, all you get is one busted knee, your athleticism is over. I mean not every singer gets a chance to be in the right recording system. But that they don't realize." He concluded that they "have a big, big problem."[121]

In trying to explain why they understood the African Americans in their narratives as deprioritizing education, some alluded to class imperatives as shown above. Others said that African American youth were unusually attracted to the status and fame of professional athletics and entertainment. Kelkar suggested that in comparing educational attainment versus the sports or entertainment, young African Americans would say, "'Well, he's a Ph.D. and he has written ten books . . . so what?'" whereas, if "he's an NBA player or he's a golfer or whatever, he's on the screen, and everybody is running around [him]. It's the glamour of Beyoncé, you know, she's singing and dancing. Just everybody looks at her."[122] Ultimately, though, Kelkar believed that African Americans have as much natural ability to succeed in school. He explained that they exhibited a low regard for educational attainment because "the majority of them, they just don't want to put the effort into it."

A few interviewees linked their perception of weak educational values among African Americans to financial hardships. Bina Parmar stated that African Americans "are also very good, but I don't know, they are not giving that much time to kids, it looks like." Because "they have so much hardship," in terms of working "minimum pay" jobs and they have to "work more," Parmar continued, they were unable to devote time to instill educational values in their children. Thus, Parmar suggested that each generation was "very hardworking" but did not use education as a ladder out of poverty. Also, repeating the damaging Reagan era stereotype of the single, poor African American mother with too many children, Parmar explained that because "they have more kids," they perpetuate the cycle of low educational attainment. She argued that, unlike African Americans who "don't put limits" on the number of children they have, Indian immigrants' choice to have smaller families contributes to their ability to teach their children the priority of academic excellence.[123]

Conversely, Parmar was the only interviewee to reason that many South Asian immigrants had implicit advantages of growing up in educated families. They could provide their children with material comforts and greater hands-on parenting time while teaching them the value of educational focus—unlike, as she understood it, less-privileged families. Parmar hinted at a "time" when African Americans were separated (she seemed to be referring to segregation) from others and struggled to "mingle" with outsiders, so that "they were also afraid from other people about 'how do we mix' [with them]. That was also hard for them."

Conclusion

Suburban flight became an established residential trend among middle-class Houstonians, intensifying in the 1970s as a result of school desegregation and perpetuated in the 1980s by the oil bust. Because white flight had become conventional among the upwardly mobile, white middle class, it gained legitimacy with the rest of the middle class.[124] Indian and Pakistani immigrants adopted a range of residential settlement options in both urban and suburban spaces over time. However, the high concentrations of South Asian residence in key suburbs, represented here by Southwest Houston and Alief, embedded neighborhood selection within racial and class discourses. South Asian immigrants' reasons for moving to these areas both remained constant and changed during these decades.

At first, immigrants embraced the class prerogatives of others in their income group. As more immigrants followed into these neighborhoods through ethnic word-of-mouth networks, proximity to coethnics emerged as an appealing social dynamic. Still, this factor could not offset the effect of so many working-class residents of color eventually moving into the vicinity. Indian and Pakistani Americans closely associated neighborhood decline with the influx of African Americans and, to a lesser extent, Hispanics. As echoed by so many immigrants, once a neighborhood "went down," then the "whole area has become more African American."[125] That a neighborhood's land and property value may have already decreased was less crucial than the different racialized groups who increasingly inhabited the neighborhood.

Ultimately, South Asian immigrants decided that Alief was "just like Houston now, it's not anything different."[126] As new neighbors replaced old, South Asians felt certain of increased crime. Although Saumitra Kelkar and his family were not victimized by crime; nevertheless, "every day you hear about it," whether "on that corner somebody shot somebody" or "at this gas station somebody shot somebody." [127] For most Alief residents, these demographic changes demanded a dramatic response. Whereas in the mid-1980s, established residents in their private conversations lamented the presence of a "different" type of neighbor, by the end of the decade, they would protest with their feet by moving away. To be sure, some early Indian and Pakistani immigrants remained in Alief, joined by a continual influx of recent immigrants, especially after housing prices collapsed. Many, however, moved elsewhere. After thirty years in the neighborhood, Rustom Mistri and his wife were seriously considering moving, most likely, they say, to Sugar Land. Once South Asian immigrants had determined that Alief schools had declined in quality, many Indian and Pakistani families relocated to affluent, majority white Sugar Land.

· ·

CHAPTER SIX

FINDING WHITER AND BROWNER PASTURES

IN THE ETHNOBURBS,

1990S–2000S

The suburbs emerged as an unexpectedly prominent site in the narrative of South Asian immigrant settlement. In the late 2010s, immigrants from the Indian subcontinent continued to live mostly in the suburbs west/southwest and north/northwest of Houston. An overwhelming majority of interviewees for this project—all chosen for their date of migration to Houston between 1960 and 1980—live in the suburbs. They moved to a suburb as soon as they could afford it, often within three or four years of arrival in the United States. When asked why they chose to live in these areas, the usual desiderata included good schools, proximity to work, friends who lived nearby, or a coworker's or friend's recommendation of a "good neighborhood." Any mention of race was conspicuously absent; however, as shown earlier, South Asians reveal both intention and meaning when they note that a particular neighborhood is "good," especially when other options for neighborhoods are closer to work. As explained in the previous chapter, the term "good" is not an empty signifier; rather, it reflects social aspirations, cultural fears, and material accessibility. Like white Americans, professionalized South Asians in Houston have historically avoided economically diverse and heavily nonwhite neighborhoods, preferring professional, majority white suburbs as home.

The suburbs to which early South Asian immigrants have moved over the past forty years have been consistent with the settlement patterns of white Houstonians in similar income brackets.[1] As engineers and physicians (among other white-collar professions), they followed the consumption patterns of other middle-class professional Americans who were mostly white, by living in majority white neighborhoods. Concerns for safety, property values, efficient public services, and competitive public education have led many middle-income city dwellers of all races and ethnicities out to Houston's suburbs. Similarly, newcomers to Houston after the 1970s frequently bypassed the city altogether, opting outright to live in the suburbs.[2] At the same time, the language of race and class explicitly marked the process of migration to the fringes of the city and beyond.

Suburbanization in the form of white and brown flight did not occur as a general pattern from the city to the suburbs, however. Rather, middle-class Houstonians moved in a targeted manner to preferred suburban neighborhoods that upheld socioeconomic hierarchies and fulfilled their aspirations. For immigrants of color, however, suburban flight also continued to facilitate the formation of new ethnic enclaves—ethnoburbs. With Houston's depressed economy heralding widespread neighborhood change, the racially whiter and browner pastures sought by middle-class Houstonians occupied a fluid space. Once located in Sharpstown and then in Alief, suburbia for the affluent was then relocated to Sugar Land, a southwesterly suburb of Houston. Race and class dimensions marked each of these spaces, and as those dimensions shifted, so did suburban space itself.

Contextualizing Suburbanization Trends

Americans may have worked in urban areas, but they often opted to live in suburban neighborhoods in detached, self-owned homes, with ample yard space and, more important, generous distance between their residence and the perceived and real dangers of the city.[3] Whereas in 1950 only 23 percent of the population of the United States resided in the suburbs, by 1980, over 40 percent did so—a greater population percentage than urban, exurban, or rural residents.[4] By 2000, that proportion had increased to 50 percent. Americans prefer to live in the suburbs, embracing its "high maintenance and long[er] commute" in exchange for larger homes in deed-restricted neighborhoods and, of course, as a result of historical events such as the desegregation of schools and neighborhoods.[5] Most Americans continue to choose the suburban periphery over the urban core.

Some scholars have predicted that gentrification—the economic revitalization of otherwise undervalued areas—suggests a national return to urban living. However, since 1990, suburban and exurban trends have continued to outpace rates of gentrification. The Houston metropolitan area provides a case in point. Houston experienced an increase of over 938,000 new residents from 1990 to 2000, of whom only 323,000 decided to live within the city limits. A majority— 65.6 percent, or 615,000—moved to the suburbs.[6] Nationally, 84 percent of metropolitan expansion between 1990 and 2000 occurred in the suburbs, rather than in gentrifying areas within the city.[7] In Houston, gentrification rates increased substantially between 2000 and 2010, but so did the pace of

TABLE 5. Comparative city, county, and metropolitan population data for Houston, 1970 and 2010.

	1970 Population Total	Percentage White		Percentage Black		Percentage Hispanic		Percentage Asian		2010 Population Total
		1970	2010	1970	2010	1970	2010	1970	2010	
SMSA	1.9 million	70	40	20	17	9*	35	**	7	5.9 million
Harris	1.7 million	70	33	20	18	9*	41	**	6	4.1 million
Houston	1.2 million	70	26	20	23	9*	44	**	6	2.1 million

Notes: All percentages are rounded to whole values. Harris County is the default geographic level for Houston census data in 1970. The city of Houston boundaries roughly correlated with the county borders.

 * "Hispanic" was not a separate category in the 1970 census; those who identified as such were counted as whites. Other 1970 census categories used to determine the population of Hispanics in Houston include "Spanish Origin and Descent," "Native Born of Foreign Stock," and "Foreign Born."

** Data not available because of small population size.

Sources: Social Explorer; U.S. Census; City of Houston Planning Department.

suburbanization, fueled especially by real estate developers and newcomers to the city.[8]

Although the Greater Houston area is often celebrated as a fantastically diverse metropolis, a closer analysis along different geographic lines complicates this narrative, bringing to light alternative possibilities. As of 2010, Houston's standard metropolitan statistical area (SMSA) of 9,432 square miles encompassed Harris County (1,778 square miles), which contains virtually the entirety of the city of Houston (655 square miles).[9] The Houston SMSA also includes eight other counties and several incorporated cities. Houston SMSA-level data is used to promote the idea of a diverse, multiethnic, tolerant Houston; when referring to "Houston," journalists and others routinely cite data using the Houston-SMSA census category. It is this category that is used to proudly state that Houston is the fourth largest city in the country, and for consistency, the same "SMSA" category is usually employed regarding other large metropolitan areas (such as Chicago and Los Angeles). Casually citing the 2010 SMSA statistics (40 percent white, 17 percent black, 35 percent Hispanic, 7 percent

Asian) to bolster claims of Houston's diversity, however, is misleading. It elides major divisions along residential lines, in particular the city-suburb boundary. It also elides change over time, which, when accounted for, suggests something rather less than "diversity." Finally, as it celebrates racial diversity, it overlooks the patterns of economic inequity that continue to divide Houston's residents.

Houston's example starkly illustrates the multifaceted meanings and significance of suburbanization—a process rooted, to be sure, in federal policy and economics but just as much in racial structure. A narrowing spatial focus on the white population is particularly illuminating. A comparison of demographic data for 1970 and 2010 shows that at the SMSA level, the metropolis is diverse and balanced (table 5).[10] Also, in 1970, the city, county, and SMSA covered roughly the same area and so reflected similar data. Where the SMSA population was once overwhelmingly (70 percent) white, that decreased in 2010 to 40 percent, with generously sized black and Hispanic populations and a growing Asian-descent population. At the city level, however, the city of Houston was only 26 percent white in 2010—a significant drop from the SMSA level of 40 percent. In 1960, whites made up 79 percent of Houston residents, but by 1980, 52 percent of Houston's residents were white. By 2000, only 30 percent remained, and in 2010, a mere 25.6 percent of Houstonians were white.[11]

Not only has the percentage of whites in the city of Houston consistently fallen, but so too have the raw numbers of white residents. Granted, the proportion of white residents relative to new immigrants of color was bound to decrease as newcomers from Latin America and Asia made Houston their home from the 1970s. Still, after peaking in 1970, *the actual numbers of white residents in the city itself has continually fallen* from just over 1 million in 1970 to roughly 538,000 in 2010.[12] That is, only 538,000 whites out of a total white SMSA population of 2.5 million choose to live within the city of Houston. Each decade since the 1960s has seen appreciable reductions in the white population, with the 1990s showing an 11.5 percent drop. Hundreds of thousands of whites have settled in the suburbs, outside the city limits, fortifying the city-suburb racial divide. Seventy-three percent of all whites in the Houston area resided in the suburbs in 2000, mostly in neighborhoods with low rates of integration.[13] The residential patterns of middle-class South Asian Houstonians (both immigrant and native-born) merged with the dominant pattern of white flight to Houston's suburbs.

Some possible explanations for the steadily declining white population inside the city limits have already been proposed. Desegregation of schools and neighborhoods played a crucial role. The city's school district, Houston Independent School District, roughly corresponds with the city limits. In suburban families' perceptions, HISD schools remain an essential marker of the city-suburb divide. Middle-class families choosing to suburbanize take into serious consideration the school district to which potential neighborhoods are zoned. In addition, as noted previously, developers and builders invested in new housing developments in a continually shifting suburban zone, attracting old and new Houstonians in the process.

Other major demographic changes may likely have contributed as well. The most obvious was the growth of the Hispanic population in the city of Houston, which though small in 1970, reached 44 percent, or over 919,000, out of total city population of about 2.1 million in 2010 (see Appendix maps 9, 11).[14] By that time, the Asian population—mainly Vietnamese and Chinese with a sizable South Asian component—mushroomed to 6 percent, or about 129,000.[15] In all, in 2010, over 20 percent of the Houston metropolitan area was foreign-born. The black population of the city shows a slight increase in its proportion over time. Where African Americans were once 20 percent of the city population in 1970, in 2010, they were 23 percent. But when compared to their 17 percent distribution across the entire SMSA in 2010, they became much more concentrated in the city.[16] By 2010, people of color vastly outnumbered Houston's white population both because of the increase in nonwhites and because of whites actively moving out of the city or bypassing the city limits altogether.

Levels of residential racial integration are yet another tool through which we can understand social hierarchies over time. Comparative demographic research on residential segregation at the national and local levels corroborates other detailed studies of white hostility toward even the idea of residence alongside black neighbors. Over the past forty years, although segregation between African Americans and whites has slightly decreased nationally, "blacks and black immigrants continue to be more segregated from whites than other groups."[17] Illustrations of the spatial distribution of African Americans and Hispanics in Houston over time and Houston-specific research on residential self-segregation show that whites usually prefer to live in neighborhoods with a ceiling of 20 percent African American or Hispanic residents (see Appendix maps 8–11).[18] Even when neighborhoods boast low crime rates, high-quality schools, and high housing values—the most commonly cited reasons for choosing a neighborhood—when asked, whites in Houston express a preference for largely non-black and non-Hispanic neighborhoods. Regarding the presence of Asians in a neighborhood, whites in Houston exhibit no negative preference at all.[19] In other words, whites do not mind living in a neighborhood with Asians but *do* mind living in a neighborhood with more than a 20 percent black or Hispanic population. Urban histories of San Francisco and Los Angeles also bear this out, concluding that Asian Americans are the least segregated group (into majority-white residential areas) of all people of color, while African Americans remain the most segregated.[20]

The patterns of South Asian American residential settlement from 1980 to 2010 show a nearly identical trajectory to whites.[21] In 1980, the U.S. Census first recognized Asian Indians, but not Pakistanis (a much smaller group), as a distinct category. In that year, they map precisely onto white areas of settlement, with exceptions for the University of Houston and the Texas Medical Center, where more Asian Indians (and, by proxy, Pakistani Americans) resided either temporarily as students and medical residents or permanently as employees (see maps 4 and 5).[22] Neighborhood clustering is already evident in Sharpstown, Alief, and Spring Branch in 1980. A decade later, while other suburban neighborhood clusters are very evident (for example, Missouri City, Clear Lake, and northwest Houston), the largest concentration of South Asian Americans is in Alief and neighboring far-southwest Houston (map 6). Maps for settlement patterns for 2010, the most recent year for which census data are available, show even more widespread suburbanization in the far west (Katy, near Interstate 10), southwest, and northwest sections of Houston and in new suburbs in Pearland, directly south of the city limits (map 7).

The overwhelmingly heaviest settlement of South Asians was in Sugar Land and neighboring Missouri City. A comparison of Houston and Sugar Land shows that while Asians made up 6 percent of Houston residents in 2010, over 35 percent of Sugar Land's inhabitants were Asian.[23] Of the Asian population, Indians and Pakistanis collectively constituted the largest percentage of all Asians in Sugar Land.[24] Vast areas of southwest and particularly west Houston essentially remain white and, increasingly, Asian American. Several large swaths of west Houston house few Hispanics and African Americans at all (see Appendix maps 10 and 11).

One notable difference between Asian Indian and white patterns is Asian Indians' preference for concentrated ethnic residential clustering. Emerging in 1980 throughout southwest Houston in Sharpstown, Fondren Southwest, and Alief, such clustering is even more pronounced thirty years later in Sugar Land, Missouri City, and, to a lesser extent, Alief and Mission Bend. As with maps 4 and 6, the city-suburb divide is also extremely apparent in 2010 (map 7).

A comparison of racial stratification and aggregate income between 1970 and 2010 across the Houston metropolitan area suggests that the concentration of poverty coincided first with the city core, then directly northeast of downtown, and with one pocket to the south of downtown (see Appendix map 12).[25] By 1990 residents of the city core and northeast Houston continued to earn the lowest incomes in the metropolitan area, whereas the wealthiest residents continued to occupy areas west and far southeast (that is, Clear Lake and the

MAP 6. Comparative spatial distribution of Asian Indian and white populations, 1990.

White Population
- <1,500
- 1,501–3,000
- 3,001–5,000
- 5,000–10,000
- >10,000
- Insufficient Data

Asian Indian
- ● 5 People
- — Harris County
- — City of Houston

Sources: City of Houston GIS; Census 1990.

MAP 7. Comparative spatial distribution of Asian Indian and white populations, 2010.

White Population
- <1,500
- 1,501–3,000
- 3,001–5,000
- 5,000–10,000
- >10,000
- Insufficient Data

Asian Indian
- ● 5 People
- — Harris County
- City of Houston

Sources: City of Houston GIS; ACS 2010.

NASA area) of the city. Residents in affluent areas thus resided largely in the west and southwest portions of the city, and for them, the line between urban and suburban ran north to south, dividing the city into halves, rather than *around* the city core, dividing the city by concentric circles.[26] The underlying logic—that of an urban versus suburban imaginary—nevertheless obtains. This is certainly the case for the Greater Houston area despite a deficit in public housing and even after accounting for specific pockets of inner city affluence such as Bellaire, West University, River Oaks, and the vicinity of the Texas Medical Center.

The key suburbs for this study—the suburbs of Houston where so many middle-class South Asian immigrants chose to live—have remained strikingly uniform over time in terms of racial and economic composition. The overall diversity of urban-to-suburban migration, however, can foster a false sense of racial integration. As whites and South Asians moved to the suburbs, so too did middle-class African Americans and Hispanics. Nationally, by 1999, 31 percent of all African Americans lived in America's suburbs.[27] Similarly, 51 and 54 percent of Asians and whites, respectively, and 44 percent of Hispanics lived in the suburbs.[28] The movement of Houston's minorities to the suburbs has mirrored this national trend. However, while all racial groups have a strong suburban presence, all racial groups do not live in the same suburbs together. Rather, multiracial, integrated neighborhoods increased by only 2 percent in Houston from 1980 to 2000.[29] Furthermore, whites showed much greater resistance to living in white-black neighborhoods than in white-Latino/a neighborhoods during the same time period. Only 1 percent of all neighborhoods in Houston were black-white in 2000, down from 6 percent in 1980.[30]

The general trend has been one of minimal progress toward actual integration. Instead, what has transpired, first, is that people of color groups (black, Latino/a, and Asian American) have clustered together residentially, leading some conservative commenters to declare that integration has been achieved and that the era of segregated cities has ended.[31] Second, though whites have been more inclined to share residential spaces with Asian Americans and Latino/as, they have been decidedly disinclined to do so with African Americans. So, in some ways, there has been greater integration—mostly among various groups of color—but in other, equally significant and troubling ways, segregation persists.

Finding Another Ethnic Enclave: Sugar Land

Asked where he would advise recent Pakistani and Indian immigrants in Houston to move, realtor Harsh Gil responded, "Honestly, I will advise them Sugar Land." His first reason was that they had "good schools," after which he noted that they also have a strong police department, newer homes, and a convenient location relative to Houston.[32] A popular suburb today, Sugar Land—of recent country music and distant sugar production fame—lies nineteen miles southwest of Houston's downtown. Its ubiquitous red-brick buildings, master-planned communities, spacious roadways, and manicured landscaping appealed to middle-class Houstonians.

Incorporated in 1959, the city of Sugar Land was established on land originally a part of the Republic of Mexico and granted to Stephen F. Austin in 1836.[33] It grew quickly on profits from the cultivation and refining of cane sugar grown in the nearby Brazos River slave plantations. Sugar cultivation ranked among the harshest of all Atlantic World plantation industries in its treatment of enslaved peoples. After emancipation, the labor source for Sugar Land's sugar industry drew on incarcerated men (mostly African American) at the local prison through the state-supported convict-lease system (a program noted for its brutality and high rates of mortality).[34] Sugar Land was also the location of large corn and cotton agricultural enterprises. By the mid-1980s, its main industries still included sugar but had expanded to tools, industrial parts, and oilfield services.[35] Major Sugar Land companies employing a large number of local engineers included Schlumberger and Fluor Corporation, which proved convenient for South Asian American engineers.[36]

More than its local industry, however, Sugar Land appealed to South Asians for many of the same reasons that did Alief over a decade earlier. "There's one reason why Sugar Land has" so many South Asians, insisted Vinod Prakash: "schools." Sugar Land has a "good education system. Fort Bend ISD, Clements, Dulles, all the high schools. That's it. Nobody cares [about] anything else. It's education." For Prakash, good schools were defined as those that had "good students, good peers." South Asian immigrants sought schools with students who had like-minded parents or, as he put it, "professional" parents—parents who had achieved material success largely through the attainment of higher education and who reinforced the same expectations for their children. It was a "combination" of this professional slant and the presence of academically strong peers that contributed to an "overall environmental psyche, so to speak." He concluded, "That's why there are so many" South Asians in Sugar Land.[37]

In casual conversation with other South Asian Americans across the United States, "Sugar Land" is a recognizable entity, part of a shared ethnic geography. "Everybody has some uncle, auntie, or friend in Sugar Land," they say. South Asian Houstonians who live away from Sugar Land often evoke the suburb when referring to the "Indian-Pakistani community." It is considered a hub of social activity with the most concentrated cluster of South Asian Americans in the Houston metropolitan area.[38] Since at least 2000, South Asian Americans along with East Asian Americans have emerged as a recognizable minority presence in this suburb. Nagaraj Shekhar, a Sugar Land resident originally from Chennai, observed, "Take Sugar Land, for example. Or Alief. Everybody lives everywhere."[39] Comparing South Asian immigrants in London, where he had lived in the late 1960s, versus those in the Houston area in the early 2000s, Shekhar noted that in England, "there was a big gap between the people from Pakistan and people from India," but in the Sugar Land, Indians and Pakistanis coexisted within the same cultural milieu, despite their differences.[40] While this may be an oversimplification, by saying that they are everywhere, Shekhar employed the notion of a shared South Asian identity that collapsed national boundaries between groups, allowing for the diffusion of potential political tension. He saw them, at least in this context, as part of a single, large, imagined community sharing similar cultural and physical spaces together, rather than in a separate "Pakistani commune or Indian commune." Shekhar was also reflecting on the high proportion of Indians, Pakistanis, and, more recently, Bangladeshis in the suburban ethnic enclaves of Sugar Land and Alief.

South Asians from India, Pakistan, and Bangladesh comprised a small but rapidly growing minority in Sugar Land between 1980 and 2000, with Bangladeshis among the more recent arrivals.[41] After 1980, Asians were by far the suburb's fastest-growing racial group, whereas, for the sake of comparison, the African American population grew by only 2 percent. The Asian population flourished, drawn by the thousands to Sugar Land's subdivisions with names like Sienna Plantation, First Colony, Plantation Bend, and Sugar Mill—which simultaneously evoke and elide Sugar Land's historical reliance on enslaved labor. Their numbers increased sharply after 2000, commensurate with the growth of the city itself; between 1980 and 2000, the population of Sugar Land expanded from 12,500 to 63,000.[42] In 2017, the population was nearly 79,000, of which 35 percent were Asian. By comparison, the city of Houston's Asian population was over 6 percent. Within the Asian population, South Asians were the largest combined subgroup, constituting over 40 percent of all Asians in Sugar Land. In Sugar Land, whites were roughly 50 percent, and African Americans only 7 percent in 2017, while the Hispanic population also remained small.[43] But for the now-shuttered Imperial Sugar factory, Sugar Land was virtually unrecognizable as a former plantation and company town.

In Sugar Land, South Asian immigrants sought and found the very features that had initially attracted immigrants to Alief in the early 1980s: high-performing public schools, professional neighbors, and a low crime rate. Although many of their children were now in college, South Asian immigrants still associated "good schools" with higher home values and a "family-oriented" resident profile. Through their experience in Alief, they came to appreciate the advantages of living near other coethnics. After 1990, as the appeal of Alief dissipated, they joined thousands of other new immigrants from India, Pakistan, and Bangladesh in Sugar Land to produce a new suburban ethnic enclave—a new ethnoburb. Meanwhile, new Pakistani and Indian families moved to Alief, continuing the process initiated in the mid-1970s. The main differences between these two neighboring South Asian communities (Alief and Sugar Land) are levels of income and educational attainment, as well as year of entry to the United States. Middle-class South Asians established ethnic enclaves in relatively affluent suburbs such as Alief in the 1970s and Sugar Land in the 1990s, seeking "good" schools in "desirable" middle-class, majority white neighborhoods—the same values evoked in white flight. However, in addition to the determinants of class and race, brown flight also accounted for ethnicity in a way that southern white flight did not.

A significant reason for ethnic clustering and brown flight was the need for safe spaces—that is, physical spaces where, because of substantial coethnic population concentration, Asian Americans felt at home. Early ethnic clustering in Alief and Sugar Land served a dual purpose. First, it facilitated ethnic community building, as coethnics assumed the responsibilities of an extended family. Second, it offered ethnic community members a sense of belonging in a dominant social landscape that indexed difference (based on "foreignness") above similarity. Ethnic residential clustering by immigrants of color reflected an attempt to mitigate the effects of social exclusion by a white majority. South Asian immigrants were tolerated by their white neighbors mostly without incident, but relationships with white neighbors often extended no further than front yard pleasantries. That is, most South Asian immigrants sensed a lack of interest in fraternizing beyond the yard. Interviewees frequently commented on the social distance their white neighbors exhibited toward them. With coethnics, those same relationships evolved into deeper, meaningful friendships. Obviously, shared cultural norms (whether real or perceived) with coethnics created a sense of familiarity, but in addition, immigrants of color chose to residentially cluster in spaces where they could minimize racial hostility.

South Asian Immigrants and the Recent
Construction of Ethnic Identity

While movement to the urban fringes of the modern Sunbelt South reveals the embedded nature of class and race hierarchies, for immigrants of color, suburban ethnic enclaves such as Sugar Land also offered safe, empowering spaces in which immigrants created a sense of belonging. Between the 1990s and the early 2000s, South Asians built an extensive ethnic infrastructure in

Sugar Land, complete with a well-developed ethnic economy and ethnic institutions. A casual drive through the commercial areas of the small city quickly
reveals Indian and Pakistani restaurants, Indo-Pak grocery stores, clothing
boutiques, party halls, beauty salons, and dance schools. In addition, South
Asian women—especially those who work as homemakers—run home-based
businesses. These include but are by no means limited to food catering and the
sale of ethnic clothing. In Sugar Land (and Alief), ethnic entrepreneurship has
flourished, supported by a large ethnic community population.

While a survey of the full range of ethnic institutions in present-day Sugar
Land is beyond the scope of this project, this section considers the continuing process and meaning of ethnic identity building for long-established immigrants. By 2010, the endpoint for this study, interviewees had lived in the
United States from roughly thirty to fifty years. Ethnicity remained a defining layer of their identity, if anything, gaining in prominence over time. For
some immigrant parents, cultural ethnicity became a central tool for shaping
their children's identities, and they expressed this through emphasis on music,
dance, language, and dress. For others, religion and ethnicity converged, with
classes at local religious centers offering spiritual training for children (for
example, Saturday and Sunday schools) and youth group activities. Some immigrants in their retirement years turned with fresh interest to ethnicity as a
defining feature of their own lives. Now retired, apparently financially secure,
and with time to invest, many established immigrants exhibited a resurgent
enthusiasm in ethnic organizations and individual acts of ethnic expression.

South Asian cultural organizations have proliferated, reflecting the linguistic and regional heterogeneity of India and Pakistan from Punjab to Bihar to
Kerala. Many of these associations were founded in the 1980s and 1990s and
have since undergone major growth. Their activities include, among many
others, the opening of language and/or dance schools for children, commemo-
rating native festivals, and hosting music shows.[44] Their stated missions often
use language along the lines of "preserving and promoting our cultural heritage," however they choose to define and reconstruct that heritage. Some also
publish and distribute newsletters. Most host social events like picnics and dinners. Specialized activities, such as weekend schools or classes, cater to children, while other social outings support seniors.

South Asian immigrants have increased the number of institutions, both
religious and cultural, in suburban Houston. While they established several
religious institutions over the decades, after the 1990s, the number and variety
of institutions across Houston flourished. By 1990, South Asian religious organizations had purchased large warehouse-style buildings or former churches
that they converted and had erected a handful of purpose-built structures.

Early places of worship included rented units in shopping strip malls or even in apartment complexes. Now, they raised sufficient funds to erect purpose-built structures that served as mosques, temples, *gurdwaras, jamatkhanas,* and churches. Additionally, established immigrants' socioeconomic status ensured their place in the congregational leadership. Within a burgeoning South Asian immigrant population, those who arrived in the 1960s and 1970s were not just the most educated; because of their professional credentials, they were often among the most financially secure. Through the 1990s, the leadership and, to a significant extent, the membership of area mosques, temples, or other in-stitutions were highly educated, white-collar professionals. According to one study, members of the Meenakshi Temple in Pearland were "almost exclusively middle and upper-middle class."[45] According to another study, 72 percent of the members at the largest mosque in north Houston had completed a college degree or advanced degree, with many congregants occupationally concen-trated in engineering and medicine.[46] Leadership positions in religious (and secular) organizations afforded affluent South Asian immigrants the "political power, status, and recognition" denied to them in mainstream white society.[47]

These congregational worship spaces offered immigrants places in which to form and expand an often new collective religious identity. Where many South Asian immigrants were not particularly religious before migration, afterward, "for the first time they had to think about the meaning of their religion and religious identity, something they could take for granted in India" and Paki-stan.[48] Also, while they might have focused less on religion in the 1970s, after immigrants had children and those children came of age, religion emerged as a way of safeguarding them through their Indian or Pakistani "heritage" from the perceived dangers of what many South Asian parents viewed as an overly individualistic, hedonistic, and promiscuous American youth culture.[49] This was not very different from the rise of Christian fundamentalism, as well as social and political conservatism in 1980s America in response to the sweep-ing social changes of the 1960s and 1970s.[50] Finally, religion took on new im-portance for South Asians in the 1980s and 1990s as another bulwark against continued marginalization from mainstream society and politics. As Prema Kurien notes, community members "participate in the activities of the religious organizations because they experience marginality and intensified religious and nationalistic commitment as a consequence of immigration."[51] Because of the concentration of Pakistanis and Indians in Sugar Land, community mem-bers have opened several houses of worship there.

At the same time, the tremendous growth of the Greater Houston area's Pakistani and Indian populations has led to deepening divisions between In-dians and Pakistanis, faith groups, and linguistic subgroups. Many Indian and Pakistani Americans continue to maintain a keen interest in the politics of their homelands, driving a wedge into any unified American panethnicity. For example, long-established Pakistani Americans in Houston and elsewhere contributed funds to support former Pakistani president Pervez Musharraf's bid (in exile) for reelection in the early 2010s.[52] Prominent Indian Houstonians have spearheaded efforts to fund the Bharatiya Janata Party (BJP) in India via U.S.-based affiliated wings of the Rashtriya Swayamsevak Sangh, the BJP's parent organization.[53] In addition, some U.S.-born South Asian Americans have embraced religion anew, in no small part due to the efforts of their parents' generation in establishing faith-based schools and camps.[54] Sometimes this, too, disrupts the formation of panethnic identity.

Individually, established South Asian immigrants expressed ethnic identity by involvement in local associations and by maintaining connections abroad. Even as immigrants established lives and livelihoods in Houston, visiting India and Pakistan helped to maintain some of the deepest ties with their homeland. "We *have* to have a connection [to India], we *have* to go there," declared Bihar-born immigrant Tariq Rahman, "to talk to people."[55] Others who used to return at least twice a year in the 1970s and 1980s have had close family members move to the United States and so have had less of a reason to return to the subcontinent in recent years. Nadia Nazir, a woman who used to return to Karachi "very frequently," has recently reduced the frequency of her visits. She said, "Because of my parents [living here], I don't have a home to go to. I have friends, but it is nothing like parents. So, I really don't go that often anymore."[56] But, Nazir continues, even if rarely, to visit Pakistan. Another woman, Uma Krishnan, whose parents remain in India, offers that "in later years, the last ten years, I felt as my parents were getting on in years, I felt a greater compulsion to visit, be there."[57] Others, particularly immigrant men, visited India only occasionally. Regarding his twice-per-decade visits, Nagaraj Shekhar counted himself among those who "didn't make it that often."[58] Nagaraj's wife, Bhanu, however, visited India annually and sometimes two or three times per year, although usually to perform classical Indian dance.[59] The ease and relative affordability of round-trip travel encouraged her to maintain strong links to India. Yet another woman, Tahira Lakhani, returned to India every year and sometimes twice per year, while her twenty-year-old son had visited India at least fifteen times.[60] Although immigrants visit and maintain contact with varying levels of frequency, they do return. Many members of this early generation of South Asian immigrants have come to believe that while the United States is their home, they cannot overlook their origins. As Tariq Rahman reflected, the United States "is my country now but I started from some other country," so much so, that "the first generation cannot break the ties."[61]

Despite the passing of decades since their arrival in the United States, some immigrants remained materially connected to their home countries by regularly sending remittances back to Pakistan and India. Pakistani businessman Javed Malhotra sent money to his family "from the first day" of his arrival.[62] Although Malhotra was speaking figuratively, soon after their arrival, immigrants supported their families in small but significant ways. Malhotra remitted roughly $200 per month during the 1970s.[63] Sara Waheed, from Pakistan, explained, "The currency rate is different—one dollar is worth more in Pakistan—so [she and her husband sent] whatever he was supposed to send them, according to them. It was not much really, though. It was $100 or less than $200. He could support them and they could live a comfortable life."[64] Her husband, Zafar Waheed, continued to send money to financially struggling relatives in *both* India and Pakistan, as some of his family members remained in India at Independence. Pakistani immigrant Yasmin Iqbal eventually assumed the responsibility from her mother in Karachi to distribute money to less fortunate family members there. She observed, "I used to get news from my mother and sometimes I do write to [other relatives] if they need help. There are a couple of family members that sometimes are in need, so we try to help them [by sending] money for business, for weddings and things like that, or if somebody is sick." She added, "Almost two or three times a year I send whatever [amount] to India."[65] Because migrants to Pakistan left so many relatives (parents, siblings, aunts, and so on) in India at Partition, as immigrants in the United States, Pakistani Americans sent remittances to both countries at high rates.[66] In 2012, the U.S. population of 339,000 Pakistanis sent a total of $1.1 billion in remittances to Pakistan.[67] The 2.6 million Indians in the United States remitted almost $13 billion to India, although Pakistani Americans presumably sent some untraceable portion of these remittances to India, as well.

Contemporary South Asian Immigration to Sugar Land

South Asian American population numbers continue to grow, in large part due to family reunification visa policies. Increasingly, recently arrived family members constitute a sizable proportion of new immigrants from Pakistan and India. This process of chain migration has pulled primarily immigrants' parents and siblings from both countries to the United States. Extended family members who enter the country without the high education or professional qualifications of earlier siblings may not possess the means to purchase property immediately in Sugar Land; nonetheless, many rent Sugar Land area apartments or small houses. Meanwhile, others live in Houston until they can afford to move to Sugar Land. Although I did not conduct formal interviews with recent immigrants, they conveyed these ideas to me in casual conversations.

Sugar Land provided a sound financial investment and an idealized upper-income suburban lifestyle, free from those residents who had brought the old neighborhood "down," so much so that even interviewees who had "stuck it out" in Alief through the 1980s and 1990s, spoke of being closer to their Sugar Land coethnics as they neared retirement age. As one immigrant said, "Our culture is community, mostly."[68] Once a critical mass of South Asians lived in Sugar Land, then other, more recent South Asians followed suit, attracted to the extensive ethnic infrastructure and kin networks. In addition, the children of professionalized immigrants from the 1960s and 1970s have returned to buy homes and raise their own children in Sugar Land. Thus, the next generations of children attend schools with large populations of South Asian Americans. In addition, other family members (grandparents, aunts, uncles, cousins) have joined earlier immigrants to create entire extended family networks in Sugar Land and the Greater Houston area. Whether the parents actively pursue it or not, Sugar Land now provides an immersive South Asian experience inside ethnic spaces—for example, dinner parties, places of worship, and weddings—as well as outside of them, at the grocery store, at the shopping mall, or in school. South Asian Americans are a visible presence in Sugar Land. Between established immigrants, their second-generation children, third-generation grandchildren, extended family, and new immigrants, Sugar Land's South Asian–descent population continues to grow.

Suburbanization and Its Further Significance for South Asian Immigrants

Though South Asian immigrants define their own suburbia by resisting exclusion from white suburban "community," they simultaneously adhere to a profile of suburbanites in terms of socioeconomic status, patterns of consumption, nuclear family structure, and child centeredness.[69] This, in turn, reinforces the divide between city and suburb in terms of interest and concern. The ways in which South Asian immigrants viewed or imagined urban and suburban landscapes were crucial to the decision-making process. South Asian immigrants and Houston's suburbanites saw the city as a place of danger, weak values, and low academic commitment, whereas key suburbs were viewed as a suburban counterpart embodying the ideals of familism, education, and professionalization. The low proportion of other people of color (non–Asian Americans) and the working class in these key suburbs was crucial. Although the urban and the suburban shift in constitution and meanings, in these immigrant imaginations, the urban seems perpetually affiliated with social stagnation and decay— a space accessed for its financial opportunities, a space to be stepped through but not stopped in. As affluent suburbanites turn their gaze toward the city, they increasingly see it through a racialized lens, meaning that the city can only be perceived as the abode of the struggling minorities assumed to be occupying virtually the entirety of it.

The relocation to key suburbs reifies this stagnant imagining of the city. In reality, the urban and suburban are in a perpetual state of flux, rendering weak the constructed boundaries erected to divide and contain them; tropes of urban decay and urban crime are also applicable in many suburbs. Even as people of color migrate into middle-class suburbs, the myth of the racial urban (versus the nonracial, white suburban) persists. If the very act of minority movement to the suburbs—in particular, Hispanic and African American migration outward—could dissolve racial myths and perceptions, it has not done so.

Residents of middle- and upper-middle-class suburbs, including South Asian immigrants, continue to uphold these imagined dichotomies. Buoyed, as they understand it, by the media's perpetuation of racial narratives, including coverage of incarceration, gang membership, and teen pregnancy rates, these suburbanites struggle to construct counternarratives. Although immigrant interviewees expressed familiarity with and support of minority successes, they nonetheless resorted to the convenience of dominant American stereotypes, maintaining further ideological distance from the city than physical proximity would suggest. They may not consciously choose to relegate others to lower rungs of the socioeconomic ladder; however, their choice to reside in exclusive areas exacerbates social distance, removing the problems of the urban poor to urban spaces.

Importantly, for South Asian immigrants, suburbanization was as much about forging ethnic community amid social marginalization as about reinforcing racial and class norms. Upper-income suburbanites in expensive incorporated suburbs such as Sugar Land show little interest in the affairs of the city core. For example, they resist public transit, which would bring urban residents into their area for economic opportunity. They pay taxes to their local government, not to the City of Houston, although they use the city's roads and freeways for a range of purposes. Their property taxes fund local suburban schools rather than underprivileged students in Houston ISD schools. Because wealth is concentrated in these upper-income suburban enclaves, the ideological distance from and disinterest for the affairs of the disadvantaged in the city thus contributes to the perpetuation of unequal access to quality education, ultimately perpetuating socioeconomic inequality. It remains to be seen whether the South Asian community will reside in Sugar Land over the next few decades. For the time being, house prices remain high, schools remain competitive, and non-Asian people of color remain few.

Conclusion

The residential patterns, rationale for public school selection, and racial sense-making of South Asian immigrants and other Houstonians from the 1960s onward illustrate the endurance of residential segregation long after the demise of Jim Crow. South Asian immigrants whose neighborhoods underwent the greatest demographic change—that is, became increasingly settled by working-class African Americans and Latinos/as—quickly relocated to whiter and browner pastures in the suburbs, affirming the endurance of entangled class and racial hierarchies in the post–Jim Crow South.

Nonetheless, as this chapter has demonstrated, although there were areas of overlap between brown and white flight, brown flight was not the same as white flight. By moving to suburbs that housed substantial South Asian minority populations, immigrants continued to build their ethnic identities. In this way, they shared something in common with white suburbanites who used suburbanization as a strategy for reinforcing whiteness. But South Asian immigrants moved to white neighborhoods not to be like whites or because they categorically ascribed to dominant racial hierarchies; South Asian immigrants sought empowerment in whatever ways they could (in this case, through class behavior) in a country that would not allow them to set aside their foreignness.

EPILOGUE

In the late 2010s, I was invited by a local college to deliver a lecture on international education. I spoke about international students and race during the Cold War. I argued that although Cold War foreign policy had reshaped the meaning of "Asian" in America and the significance of Asia to the United States, the lived experience of international Asian students suggests that the traditional meanings of racial categories continued to resonate with Americans through the early decades of the Cold War. I provided multiple examples of how international students experienced racialization in Houston. Much of that material is included in this book and an article that I wrote on the topic. During the question-and-answer session after my lecture, a self-identified Indian immigrant stood up to make a comment. He stated that he could not understand why I focused on race or class at all when speaking about Indian immigrants. They were simply, in his words, "economic migrants." In his eyes, this categorization made Indian immigrants immune to other hierarchical structures that govern American society—presumably gender and class, but especially race.

In February 2017, an Asian family in an affluent subdivision of Sugar Land found an anonymous letter tacked to their front door.[1] The letter writer yearned for a return to a "white nation," stating that to get "back on the right track, we need to get rid of Muslims, Indians, Blacks and Jews." The writer concluded, "If you are one of the above mentioned race then this is a warning to leave Texas or better yet go back to where you came from. If you don't heed this warning then we are not responsible for the torture starting now." In another incident that same month, two Sugar Land families of color found swastikas painted on their property. An Indian neighbor, however, offered that perhaps this was not a hate crime but just a teenage prank.[2]

I mention these anecdotes to draw attention to the enduring lived reality of race, class, and ethnicity in South Asian immigrants' lives, and immigrants' conflicting understandings about identity. Like many other highly skilled immigrants of color, the Indian "economic migrant" above preferred to avoid any association with race in favor of a class identity. He might, I presume, challenge the reading of the history presented in these pages, saying that his experience (and success) exists outside of or, at least, in spite of hierarchies and frameworks of immigration selectivity, racial duality, and class privilege. As other scholars have noted and as is shown in this book, South Asians do not deny the concept of race but reject the "idea of being raced."[3] They do so as a strategy of empowerment despite and because of personal experiences of racialization. In crafting their own narrative, they can exercise some measure of control over the forced racial scripting prevalent in American society and place distance between themselves and the stained association with race.

Certainly, the trajectory of middle-class Indians and Pakistanis joining American universities and white-collar jobs in the 1960s and 1970s and finally settling in Sugar Land does not comprehensively represent the full range of South Asian experiences in the Greater Houston area. The history proffered here is by no means exhaustive or absolute. It offers a historical interpretation that I hope expands our understanding of the past and informs our decisions looking forward. Throughout, I have focused on questions of class, race, and ethnicity to explore the hierarchies of privilege that have shaped southern and American society in the postwar era. South Asians who entered the United States on educational or professional visas met with material success in a boomtown economy. This produced some paradoxes. On the one hand, they were socially tolerated because of U.S. Cold War priorities and because most Asian immigrants arriving in the 1960s and 1970s eschewed domestic politics and controversy in favor of establishing themselves financially. To the extent possible, South Asian immigrants merged with Houston's white middle class, at least in terms of residential and public school patterns. Yet, despite the immigrants' English-language fluency, basic familiarity with Western norms, and high levels of education, white Americans' tolerance of them did not equate with full acceptance. Consequently, South Asian immigrants sought to establish ethnic enclaves in which they could experience a greater degree of social acceptance. Unfortunately, their own experiences with racism have not prevented them from racializing other people of color. In the post–Civil Rights era, South Asian immigrants resided alongside the white middle class, partly adopting their racial ideology but failing to fully realize the racial history that preceded and included them, even as they continued to occupy a racial space apart.

TABLE 6. Oral history interviews conducted by author.

Pseudonym	Ethnicity	Gender	Religious Affiliation	Birthplace (City and/or State, Country)	Grew Up in (City or State)
Sanjay Bavare	Indian	M	Hindu	Maharashtra, India	Maharashtra
Mrudula Bavare	Indian	W	Hindu	Maharashtra, India	Maharashtra
Suresh Bhatt	Indian	M	Sai Baba	Bombay, India	Bombay
Raj Bindal	Indian	M	Hindu	Punjab, India	Punjab
Namrata Chandra	Indian	W	Hindu	Poona, India	Poona and Bombay
Hemant Chokshi	Indian	M	NA	Bombay, India	Bombay
Ashok Dani	Indian	M	Hindu	Baroda, India	Poona and Bombay
Lata Dani	Indian	W	Hindu	Bombay, India	Poona
Harun Farid	Pakistani	M	Muslim	Rampur, Uttar Pradesh, India	Rampur
Varuni Gil	Pakistani	W	Hindu	Shikarpur, Sindh, Pakistan	Shikarpur
Harsh Gil	Pakistani	M	Hindu	Rohri, Sindh, Pakistan	Karachi
Nadia Hasan	Pakistani	W	Muslim	Karachi, Pakistan	Karachi
Jamal Iqbal	Pakistani	M	Muslim	Sultanpur, India	Karachi

TABLE 6. (*Continued*)

Pseudonym	Ethnicity	Gender	Religious Affiliation	Birthplace (City and/or State, Country)	Grew Up in (City or State)
Yasmin Iqbal	Pakistani	W	Muslim	Nowgong, India	Karachi
Mukhtar Jafri	Pakistani	M	Muslim	Karachi, Pakistan	Karachi
Keshav Jagadish	Indian	M	Hindu	Rajahmundry, Andhra Pradesh, India	Rajahmundry
Saumitra Kelkar	Indian	M	Hindu	Parla, Bombay, India	Parla, Bombay
Shalini Kelkar	Indian	W	Hindu	Parla, Bombay, India	Parla, Bombay Mumbai
Vera Khatri	Indian	W	Hindu	Karol Bagh, Delhi, India	Delhi
Kumar Krishnan	Indian	M	Hindu	Madurai, Tamil Nadu, India	Delhi
Uma Krishnan	Indian	W	Hindu	Simla, India	Delhi and Madras
Tahira Lakhani and Idris Lakhani	Indian	W M	Muslim	Gujarat, India	Gujarat
Ramesh Lal	Indian	M	Hindu	South Bombay, India	Bombay
Shiv Majumdar	Indian	M	Hindu	Baroda, Gujarat, India	Baroda
Javed Malhotra	Pakistani	M	Muslim	Karachi, Pakistan	Karachi
Rustom Mistri	Indian	M	Zoroastrian	Faizabad, Uttar Pradesh, India	Nainital and Dehradun
Suman Parikh	Indian	M	Hindu	Gujarat, India	Gujarat

TABLE 6. (*Continued*)

Pseudonym	Ethnicity	Gender	Religious Affiliation	Birthplace (City and/or State, Country)	Grew Up in (City or State)
Jyoti Patel	Indian	W	Hindu	Dahod, Gujarat, India	Dahod
Rohan Patil	Indian	M	Hindu	Kanpur, Maharashtra, India	Kanpur
Bina Parmar	Indian	W	Hindu	Gabat, Gujarat, India	Bombay
Vinod Prakash	Indian	M	Hindu	Bombay, India	Bombay
Tariq Rahman	Indian	M	Muslim	Bihar, India	Bihar
Anita Sharma	Indian	W	Hindu	Saran District, Bihar, India	N/A
Bhanu Shekhar	Indian	W	Hindu	Chennai, India	Chennai
Nagaraj Shekhar	Indian	M	Hindu	Chennai, India	Chennai
Sara Waheed	Pakistani	W	Muslim	Bilaspur, India	Karachi
Zafar Waheed	Pakistani	M	Muslim	Jabalpur, India	Karachi

Notes: All names are carefully selected pseudonyms that reflect point of origin, linguistic background, and, where applicable, caste affiliation. Most of the interviews are archived with the Oral Histories–Houston History Project, Special Collections, University of Houston Libraries.

N/A = Information not available

TABLE 7. Immigration preference system, Immigration and Nationality Act of 1965.

First preference	Unmarried sons and daughters of U.S. citizens	Not more than 20%
Second preference	Spouse and unmarried sons and daughters of an alien lawfully admitted for permanent residence	20% plus any unused portion of first preference
Third preference	Members of the professions, scientists, artists of exceptional ability	Not more than 10%
Fourth preference	Married sons and daughters of U.S. citizens	10% plus any unused portion of first three preferences
Fifth preference	Brothers and sisters of U.S. citizens	24% plus any unused portion of first four preferences
Sixth preference	Skilled and unskilled workers in occupations for which labor is in short supply in U.S.	Not more than 10%
Seventh preference	Refugees to whom conditional entry or adjustment of status may be granted	Not more than 6%
Nonpreference	Any applicant not entitled to one of the above preferences	Any unused portion of first through seventh preferences

Source: Department of State, Bureau of Security and Consular Affairs, *Annual Report of the Visa Office*, 1968, 68.

TABLE 8. Asian American population decadal totals in the United States, 1900–2010.

Year	Total U.S. Population	Total Asians in U.S. +	Japanese	Chinese	Filipino	Korea +	Vietnamese	Asian Indian	Pakistani	Bangladeshi
1900	76,212	204,500	85,716	118,746	NA	NA	NA	2,050	NA	NA
1910	92,229	250,000	152,745	94,414	2,767	5,000	NA	2,546	NA	NA
1920	106,022	332,000	220,596	85,202	26,634	6,000	NA	2,495	NA	NA
1930	123,205	489,000	278,743	102,159	108,424	8,000	NA	3,130	NA	NA
1940	132,165	490,000	285,115	106,334	98,535	9,000	NA	2,405	NA	NA
1950	151,326	599,000	326,379	150,005	122,707	*7,030	NA	2,398	NA	NA
1960	179,323	878,000	464,332	237,292	176,310	NA	NA	8,746	NA	NA
1970	203,212	1,430,000	591,290	435,062	343,060	69,000	NA	13,149	1,708	NA
1980	226,546	3,466,847	700,974	806,040	774,652	354,593	261,729	361,531	6,182	NA
1990	248,709,873	6,908,638	847,562	1,645,472	1,406,770	798,849	614,547	815,447	81,371	11,838
2000**	281,421,906	11,898,828	1,148,932	2,865,232	2,364,815	1,228,427	1,223,736	1,899,599	204,309	57,412
2010**	308,745,538	17,320,856	1,304,286	4,010,114	3,416,840	1,706,822	1,737,433	3,183,063	409,163	147,300

Notes:

+ Rounded estimates before 1980. Source: Xenos et al., Asian Indians in the United States.

* Data available for Hawaii only.

** The data for 2000 and 2010 reflect the category of an ethnic group "alone or in combination with another," which is not consistently available for earlier decades. Before 2000, the data above reflects an ethnic group "alone."

Sources: U.S. Census Bureau 1980 (table 40), 1990 (table 3), 2010, and various census reports; Xenos et al., Asian Indians in the United States.

TABLE 9. Foreign-born population of major U.S. cities, 1960.

	Total Population	Native-Born Population	Foreign-Born Population	Foreign-Born (Percentage)
United States	179,326,000	169,588,000	9,738,000	5.7
Texas				
Houston (city)	938,219	913,920	24,299	2.6
Dallas	679,684	666,964	12,720	1.9
San Antonio	588,042	548,258	39,784	6.8
El Paso	276,687	233,673	43,014	15.5
Major U.S. Cities				
New York City	7,783,314	6,224,624	1,558,690	20.0
Los Angeles	2,481,456	2,169,779	311,677	12.6
Chicago	3,550,404	3,112,012	438,392	12.3
Philadelphia	2,002,509	1,824,082	178,427	8.9
Detroit	1,670,144	1,468,431	201,713	12.1
South/Southwest Region				
Atlanta	487,275	482,680	4,595	0.9
Phoenix	439,170	419,732	19,438	4.4
Miami	291,688	242,442	49,246	16.9

Source: U.S. Bureau of the Census, table 19: "Nativity of the Population for the 50 Largest Urban Places, 1870 to 1990."

TABLE 10. Foreign-born population of major U.S. cities, 1970.

	Total Population	Native-Born Population	Foreign-Born Population	Foreign-Born (Percentage)
United States	203,210, 000	193,591,000	9,619,000	4.9
Texas				
Houston (city)	1,231,572	1,194,071	37,501	3.0
Dallas	844,280	826,854	17,426	2.1
San Antonio	654,468	615,779	38,689	5.9
El Paso	322,261	277,919	44,342	13.8
Major U.S. Cities				
New York City	7,894,798	6,457,740	1,437,058	18.2
Los Angeles	2,815,998	2,405,128	410,870	14.6
Chicago	3,362,947	2,989,028	373,919	11.1
Philadelphia	1,948,608	1,821,712	126,896	6.5
Detroit	1,511,322	1,391,975	119,347	7.9
South/Southwest Region				
Atlanta	497,046	491,194	5,852	1.2
Phoenix	581,466	559,810	21,656	3.7
Miami	335,062	194,855	140,207	41.8

Source: U.S. Bureau of the Census, table 19: "Nativity of the Population for the 50 Largest Urban Places, 1870 to 1990."

TABLE 11. Foreign-born population of major U.S. cities, 1980.

	Total Population	Native-Born Population	Foreign-Born Population	Foreign-Born (Percentage)
United States	226,546,000	212,466,000	14,080,000	6.6
Texas				
Houston (city)	1,595,167	1,439,590	155,577	9.8
Dallas	904,074	849,162	54,912	6.1
San Antonio	785,809	720,933	64,876	8.3
El Paso	425,259	334,352	90,907	21.4
Major U.S. Cities				
New York City	7,071,639	5,401,440	1,670,199	23.6
Los Angeles	2,966,850	2,162,032	804,818	27.1
Chicago	3,005,078	2,569,846	435,232	14.5
Philadelphia	1,688,210	1,580,259	107,951	6.4
Detroit	1,203,339	1,135,036	68,303	5.7
South/Southwest Region				
Atlanta	425,022	415,245	9,777	2.3
Phoenix	789,704	745,042	44,662	5.7
Miami	346,865	160,585	186,280	53.7

Source: U.S. Bureau of the Census, table 19: "Nativity of the Population for the 50 Largest Urban Places, 1870 to 1990."

MAP 8. Black/African American population, Houston, 1970.

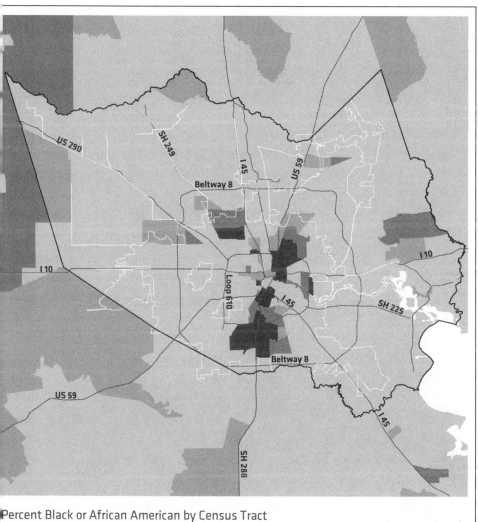

Percent Black or African American by Census Tract

    <25%

    25%–50%

    50%–75%

    >75%

— Harris County

  City of Houston

Sources: City of Houston GIS; Census 1970.

MAP 9. Hispanic origin/descent population, Houston, 1970.

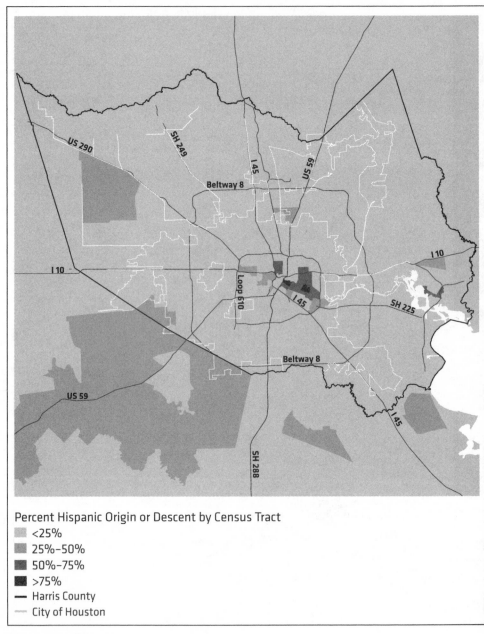

Percent Hispanic Origin or Descent by Census Tract
- <25%
- 25%–50%
- 50%–75%
- >75%
- Harris County
- City of Houston

Sources: City of Houston GIS; Census 1970.

MAP 10. Black/African American population, Houston, 2010.

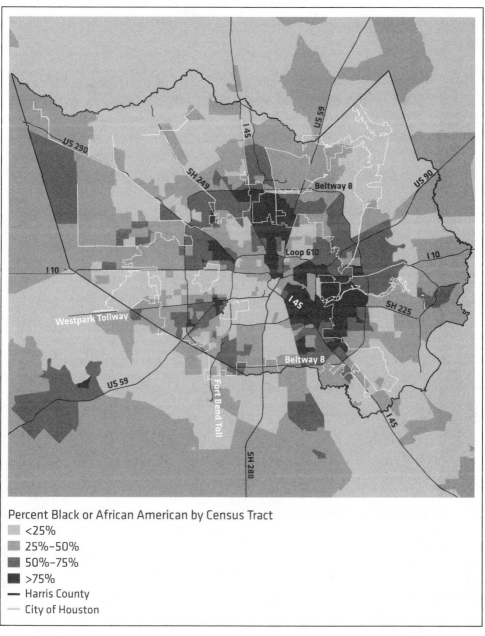

Percent Black or African American by Census Tract

    <25%
    25%–50%
    50%–75%
    >75%
— Harris County
— City of Houston

Sources: City of Houston GIS; ACS 2010.

MAP 11. Hispanic origin/descent population, Houston, 2010.

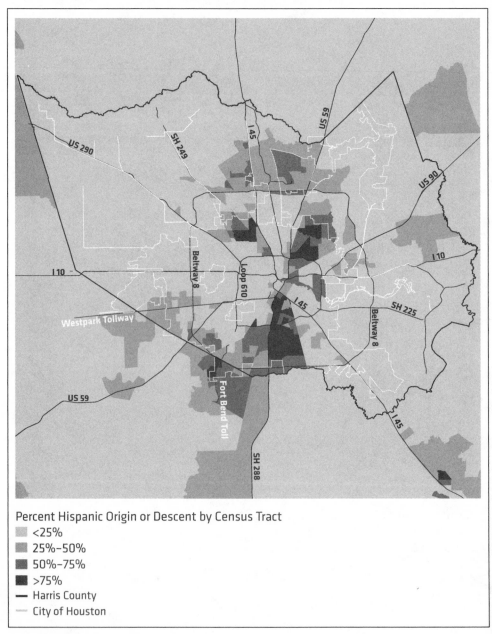

Percent Hispanic Origin or Descent by Census Tract
- <25%
- 25%–50%
- 50%–75%
- >75%
— Harris County
— City of Houston

Sources: City of Houston GIS; ACS 2010.

MAP 12. Aggregate family income by total population, Houston, 1970, 1990, 2010.

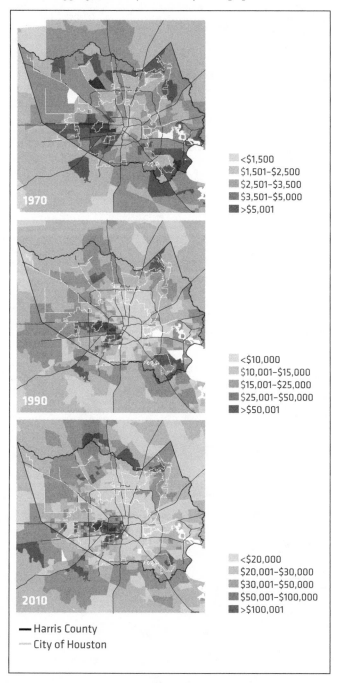

<$1,500
$1,501–$2,500
$2,501–$3,500
$3,501–$5,000
>$5,001

<$10,000
$10,001–$15,000
$15,001–$25,000
$25,001–$50,000
>$50,001

<$20,000
$20,001–$30,000
$30,001–$50,000
$50,001–$100,000
>$100,001

1970

1990

2010

— Harris County
— City of Houston

Sources: City of Houston GIS; Census 1970; Census 1990; ACS 2010.

NOTES

Abbreviations

DOS	U.S. Department of State
EPL	Dwight D. Eisenhower Presidential Library
FSD	Foreign Service Despatch
HAAA	Houston Asian American Archive, Rice University
HHP	Oral Histories–Houston History Project, Special Collections, University of Houston Libraries
HMRC	Houston Metropolitan Research Center
NACP	National Archives at College Park
NSC	National Security Council
OCB	Operations Coordinating Board
RG	Record Group
SAADA	South Asian American Digital Archive
TPL	Harry S. Truman Presidential Library
USIA	United States Information Agency
USIS	United States Information Service
UH	University of Houston

Introduction

1. Rohan Patil, interview with author, 2011, HHP.

2. I capitalize the word "State" in reference to the federal government and, at times, to denote the U.S. State Department.

3. For more on Asian international students in the early Cold War years, see Hsu, *Good Immigrants*; Schreuder, *Universities for a New World*; and Bevis, *History of Higher Education Exchange*.

4. I prefer to use the term "Latino/a" instead of "Hispanic" because many Latino/as regard "Hispanic" as a label imposed on Spanish-speaking peoples by the U.S. government. However, when referring to U.S. census data or other population-related data, I use the label "Hispanic" to reflect the terminology of the census since 1980. For a discussion of labels used for and within the Latino/a community, see Cohn, "Census History"; and Ramón A. Gutiérrez, "What's in a Name?," in Gutiérrez and Almaguer, *New Latino Studies Reader*.

5. The Luce-Celler Act of 1946 permitted entry of 100 Indians and 100 Filipinos annually. The act was inspired by passage of the Magnuson Act (or Chinese Repealer, which allowed for the entry of 103 Chinese annually) passed in 1943 to foment positive Allied relations. See also Hing, *Making and Remaking Asian America*; Hing, *Defining America*; Reimers, *Other Immigrants*; and Danico, *Asian American Society*.

6. Emma Lazarus, "The New Colossus" (1883).

7. For general Cold War histories, see Gaddis, *Cold War*; Westad, *Cold War*; and Leffler, *Specter of Communism*.

8. Lee and Yung, *Angel Island*.

9. Overviews of immigration to the United States include Dinnerstein and Reimers, *Ethnic Americans*; Kraut, *Huddled Masses*; Daniels, *Coming to America*; Takaki, *Different Mirror*; Gerber, *American Immigration*; and Gabaccia, *From Sicily to Elizabeth Street*.

10. On the development of the postwar economy, see Neumann, *Remaking the Rust Belt*; Wells, *American Capitalism, 1945–2000*; Rosenberg, *American Economic Development since 1945*; and McDonald, *Postwar Urban America*.

11. There is a rich and varied literature—especially in the social sciences—on the second generation and emerging work on the working class, although many fruitful lines of inquiry remain open.

12. By 2010, Indians and Pakistanis were still among the most educated segments of American society, but Pakistanis, in particular, also had high poverty levels similar to African Americans and Hispanics. For data on Houston and other cities, see Asian Americans Advancing Justice (AAAJ), "Community of Contrasts."

13. Wong and Hirschman, "New Asian Immigrants," 396.

14. Xenos et al., *Asian Indians in the United States*, 16.

15. Wong and Hirschman, "New Asian Immigrants," 391.

16. Morrison Wong and Charles Hirschman define nonpreference immigrants as "applicants not entitled to any other preferences but admitted because the 170,000 overall maximum for the Eastern hemisphere was not reached" ("New Asian Immigrants," 389).

17. Wong and Hirschman, "New Asian Immigrants."

18. Klineberg, *Houston Area Asian Survey: Diversity and Transformation Among Asians in Houston*; Helweg and Helweg, *Immigrant Success Story*; Helweg, *Strangers in a Not-So-Strange Land*.

19. Pratt, "Coming to Houston," 8; Klineberg, *Houston Area Survey 1982–2005: Public Perceptions in Remarkable Times*, 5-6.

20. Pratt, "Coming to Houston," 9.

21. Klineberg, *Houston Area Survey 1982–2005: Public Perceptions in Remarkable Times*, 15. The term "majority minority" is problematic for at least two reasons. First, if one regards minorities as a group, then their increase in number—that is, their emergence as a collective majority—destabilizes and indeed undermines the very categories of "majority" and "minority." Second, neither of these "groups" necessarily claims solidarity with the other, so there are, instead, many majorities and minorities, often allied along different intersections.

22. AAAJ, "Community of Contrasts," 35. The two largest population centers in the

metropolitan area are Harris County, with 253,092 Asian American residents, and Fort Bend County, with 97,597 (Census 2010).

23. Klineberg, *Houston Area Asian Survey: Diversity and Transformation Among Asians in Houston*. South Asians, especially Pakistanis and Bangladeshis, are also among the poorest of immigrant groups. They occupy two extremes, reflecting differences of selectivity between earlier and later immigrants.

24. Lassiter, *Silent Majority*, 15–16.

25. Bartley, "Social Change and Sectional Identity," 4.

26. Edwards, "Southern History as U.S. History," 534.

27. Randolph B. Campbell, "History and Collective Memory in Texas," in Cantrell and Turner, *Lone Star Pasts*, 279.

28. Campbell, "History and Collective Memory in Texas," 279.

29. Baker, "From Rural South to Metropolitan Sunbelt," 2.

30. Fairbanks and Underwood, *Essays on Sunbelt Cities*; Nickerson and Dochuk, *Sunbelt Rising*.

31. Nickerson and Dochuk, *Sunbelt Rising*, 9.

32. Elizabeth Tandy Shermer, "Sunbelt Boosterism: Industrial Recruitment, Economic Development, and Growth Politics in the Developing South," in Nickerson and Dochuk, *Sunbelt Rising*, 37.

33. See Nickerson and Dochuck, *Sunbelt Rising*.

34. See, e.g., Hobbs and Stoops, "Demographic Trends in the 20th Century."

35. Myrdal, *American Dilemma*.

36. See the Appendix, table 6, for more information on the interviewees.

37. I am indebted to cinema studies scholar Samhita Sunya for helping me to create suitable pseudonyms.

38. Abrams, *Oral History Theory*, 71.

39. Several important studies address some of the groups not extensively included here. See, e.g., Reddy, *Nursing and Empire*; Bhatia, *American Karma*; Geiger, *Subverting Exclusion*; Sircar, *Work Roles, Gender Roles, and Asian Indian Immigrant Women*; Mishra, *Desis Divided*; Bald, Chatterji, Reddy, and Vimalassery, *Sun Never Sets*.

40. My engagement with interviewees involved mainly oral history interviews. Though I did not conduct formal anthropological fieldwork, to the extent that I am of Pakistani descent, grew up in Houston's Pakistani community, and now write about this community, I have long been both a participant and observer. See Geertz, *The Interpretation of Cultures*.

41. See Reddy, *Nursing sand Empire*.

42. Xenos et al., *Asian Indians*.

43. Ternikar, "Revisioning the Ethnic Family."

44. Fenton, *Transplanting Religious Traditions*.

45. Patel, "Complicating the Tale of 'Two Indians,'" n.p.

46. Madrasi: a person with origins in the city of Chennai, formerly Madras, in southern India.

47. See Jalal, *Democracy and Authoritarianism in South Asia*.

48. Kibria, "Diaspora Diversity."

49. Schiller, Basch, and Blanc, "From Immigrant to Transmigrant"; Purkayastha,

Negotiating Ethnicity; Afzal, "Transnational Religious and Citizenship Practices"; Lin, Song, and Ball-Rokeach, "Localizing the Global."

50. Gail Sutherland notes that Indian Hindu immigrants in Houston frequently "distinguish[ed] themselves from Muslims" ("Wedding Pavilion," 122).

51. Maira, *9/11 Generation*; Ewing, *Being and Belonging*; Rana, *Terrifying Muslims*.

52. Vinod Prakash, interview with author, 2011, HHP.

53. Westad, *Global Cold War*, 3.

54. Cull, *Cold War and the United States*, xvi.

55. For further discussion of the use of this term, see Cull, *Cold War and the United States*; and Osgood, *Total Cold War*.

56. See Leonard, *Making Ethnic Choices*; Shah, *Stranger Intimacy*; Bhatt and Iyer, *Roots and Reflections*; Bald, *Bengali Harlem*; and Visram, *Asians in Britain*.

57. Sanjay Joshi, "The Spectre of Comparisons: Studying the Middle Class of Colonial India," in Baviskar and Ray, *Elite and Everyman*, 49–53; Joshi, *Middle Class in Colonial India*.

58. Joshi, "Spectre of Comparisons," 57. See also Joshi, *Middle Class in Colonial India*; Bayly, *Rulers, Townsmen and Bazaars*; and Lockwood, *Indian Bourgeoisie*.

59. Prashant Kidambi, "Consumption, Domestic Economy, and the Idea of the 'Middle Class' in Late Colonial Bombay," in Joshi, *Middle Class in Colonial India*, 133, 142.

60. See Metcalf and Metcalf, *Concise History of Modern India*; and Bose and Jalal, *Modern South Asia*.

61. S. N. Mukherjee, "Class, Caste and Politics in Calcutta, 1815–1838," in Leach and Mukherjee, *Elites in South Asia*, 33–78.

62. Johnson, *Middle Classes in Dependent Countries*, 145.

63. Hossain, Islam, and Kibria, *South Asian Economic Development*, 15.

64. Johnson, *Middle Classes in Dependent Countries*, 15.

65. Hossain, Islam, and Kibria, *South Asian Economic Development*, 13, 19–20.

66. After independence, India built on iron and steel, Pakistan on cotton textiles; Bangladesh mainly produced jute. Hossain, Islam, and Kibria, *South Asian Economic Development*, 20.

67. Driver and Driver, *Social Class in Urban India*, 47. Retabulated from data in table 4.

68. It should be noted that these occupations were quite varied, including at the higher end—for example, architects, chemists, physicians, journalists, and professors. "Lower professional" occupations could be said to include auditors, clerks, sales workers, and brokers. Also, incomes for the latter set of occupations occasionally overlapped with the higher grade of manual workers, such as electricians and artisans. Driver and Driver, *Social Class in Urban India*, 42.

69. López and Weinstein, *Making of the Middle Class*, 18–19.

70. Joshi, "Spectre of Comparisons," 90–91.

71. Driver and Driver, *Social Class in Urban India*, 19.

72. Driver and Driver, *Social Class in Urban India*, 19–20.

73. López and Weinstein, *Making of the Middle Class*, 4.

74. Joshi, *Fractured Modernity*, 60.

75. Kim, "Racial Triangulation of Asian Americans," 105–7.

76. Hsu and Wu, "'Smoke and Mirrors,'" 43.

77. A vast body of literature documents the rise of the model minority myth. See, e.g., Ellen Wu, *Color of Success*; Chou and Feagin, *Myth of the Model Minority*; and Chung, *Saving Face*.

78. Parker, *Hearts, Minds, Voices*.

79. Although I did not pursue a line of questioning specifically regarding caste in my interviews, presumably some Indian student immigrants to the United States were of Dalit descent. As early as the 1910s, B. R. Ambedkar, an Indian political leader and a member of the group marked as "Untouchable" in India, obtained his doctorate in economics from Columbia University.

80. Hemalatha Ganapathy-Coleman notes that "the participants in this study belonged to the top three castes in the Hindu hierarchy" ("Raising 'Authentic' Indian Children in the United States," 381).

81. Lessinger, *From the Ganges to the Hudson*.

82. Kurien, "Religion, Ethnicity and Politics," 267.

83. Bhatia, *American Karma*.

84. For a compelling discussion of the complexities of racial and caste solidarity in the United States, see Patel, "Complicating the Tale."

85. Pandey, *History of Prejudice*, 6.

86. Pandey, *History of Prejudice*, 8. In addition, the many authors included in Sukhadeo Thorat and Umakant's edited collection, *Caste, Race, and Discrimination*, insist on fundamental differences between caste and race. Dipankar Gupta reiterates the same position—namely, that he understands caste to be more complex and entrenched than race, based on multiple hierarchies, and not tied to phenotype (*Interrogating Caste*, 86–95).

87. Kurien, "Religion, Ethnicity and Politics," 269; Patel, "Complicating the Tale."

88. See Hasan, "Twentieth-Century Indian Immigration to Chicago"; Rangaswamy, *Namasté America*; and Skop, *Immigration and Settlement of Asian Indians in Phoenix*. For an extensive discussion of the early formation of Philadelphia's South Asian community, see Khan, "In/Visibility of South Asian Muslim Americans."

89. Sutherland, "Wedding Pavilion," 122.

90. U.S. Department of Justice, Immigration and Naturalization Service, *Annual Report for years 1967–72*.

91. Surinder M. Bhardwaj and N. Madhusudana Rao, "Asian Indians in the United States: A Geographic Appraisal," in Clarke, Peach, and Vertovec, *South Asians Overseas*, 200. Maxine Fisher writes, "Of the 14,939 Indians admitted as immigrants in 1975, 6,156 were classified by the U.S. Immigration Service as 'professional/technical workers.' An additional 7,763 were classified as 'spouses and children of professional/technical workers.' The combined figures account for 93% of the Indian immigrants admitted during that year" ("Creating Ethnic Identity," 272).

92. Chandrasekhar, *From India to America*; Census 1990.

93. Census 2010.

94. Bhardwaj and Rao, "Asians Indians in the United States," 206–7.

95. AAAJ, "Community of Contrasts," 35, 8.

96. AAAJ, "Community of Contrasts," 36.

97. Afzal, "Transnational Religious and Citizenship Practices," 8.

98. See Jason C. Parker, *Hearts, Minds, Voices*; McMahon, *Cold War in the Third World*.

Prologue

1. On pre-1965 anti-Asian immigration laws and race relations, see Hing, *Making and Remaking Asian America*; and Kurashige, *Two Faces of Exclusion*.

2. Japanese emigrants were heavily screened by Japan, ensuring that they were literate and more financially secure than earlier Chinese or later Indian immigrants. See Takaki, *Strangers from a Different Shore*; and Hing, *Defining America*.

3. Bald, *Bengali Harlem*, 7.

4. Bald, *Bengali Harlem*, 24, 28. Several of the passages regarding Bengali immigrants in this prologue appeared originally in my review of Bald's *Bengali Harlem* in the *Journal of Southern History* 81, no. 4 (November 2015). They are reprinted here by permission of the journal.

5. Bald, *Bengali Harlem*, 35, 98, 134.

6. Jensen, "Apartheid," 339.

7. Melendy, *Asians in America*, 255. Melendy draws his data directly from Immigration and Naturalization Service and census records. Other studies note different numbers. In particular, Gary Hess, in an oft-cited essay, states that between 1907 and 1920, some 6,400 Indian laborers arrived and settled in the United States, with more than 2,700 in central California. Hess, however, bases his numbers on the records of the anti-Asian organization the Asiatic Exclusion League. Hess, "Forgotten Asian Americans," 576.

8. Hess, "Forgotten Asian Americans," 578.

9. Takaki, *Strangers from a Different Shore*, 295–98.

10. Shah, *Stranger Intimacy*, 28.

11. Hess, "Forgotten Asian Americans," 580; See also Jensen, "Apartheid."

12. Hess, "Forgotten Asian Americans," 580.

13. On passage of the Chinese Exclusion Act, see Gyory, *Closing the Gate*; Lew-Williams, *Chinese Must Go*.

14. Immigration Act of 1917, quoted in Hing, *Making and Remaking Asian America*, 32.

15. Takaki, *Strangers from a Different Shore*, 297.

16. Hing, *Making and Remaking Asian America*, 70.

17. Quoted in López, *White by Law*, 31, 35–37, 193.

18. Quoted in Tragen, "Statutory Prohibitions against Interracial Marriage," 269.

19. Tragen, "Statutory Prohibitions."

20. Leonard, *Making Ethnic Choices*, 57.

21. Leonard, *Making Ethnic Choices*, 56.

22. Leonard, *Making Ethnic Choices*, 57.

23. Hess, "Forgotten Asian Americans," 584.

24. Quoted in Takaki, *Strangers from a Different Shore*, 306.

25. Jensen, "Apartheid," 339–40; Gould, *Sikhs, Swamis, Students and Spies*, 293.

26. Bald, *Bengali Harlem*, 49–50.

27. Leonard, *Making Ethnic Choices*, 33, 42.

28. Leonard, *Making Ethnic Choices*, 42, 133–34.

29. Leonard, *Making Ethnic Choices*, 134.

30. Leonard, *Making Ethnic Choices*, 133.

31. Leonard, *Making Ethnic Choices*, 133.

32. Takaki, *Strangers from a Different Shore*, 295–97; Bhatt and Iyer, *Roots and Reflections*, 35.

33. López, *White by Law*, esp. 4, 45, 54.

34. *Takao Ozawa v. U.S.* (1922) and *U.S. v Bhagat Singh Thind* (1923), quoted in López, *White by Law*, 176–82.

35. Hing, *Defining America*, 45.

36. López, *White by Law*, 90.

37. Mae M. Ngai, "The Unlovely Residue of Outworn Prejudices: The Hart-Celler Act and the Politics of Immigration Reform, 1945–1965," in Kazin and McCartin, *Americanism*, 3–14.

38. Hing, *Making and Remaking Asian America*, 32–33.

39. Hing, *Making and Remaking Asian America*, 33. Though enrollment numbers declined by about half in the decades following the National Origins Act, Asian international students nevertheless continued to attend U.S. universities with the aid of the Institute of International Education, founded in 1919, and missionary groups. See Paul A. Kramer, "Is the World Our Campus?," 790–91, 788; and Ling, "History of Chinese Female Students," 84–85.

40. Gould, *Sikhs, Swamis, Students and Spies*, 142–43. Asian students in U.S. universities during the exclusion years hailed mainly from China, Japan, the Philippines, and India. See also Hsu, *Good Immigrants*.

41. Almaguer, *Racial Fault Lines*, 11.

42. Shaffer, "J. J. Singh and the India League of America"; Gould, *Sikhs, Swamis, Students and Spies*. Gould's book, though often overlooked, is a valuable source on Indian resistance and agency in the United States.

43. Gould, *Sikhs, Swamis, Students and Spies*, 400–431.

44. Gould, *Sikhs, Swamis, Students and Spies*, 393–431.

45. Hess, "Forgotten Asian Americans," 592.

46. Gould, *Sikhs, Swamis, Students and Spies*, 400–431; McClain, *Asian Indians, Filipinos, Other Asian Communities, and the Law*.

47. Gould, *Sikhs, Swamis, Students and Spies*, 410.

48. Hing, *Making and Remaking Asian America*, 37.

49. Filipino and Indian Naturalization Act, 60 Stat. 416 (July 2, 1946), quoted in Hing, *Making and Remaking Asian America*, 215.

50. Hsu and Wu, "'Smoke and Mirrors,'" 44.

51. Hsu and Wu, "'Smoke and Mirrors.'"

52. Hsu, *Good Immigrants*, 126.

53. Reimers, "Unintended Reform."

54. Memorandum by the Director of the Bureau of the Budget to the President, May 9, 1952, quoted in Chin, "Civil Rights Revolution," 292.

55. Quoted in Chin, "Civil Rights Revolution," 293.

56. Quoted in Chin, "Civil Rights Revolution," 296.

57. U.S. Congress, Senate, *Congressional Record*, February 28, 1950, 96:2476, quoted in Reimers, "Unintended Reform," 11. After much debate and anti-semitic discourse, the Displaced Persons Act of 1950 finally permitted some 400,000 Jewish refugees into the United States.

58. Wartime and postwar laws regarding China include the Magnuson Act, 1943; Alien Fiancées and Fiancés Act, 1946; and Chinese Alien Wives of American Citizens Act, 1946. Concerning the Philippines and India, Congress passed the act of July 2, 1946, that granted naturalized citizenship and an Indian quota of one hundred per year.

59. David M. Reimers, "Unintended Reform," 10; Ngai, "Unlovely Residue of Outworn Prejudices."

60. See Asian Americans Advancing Justice (AAAJ), "Community of Contrasts."

61. Hilliker, "Lord William Bentinck's Resolution of 1835," 40–45; Aparna Basu, "Indian Higher Education: Colonialism and Beyond," in Altbach and Selvaratnam, *From Dependence to Autonomy*, 169. The sentiment was introduced by parliamentarian Thomas Macaulay in his "Minute" on Indian education (February 2, 1835), known as Macualay's Minute.

62. Peshkin, "Education, Muslim Elite, and Creation of Pakistan," 154. Funding for traditional education actually continued but was exceptional. Slowly, it ended altogether.

63. Roy, "Englishing of India," 71.

64. Roy, "Englishing of India."

65. Roy, "Englishing of India."

66. Roy, "Englishing of India," 42–43.

67. Basu, "Indian Higher Education," 171.

68. Peshkin, "Education, the Muslim Elite,"155.

69. Roy, "Englishing of India," 50.

70. Prashad, *Karma of Brown Folk*, 75. See also Prakash, *Another Reason*.

71. Béteille, *Universities at the Crossroads* , 3.

72. Pawan Agarwal, "Asia: Higher Education in India and Pakistan—Common Origin, Different Trajectories," in Schreuder, *Universities for a New World*, 254–83.

73. Lux, "Technical Education in India," 301.

74. "Report: The Indian Student," 78, September 1954, Folder: IEV IND 55-2768, Box 29, International Survey Research Reports, 1953–1964, RG 306, NACP.

75. Agarwal, "Asia: Higher Education," 258. As Ross Basset notes, even these engineering colleges were intended "to prepare Indians to work in subsidiary positions under British rule" ("Aligning India in the Cold War," 786).

76. Ross Bassett, "Aligning India in the Cold War," 787. These countries included the United States, Soviet Union, West Germany, and United Kingdom.

77. N. Jayaram, "Higher Education in India: Massification and Change," in Altbach and Umakoshi, *Asian Universities*, 91. See also Béteille, *Universities at the Crossroads*, 45. Estimates vary, with Béteille stating that India had thirty universities at Independence, Jayaram calculating twenty universities, and USIA estimating twenty-four to thirty universities.

78. Agarwal, "Asia: Higher Education," 258.

79. Jayaram, "Higher Education in India," 88.

80. Béteille, *Universities at the Crossroads*, 4.

81. Mukerji, *History of Education in India*, 319.

82. Béteille, *Universities at the Crossroads*, 17, 47.

83. Kibbee, "Higher Education in Pakistan," 182.

84. Salam, "Pakistan," 3.

85. Gant, "Ford Foundation and Pakistan," 152. The role of the Ford Foundation is examined more fully later in this chapter.

86. Galvani, "Introduction to Pakistan," 4.

87. Lall, "Educate to Hate," 103–19, 107.

88. Lall, "Educate to Hate."

89. Roy, "Englishing of India," 54.

90. Roy, "Englishing of India," 55; Basu, "Indian Higher Education," 178.

Chapter One

1. Hsu, *Good Immigrants*.

2. In addition to the abundant literature on anti-Chinese exclusion, on anti-Asian xenophobia see Kurashige, *Two Faces of Exclusion*; and Tchen and Yeats, *Yellow Peril!*

3. For a detailed account of the political relations among the United States, India, and Pakistan, see McMahon, *Cold War on the Periphery*. See also Sattar, *Pakistan's Foreign Policy*; Kux, *India and the United States*; Kux, *United States and Pakistan*; Tahir-Kheli, *India, Pakistan, and the United States*; Jalal, *Struggle for Pakistan*; Ganguly, *Engaging the World*; and Ganguly, *Conflict Unending*.

4. McMahon, *Cold War on the Periphery*, 333.

5. Sassen, *Globalization and Its Discontents*.

6. Sassen, *Globalization and Its Discontents*, 40. See also Wallerstein, *Modern World-System*.

7. Chan, *Asian Americans*, 151; Sassen, *Globalization and Its Discontents*, 40, 45.

8. Unger, "Towards Global Equilibrium." Over time, India's increasing dependence on U.S. aid led to resentment among Indians and the charge of American imperialism. This was compounded by India's slow economic growth, inhibited by poor harvests, sluggish rates of export, and a currency crisis. See David C. Engerman, "South Asia and the Cold War," in McMahon, *Cold War in the Third World*, 74–75; and McGarr, "'Quiet Americans in India.'"

9. McMahon, *Cold War on the Periphery*; Tahir-Kheli. *India, Pakistan, and the United States*.

10. Leffler, "American Conception of National Security." See also Gaddis, *United States and Origins of the Cold War*; and Westad, *Global Cold War*.

11. Sattar, *Pakistan's Foreign Policy*, 51; Engerman, "South Asia and the Cold War," 74–75.

12. "U.S. Information Agency Conference on India," September 11–12, 1961, 1960–1963 Central Decimal File, Box 1081, RG 59, NACP.

13. McMahon, *Cold War on the Periphery*, 36–79. In the early 1960s, the U.S.-based

Asia Society toyed with the idea of establishing an India-Pakistan Society "to point out U.S. interest in the sub-continent as a whole." Politically, however, this was never the most expedient path. See "U.S. Information Agency Conference on India," 8.

14. Henry Cabot Lodge to President Dwight D. Eisenhower, February 21, 1958, Box 24, A75-22, Administration Series, DDE: Papers as President, 1953–1961 (Ann Whitman File), EPL.

15. *The Pakistan-American Alliance: Stresses and Strains*, reprinted from *Foreign Affairs*, January 1964, Folder: Name File, Box 104, Papers of Harry S. Truman, Post-Presidential Papers, TPL.

16. American foreign policy goals for Vietnam and ongoing military and financial support in South Vietnam dictated that that country received the bulk of USIA's attention in Asia.

17. McMahon, *Cold War on the Periphery*, 8. Economist Anne Krueger calculates that between 1953 and 1961, India and Pakistan received a combined total of $3.8 million in aid. The highest recipients of aid were Korea and India, with each given over $2.4 million. Other major recipients of U.S. aid from the mid-1960s were Israel, Egypt, Vietnam, and Indonesia. Krueger, *Economic Policies at Cross-Purposes*, 45.

18. McGarr, *Cold War in South Asia*, 43–46; Rakove, *Kennedy, Johnson, and the Nonaligned World*.

19. Although Pakistan initially toyed with the idea of nonalignment, with Jawaharlal Nehru's championing of nonalignment and Pakistan's comparatively weak position, Pakistan opted to move squarely in the opposite camp: alignment with the United States.

20. Osgood, *Total Cold War*, 9.

21. Cull, *Cold War and the United States*, 15.

22. "Chronological Background of U.S. Information Activities," Advisory Commission on Information, n.d., Box 4, P215: Records Relating to Information Programs, 1948–1953, RG 306, NACP.

23. USIS India was named USIE at the time. India Semi-Annual Report, USIE Field Reporting, June 1–November 30, 1950, Box 10, P265: Records Relating to India, 1952–1956, RG 306, NACP.

24. Osgood, *Total Cold War*, 93.

25. Osgood, *Total Cold War*, 9.

26. Office Memorandum, "Outline Plan of Operations on NSC-5409," Jones in DOS to Landon in OCB, March 2, 1955, Folder: OCB 091, Pakistan (File #1) (3) [June 1954–June 1955], Box 51, A-82-18, White House Office, National Security Council Staff: Papers, 1948–1961, OCB Central File Series, EPL.

27. Osgood, *Total Cold War*, 93. In 1955, for example, USIA requested $965,000 "for Pakistan for indigenous propaganda groups, anti-communist pamphlets, films and books, atomic energy exhibit, and anti-communist radio programs," labeled "high priority items." Memorandum for Harold E. Stassen, February 2, 1955, Folder: OCB 091, Pakistan (File #1) (2) [June 1954–June 1955], Box 51, A82-18, White House Office, National Security Council Staff: Papers, 1948–61, OCB Central File Series, EPL.

28. Secret Memorandum, USIA Policy Officer N. Paul Neilson to Marion Boggs at NSC, September 24, 1958, and Draft of USIA Annual Report in Secret Memorandum

from Oren Stephens, September 9, 1957, Box 2, P253: Subject Files, 1953–1959, RG 306, NACP.

29. Public Law 80-402, January 27, 1948, United States Information and Cultural Exchange Act of 1948.

30. Osgood, *Total Cold War*, 219. Per the Smith-Mundt Act and Fulbright Act, the State Department maintained control of cultural and educational exchange, while propaganda work (which would have tainted the department) was carried out by a separate agency (after 1953, USIA).

31. Osgood, *Total Cold War*.

32. "India Semi-Annual Report"; "Confidential Security Information: India Country Program," 1954, Box 6, P265: Records Relating to India, 1952–1956, RG 306, NACP.

33. "Confidential Security Information: India Country Program.".

34. SyamRoy, *India's Journey towards Sustainable Population*, 10; Hashmi and Sultan, "Population Trends and Rates of Population Growth in Pakistan," 486–97.

35. Parker, *Hearts, Minds, Voices*; Cull, *Cold War and the United States*; Bu, *Making the World Like Us*.

36. Parker, *Hearts, Minds, Voices*, 11.

37. "Some Highlights of the USIS Program in India," November 16, 1953, Folder: India, Program–1954, Box 6, P265: Records Relating to India, 1952–1956, RG 306, NACP; "Confidential Security Information: India Country Program."

38. USIS, "Country Plan: Pakistan," April 4, 1953, Folder: Pakistan, 1954–1955, Box 1, P267: Records Relating to Pakistan, 1952–1955, RG 306, NACP.

39. *Saptarshi* newsletter, Dacca, September 1961, Folder: Dacca Tenth Anniversary of USIS in East Pakistan, Box 213, U.S. Information Agency, 1951–1979, RG 306, NACP. East Pakistan alone had 113 staff members.

40. *Saptarshi* newsletter. Branch centers included Barisal, Mymensingh, Sylhet, Chittagong, and Rajshahi.

41. DOS to Embassy of Pakistan, January 4, 1955, 1955–1959 Central Decimal File, Box 2227, RG 59, NACP.

42. Am Embassy Karachi to DOS, "Public Law 402 Foreign Leader Program," October 28, 1955, 1955–1959 Central Decimal File, Box 2227, RG 306, NACP; DOS to Saltonstall, January 21, 1960, 1960–1963 Central Decimal File, Box 1081, RG 59, NACP.

43. Telegram, U.S. Ambassador to Pakistan Horace A. Hildreth to Secy of State, August 26, 1955, Folder 511.90D3, 1955–1959 Central Decimal File, Box 2227, RG 59, NACP.

44. Am Embassy Karachi to DOS, January 6, 1956, 1955–1959 Central Decimal File, Box 2227, RG 59, NACP.

45. C. Subramaniam to Dean Rusk, August 25, 1961, 1960–1963 Central Decimal File, Box 1081, RG 59, NACP.

46. Field Message 52, Carl Gebuhr, Public Affairs Officer, USIS Lahore, to USIA Washington, April 30, 1962, Box 30, A1 1039: Records Concerning Exhibits in Foreign Countries, 1955–1967, RG 306, NACP.

47. FSD, Alexander Daspit, First Secretary, Am Embassy Karachi, to DOS, April 27, 1956, Folder 511.90D3, 1955–1959 Central Decimal File, Box 2227, RG 59, NACP.

48. FSD, Public Affairs Officer Thomas J. Needham in USIS Calcutta to USIA,

June 14, 1954, Folder: India Records–1955, Box 11, P265: Records Relating to India, 1952–1956, RG 306, NACP.

49. Williams in Am Con Gen Dacca to DOS, 1955–1959 Central Decimal File, Box 2227, RG 59, NACP.

50. "A Pakistani Looks at America," text of M. A. Azam speech, FSD from USIS Dacca to USIA Washington, December 3, 1954, Box 2, P267: Records Related to Pakistan, 1952–1955, RG 306, NACP.

51. Joseph, *Amiable American*, 38.

52. FSD, Cultural Affairs Officer Edwin C. Kirkland in Am Con Gen Bombay to DOS, August 2, 1955, Folder: India Records–1955, Box 11, P265: Records Relating to India, 1952–1956, RG 306, NACP.

53. Kirkland to DOS, August 2, 1955.

54. On the difficulties experienced by the refugees during Partition, see Khan, *Great Partition*.

55. Yasmin Iqbal, interview with author, 2007, HHP.

56. Pierre Bourdieu, "The Forms of Capital," in Richardson, *Handbook of Theory and Research*, 241–58.

57. Alfred V. Boerner (Asst Secy, Educational and Cultural Affairs) to John S. Cooper, November 14, 1962, 1960–1963 Central Decimal File, Box 1081, RG 59, NACP.

58. FSD, John K. Emerson to DOS, June 7, 1954, Doc 511.90D3/6-754, Box 2, P267: Records Relating to Pakistan, 1952–1955, RG 306, NACP.

59. Lebovic, "From War Junk to Educational Exchange"; Lonnie R. Johnson, "The Fulbright Program and the Philosophy and Geography of U.S. Exchange Programs since World War II," in Tournès and Giles Scott-Smith, *Global Exchanges*.

60. Khaliq in Pak Embassy DC to Hawkins in DOS, November 17, 1955, 1955–1959 Central Decimal File, Box 2227, RG 59, NACP.

61. FSD, Garrett H. Soulen, First Secretary, USIS Karachi, to USIA Washington, April 5, 1955, Folder 511.90D3, 1955–1959 Central Decimal File, Box 2227, RG 59, NACP.

62. FSD, Arthur Z. Gardiner, Deputy Chief of Mission, Am Embassy Karachi, to DOS, July 15, 1955, Folder 511.90D3, 1955–1959 Central Decimal File, Box 2227, RG 59, NACP.

63. Announcement of Award, 1960–63 Central Decimal File, Box 1081, RG 59, NACP.

64. Norman D. Palmer and Friends of India to Chester Bowles, April 1961, 1960–1963 Central Decimal File, Folder 511.913/1-461, Box 1081, RG 59, NACP.

65. Dean Rusk to Norman Palmer, April 21, 1961, 1960–1963 Central Decimal File, Box 1081, RG 59, NACP.

66. Brooks Hays to Jack Miller (Senator, Iowa), May 17, 1961, 1960–63 Central Decimal File, Box 1081, RG 59, NACP.

67. Soulen to USIA Washington, April 5, 1955.

68. Report, "Improving the Service of Research and Information Concerning International Educational Exchange Activities, 1949," DOS and American Council on Education, Folder: Dept. of State Info Programs, 1949—International Educational Exchange Act, Box 11, Charles M. Hulten Papers, TPL.

69. FSD (Semi-Annual Report), Alexander Daspit, First Secretary, Am Embassy

Karachi, to DOS, March 14, 1956, Folder 511.90D3, 1955–1959 Central Decimal File, Box 2227, RG 59, NACP.

70. Rotter, *Comrades at Odds*; Chaudhuri, *Forged in Crisis*; Rakove, *Kennedy, Johnson, and the Nonaligned World*.

71. William K. Cummings, "Foreign Students," in Altbach, *International Higher Education*, 118.

72. "Confidential Security Information: India Report for Jackson Committee," 1954, Box 6, P265: Records Relating to India, 1952–1956, RG 306, NACP.

73. Gardiner in Am Embassy Karachi to DOS, February 16, 1956, 1955–1959 Central Decimal File, Box 2227, RG 59, NACP; "Report: The Indian Student," September 1954, Folder: IEV IND 55, Box 29, P78: International Survey Research Reports, 1953–1964, RG 306, NACP; "Country Plan: Pakistan," USIS, April 4, 1953, Folder: Pakistan, 1954 and 1955, Box 1, P267: Records Relating to Pakistan, 1952–1955, RG 306, NACP. By comparison, more than 2.6 million American students were enrolled in U.S. universities.

74. "Country Plan: Pakistan," 11.

75. "Overt Information and Propaganda/Confidential Security Information: India," n.d., Folder: General-Reports-Misc-1953, Box 1, P268: Records Relating to South Asia, 1952–1956, RG 306, NACP.

76. "Confidential Security Information: India Country Program," 1954, Box 6, P265: Records Relating to India, 1952–1956, RG 306, NACP.

77. "Confidential Security Information: India Country Program."

78. "Operations Memorandum: Greater Utilization of U.S. College and University Resources in the Agency's Programs," USIS Bombay to USIA, December 13, 1954, Box 7, P265: Records Relating to India, 1952–1956, RG 306, NACP.

79. "Minutes of Conference on College Contact Program, Madras, March 2–4, 1953," enclosure in FSD, Teg C. Grondahl, Counselor and Chief Public Affairs Officer at Am Embassy New Delhi, to DOS, March 13, 1953, Folder: USIA Cultural Program India, 1954, Box 2, P265: Records Relating to India, 1952–1956, RG 306, NACP.

80. "Confidential Security Information: India Country Program."

81. "Minutes of Conference on College Contact Program, Madras."

82. "Summary: USIS Accomplishments during Its First Ten Years in E. Pakistan," Field Message 36 from Public Affairs Officer Wilson P. Dizard at USIS Dacca to USIA Washington, October 24, 1961, Box 30, A1 1039: Records Concerning Exhibits in Foreign Countries, 1955–1967, RG 306, NACP.

83. "Minutes of Conference on College Contact Program, Madras."

84. Harun Farid, interview with author, 2011, HHP.

85. Benjamin Cohen defines *jagir* as "a grant of land made for military support or as a personal honor by the ruler upon a subordinate" (*Kingship and Colonialism in India's Deccan*, 22–23). Barbara Metcalf and Thomas Metcalf define a *jagir* as "the right to the assessed tax revenue of a piece of land, given for a limited term by the Mughals as a reward for service" (*Concise History of Modern India*, xxii).

86. The gender breakdown among South Asian international students is discussed in a later chapter.

87. Joseph, *Amiable American*, 1–2.

88. "Monthly Report of the Library in Bombay, March 1–31, 1946," Consulate General of the U.S., Public Affairs Branch, Folder: Dept. of State Info Programs, 1946—Monthly Reports—India, Box 8, Charles M. Hulten Papers, TPL.

89. "Stereotyped Concepts . . . ," Intelligence Research Report OCL–4242, February 5, 1947, DOS, Folder: Dept. of State Info Programs, 1947—Stereotyped Concepts of U.S., Box 9, Charles M. Hulten Papers, TPL.

90. Gardiner in Am Embassy Karachi to DOS, October 10, 1955, 1955–1959 Central Decimal File, Box 2227, RG 59, NACP.

91. Williams in Am Embassy Dacca to DOS, February 17, 1956, 1955–1959 Central Decimal File, Box 2227, RG 59, NACP.

92. Soulen to USIA Washington.

93. FSD, Alexander Daspit, First Secretary, Am Embassy Karachi, to DOS, April 28, 1956, Folder: 511.90D3, 1955–1959 Central Decimal File, Box 2227, RG 59, NACP.

94. Field Message 53, Public Affairs Officer Wilson P. Dizard at USIS Dacca to USIA Washington, February 28, 1962, Box 30, A1 1039: Records Concerning Exhibits in Foreign Countries, 1955–1967, RG 306, NACP.

95. Gardiner in Am Embassy Karachi to DOS, February 16, 1956, 1955–1959 Central Decimal File, Box 2227, RG 59, NACP. Several works address U.S. cultural diplomacy abroad, including Von Eschen, *Satchmo Blows Up the World*; Prevots, *Dance for Export*; and Wulf, *U.S. International Exhibitions during the Cold War*.

96. FSD (Semi-Annual Report), Daspit to DOS.

97. Yasmin Iqbal, interview

98. Sara Waheed, interview with author, 2007, HHP.

99. FSD (Semi-Annual Report), Daspit to DOS.

100. FSD, Chargé d'Affaires ad Interim Arthur Z. Gardiner in Am Embassy Karachi to DOS, September 12, 1955, Box 1, P267: Records Relating to Pakistan, 1952–1955, RG 306, NACP.

101. DOS to Ambassador of Pakistan, "Secretary of State Presents . . . ," 1954–1955, Folder 5.11.90D3/1-455 to 12-3/56, 1955–1959 Central Decimal File, Box 2227, RG 59, NACP.

102. "Confidential Security Information: India Country Program."

103. "Summary: USIS Accomplishments during Its First Ten Years in E. Pakistan."

104. USIA correspondence, Public Affairs Officer Renzo Pagin to USIA Washington, October 26, 1961, and letter to Senator Harry F. Byrd, October 26, 1962, Doc. 511.913/10–462, both in Folder 511.913/8–1062, 1960–1963 Central Decimal File, Box 1081, RG 59, NACP.

105. "Summary: USIS Accomplishments during Its First Ten Years in E. Pakistan."

106. Oliver Schmidt, "Small Atlantic World: U.S. Philanthropy and the Expanding International Exchange of Scholars after 1945," in Gienow-Hecht and Schumacher, *Culture and International History*; David Engerman, "Solidarity, Development, and Non-Alignment: Foreign Economic Advisors and Indian Planning in the 1950s and 1960s," in Unfried, *Practices of International Solidarity*.

107. Selina Ahmed, oral history interview, July 11, 2013HAAA. See also *Development of Home Economics in Pakistan*; Berry, "Lakshmi and the Scientific Housewife."

108. Jamal Iqbal, interview with author, 2007, HHP.

109. DOS to Menon, January 22, 1960, 1960–1963 Central Decimal File, Box 1081, RG 59, NACP.

110. Hays to Fisher, August 15, 1961, 1960–1963 Central Decimal File, Box 1081, RG 59, NACP.

111. FSD (Semi-Annual Report), Daspit to DOS.

112. Hays to Wilson, September 12, 1961, 1960–1963 Central Decimal File, Box 1081, RG 59, NACP; Correspondence from Moses Hirschtritt of International Exchange Service to Donnal Smith, President, Cortland State Teachers College, May 16, 1956, Folder 511.90D3, 1955–1959 Central Decimal File, Box 2227, RG 59, NACP.

113. Williams in Am Consul Gen Dacca to DOS, Conference with Dr. W. A. Jenkins, September 21, 1955, 1955–1959 Central Decimal File, Box 2227, RG 59, NACP.

114. Correspondence, Gertrude G. Cameron, Chief of Program Reporting at IEES, to the President of Southern Methodist University, August 10, 1955, Folder 511.90D3, 1955–1959 Central Decimal File, Box 2227, RG 59, NACP.

115. William Phillips Talbot was U.S. assistant secretary of state for Near Eastern and South Asian affairs.

116. Talbot to Samuel B. Gould, September 8, 1961, 1960–1963 Central Decimal File, Box 1081, RG 59, NACP.

117. Benjamin Read to Walt W. Rostow (White House), July 13, 1966, 1964–1966 Central Foreign Policy Files, Box 396, RG 59, NACP.

118. "Confidential Security Information: India Country Program."

119. Field Message 36, USIS Karachi to USIA Washington, November 20, 1964, Box 29, A1 1039: Records Concerning Exhibits in Foreign Countries, 1955–1967, RG 306, NACP.

120. "Outgoing Message: Development of American Studies," USIA to All USIS Mission Posts, August 31, 1959, Box 1, P253: Subject Files, 1953–1959, RG 306, NACP.

121. Field Message 36 USIS Karachi to USIA Washington.

122. Airgram, Am Embassy Karachi to DOS, July 2, 1965, Folder EDU Neth Ant 1/1/64 to EDU Par 1/1/64, 1964–1966 Central Foreign Policy Files, Box 370, RG 59, NACP.

123. "Office Memorandum: Pak Student Convention," June 23, 1954, Box 1, P267: Records Relating to Pakistan, 1952–1955, RG 306, NACP.

124. "Outgoing Message: Coverage of Foreign Students in U.S.," USIS Karachi to USIS Lahore, December 29, 1955, Box 1, P267: Records Relating to Pakistan, 1952–1955, RG 306, NACP.

125. "Office Memorandum: Pak Student Convention."

126. "Office Memorandum: Pak Student Convention."

127. "Office Memorandum: Pak Student Convention."

128. Photo No. 57-16526, "Foreign Students in U.S.-Pakistan," July 26, 1957, Records of the United States Information Agency, Still Picture Branch, NACP.

129. "USIA: Incoming Telegram," June 14, 1955, Box 2, P267: Records Relating to Pakistan, 1952–1955, RG 306, NACP.

130. Photo No. 65-3318 (306-PSD-65-3318), September 1965, Records of the United States Information Agency, Still Picture Branch, NACP.

131. M. Brewster Smith for the *Journal of Higher Education* (1955), quoted in Bevis and Lucas, *International Students*, 136.

132. Lyndon Johnson quoted in Bevis and Lucas, *International Students*, 157.

133. Lyndon Johnson quoted in Bevis and Lucas, *International Students*, 157.

134. Editorial, "IIE Caps Students' American Years," *Houston Chronicle*, June 17, 1962.

135. Editorial, "IIE Caps Students' American Years."

136. Editorial, "IIE Caps Students' American Years."

137. Operations Memorandum, USIS Dacca to USIA Washington, April 12, 1961, Box 30, A1 1039: Records Concerning Exhibits in Foreign Countries, 1955–1967, RG 306, NACP.

138. Joseph, *Amiable American*, 34.

139. Operations Memorandum, USIS Dacca to USIA, April 12, 1961, Box 30, A1 1039: Records Concerning Exhibits in Foreign Countries, 1955–1967, RG 306, NACP.

140. Am Embassy Karachi to Sec State Washington, May 21, 1965, 1964–1966 Central Foreign Policy Files, Box 370, RG 59, NACP.

141. Airgram, "Youth Activities," Am Embassy New Delhi to DOS, September 2, 1966, File India EDX 6, 1964–1966 Central Foreign Policy Files, Box 396, RG 59, NACP.

142. Airgram, "Youth Activities."

143. Airgram, "Emphasis on Youth," Am Embassy Karachi to DOS, July 2, 1965, file CA-11045, 1964–1966 Central Foreign Policy Files, Box 370, RG 59, NACP.

144. Airgram, "Emphasis on Youth."

145. Hing, *Making and Remaking Asian America*, 39.

146. Hsu, *Good Immigrants*, 213. Though Hsu writes specifically of Chinese Americans and their crucial role in challenging immigration restrictions, she also references the actions of other ethnic Americans equally anxious to repeal immigration restriction.

147. Surinder M. Bhardwaj and N. Madhusudana Rao, "Asian Indians in the United States: A Geographic Appraisal," in Clarke, Peach, and Vertovec, *South Asians Overseas*, 199.

148. U.S. Congress, House, Subcommittee No. 1 of the Committee on the Judiciary, Immigration, *Hearings*, 88th Cong., 2d sess., 1964, 418, quoted in Reimers, "Unintended Reform," 16.

149. U.S. Congress, House, *Congressional Record*, August 25, 1965, 111:21758, quoted in Reimers, "Unintended Reform," 16.

150. Chin, "Civil Rights Revolution Comes to Immigration Law."

151. Weekly Compilation of Presidential Documents, 1 (October 11, 1965): 364–65, quoted in Reimers, "Unintended Reform," 16.

152. Appendix, table 7. See also Keely, "Immigration Composition and Population Policy."

153. Fisher, "Creating Ethnic Identity," 272.

154. Bhardwaj and Rao, "Asians Indians in the United States," 199.

155. Godfrey, "Migration of Professionals from Commonwealth Developing Countries," 642.

156. Sohi, *Echoes of Mutiny*, 22–23.

157. Lambert and Bressler, *Indian Students on an American Campus*, 42–43.

158. Joseph, *Amiable American*, 35.

159. Joseph, *Amiable American*, 38, 43.

160. Bassett, "Aligning India in the Cold War," 789.

161. Jamal Iqbal, interview.

162. The first Commonwealth Immigrants Act (1962) required immigrants to obtain employment vouchers before entry. The white paper of 1965 set a quota of 8,500 work vouchers.

163. Based on several oral history interviews conducted by the author.

164. Jamal Iqbal, interview.

165. Joseph, *Amiable American*, 37. Several oral history interviews conducted by the author also reveal the presence of generous financial assistance.

166. Statistics and Information Division, Ministry of Education and Social Welfare, "Studies in Educational Statistics." Between 1965 and 1966, 127 Indian students left India to pursue study in the Soviet Union; in subsequent years, the number fluctuated between 32 and 200 students per year. I was unable to locate statistical reports for East and West Pakistan.

167. Cummings, "Foreign Students," 119.

168. Adams, *Brain Drain*. See also Saxenian, *New Argonauts*.

169. Fortney, "International Migration of Professionals," 229.

170. Pawan Agarwal, "Asia: Higher Education in India and Pakistan—Common Origin, Different Trajectories," in Schreuder, *Universities for a New World*, 203.

171. Prashad, *Karma of Brown Folk*, 76.

172. Ghaswala, "Using What's Available," 314.

173. Fisher, Lahiri, and Thandi, *South-Asian History of Britain*, 162.

174. Ghaswala, "Using What's Available," 314.

175. Ghaswala, "Using What's Available," 314.

176. Naik, *Education Commission and After*. Quoted by N. Jayaram, "Higher Education in India: Massification and Change," in Altbach and Umakoshi, *Asian Universities*, 91.

177. See tables in the Appendix for more data on immigration.

178. Kizilbash, "Employment of Returning U.S. Educated Indians," 320.

179. Godfrey, "Migration of Professionals," 642; Bu, *Making the World Like Us*.

180. Herbert Baumgartner (Public Affairs Office, USIS Bombay) to USIA Washington, October 12, 1964, 1964–1966 Central Foreign Policy Files, Box 365, RG 59, NACP.

181. F visa adjustment was easy, especially in contrast to the J visa, which permitted students to enter the United States for exchange visitor programs, such as fellowships and trainee programs, but required them to leave the country for two years on completion of their course of study. Some temporarily relocated to Canada to work and wait for the two-year period to pass. See Bayer, "Foreign Students in American Colleges."

182. Oh, "Estimating Migration of U.S.-Educated Manpower," 343.

183. Oh, "Estimating Migration of U.S.-Educated Manpower," 345, emphasis added.

184. Oh, "Estimating Migration of U.S.-Educated Manpower," 337.

185. USIS Bombay to USIA Washington, "Educational and Culture Program Co-Sponsored with Sardar Vallabhbhai Vidyapeeth," October 12, 1964, file EDU 9-4 India 1/1/64, 1964–1966 Central Foreign Policy Files, Box 365, RG 59, NACP.

186. Tariq Rahman, interview with author, 2007, HHP; Nagaraj Shekhar, interview with author, 2007, HHP.

187. See Wu, *Color of Success*, and Hsu, *Good Immigrants*, for an excellent, thorough discussion of this phenomenon.

188. Schreuder, *Universities for a New World*; Bevis, *History of Higher Education Exchange*.

189. For a full discussion of U.S. educational exchange efforts as soft power in other countries, see Bu, *Making the World Like Us*.

190. FSD, Alexander Daspit, First Secretary, Am Embassy Karachi, to DOS, April 4, 1956, Folder 511.90D3, 1955–1959 Central Decimal File, Box 2227, RG 59, NACP.

Chapter Two

1. Hsu, *Good Immigrants*, 5.

2. Ritterband, "Law, Policy, and Behavior," 72; Hing, *Making and Remaking Asian America*; Liu, *Chinese Student Migration and Selective Citizenship*. Liu writes, "Foreign students born in countries restricted by the national origins quota (European, South African and Oriental countries) or born of races ineligible for US citizenship were to obtain a nonquota student visa to enter the United States under Section 4(e) of the 1924 Act" (89).

3. Gmelch, "Return Migration."

4. Houston International Airport was renamed William P. Hobby Airport in 1967 after the former Texas governor but also in anticipation of the opening of newer, larger Houston Intercontinental Airport, which opened in 1969.

5. "Bayou Wilderness," Houston Wilderness, http://houstonwilderness.org/bayou -wilderness/. Houston has 2,500 miles of bayous and waterways.

6. General histories of Houston include Fuermann, "Houston, 1880–1910"; Johnston, *Houston: The Unknown City*; McComb, *Houston, the Bayou City*; Platt, *City Building in the New South*; and Siegel, *Houston: A Chronicle*.

7. Potts, *Railroad Transportation in Texas*, 19.

8. See Kreneck, *Del Pueblo*; De León, *Ethnicity in the Sunbelt*; and Beeth and Wintz, *Black Dixie*.

9. Von der Mehden, *Ethnic Groups of Houston*.

10. Glasrud, "Asians in Texas."

11. Glasrud, "Asians in Texas," 15–16.

12. Martha Wong, interview with author, 2007, HHP. Wong was one of the first Asian American members of Houston City Council and the Texas State Legislature. She recalls that while she lived in an all-white neighborhood in the Heights and attended white public schools in the 1940s and 1950s, she had Chinese American friends who lived in African American neighborhoods and attended black schools.

13. De León, *Ethnicity in the Sunbelt*, 23.

14. Feagin, *Free Enterprise City*. See also Levengood, "For the Duration and Beyond." Levengood documents the many war-industry training programs in Houston available privately and through the Houston Independent School District, University of Houston, and so on.

15. Feagin, *Free Enterprise City*, 70. Carleton writes that because of World War II, Houston led the United States in industrial construction by war's end. See Don E. Carleton, *Red Scare!*, 12.

16. Mollenkopf, *Contested City*, 217–18; McComb, *Houston, the Bayou City*, 131.

17. Based on oral history interviews and records in the College of Technology Collection, Special Collections, UH Libraries.

18. Robert Fisher, "The Urban Sunbelt in Comparative Perspective," in Fairbanks and Underwood, *Essays on Sunbelt Cities and Recent Urban America*, 34.

19. Feagin, "Global Context of Metropolitan Growth," 1219.

20. See Nickerson and Dochuk, *Sunbelt Rising*, esp. 85, 146.

21. Social Explorer Tables (SE), Census 1970, Social Explorer and U.S. Census Bureau.

22. Bevis and Lucas, *International Students*, 144.

23. "All Places of Origin of International Students, Selected Years: 1949/50–1999/00," *Open Doors Report on International Educational Exchange*, Institute of International Education, 2009, http://www.iie.org/opendoors.

24. Interactive graph, "Pride Origins: Coogs from across the United States and Texas, Fall 2016," Office of Institutional Research, UH, http://www.uh.edu/ir/.

25. Edison E. Oberholtzer, *The Growth and Development of the University of Houston, A Summation, March 1927–May 1950*, quoted from inside cover text, *Charter of the University of Houston, April 1945* (Houston: University of Houston, 1950), 2, Houston Metropolitan Research Center.

26. Not all the immigrants that I interviewed attended UH, though all were middle class and college educated.

27. The cities were Ahmedabad, Chandigarh, Jadavpur, Madras, Lucknow, Bangalore, Dhanbad, and Bhopal.

28. "Summer Institutes for Polytechnic Faculties," College of Technology Records, 1940–2009, Courtesy of Special Collections, UH Libraries. My thanks to Bryant Etheridge for alerting me to this collection.

29. The topic of international students at Houston's historically segregated university remains a fascinating area for further study.

30. Complete international enrollment data were not available but were aggregated from the following institutions. For University of Houston: *Annual Enrollment Reports*, various, 1969–80, Office of International Student Admissions, College of Arts and Sciences Collection, Special Collections, UH Libraries; *Directory of International Students, 1969–1970; 1974–1975;* and *1977–1978*, International Student Office, College of Arts and Sciences Collection, Box 14, Folder 1, Special Collections, UH Libraries. For Texas Southern University: "Archived International Student Admissions Records," data request, December 8, 2016, Office of the Registrar, Texas Southern University (1960–80). Sincere thanks to TSU registrar Marilyn Square and her staff for tabulating this data. For Rice University: *Rice World* newsletter, Office of International Students and Scholars (Houston: Rice University 1988–2008); *Registrar's Reports to the President* (Houston: Rice University, 1958–84).

31. Kurien, *Place at the Multicultural Table*, 45.

32. Bevis and Lucas, *International Students*, 135.

33. Syamroy, *India's Journey towards Sustainable Population*, 10; Hashmi and Sultan, "Population Trends and Rates of Population Growth in Pakistan," 496.

34. Bevis and Lucas, *International Students*, 152. The largest percentage of graduate students in U.S. universities from any one country was India (67 percent).

35. Bevis and Lucas, *International Students*, 157.

36. Statistics and Information Division, "Studies in Educational Statistics." I was unable to locate statistical reports for East and West Pakistan.

37. Barbara Weinstein, "Commentary on Part I," in López and Barbara Weinstein, *Making of the Middle Class*, 108–9.

38. Suman Parikh, interview with author, 2008, in author's possession.

39. Bevis and Lucas, *International Students*, 147, 152.

40. Kizilbash, "Employment of Returning U.S. Educated Indians," 322.

41. Ong, Cheng, and Evans, "Migration of Highly Educated Asians."

42. Quoted in Helweg, *Strangers in a Not-So-Strange Land*, 46.

43. Betty Ewing, "IIE Calls Them Main Street Diplomats," *Houston Chronicle*, April 28, 1965.

44. Society Today, "IIE Family Program Co-Chairmen Won," *Houston Chronicle*, May 12, 1967.

45. "Statement by J. William Fulbright of Arkansas," Washington, D.C., September, 1945, Fulbright Papers, box 8, file 6. Quoted in Lebovic, "From War Junk to Educational Exchange," 286.

46. "Students Talk Freely about Soviet Study," *Houston Chronicle*, October 19, 1960.

47. Maryrice Brogan, "W.A.D.s Plan 'Blitz Party' to Meet Foreign Students," *Houston Chronicle*, October 16, 1960.

48. "Top Fashions Are Ready for Tuesday's Fete Francais," *Houston Chronicle*, September 15, 1963.

49. "Valentine's Day Tea for Foreign Students," *Houston Chronicle*, February 13, 1966.

50. Committee on International Student Problems, *Report on the International Student at the University of Houston*, July 20, 1968, College of Arts and Sciences Collection, box 14, folder 2, Special Collections, UH Libraries, 73.

51. Marie David, "College Is 'Another World' When You Come from London or Bombay," *Houston Chronicle*, September 17, 1967.

52. Betty Ewing, "IIE Calls Them Main Street Diplomats," *Houston Chronicle*, April 28, 1965.

53. Zafar Waheed, interview with author, 2007, HHP. Although I have not located solid evidence for this, those individuals who I have found were involved in organizing host family efforts were white.

54. Parts of the sections on host families and the church are found in Quraishi, "Educationally Empowered."

55. Sara Waheed, interview with author, 2007, HHP.

56. Ramesh Lal, interview with author, 2011, HHP.

57. Ramesh Lal, intervew.

58. Ramesh Lal, intervew.

59. Ramesh Lal, interview.

60. Yasmin Iqbal, interview with author, 2007, HHP.

61. *Report on the International Student*, 45.

62. *Report on the International Student*, 72.

63. *International News*, UH newsletter, International Student Services, University of Houston, 1968 (complete date unavailable), Special Collections, UH Libraries.

64. *International News*, UH newsletter, 1968 (complete date unavailable), Special Collections, UH Libraries.

65. *International News*, UH newsletter, October 29, 1969 (no volume number listed), Special Collections, UH Libraries.

66. *International News*, UH newsletter, April 21, 1971, vol. 2:28, Special Collections, UH Libraries.

67. Varuni Gil, interview with author, 2007, HHP.

68. The church was possibly the South Main Baptist Church.

69. Sara Waheed, interview.

70. Sara Waheed, interview.

71. "Foreigners in Demand as Guests," *New York Times*, November 16, 1962.

72. *International News*, UH newsletter, November 5, 1969, vol. 1:8; *International News*, November 18, 1970, Special Collections, UH Libraries.

73. *International News*, UH newsletter, December 3, 1969, vol. 1:12, Special Collections, UH Libraries.

74. Tahira Lakhani, interview with author, 2007, HHP.

75. Oral history interview with Najma Rizvi, 2007, South Asian Oral History Project at the University of Washington, accessed through SAADA, https://www.saada.org/item/20170122-4904.

76. For a discussion of caste, see the Introduction.

77. Suman Parikh, interview.

78. Joseph, *Amiable American*, 3.

79. Kizilbash, "Employment of Returning U.S. Educated Indians," 320. This amount excluded extraneous costs.

80. Bevis and Lucas, *International Students*, 156; Wolf, "Anatomy of the Problem," 159.

81. Bevis and Lucas, *International Students*, 195.

82. Zafar Waheed, interview.

83. *Report on the International Student*, 33.

84. *Report on the International Student*, 32.

85. Wolf, "Anatomy of the Problem," 159.

86. Jamal Iqbal, interview with author, 2007, HHP.

87. Less commonly, students applied for immigrant visas, as in the case of Zafar Waheed. Because he had previously lived in Houston while working toward his master's degree, he developed a close relationship with an American family. On the basis of that family's vouching for Waheed's financial solvency, he applied for and received an immigrant visa. After returning to Houston—this time as an "immigrant"—Waheed enrolled at UH for another advanced degree.

88. Yasmin Iqbal, interview.

89. Bald, *Bengali Harlem*; Jensen, *Passage from India*; Leonard, *Making Ethnic Choices*; Takaki, *Strangers from a Different Shore*.

90. "University of Houston Integration Records," Digital Library, UH Libraries, http://digital.lib.uh.edu/collection/integ; Pegoda, "University of Houston and Texas Southern University."

91. Social Explorer, Census 1960. By 1960, Third Ward was 98 percent African American.

92. Pegoda, "University of Houston," 19; Shabazz, *Advancing Democracy*, 206. See also Pegoda, "Watchful Eyes."

93. "University of Houston Integration Records."

94. "Negro Student Survey, Public Senior Colleges and Universities in Texas," November 1966, ID 1985-005, Box 29, Folder 19, President's Office Records, UH Integration Records, Special Collections, UH Libraries.

95. "Headcount Enrollment by Ethnicity, 1971–2014," data generated by Office of Institutional Research, UH, November 10, 2016, at author's request. In 2011, 10 percent of UH's student body was African American. See http://www.uh.edu/about/uh-glance/facts-figures/index.php.

96. San Miguel, *"Let All of Them Take Heed"*; Shabazz, *Advancing Democracy*, 5.

97. San Miguel, *Brown, Not White*, 68. Chicano activists in the group ARMAS protested this discrepancy on September 16, 1969.

98. "Headcount Enrollment by Ethnicity, 1971–2014."

99. Boles, *A University So Conceived*.

100. Kean, *Desegregating Private Higher Education*, 220–33. In 1962, at the urging of Rice University president Kenneth Pitzer, the board of trustees unanimously passed a resolution to desegregate the university, but soon thereafter, two Rice alumni passed a counterresolution to maintain racial exclusion. The lawsuit was not resolved until 1966.

101. Oral history interview with Najma Rizvi, 2007, South Asian Oral History Project at the University of Washington, accessed through SAADA, https://www.saada.org/item/20170122-4904.

102. This term is borrowed from the sociological "gateway city" to denote a common geographic point of entry before more permanent settlement. See the example of Gulfton in Southwest Houston in Rogers, "Superneighborhood 27."

103. Wilson, "Third Ward, Steeped in Tradition," 31; Bullard, *Invisible Houston*, 30.

104. Bullard, *Invisible Houston*, 24; Lipsitz, *How Racism Takes Place*, 151; Robert D. Bullard, "Blacks in Heavenly Houston," in Bullard *In Search of the New South*, 17. The city charter of 1839 divided Houston into four sections—First through Fourth Wards—though more wards would be added later. After emancipation, formerly enslaved peoples took up residence in Fourth Ward, establishing Freedman's Town. Eventually, they also settled predominantly in Fifth and Third Wards.

105. Social Explorer Tables (SE), Census 1940, Social Explorer and U.S. Census Bureau.

106. Robert Bullard, *Invisible Houston*.

107. Bullard, *Invisible Houston*, 24–25. The construction of Interstate 45 divided the Fourth Ward neighborhood, rendering the unstable neighborhood more susceptible

to the expanding central business district on its border; see also Lipsitz, *How Racism Takes Place*, 151.

108. Houston City Planning Department, *Third Ward Data Book*, 1.

109. Bullard, *Invisible Houston*, 30.

110. Houston City Planning Department, *Third Ward Data Book*, 1.

111. A "lifeworld" or *lebenswelt* (from Edmund Husserl) can be defined as the reality produced through the individual's interactions with and in society. See Schwandt, *SAGE Dictionary of Qualitative Inquiry*.

112. Zafar Waheed, interview.

113. International Student Office, "International Student Roster," various, Fall 1966 through Summer 1968, College of Arts and Sciences Collection, Box 14, Folder 1, Special Collections, UH Libraries; *A Report on the International Student*, 52.

114. Suresh Bhatt, interview with author, 2011, HHP.

115. Jamal Iqbal, interview with author, 2007, HHP.

116. Rohan Patil, interview with author, 2011, HHP.

117. Suresh Bhatt, interview.

118. Suresh Bhatt, interview. According to Bhatt, there were not many white American or Hispanic American engineering graduate students either. International students constituted the bulk of students. His own cohort, matriculating in 1974, entailed one student each from Mexico, Israel, Iran, Argentina, and Chile, perhaps two from the United States, and three from India.

119. Suresh Bhatt, interview.

120. Ramesh Lal, interview.

121. Ramesh Lal, interview.

122. Suresh Bhatt, interview.

123. Raman, *Hindu in America*, 65–66.

124. Raman, *Hindu in America*, 66.

125. Raman, *Hindu in America*, 66.

126. Raman, *Hindu in America*, 66.

127. Raman, *Hindu in America*, 65.

128. Raman, *Hindu in America*, 65.

129. Yasmin Iqbal, interview.

130. Varuni Gil, interview.

131. Ramesh Lal, interview.

132. Tatum, *"Why Are All the Black Kids Sitting Together in the Cafeteria?"*

133. Omi and Winant, *Racial Formation in the United States*; Bonilla-Silva, *White Supremacy and Racism*.

134. Ramesh Lal, interview.

135. Bhatia, *American Karma*, 198. Quoted from George, "'From Expatriate Aristocrat to Immigrant Nobody.'"

136. Ashok Dani and Lata Dani, interview with author, 2011, HHP. See also Bevis and Lucas, *International Students*, 244.

137. Bevis and Lucas, *International Students*, 244.

138. Vinay Harpalani, building on previous work by Nazli Kibria, offers a theorization of South Asian "racial ambiguity" in which he suggests that South Asians,

biracial, and multiracial individuals, along with "other groups, such as Latinos and Arab Americans, can be racially ambiguous." See Harpalani, "Desicrit." Kibria proposed the idea of Asian American racial ambiguity in her article "The Contested Meanings of 'Asian American.'"

139. Mrudula Bavare, interview with author, 2007, in author's possession.

140. Maira, *Desis in the House*. Maira demonstrates that second-generation South Asian youth use ethnic identity as a way to transcend and bypass racial assignations.

141. Zafar Waheed, interview.

142. Ian Haney López, *White by Law*, quoted in Koshy, "Category Crisis," 291–92.

143. "Indian Envoy Gets Snub at Airport Here," *Houston Chronicle*, August 23, 1955.

144. "Cafe Manager Denies Charge," *Beaumont Enterprise*, August 25, 1955. After much publicity of the incident, Alley quickly shifted stories, claiming that she recognized Mehta as a dignitary and so invited him to dine in a more comfortable private area. See also "Claim Indian Envoy Was Not Snubbed Here," *Houston Chronicle*, August 24, 1955.

145. "Bulletin," *Houston Chronicle*, August 23, 1955; "India Unruffled by Texas Incident," *New York Times*, August 25, 1955. For information on other such incidents throughout the United States, see Layton, *International Politics and Civil Rights Policies*.

146. Carleton, *Red Scare*. Klan-sponsored barbeques and parades in Houston attracted several thousand attendees from the 1920s. In addition, the statewide Klan newspaper, *Colonel's Mayfield's Weekly*, was published in Houston. See Greene, "Guardians against Change."

147. Kreneck, *Del Pueblo*, 34. In the 1920s, Mexicans were vilified in the press for their supposedly weak English skills, lack of religiosity (and concurrent overreligiosity, perceived as a papal threat), and presumed general "ignorance."

148. Carleton, *Red Scare*. Carleton writes of a lesser-known incident involving anticommunist groups in Houston and an Indian dignitary. After a lecture in Dallas in which Dr. Bharatan Kumarappa, a U.N. representative, spoke in critical terms about Western colonialism and the United States, Kumarappa's subsequent lectures in Houston were canceled. *Red Scare*, 138.

149. Carleton, *Red Scare*, 296–309.

150. Rohan Patil, interview.

151. Watson, *Race and the Houston Police Department*.

152. Rohan Patil, interview.

153. Emphasis mine. Raj Bindal, interview with author, 2011, HHP.

154. Raj Bindal, interview.

155. Yancy, *Black Bodies, White Gazes*, xix–xx.

156. When asked to discuss their lives as immigrants, interviewees usually began their narratives with their arrival in the United States. The problem with this starting point is that they arrived in the United States with cultural capital, not with a blank slate, and certainly not disadvantaged. Obviously, not every immigrant would describe the journey in this way, but for those with whom I spoke, the rags to riches trope emerged very clearly. As noted in the Introduction, I have not attempted to identify universal patterns across entire subcommunities; however, this pattern, no

matter how uncomfortable to South Asians, is a powerful evasion of American society's historical, systematic, structural discrimination against African Americans.

157. The American Dream, model minority myth, and affirmative action are discussed at greater length in other chapters. See also Hayden, *Redesigning the American Dream*.

158. Hsu and Wu, "'Smoke and Mirrors,'" 43.

159. Chung, *Saving Face*; Chou and Feagin, *Myth of the Model Minority*.

160. Kim, "Racial Triangulation of Asian Americans," 105–7.

161. Hsu, *Good Immigrants*.

162. Wu, *Color of Success*.

163. See Hsu, *Good Immigrants*.

164. Xu and Lee, "The Marginalized 'Model' Minority"; Kim, "Racial Triangulation of Asian Americans."

165. Hsu and Wu, "'Smoke and Mirrors'"; Prashad, *Karma of Brown Folk*.

Chapter Three

1. Jamal Iqbal, interview with author, 2007, HHP.

2. Feagin, *Free Enterprise City*, 197–99.

3. Jamal Iqbal, interview.

4. City of Houston, Planning and Development Department, *Historical Population: 1900 to 2017*. See also table 4.

5. Social Explorer Tables (SE), Census 1970, Social Explorer and U.S. Census Bureau.

6. Social Explorer Tables, made from Census 1980 Summary File 1 and Summary File 3, U.S. Census Bureau.

7. This shift in orientation was initially proposed by Clifford Geertz in his landmark work *The Interpretation of Cultures*. See also Swidler, "Culture in Action," 273.

8. Espiritu, *Asian American Panethnicity*; Portes, "Rise of Ethnicity"; Okamoto, "Toward a Theory of Panethnicity"; Lopez and Espiritu, "Panethnicity in the United States."

9. See Diner, *Jews of the United States*; and Gabaccia, *From Sicily to Elizabeth Street*.

10. Espiritu, *Asian American Panethnicity*, 3.

11. Espiritu, *Asian American Panethnicity*, 2.

12. Espiritu, *Asian American Panethnicity*, 6.

13. Ayesha Jalal unconventionally argues that Jinnah preferred an autonomous "Pakistan" *within* and as part of independent India. Though the idea of an autonomous and sovereign Muslim nation had been championed for many years before Pakistan, in the haste of British Partition plans, Jinnah was forced to accept the idea of a "moth-eaten and truncated" Pakistan in 1947. See Jalal, *Sole Spokesman*, 260. See also Malik, *Making of the Pakistan Resolution*; Sattar, *Pakistan's Foreign Policy*; and Jalal, *Struggle for Pakistan*.

14. Wiebe, *Who We Are*.

15. For readings on ethnicity, see Bhatia, *American Karma*; Brah, *Cartographies of Diaspora*; Espiritu, *Asian American Panethnicity*; Hall, "Ethnicity: Identity, and

Difference"; Lowe, "Heterogeneity, Hybridity, Multiplicity"; Nagel, "Constructing Ethnicity"; Rudrappa, *Ethnic Routes to Becoming American*; and Shukla, *India
Abroad.*

16. Shankar, *A Part, Yet Apart.*

17. For readings on ethnicity, see Shukla, *India Abroad*; and Shankar, *A Part, Yet
Apart.*

18. I define these as nonradical in the context of this South Asian diaspora, though
in other places and times, these art forms may very well have been.

19. "Pakistani Ambassador Visits," *Houston Chronicle*, April 7, 1974.

20. Jyoti Patel, interview with author, 2011, HHP.

21. Helweg, *Strangers in a Not-so-Strange Land*, 110.

22. *International News* UH newsletter, International Student Services, University of
Houston, September 4, 1974, vol. 6:1, Presidents Office Collection, Box 29, Folder 32,
Special Collections, UH Libraries.

23. Frances Victory, "Indians to Celebrate Here," *Houston Post*, August 15, 1977.

24. Bhanu Shekhar, interview with author, 2007, HHP.

25. Nadia Hasan, interview with author, 2007, HHP.

26. Nagaraj Shekhar, interview with author, 2007, HHP.

27. Anita Sharma, interview with author, 2011, in author's possession. Mukesh
Chand Mathur, popularly known as Mukesh, was a playback singer for the Hindi film
industry from 1941 to 1976. Asha Parekh was active in the Hindi film industry as an
actress since childhood and as a director and producer since the 1990s.

28. "Dress Rehearsal," *Houston Chronicle*, March 1, 1968.

29. Nagaraj Shekhar, interview.

30. Nagaraj Shekhar, interview.

31. *International News* UH newsletter, International Student Services, University of
Houston, October 29, 1969, vol. 1:6, Special Collections, UH Libraries.

32. Suman Parikh, interview with author, 2008, in author's possession.

33. Yasmin Iqbal, interview with author, 2007, HHP. Javed Malhotra, interview
with author, 2007, HHP.

34. Tahira Lakhani, interview with author, 2007, HHP.

35. Xenos et al., *Asian Indians in the United States*, 16; Morrison G. Wong and
Charles Hirschman, "The New Asian Immigrants," in McCready, *Culture, Ethnicity,
and Identity*, 381–403.

36. Xenos et al., *Asian Indians*; by 1984 about 50 percent of Indian immigrants were
women (*Asian Indians*, 16). Reddy, *Nursing and Empire.*

37. For studies that elaborate exclusively on Indian women's experiences, see
George, *When Women Come First*; Sircar, *Work Roles, Gender Roles, and Asian
Indian Immigrant Women*; Thacker, "Homeward Bound"; and Reddy, *Nursing and
Empire.*

38. Church groups will be discussed further in this chapter.

39. Sara Waheed, interview with author, 2007, HHP.

40. Yasmin Iqbal, interview.

41. Nadia Hasan, interview.

42. Tahira Lakhani, interview.

43. Nagaraj Shekhar, interview.

44. Sara Waheed, interview.

45. See Das, *Desi Dreams*; Vasudhaiva Kutumbakam, "Family in the Knowledge Economy," in Opitz, Staffan Bergwik, and Van Tiggelen, *Domesticity in the Making of Modern Science*.

46. Nadia Hasan, interview.

47. Yasmin Iqbal, interview.

48. Sara Waheed, interview.

49. Sara Waheed, interview.

50. One interviewee, Tahira Lakhani, had planned to pursue higher education as soon as she arrived in the United States in 1972 after her marriage to an Indian immigrant.

51. Varuni Gil, interview with author, 2007, HHP.

52. Yasmin Iqbal, interview.

53. Xenos et al., *Asian Indians*.

54. Namrata Chandra, interview with author, 2011, HHP.

55. Vera Khatri, interview with author, 2011, HHP.

56. Nadia Hasan, interview.

57. Varuni Gil, interview.

58. Yasmin Iqbal, interview.

59. Tariq Rahman, interview with author, 2007, HHP; Rustom Mistri, interview with author, 2011, HHP; Zafar Waheed, interview with author, 2007, HHP.

60. Jamal Iqbal, interview.

61. Saumitra Kelkar, interview with author, 2011, HHP.

62. Javed Malhotra, interview with author, 2007, HHP.

63. Yasmin Iqbal, interview.

64. Sara Waheed, interview.

65. Stuart Hall, "Cultural Identity and Diaspora," in Rutherford, *Identity, Community, Culture, Difference*, 225.

66. Zafar Waheed, interview.

67. Sattar, *Pakistan's Foreign Policy*, 160–69.

68. Nagaraj Shekhar, interview. Ragas are musical scales upon which South Asian music is based.

69. *Indo American News*, June 9, 1984.

70. Shaila Dewan, "Desi Dance," *Houston Press*, September 25, 1997.

71. In addition, Ahmed Afzal writes about post-2000 Desi radio programs on Houston's airwaves in *Lone Star Muslims*.

72. The Mughal court used Urdu as the language of the literati, regardless of religion. Urdu was thus elevated as an art form, enjoyed for its poetic and expressive qualities. In India and Pakistan today, enthusiasts regularly gather to enjoy recitals. Modern India is home to more than twenty major languages, while more than ten major languages are spoken within Pakistan's borders.

73. Ahmad, "Scripting a New Identity," 1167.

74. Dalby, *Dictionary of Languages*, 663.

75. Farooqi, "'Hindi' of the 'Urdu,'" 18–20.

76. Farooqi, "'Hindi' of the 'Urdu,'" 20.

77. Ahmad, "Scripting a New Identity," 1164.

78. Ahmad, "Scripting a New Identity," 1164, 1170.

79. Metcalf and Metcalf, *Concise History of Modern India*, 134.

80. Ahmad, "Scripting a New Identity," 1181. Modern Urdu contains more loan words from Persian and is written in the Indo-Persian script, whereas Hindi increasingly draws more from Sanskrit. The newly created independent nation of Pakistan adopted Urdu and English as its official languages.

81. Sara Waheed, interview.

82. Sara Waheed, interview.

83. Metcalf, "Urdu in India the 21st Century," 30. According to Metcalf, Urdu, a language that emerged as a "highly developed language of poetry" in the eighteenth century, was spoken by educated, elite Muslims and Hindus across broad areas of north India. The new intelligentsia used Urdu in new genres of expression like journalism and novels, while scribes of all religions wrote in Urdu. Thus, as Benedict Anderson indicates in *Imagined Communities,* the literate or "reading classes" were both the producers and consumers of the print market, linked as a community through the "silent bazaar" of print capitalism. It is therefore unsurprising that the debates regarding Urdu and Hindi were waged by civil servants and "prominent Hindus" through official memoranda and, especially, through local language newspapers. See Ahmad, "Scripting a New Identity," 1167–68; and Anderson, *Imagined Communities*.

84. Yasmin Iqbal, interview.

85. Nadia Hasan, interview. Hasan added, "With Mom, I used to talk to her over the phone because she would not speak in English. I was not very good at writing in Urdu although I did write, but it would take me forever to write so [we] talked on the phone. But with Father and with the rest of the family, I always wrote to them in English. So, we never had problems communicating that way."

86. Tahira Lakhani, interview.

87. Yasmin Iqbal, interview.

88. Yasmin Iqbal, interview.

89. Diwali (Deepavali) is a festival of lights that originates in a scriptural story of good triumphing over evil.

90. Williams, *Religions of Immigrants from India and Pakistan*; Ebaugh and Chafetz, *Religion and the New Immigrants*; Fenton, *Transplanting Religious Traditions*; Kurien, *Place at the Multicultural Table*.

91. Ebaugh and Chafetz, *Religion and the New Immigrants*; Kurien, *A Place*; Kurien, "Religion, Ethnicity and Politics."

92. Williams, *Religions of Immigrants*, 11.

93. Williams, *Religions of Immigrants*, 3.

94. Varuni Gil, interview.

95. Varuni Gil, interview.

96. Yasmin Iqbal, interview.

97. The first president of MSA at UH was Khalil Yazdi while the general secretary was Zia Haque. *International News*, UH newsletter, International Student Services, University of Houston, October 2, 1974, vol. 6:14, Presidents Office Collection, Box 29, Folder 32, Special Collections, UH Libraries.

98. *International News*, UH newsletter, October 2, 1974, vol. 6:14, Special Collections, Presidents Office Collection, UH Libraries.

99. Jamal Iqbal, interview.

100. Sara Waheed, interview, HHP; Zafar Waheed, interview; Yasmin Iqbal, interview; Jamal Iqbal, interview.

101. The Islamic Society of Greater Houston, "Resolution Adopted by the Executive Committee," November 4, 1971. For more on ISGH, see Hoda Badr, "Al-Noor Mosque: Strength through Unity," in Ebaugh and Chafetz, *Religion and the New Immigrants*.

102. Louis Moore, "Moslems Open Mosque in Houston; First in the South," *Houston Chronicle*, August 11, 1972.

103. Diouf, *Servants of Allah*; Curtis, *Encyclopedia of Muslim-American History*.

104. Religious studies scholar Jane I. Smith writes that mainstream Muslims find the teaching of the NOI "irreconcilable with the tradition of Islam," largely because of NOI founders' claims to prophethood. Smith, *Islam in America*, 83.

105. "Founded in the 1950's," Masjid Warithuddeen Mohammed, http://masjidwd mohammed.com/history/.

106. "Moslems Open Mosque in Houston; First in the South," *Houston Chronicle*, August 11, 1972.

107. Burke Watson, "About 5,000 Families Comprise Burgeoning Hindu Community," *Houston Chronicle*, July 10, 1982.

108. Williamson, *Transcendent in America*.

109. Barbara Karkabi, "A Bit of India Comes to Texas," *Houston Chronicle*, July 29, 19821; "Temple of Faith: Houston Area Hindu Community Erects Religious Shrine," *Houston Chronicle*, July 29, 1982.

110. Simon Jacob and Pallavi Thaku, "Jyoti Hindu Temple: One Religion, Many Practices," in Ebaugh and Chafetz, *Religion and the New Immigrants*. "Jyoti Temple" is a pseudonym for Meenakshi Temple as selected by the authors.

111. "Collection Plate: To Inaugurate New Shrine," *Houston Chronicle*, August 18, 1979.

112. Karkabi, "Bit of India Comes to Texas"; "Temple of Faith."

113. "Temple Society Dinner," *Houston Chronicle*, May 15, 1982; "First Hindu Temple," *Houston Chronicle*, May 22, 1982; "Hindu Temple Inauguration Set," *Houston Chronicle*, June 26, 1982.

114. Karkabi, "Bit of India Comes to Texas"; "Temple of Faith."

115. Karkabi, "Bit of India Comes to Texas"; "Temple of Faith."

116. "Sri Meenakshi Devasthanam," Meenakshi Temple, https://www.emeenakshi .org/StaticContentMenu.aspx?PN=Temple_History.htm.

117. Karkabi, "Bit of India Comes to Texas"; "Temple of Faith."

118. Advertisement, "Ravi Shankar in Concert," *Houston Chronicle*, May 1, 1983.

119. Karkabi, "Bit of India Comes to Texas"; "Temple of Faith."

120. Karkabi, "Bit of India Comes to Texas"; "Temple of Faith."

121. Jacob and Thaku, "Jyoti Hindu Temple," 231.

122. Jamal Iqbal, interview.

123. Ebrahim Yazdi, "Islam Report Brings Protest from Reader," letter to the editor, *Houston Chronicle*, January 9, 1970.

124. By the mid-1980s, Houston's Shi'a community had established a separate

worship and community center, the Islamic Education Center, in west Houston. The location was later shifted to Voss Street in central Houston.

125. Betty Ewing, "Trade Wonders: Taj Mahal-Dome," *Houston Chronicle*, December 5, 1973.

126. Ewing, "Trade Wonders."

127. Ewing, "Trade Wonders."

128. Ewing, "Trade Wonders."

129. *India Week*, September 27–October 5, 1986.

130. I was unable to find any mainstream newspaper accounts about PAGH in the 1970s, although the organization was established in that decade. After the events of September 11, PAGH was renamed the Pakistan American Association of Greater Houston.

131. Hasan, "Twentieth-Century Indian Immigration to Chicago."

132. George Rosenblatt, "Gujarati Community Here among Largest outside India," *Houston Chronicle*, May 13, 1979.

133. Rosenblatt, "Gujarati Community"; *India Week*, September 27–October 5, 1986.

134. Rosenblatt, "Gujarati Community."

135. Sara Waheed, interview.

136. Uma Krishnan, interview with author, 2007, HHP.

137. Mrudula Bavare, interview with author, 2007, in author's possession; Lal Sardana, interview by Ahmed Afzal, in Afzal, "Transnational Religious and Citizenship Practices," 200; Tahira Lakhani, interview.

138. Mrudula Bavare, interview with author, 2007, in author's possession; Suman Parikh, interview.

139. Jensen, *Passage from India*.

140. Sanjay Bavare, interview with author, 2007, in author's possession.

141. Nagaraj Shekhar, interview.

142. Nagaraj Shekhar, interview. See also Bhanu Shekhar, interview with author, 2007, HHP. According to Bhanu, Devi served as "head of the Vegetarian Congress and she had come to Houston a couple of times with "a big delegation."

143. Nagaraj Shekhar, interview.

144. Nagaraj Shekhar, interview.

145. Nagaraj Shekhar, interview.

146. Mary Lu Abbott, "Quickly Americanized Children of India Get Lessons in Traditions," *Houston Chronicle*, April 30, 1978.

147. Abbott, "Quickly Americanized Children."

148. Uma Krishnan, interview.

149. Yasmin Iqbal, interview.

150. Sara Waheed, interview.

151. Nagaraj Shekhar, interview.

152. This is a good example of how the transitions—the searching for the right words—between thoughts are as revealing as the main ideas expressed in an oral history passage.

153. Brah, *Cartographies of Diaspora*, 3.

Chapter Four

1. Yasmin Iqbal and Jamal Iqbal, interviews with author, 2007, HHP.

2. The development of class in urban India is discussed in further detail in the introduction of this book. See also Driver and Driver, *Social Class in Urban India*.

3. López and Weinstein, *Making of the Middle Class*.

4. Johnson, *Middle Classes in Dependent Countries*, 48.

5. Noel F. Busch, "Dizzying, Dazzling Houston: America's Fastest-Growing Big City Displays a Go-Go Vitality Unmatched Anywhere Else Today," *Reader's Digest*, April 1975, 114.

6. Busch, "Dizzying, Dazzling Houston."

7. Schulman, *From Cotton Belt to Sunbelt*, 149.

8. Feagin, *Free Enterprise City*, 76.

9. Feagin, *Free Enterprise City*, 76.

10. Feagin, *Free Enterprise City*, 77.

11. Advertisement for Armco, *Houston Chronicle*, June 2, 1975.

12. See Feagin, *Free Enterprise City*.

13. Advertisement for Armco, *Houston Chronicle*.

14. See Hobbs and Stoops, *Demographic Trends*, table 4, A-6.

15. Greater Houston Partnership, "Houston Facts," 5.

16. Research Bureau Community Council, *Demographic Characteristics of Harris County, Part I*, 1.

17. Greater Houston Partnership, "Houston Facts."

18. "Houston Area's Growth by Far Highest in State," *Houston Chronicle*, June 18, 1970.

19. Hobbs and Stoops, *Demographic Trends*.

20. Hobbs and Stoops, *Demographic Trends*, table 4, A-6.

21. This growth intersected with other factors, such as an increase in the population ceiling of large American cities in the postwar era, as well as overall increasing rates of urbanization in Texas.

22. Carleton, *Red Scare*, 13.

23. Social Explorer Tables (SE), Census 1970, Social Explorer and U.S. Census Bureau.

24. Davis, *Houston, a Historical Portrait*, 38.

25. Busch, "Dizzying, Dazzling Houston," 115.

26. The foreign-born populations in New York and California were 39 and 25 percent, respectively, compared to 11 percent in Texas in 1960. Social Explorer Tables (SE), Census 1960 (U.S., County, and State), Social Explorer and U.S. Census Bureau. Even fewer immigrants lived in the Greater Houston area (Harris County) at that time. On the history of Mexican Americans in Houston, see De León, *Ethnicity in the Sunbelt*. On Vietnamese immigration to Houston, see Vu, "Rising from the Cold War Ashes." On Chinese in Houston, see Ng, *Adaptation, Acculturation, and Transnational Ties*.

27. These are the official census numbers and likely undercount the number of

unauthorized Mexican immigrants. In addition, the 1970 census shows 212,000 Houstonians of "Spanish Origin," plus 47,156 who claimed "Mexican" descent but were born in the United States, most of whom probably self-identified as "white" on the census, given the narrow choices available.

28. Social Explorer Tables (SE), Census 1960 and 1970, Social Explorer and U.S. Census Bureau.

29. The primary labor market refers to jobs that offer high rates of upward mobility; these are largely white-collar jobs. Though I did not interview any physicians or nurses, these two educational categories were a sizable component of the high-skills immigration stream from India and Pakistan in the 1960s and after. Two doctoral dissertations that skillfully examine the racial experiences of Asian Indian doctors and nurses are Murti, "With and without the White Coat"; and Thacker, "Homeward Bound." See also Reddy, *Nursing and Empire*.

30. See Shelton, *Power Moves*; and McKinney, "Superhighway Deluxe."

31. George Rosenblatt, "Recruiting: Jobs Still Seeking People," *Houston Chronicle*, June 1, 1975; Charlie Evans, "Developers Go West of the City," *Houston Chronicle*, June 1, 1975.

32. Pando, "Oveta Culp Hobby," 132n26. Brown & Root, founded by Herman and George R. Brown, was acquired by Halliburton Corporation in 1962, following the death of one of the founders. See Bryce, *Pipe Dreams*.

33. Meyer, *Days of My Years*, 138–39.

34. Ashok Dani and Lata Dani, interview with author, 2011, HHP.

35. Ashok Dani and Lata Dani, interview.

36. Ashok Dani and Lata Dani, interview.

37. Ashok Dani and Lata Dani, interview. The gendered power dynamics at play in the following exchange, though not directly germane to the overall argument of this study, offer some possible insight into the uniquely gendered experiences of South Asian immigrant women and men. The exact exchange is as follows:

> *Ashok*: At work, these people are really rough. No kind of manners or anything and they would talk and treat you like something different.
> *Lata*: Maybe *he* found that in his office, [but] not everywhere.
> *Ashok*: Everywhere! Everywhere!
> *Lata*: Because for me I was not working at that time.
> *Ashok*: Right. Ladies, they are not exposed to outside. Gents, they face this and to live this every time, you know, this is very difficult.

38. Ashok Dani and Lata Dani, interview.

39. Where Sassen emphasizes the "new" interconnectedness of economies, capital, and people around the world, Chatterjee reminds us that nations had far higher rates of foreign investment and migration in the late nineteenth century. See Chatterjee, *Politics of the Governed*, 87–90; and Sassen, *Global City*.

40. Feagin, "Global Context of Metropolitan Growth," 1218–19. Feagin writes, "When the major oil companies began to develop international operations in the 1920s and 1930s, the city developed ties outside the U.S. economy. By the 1960s and 1970s, Houston had become an international city whose economic base was

as much affected by international as by national events" (1220); Quraishi, "Racial Calculations."

41. Vinod Prakash, interview with author, 2011, HHP.

42. College Station is the location of Texas A&M University, which was attended in 1964 exclusively by white men and some few international male students.

43. Saumitra Kelkar, interview with author, 2011, HHP.

44. Tariq Rahman, interview with author, 2007, HHP.

45. Rohan Patil, interview with author, 2011, HHP.

46. Saumitra Kelkar, interview, emphasis added.

47. Nagaraj Shekhar, interview with author, 2007, HHP.

48. Lipsitz, *Possessive Investment in Whiteness.*

49. GIS maps, created by author. Sources: Social Explorer and U.S. Census.

50. One of the most striking patterns to emerge during the 1970s was the availability for African Americans of new residential developments in the outskirts and suburbs of Houston. These neighborhoods were planned and built starting in the 1960s, and given new postwar technologies in housing construction, along with financing options, they proved to be an affordable stepping stone for some first-time, middle-class home buyers. Neighborhoods such as Westbury quickly became multiracial. A similar phenomenon could be identified in neighborhoods like Ridgemont and Briargate in suburban Missouri City from the mid- to late 1970s, where, for the first time, many could purchase new housing stock at affordable prices. African Americans also flocked to areas with a high proportion of rentable multifamily housing. During this decade of Houston's housing boom, this was most apparent in the greater Fondren area of Southwest Houston, where rows of new apartment complexes lined street after street. With limited public housing options in Houston, Fondren's scores of new apartments nonetheless offered an affordable option for old and new Houstonians.

51. Houston City Planning Department, *City Wide Study*, 18–19.

52. Phelps, *People's War on Poverty.* "For a short period of time," Phelps argues, "grassroots activists and poor Houston residents were able to transform a federal policy program into a vehicle for social change" (12).

53. The first African American elected to public office in Texas was Hattie Mae White, who secured a seat on the Houston School Board in 1958. After 1966, several other African Americans served in public office, including Curtis Graves, Barbara Jordan, and Judson Robinson Jr.

54. "Housing Ruling Effects Not Expected," *Houston Post*, April 21, 1977.

55. Clayton Cox, "Houston Eligible for Jobless Program," *Houston Post*, March 27, 1977.

56. Bullard, *Black Metropolis in the Twenty-First Century.*

57. Skop, *Immigration and Settlement of Asian Indians in Phoenix.*

58. Clear Lake is officially part of the city of Houston but falls some distance away from the city center. Though Clear Lake residents pay taxes to the city of Houston (as well as to the local water authority and school district), Clear Lake features a suburban layout and maintains a suburban identity.

59. Rohan Patil, interview.

60. Tariq Rahman, interview with author, 2007, HHP.

61. Uma Krishnan, interview with author, 2007, HHP.

62. Uma Krishnan and her family lived in the Glenshire subdivision. Their son first attended private Montessori preschool, then Bell Elementary School, and one year at Welch Middle School (both public) before completing his remaining years at St. John's School, one of Houston's most elite private schools.

63. Houston City Planning Department, *City Wide Study*; Bullard, *Invisible Houston*. See *The Handbook of Texas Online*, Texas State Historical Association, http://www.tshaonline.org/handbook/online/articles/hrrsm.

64. Robert S. Thompson, "The Air Conditioning Capital of the World: Houston and Climate Control," in Melosi and Pratt, *Energy Metropolis*, 100.

65. Bhanu Shekhar and Nagaraj Shekhar, interviews with author, 2007, HHP.

66. This area would become modern-day Gulfton, recognized as one of the main "gateway neighborhoods" for unauthorized Latinos to transition into the United States. See Rogers, "Superneighborhood 27."

67. Houston City Planning Department, *City Wide Study*, 49.

68. Houston City Planning Department, *1973 Annual Report*; Houston City Planning Department, *City Wide Study*, 49, 52, 55.

69. Saumitra Kelkar, interview.

70. Sharp was indicted after the Sharpstown Bank Stock Fraud Scandal came to light. Sharp and nearly two dozen other state officials including the former state attorney general were charged. See Herskowitz, *Sharpstown Revisited*.

71. McComb, *Houston, the Bayou City*, 124.

72. R. E. Connor, "Sharpstown Called Model at Its Opening," *Houston Chronicle*, March 14, 1955.

73. Herskowitz, *Sharpstown Revisited*, 52–59.

74. Jamal Iqbal, interview.

75. Suburbs have been variously read by critics and the broader public as stifling, conformist, and exclusive, as well as both excessively community oriented and not community oriented enough. Post–World War II urban critics insisted on the "environmental determinism" of the suburbs as a place that determined the culture it produced, and even more recent historians suggest that the built space surrounding us "sets up living patterns that condition our behavior." While some academics decry the city as a place that obliterated community relations because of the impersonality of its interactions, others argue that the increased density, diversity, and foot traffic of the city created the ideal conditions for creativity and sociality. William H. Whyte cautions that the concept of community, especially as it existed in the suburbs, was crushing in its pressure to join the "group." Still, such critics neglect to explain why, if the suburbs were confining to a fault, people continue to flock to them. Even today, far from fleeing "suburban traps," Americans continue to gravitate toward suburbs. See Becky Nicolaides, "How Hell Moved from the City to the Suburbs: Urban Scholars and Changing Perceptions of Authentic Community," in Kruse and Sugrue, *New Suburban History*, 80–90.

76. "Sharp to Enlarge Homesite Project," *Houston Chronicle*, August 6, 1954. The new land abutted Westheimer Road to the west.

77. Uma Krishnan, interview.

78. Namrata Chandra, interview with author, 2011, HHP.

79. Saumitra Kelkar, interview.

80. Research Bureau Community Council, *Demographic Characteristics of Harris County, Part II*, 27.

81. Research Bureau Community Council, *Demographic Characteristics of Harris County, Part II*. River Oaks was established and developed by two affluent Houstonians, Mike Hogg and Hugh Potter, beginning in 1924. See Barry J. Kaplan and Charles Orson Cook, "Civic Elites and Urban Planning: Houston's River Oaks," in Rosales and Kaplan. *Houston: A Twentieth Century Urban Frontier*, 24.

82. Namrata Chandra, interview. She and her husband eventually moved to a large new house in Sugar Land's Greatwood subdivision.

83. Hemant Chokshi, interview with author, 2011, HHP.

84. Hemant Chokshi, interview with author, 2011, HHP.

85. Anita Sharma, interview with author, 2011, in author's possession. The act of searching for words, such as the interviewee does in this quotation, is discussed further elsewhere in this book. The ellipses in this quotation mark Sharma's pauses as she struggled to articulate herself, not gaps in the statement. I discuss the meanings of the term "good" elsewhere.

86. Charlie Evans, "Developers Go West of City," *Houston Chronicle*, June 1, 1975.

87. Regency Square Newsletter, Summer 1975, VF Real Estate—1970s, Houston Metropolitan Research Center, Bob Bailey Studios Photographic Archive, Box 3N364, Dolph Briscoe Center for American History, University of Texas at Austin. The photographic collection at UT Austin includes several historical images of Sharpstown in the early 1960s.

88. Charlie Evans, "Escalating Land Costs Will Spur Flight to the Suburbs," *Houston Chronicle*, November 29, 1970.

89. Charlie Evans, "Developers Go West," *Houston Chronicle*, June 1, 1975; Evans, "Escalating Land Costs Will Spur Flight."

Chapter Five

1. I use the terms "metropolis" and "metropolitan area" to signify Houston and its environs. It includes the city of Houston, incorporated cities within (e.g., Bellaire), surrounding suburbs (e.g., Sugar Land), and smaller satellite cities that are economically and culturally tied to the city (e.g., Pasadena). Robert D. Bullard writes extensively about how Houston's boom cycle bypassed the city's African Americans in *Invisible Houston*.

2. Klineberg, *Houston Area Survey 1982–2005: Public Perceptions in Remarkable Times*, 7.

3. Shelton, *Houston*, 24.

4. Major imports included (in order) oil, steel, cars, and transportation equipment. The top exports were construction, mining, oilfield machinery, unmilled grain, and organic chemicals. Shelton, *Houston*, 25.

5. Smith, *Recent Developments in Houston Home Prices*, 1.

6. Federal Reserve Bank of Dallas, *Houston Business*; City of Houston, "Fiscal Year

2015 Budget." In *Free Market City*, 85–86, Joe Feagin places this figure at 55 percent. A *Houston Chronicle* article, however, places the percentage of jobs directly or indirectly related to the oil industry at a whopping 70 percent. See "Oil Bust, Space Tragedy and Chronicle Sale," *Houston Chronicle*, October 14, 2001.

7. Robert W. Gilmer, "Oil Prices and Manufacturing Growth: Their Contribution to Houston's Economic Recovery," *Economic Review*, March 1990.

8. Robert G. Fichenberg, "Americans Forestalling Recession," *Houston Chronicle*, January 8, 1980; and *Houston Chronicle*, January 12, 1980.

9. Gilmer, "Oil Prices and Manufacturing."

10. Orfield, *Minority Suburbanization*, 8.

11. Arthur Weise, "Houston's Economy Keyed to Expansion," *Houston Post*, March 20, 1977.

12. By 1980, the land within the city limits sprawled to 556 square miles. Fisher, "Urban Policy in Houston."

13. Kruse, *White Flight*, 8.

14. Lassiter, *Silent Majority*, 2.

15. Charlie Evans, "Some Builders Offer Lower Mortgage Rates in the Houston Area," *Houston Chronicle*, January 13, 1980.

16. Plaut, *Houston Metropolitan Area Profile*, 4, fig. 3.

17. Plaut, *Houston Metropolitan Area Profile*, 4, fig. 3.

18. Plaut, *Houston Metropolitan Area Profile*.

19. Social Explorer Maps (SE), Census 1980, Social Explorer and U.S. Census Bureau (table SE:T53).

20. Smith, *Recent Developments*, 5.

21. Hansen, "Invitation to Annexation," 329.

22. Social Explorer Tables (SE), Census 1970, Social Explorer and U.S. Census Bureau (table SE:T65).

23. Social Explorer Tables (SE), Census 1970, Social Explorer and U.S. Census Bureau (table SE:T1; T107), for Census Tracts 437 and 438, which contain the fuzzy boundaries of Alief.

24. Social Explorer Tables (SE), Census 1980, Social Explorer and U.S. Census Bureau (table SE:T12; T13; T18), for Census Tracts 437.1, 437.2, and 438.6.

25. In the city of Houston, 20 percent of Asians were Asian Indian. There are no data available for Pakistanis as a subgroup, but oral history interviews reveal the extensive presence of Pakistani immigrant families in Alief. Social Explorer Tables (SE), Census 1980, Social Explorer and U.S. Census Bureau (table SE:T12), for Census Tracts 437.1, 437.2, and 438.6. Chinese, Vietnamese, and Filipino were 27.3, 15.5, and 14.4 percent, respectively.

26. In this section I use a GIS map that layers populations according to census data in order to find similarities and identify patterns among racial groups.

27. In only a decade, significant residential shifts among all racial groups stemmed from the desegregation of schools and neighborhoods. By 1980, African American residents began to move beyond the borders of historically black areas, flowing into immediately adjacent areas. In addition, small populations of African Americans

began to emerge in new pockets throughout the western portion of the city, but many subdivisions remained majority white. The rural African American communities around the periphery of Harris County, meanwhile, remained somewhat consistent but with a slight decrease in overall numbers. GIS maps, created by author, based on Social Explorer and U.S. Decennial Census.

28. Social Explorer Tables (SE), Census 1980, Social Explorer and U.S. Census Bureau (table SE:T85), for Census Tracts 437.1, 437.2, and 438.6.

29. Houston City Planning Department, *Annexation*, 2–3, quoted in Hansen, "Invitation to Annexation," 328.

30. "Real Estate Supplement," *Houston Post*, August 14, 1977.

31. Social Explorer Tables (SE), Census 1980, Social Explorer and U.S. Census Bureau (table SE:T50; TE59), for Census Tracts 437.1, 437.2, and 438.6 and Houston city.

32. Suresh Bhatt, interview with author, 2011, HHP .

33. Bina Parmar, interview with author, 2011, HHP.

34. Emily Skop and Wei Li, "Enclaves, Ethnoburbs, and New Patterns of Settlement among Asian Immigrants," in Zhou and Gatewood, *Contemporary Asian America*, 234.

35. See Lee and Zhou, *Asian American Youth*; Maira, *Desis in the House*; and Shankar, *Desi Land*.

36. Indians and Pakistanis continued to gather at the University of Houston for major ethnic and national events, though to a lesser extent, as the formation of ethnic residential fulfilled some of the social function of the earlier university affairs.

37. *Indo-American News*, December 30, 1985.

38. See Afzal, *Lone Star Muslims*.

39. *India Week*, September 27–October 5, 1986, 31.

40. *India Week*, September 27–October 5, 1986, 35.

41. See Lee and Zhou, *Asian American Achievement Paradox*.

42. In accordance with the status attainment model, it is the children of these Asian immigrants who have often secured high class ranks at high schools across the nation, though of course not all Asian Americans invest heavily in education. Lee and Zhou argue, however, that highly educated immigrants create an achievement-based cultural frame that also relies on external resources to encourage positive educational outcomes for their children (*Asian American Achievement Paradox*, 8).

43. See Molina, *How Race Is Made in America*.

44. Kellar, *Make Haste Slowly*.

45. Kluger, *Simple Justice*, 744; Berman, *It Is So Ordered*.

46. Kluger, *Simple Justice*, 743.

47. Kellar, *Make Haste Slowly*.

48. HISD was formed in 1924 and was, in theory, independent of the municipal government's control. In reality, the HISD leadership was populated with Houston's business elite, who in turn controlled the city's politics and growth. For example, William G. Farrington was chairman of HISD's board of trustees and also the wealthy developer of the exclusive Tanglewood subdivision. He played a role in securing land for new schools. See Koush, "Houston Lives the Life," 18.

49. Kellar, *Make Haste Slowly*, 138.

50. Kellar, *Make Haste Slowly*, 155. Only 3 percent of the 39,000 eligible black elementary students attended desegregated schools in fall 1964.

51. Kellar, *Make Haste Slowly*, 163.

52. Breeden, "Race and Educational Politics."

53. Kellar, *Make Haste Slowly*, 162.

54. Kellar, *Make Haste Slowly*, 162.

55. Harsh Gil, interview with author, 2012, HHP.

56. Harsh Gil, interview.

57. Saumitra Kelkar, interview with author, 2011, HHP.

58. Ashok Dani and Lata Dani, interview with author, 2011, HHP.

59. Harsh Gil, interview.

60. Fondren Southwest advertisement, *Houston Post*, August 14, 1977, BB-25.

61. Quail Valley advertisement, *Houston Post*, August 14, 1977, BB-29.

62. Advertisement, *Houston Post*, August 14, 1977, BB-28.

63. Bina Parmar, interview.

64. Saumitra Kelkar, interview.

65. Anita Sharma, interview with author, 2011, in author's possession.

66. Ashok Dani and Lata Dani, interview.

67. Ashok Dani and Lata Dani, interview.

68. Saumitra Kelkar, interview.

69. Saumitra Kelkar, interview.

70. Jim Craig, "Most City Grade Schools Fail in Academic Study," *Houston Post*, March 9, 1976, 1A.

71. Craig, "Most City Grade Schools Fail."

72. Nationally, the 1970s recession was driven by rising inflation after the Vietnam War, two oil-price spikes, and higher short-term interest rates. Federal Reserve Bank of Dallas, *Houston Business*.

73. Bureau of Labor Statistics, U.S. Department of Labor, Labor Force Statistics from the Current Population Survey, https://www.bls.gov/cps/.

74. Federal Reserve Bank of Dallas, *1982–1990*.

75. Diwan and Mohamedi, "Gulf Comes Down to Earth," 6–11; Federal Reserve Bank of Dallas, *Houston Business*, 13–15.

76. Federal Reserve Bank of Dallas, *1982–1990*.

77. Federal Reserve Bank of Dallas, *Houston Business*.

78. Federal Reserve Bank of Dallas, *1982–1990*.

79. Federal Reserve Bank of Dallas, *Houston Business*.

80. Shelton et al., *Houston*, 125–26.

81. "Population Data for Houston–The Woodlands–Sugar Land, TX," Texas A&M University, Real Estate Center, https://www.recenter.tamu.edu/data/population#!/msa /Houston-The_Woodlands-Sugar_Land%2C_TX.

82. City of Houston, *Economic Profile*.

83. Saumitra Kelkar, interview.

84. Smith, *Recent Developments*.

85. South Asians opted to live in Fondren Southwest in the 1970s in high numbers.

86. Smith, *Recent Developments*, esp. 5; Nestor P. Rodriguez and Jacqueline Maria Hagan, "Apartment Restructuring and Latino Immigrant Tenant Struggles: A Case Study of Human Agency," in Smith, *After Modernism*, 164–80.

87. Saumitra Kelkar, interview.

88. Harun Farid, interview with author, 2011, HHP. It is revealing that Farid does not mean "central area" to indicate truly centrally located neighborhoods—that is, neighborhoods with high numbers of nonwhite residents. Instead, he means those "central but not too central" neighborhoods at enough distance from the city core to maintain high house values.

89. Harun Farid, interview.

90. Saumitra Kelkar, interview.

91. Saumitra Kelkar, interview.

92. Saumitra Kelkar, interview.

93. Zafar Waheed, interview with author, 2007, HHP.

94. Harsh Gil, interview.

95. Census 2000 and 2010.

96. Lewis, Emerson, and Klineberg, "Who We'll Live With"; Emerson, Chai, and Yancey, "Does Race Matter in Residential Segregation?"; Orfield and Lee, *Why Segregation Matters*.

97. Sikkink and Emerson, "School Choice and Racial Segregation."

98. Sikkink and Emerson, "School Choice and Racial Segregation," 275.

99. Sikkink and Emerson, "School Choice and Racial Segregation," 277–79.

100. Kao, "Asian Americans as Model Minorities?," 130–31.

101. Kao, "School Choice and Racial Segregation," 131.

102. Saumitra Kelkar, interview.

103. Saumitra Kelkar, interview.

104. Bina Parmar, interview.

105. Bina Parmar, interview.

106. Saumitra Kelkar, interview.

107. Suresh Bhatt, interview.

108. Rohan Patil, interview with author, 2011, HHP.

109. Ashok Dani and Lata Dani, interview.

110. Saumitra Kelkar, interview.

111. Ashok Dani and Lata Dani, interview.

112. Hemant Chokshi, interview with author, 2011, HHP.

113. Suresh Bhatt, interview.

114. Saumitra Kelkar, interview.

115. Ashok Dani and Lata Dani, interview.

116. Bina Parmar, interview.

117. Hemant Chokshi, interview.

118. Bina Parmar, interview.

119. Ashok Dani, interview.

120. Bina Parmar, interview.

121. Saumitra Kelkar, interview.

122. Saumitra Kelkar, interview.

123. Bina Parmar, interview.

124. Kevin Kruse, *White Flight*, 77.

125. Suresh Bhatt, interview.

126. Saumitra Kelkar, interview.

127. Saumitra Kelkar, interview.

Chapter Six

1. This is correlated by other studies such as John Iceland's *Where We Now Live*. Iceland finds that "those with greater income are more likely than lower-income immigrants to share neighborhoods with whites" (*Where We Live Now*, 12).

2. Skop, *Immigration and Settlement of Asian Indians in Phoenix*.

3. Jackson, *Crabgrass Frontier*, 6.

4. Short, *Urban Theory*, 8; Jackson, *Crabgrass Frontier*, 4. With the aid of postwar federal dollars (FHA loans, GI Bill, and VA loans), suburban expansion in the United States occurred mainly after 1945.

5. Becky Nicolaides, "'How Hell Moved from the City to the Suburbs': Urban Scholars and Changing Perceptions of Authentic Community," in Kruse and Sugrue, *New Suburban History*, 93.

6. Gordon, Richardson, and Kim, "Where Americans Live, Work and Do Business."

7. Gordon, Richardson, and Kim, "Where Americans Live, Work and Do Business," 2–3.

8. Wendie Choudary, Jie Wu, and Mingming Zhang state that gentrification across Houston has accelerated since 2000. Very little gentrification occurred from 1990 to 2000, while the period between 2000 and 2010 saw the greatest change. Growing gentrification patterns emerge during the time period between 2010 and 2016" (Kinder Institute for Urban Research, Rice University, *Neighborhood Gentrification across Harris County*). On the other hand, Gordon Wittenburg and Amanda Chang note the continued pace of sprawl well beyond the city limits, due in large part to the new construction of highways distant from the city core (Kinder Institute for Urban Research, Rice University, *Mapping Houston Development*).

9. See Greater Houston Partnership, "Houston Facts," 5. See, for e.g., other publications by the Greater Houston Partnership, whose data are presumably used widely. The nine-county region SMSA consists of: Harris, Montgomery, Liberty, Chambers, Galveston, Brazoria, Fort Bend, Austin, and Waller. Other frequently used census areas for Houston (e.g., used by the city of Houston) include the Consolidated Metropolitan Statistical Area (CMSA), an eight-county region that omits Austin County.

10. It is important to note that some Hispanics self-identify as white and that the census categorized Hispanics as white in 1970. In 1970, the U.S. Census lists 185,715 individuals of "Spanish Origin or Descent" in Harris County, likely including 41,467 native born but of Mexican descent and 16,275 foreign-born Mexicans.

11. City of Houston, *Population by Race/Ethnicity*, based on U.S. Census Bureau 1980–2010 and Census 2010 redistricting data.

12. City of Houston, *Population by Race/Ethnicity*.

13. Orfield, *Minority Suburbanization, Stable Integration*.

14. City of Houston, *Population by Race/Ethnicity.*

15. City of Houston, *Population by Race/Ethnicity.*

16. City of Houston, *Population by Race/Ethnicity,* and data calculated from the U.S. census.

17. Iceland, *Where We Live Now,* 64–71.

18. Lewis, Emerson, and Klineberg, "Who We'll Live With," 1385.

19. Emerson, Chai, and Yancey, "Does Race Matter in Residential Segregation?," 927; Lewis, Emerson, and Klineberg, "Who We'll Live With," 1397.

20. Brooks, *Alien Neighbors, Foreign Friends.*

21. In this final chapter of the book, where applicable, I transition from using the term "South Asian immigrant" to "South Asian American" for the following reasons. First, 2000 and 2010 census data reflect a more generationally varied profile, including immigrants, their children, and a third generation of South Asian Americans. Second, most of my interlocutors routinely referred to themselves as immigrants out of recognition of their foreign birthplace but, by the 2000s, identified strongly as "Indian" or "Pakistani" *and* "American." They had also obtained U.S. citizenship, though my use of "South Asian Americans" reflects their own recent self-identification more than their legal status.

22. I extrapolate Pakistani American spatial distribution based on GIS maps for Houston's Asian Indian population and oral history.

23. Social Explorer Tables for percentage of total population.

24. Taken separately, Indians and Pakistanis in Sugar Land were 31 and 12 percent, respectively. Social Explorer and U.S. Census Bureau 2010 (tables SE:T54; T57), for Sugar Land city.

25. Rural areas well beyond the city limits but still part of the metropolitan area obviously had very low median income levels, similar to those found in the city core. See the maps in the Appendix.

26. In the older industrial cities of the Northeast and Midwest (e.g., Chicago, Detroit, and Philadelphia) because of the concentration of public housing, low-income neighborhoods and preponderance of historically black neighborhoods near city cores, wealth increases incrementally the farther one moves from the core. Jackson, *Crabgrass Frontier,* 8.

27. Michael Jones-Correa, "Reshaping the American Dream: Immigrants, Ethnic Minorities, and the Politics of the New Suburbs," in Kruse and Sugrue, *New Suburban History,* 184.

28. Jones-Correa, "Reshaping the American Dream," 184.

29. Orfield, *Minority Suburbanization, Stable Integration,* 10.

30. Orfield, *Minority Suburbanization, Stable Integration.*

31. Sam Roberts, "Segregation Curtailed in U.S. Cities, Study Finds," *New York Times,* January 30, 2012.

32. Harsh Gil, interview with author, 2012, HHP. Sugar Land is located roughly ten miles from the city of Houston's southwest boundary.

33. City of Sugar Land, *Sugar Land,* 7.

34. Thomas Kreneck writes that both the sugar refining factory and the surrounding corn and cotton fields were co-owned by W. T. Eldridge and I. H. Kempner.

After the turn of the twentieth century, Mexican immigrants provided a bulk of the labor for Sugar Land's fields, replacing the mostly African American labor procured through the nearby state prison's convict-lease program. Mexican Americans clustered residentially in order to avoid racist confrontations in an era of hostility and discrimination toward the region's minority populations. See Kreneck, *Mexican American Odyssey*, 25–27.

35. "Sugar Land, Texas," fact sheet, October 16, 1985, Richmond County Library (RCL), Vertical Files.

36. "City of Sugar Land Brochure," n.d. (Sugar Land, Tex.), RCL, Vertical Files.

37. Vinod Prakash, interview with author, 2011, HHP.

38. By this point, many of the early immigrants had committed to permanent residence in the United States. Reflecting this shift, I transition to frequent use of the term "South Asian American" in addition to "South Asian immigrant," whenever relevant.

39. Nagaraj Shekhar, interview with author, 2007, HHP.

40. Nagaraj Shakhar, interview.

41. Like other South Asian immigrants in the United States, Bangladeshis are mostly middle class, with high levels of education, and originating from urban areas in Bangladesh. Kibria, "Diaspora Diversity," 142–43.

42. Don Munsch, "Sugar Land Still Home to Its Namesake, Imperial Sugar," *Fort Bend Herald*, July 14, 2009; Social Explorer Tables (SE), Census 1980, Social Explorer and U.S. Census Bureau (table SE:T13), for Census Tracts 702.1–.4.

43. Social Explorer Tables (SE), Census 1980, 2010, Social Explorer and U.S. Census Bureau (table SE:T54; TE57).

44. I researched websites of several organizations, including, e.g., Houston Telugu Cultural Association (http://www.houstontca.org), Bihar Association of North America (www.banahouston.org), and Gujarati Samaj of Houston (www.gshouston.org/).

45. Simon Jacob and Pallavi Thaku, "Jyoti Hindu Temple: One Religion, Many Practices," in Ebaugh and Chafetz, *Religion and the New Immigrants*, 231.

46. Hoda Badr, "Al Noor Mosque: Strength through Unity," in Ebaugh and Chafetz, *Religion and the New Immigrants*.

47. Kurien, "Religion, Ethnicity and Politics," 283. Prema Kurien's study delves deeply into the significance of participation and leadership in religious organizations in southern California.

48. Kurien, "Religion, Ethnicity and Politics," 279.

49. Kurien, "Religion, Ethnicity and Politics," 278.

50. Williams, *God's Own Party*; Lassiter, *Silent Majority*; Schulman and Zelizer, *Rightward Bound*.

51. Kurien, "Religion, Ethnicity and Politics," 283.

52. Zain Shauk, "Pakistan's Musharraf Brings His Long-shot Bid to Houston," *Houston Chronicle*, October 19, 2010.

53. Pieter Friedrich, "All in the Family: The American Sangh's Affair with Tulsi Gabbard," *The Caravan*, August 1, 2019.

54. Falcone, "Putting the 'Fun' in Fundamentalism."

55. Tariq Rahman, interview with author, 2007, HHP.

56. Nadia Nazir, interview with author, 2007, HHP.

57. Uma Krishnan, interview with author, 2007, HHP.

58. Nagaraj Shekhar, interview.

59. Bhanu Shekhar, interview with author, 2007, HHP.

60. Tahira Lakhani, interview with author, 2007, HHP.

61. Tariq Rahman, interview with author, 2007, HHP.

62. Javed Malhotra, interview with author, 2007, HHP.

63. Javed Malhotra, interview.

64. Sara Waheed, interview with author, 2007, HHP.

65. Yasmin Iqbal, interview with author, 2007, HHP.

66. "Asian Indian" is a U.S. census category created in 1980 denoting Americans residents of Asian Indian descent.

67. Migration Policy Institute, *Pakistani Diaspora in the United States.* The highest sending countries for remittances to Pakistan are Saudi Arabia, India, United Arab Emirates, United Kingdom, Qatar, and the United States, in that order; Migration Policy Institute, *Indian Diaspora in the United States.* United Arab Emirates and the United States are the top remitting countries to India.

68. Tariq Rahman, interview with author, 2007, HHP.

69. Several interviewees allude to the social distance between themselves and non–South Asian neighbors. Simultaneously, they create community with coethnics both far and near. Nicolaides, "How Hell Moved," 80–98.

Epilogue

1. Deborah Wrigley, "Letter Spewing Hate Left on Fort Bend County Home," ABC 13 Eyewitness News, February 3, 2017, https://abc13.com/1734776/. The incidents were widely reported by local and ethnic Indian news media.

2. Kevin Quinn, "Swastikas Found Spray Painted in Sienna Plantation," ABC 13 Eyewitness News, February 1, 2017, https://abc13.com/news/swastikas-found-spray-painted-in-sienna-plantation/1732186/.

3. Bhatia, *American Karma*, 197–206; George, "'From Expatriate Aristocrat to Immigrant Nobody.'"

BIBLIOGRAPHY

Archives

Houston area
  African American Archives at the Gregory School, Houston Public Library
  Houston Metropolitan Research Center
  Richmond County Library, Richmond, Tex.
  Special Collections, University of Houston Libraries
  Woodson Research Center, Fondren Library, Rice University
United States
  Dwight D. Eisenhower Presidential Library, Abilene, Kans.
  Library of Congress, Washington, D.C.
    Law Library of Congress
    Newspaper and Current Periodical Collection
  National Archives and Records Administration, College Park, Md.
    Record Group 59
    Record Group 306
    Still Picture Branch
  Harry S. Truman Presidential Library, Independence, Mo.

Oral History Interviews

Houston Asian American Archive, Woodson Research Center, Fondren Library,
  Rice University
Indo-American Oral History Project, Houston Public Library
Interviews in author's possession
Oral History of Houston Project, M. D. Anderson Library, University of Houston
  (Appendix, table 6, for detailed list)
South Asian American Digital Archive (SAADA), www.saada.org

Unrecorded, Annotated Interviews

Kamran Riaz, associate dean of students, University of Houston, February 15, 2008
Patrick M. Walsh, director of transportation, City of Sugar Land, Texas, May 3, 2012

Reports, Records, and Statistical Databases

INTERNATIONAL

Development of Home Economics in Pakistan: Significant Contribution to the Education of Women, 1952–1972. Washington, D.C.: Ford Foundation, 1972.

Government of India. Ministry of Education and Welfare. Statistics and Information Division. *Studies in Educational Statistics, No. 4–1977: Indian Students Going Abroad and Foreign Students in India, 1965–66 to 1974–75.* New Delhi: Department of Education, 1977.

MUNICIPAL

City of Houston. "Economic Profile." Houston, 1994.

———. "Fiscal Year 2015 Budget: Demographic/Economic Summary of the City." http://www.houstontx.gov/budget/15budprop/I_EO.pdf.

City of Houston. Planning and Development Department. *Historical Population: 1900 to 2017 City of Houston.* January 2017. https://www.houstontx.gov/planning /Demographics/docs_pdfs/Cy/hist_pop_1900_2017.pdf.

———. *Historical Population Growth: 1850–2010, City of Houston Data Sheet.* February 24, 2010.

———. *Population by Race/Ethnicity, City of Houston: 1980–2010, COH Data.* N.d.

des Jarlais, Don, and Mary Ellen Goodman. "Houstonians of Mexican Ancestry: The Spanish Surname Population of Houston: A Demographic Sketch." Houston: Rice University, 1968.

Federal Reserve Bank of Dallas. Houston Branch. *Houston Business: A Perspective on the Houston Economy.* Houston, June 2003. https://www.dallasfed.org/~/media /documents/research/houston/2003/hb0304.pdf.

———. *1982–1990: When Times Were Bad in Houston.* Houston, June 2003.

Greater Houston Partnership. "Houston Facts." 2018. https://www.houston.org/assets /pdf/economy/Houston%20Facts_web.pdf.

Houston City Planning Department. *City Wide Study.* Houston, July 1973.

———. *1973 Annual Report.* Houston, 1973.

———. *Third Ward Data Book.* Houston, July 1976.

Houston Independent School District. *HISD, 2011–2012, Facts and Figures.* https:// www.houstonisd.org, HISDFactsFigures2012Final.pdf.

Kinder Institute for Urban Research, Rice University. Gordon Wittenberg and Amanda Chang, authors. "Mapping Houston Development." https://doi.org /10.25612/837.za4dlb04k1kz.

———. Wendie Choudary, Jie Wu, and Mingming Zhang, contributors. "Neighborhood Gentrification across Harris County: 1990 to 2016." December 2018. https:// kinder.rice.edu.

Klineberg, Stephen L. *An Historical Overview of Immigration in Houston, Based on the Houston Area Survey.* Houston: Rice University, 2008. https://doi.org/10.25611 /z1dn-cvj.

———. *Houston Area Asian Survey: Diversity and Transformation among Asians in Houston*. Houston: Rice University, February 2013.

———. *The Houston Area Survey: Houston's Economic and Demographic Transformations*. Houston: Rice University, 2002.

———. *The Houston Area Survey, 1982–2005: Public Perception in Remarkable Times*. Houston: Rice University, 2005.

Plaut, Thomas R. *Houston: Metropolitan Area Profile*. Austin: University of Texas at Austin–Bureau of Business Research, 1985.

Research Bureau Community Council. *Demographic Characteristics of Harris County, Part I: Population Change*. Houston, February 1963.

———. *Demographic Characteristics of Harris County, Part II: Social and Economic Variables*. Houston, December 1963.

Rice Center. *Phase One Technical Report: Economic Base Analysis for the Houston-Galveston Region*. Houston, April 1979.

Smith, Barton. *Recent Developments in Houston Home Prices*. Houston: University of Houston Center for Public Policy, February 1985.

Stafford, James E., and Robert G. Lehnen. "Houston Community Study." Houston: Alumni Educational Foundation, University of Houston College of Business Administration, August 1976.

Turrentine, Gordon. "City Planning in Houston: A Review of the Planning Foundations upon Which the Community Has Been Built." Houston: Houston Chamber of Commerce, April 1971.

NATIONAL

Asian Americans Advancing Justice. *A Community of Contrasts: Asian Americans, Native Americans and Pacific Islanders in the South*. Washington, D.C., 2014.

Chatten, Robert, Lois Herrmann, Theresa Markiw, and Frances Sullinger. *The United States Information Agency: A Commemoration; Public Diplomacy, Looking Back, Looking Forward*. Washington, D.C.: U.S. Information Agency, 1999.

Cohn, D'Vera. "Census History: Counting Hispanics." Washington, D.C.: Pew Research Center, March 3, 2010. https://www.pewsocialtrends.org/2010/03/03/census-history-counting-hispanics-2/.

Gibson, Campbell, and Kay Jung. *Historical Census Statistics on the Foreign-Born Population of the United States: 1850 to 2000*. Washington, D.C.: U.S. Census Bureau, February 2006. https://www.census.gov/population/www/documentation/twps0081/twps0081.pdf.

Hobbs, Frank, and Nicole Stoops. *Demographic Trends in the 20th Century*. Washington, D.C.: U.S. Census Bureau, November 2002. https://www.census.gov/prod/2002pubs/censr-4.pdf.

Institute of International Education. *Open Doors Report on International Educational Exchange*. http://www.iie.org/opendoors.

Kochhar, Rakesh, Richard Fry, and Paul Taylor. *Wealth Gap Rise to Record Highs between Whites, Blacks and Hispanics*. Washington, D.C.: Pew Research Center, July 26, 2011.

Migration Policy Institute. *The Indian Diaspora in the United States*. New York: Rockefeller Foundation, July 2014.

——. *The Pakistani Diaspora in the United States*. New York: Rockefeller Foundation, June 2015.

Orfield, Myron. *Minority Suburbanization, Stable Integration, and Economic Opportunity in Fifteen Metropolitan Regions*. Minneapolis: Institute on Race and Poverty, February 2006.

Reeves, Terrance J., and Claudette E. Bennett. *We the People: Asians in the United States*. Census 2000 Special Reports. Washington, D.C.: Bureau of the Census, Economics and Statistics Administration, December 2004.

Taylor, Paul et al. "The Rise of Asian Americans." Washington, D.C.: Pew Research Center, 2013. http://www.pewsocialtrends.org/wp-content/uploads/sites/3/2013/04/Asian-Americans-new-full-report-04-2013.pdf.

U.S. Census Bureau. *United States Census*, 1960–2010.

U.S. Department of Justice. Immigration and Naturalization Service. *Annual Report*. Washington, D.C.: Department of Justice, 1967–72.–

U.S. Department of State. Bureau of Security and Consular Affairs. *Annual Report of the Visa Office*, 1968.

STATE

Combs, Susan. *Window on State Government: Fiscal Notes*. Texas Comptroller of Public Accounts. May 2007.

Texas Department of Insurance. State Planning Grant Project. *Working Together for a Healthy Texas*. September 2003.

UNIVERSITY

University of Houston

Annual Enrollment Report. Office of International Student Admissions, 1969–80.

Directory of International Students. International Student Office, 1969–70, 1974–75, 1977–78.

International Student Roster. International Student Office, Fall 1966.

International News. International Student Services, 1960–68.

A Report on the International Student at the University of Houston. Committee on International Student Problems, July 20, 1968.

Rice University

Registrar's Report to the President. Registrar's Office, 1958–84.

Rice World (newsletter). Office of International Students and Scholars, 1988–2008.

Dissertations and Theses

Afzal, Ahmed. "Transnational Religious and Citizenship Practices and the Pakistani Immigrant Experience in Houston, Texas." Ph.D. diss., Yale University, 2005.

Breeden, Edwin. "Race and Educational Politics at the Advent of Mandatory Integration, Houston, Texas, 1969–1975." Ph.D. diss., Rice University, 2017.

Hansen, Roger C. "Invitation to Annexation: Metropolitan Fragmentation and Community in Cincinnati and Houston, 1920–1980." Ph.D. diss., University of Cincinnati, 1993.

Hasan, Tajiya. "Twentieth-Century Indian Immigration to Chicago." M.A. thesis, Roosevelt University, 2005.

Koush, Ben. "Houston Lives the Life: Modern Houses in the Suburbs, 1952–1962." Ph.D. diss., Rice University, 2002.

Levengood, Paul Alejandro. "For the Duration and beyond: World War II and the Creation of Modern Houston, Texas." Ph.D. diss., Rice University, 1999.

McKinney, Tom Watson. "Superhighway Deluxe: Houston's Gulf Freeway." Ph.D. diss., University of Houston, 2006.

Murti, Lata. "With and without the White Coat: The Racialization of Southern California's Indian Physicians." Ph.D. diss., University of Southern California, 2010.

Pando, Robert T. "Oveta Culp Hobby: A Study of Power and Control." Ph.D. diss., Florida State University, 2008.

Pegoda, Andrew Joseph. "Watchful Eyes: An Examination of the Struggle for African-Americans to Receive Admission and Equality at the University of Houston, 1927–1969." Ph.D. diss., University of Houston, 2010.

Quraishi, Uzma. "Educationally Empowered: The Indian and Pakistani Student Community in Houston, Texas, 1960–1975." M.A. thesis, University of Houston, 2008.

———. "Multiple Mobilities: Race, Capital, and South Asian Migrations to and through Houston." Ph.D. diss., Rice University, 2013.

Ternikar, Farha Bano. "Revisioning the Ethnic Family: An Analysis of Marriage Patterns among Hindu, Muslim and Christian South Asian Immigrants." Ph.D. diss., Loyola University Chicago, 2004.

Thacker, Bela. "Homeward Bound: Asian-Indian Women Putting Down Roots in Houston, TX." Ph.D. diss., State University of New York at Buffalo, 2004.

Vu, Roy. "Rising from the Cold War Ashes: Construction of a Vietnamese American Community in Houston, 1975–2005." Ph.D. diss., University of Houston, 2006.

Newspapers and Periodicals

The Caravan
Economic and Political Weekly
Fort Bend Herald
The Hindu
Houston Chronicle
Houston Post
Houston Press
India Week
Indo American News
International Students
New York Times
Reader's Digest
Voice of Asia
Wall Street Journal

Secondary Sources

Abrams, Lynn. *Oral History Theory.* New York: Routledge, 2010.

Adams, Walter. *The Brain Drain.* New York: Macmillan, 1968.

Afzal, Ahmed. *Lone Star Muslims: Transnational Lives and the South Asian Experience in Texas.* New York: New York University Press, 2015.

Agarwal, Pawan. "Higher Education in India: Growth, Concerns and Change Agenda." *Higher Education Quarterly* 61, no. 2 (April 2007): 197–207.

Ahmad, Rizwan. "Scripting a New Identity: The Battle for Devanagari in Nineteenth Century India." *Journal of Pragmatics* 40, no. 7 (July 2008): 1163–83.

Ahmed, Akbar S. *Jinnah, Pakistan and Islamic Identity: The Search for Saladin.* New York: Routledge, 1997.

Ahmed, Ishtiaq. *The Punjab Bloodied, Partitioned and Cleansed: Unravelling the 1947 Tragedy through Secret British Reports and First-Person Accounts.* Karachi: Oxford University Press, 2012.

Ainsworth-Darnell, James W., and Douglas B. Downey. "Assessing the Oppositional Culture Explanation for Racial/Ethnic Differences in School Performance." *American Sociological Review* 63, no. 4 (August 1998): 536–53.

Ali, Kamran Asdar. *Communism in Pakistan: Politics and Class Activism, 1947–1972.* London: I. B. Tauris, 2015.

Almaguer, Tomás. *Racial Fault Lines: The Historical Origins of White Supremacy in California.* Berkeley: University of California Press, 2008.

Alsultany, Evelyn. *Arabs and Muslims in the Media: Race and Representation after 9/11.* New York: New York University Press, 2012.

Altbach, Philip G., ed. *International Higher Education: An Encyclopedia.* New York: Garland, 1991.

Altbach, Philip G., and Viswanathan Selvaratnam, eds. *From Dependence to Autonomy: The Development of Asian Universities.* Dordrecht: Kluwer Academic, 1989.

Altbach, Philip G., and Tōru Umakoshi, eds. *Asian Universities: Historical Perspectives and Contemporary Challenges.* Baltimore: Johns Hopkins University Press, 2004.

Amin, Shahid M. *Pakistan's Foreign Policy: A Reappraisal.* New York: Oxford University Press, 2003.

Anderson, Benedict R. *Imagined Communities: Reflections on the Origin and Spread of Nationalism.* New York: Verso, 1991.

Azam, Qazi Tauqir, and Robert E. Evenson. *Agricultural Research Productivity in Pakistan.* New Haven, Conn.: Pakistan Agricultural Research Council/Economic Growth Center, Yale University, 1990.

Baker, Andrew C. "From Rural South to Metropolitan Sunbelt: Creating a Cowboy Identity in the Shadow of Houston." *Southwestern Historical Quarterly* 118, no. 1 (2014): viii–22.

Bald, Vivek. *Bengali Harlem and the Lost Histories of South Asian America.* Cambridge, Mass.: Harvard University Press, 2013.

Bald, Vivek, Miabi Chatterji, Sujani Reddy, and Manu Vimalassery, eds. *The Sun*

Never Sets: South Asian Migrants in an Age of U.S. Power. NYU Series in Social and Cultural Analysis. New York: New York University Press, 2013.

Baldwin, George B. "Brain Drain or Overflow?" *Foreign Affairs* 48, no. 2 (1970): 358–72.

Barringer, Herbert R., David T. Takeuchi, and Peter Xenos. "Education, Occupational Prestige, and Income of Asian Americans." *Sociology of Education* 63, no. 1 (January 1990): 27–43.

Bartley, Numan V. "Social Change and Sectional Identity." *Journal of Southern History* 61, no. 1 (1995): 3–16.

Bassett, Ross. "Aligning India in the Cold War Era: Indian Technical Elites, the Indian Institute of Technology at Kanpur, and Computing in India and the United States." *Technology and Culture* 50, no. 4 (2009): 783–810.

Baviskar, Amita, and Raka Ray, eds. *Elite and Everyman: The Cultural Politics of the Indian Middle Classes.* New York: Routledge, 2011.

Bayer, Alan E. "Foreign Students in American Colleges: Time for Change in Policy and Practice." *Research in Higher Education* 1, no. 4 (1973): 389–400.

Bayly, C. A. *Rulers, Townsmen and Bazaars: North Indian Society in the Age of British Expansion, 1770–1870.* Cambridge: Cambridge University Press, 1983.

Bean, Susan S., and Peabody Essex Museum. *Yankee India: American Commercial and Cultural Encounters with India in the Age of Sail, 1784–1860.* Salem, Mass.: Mapin, 2001.

Beaudoin, Christopher E. "The Impact of News Use and Social Capital on Youth Wellbeing: An Aggregate-Level Analysis." *Journal of Community Psychology* 35, no. 8 (2007): 947–65.

Beeth, Howard, and Cary D. Wintz, eds. *Black Dixie: Afro-Texan History and Culture in Houston.* College Station: Texas A&M University Press, 1992.

Bernard, Richard M., and Bradley Robert Rice, eds. *Sunbelt Cities: Politics and Growth since World War II.* Austin: University of Texas Press, 1983.

Berry, Kim. "Lakshmi and the Scientific Housewife: A Transnational Account of Indian Women's Development and Production of an Indian Modernity." *Economic and Political Weekly* 38, no. 11 (2003): 1055–68.

Béteille, André. *Universities at the Crossroads.* New York: Oxford University Press, 2010.

Bevis, Teresa B. *A History of Higher Education Exchange: China and America.* New York: Taylor and Francis Group, 2013.

Bhagavan, Manu. *India and the Quest for One World: The Peacemakers.* Basingstoke, U.K.: Palgrave Macmillan, 2013.

Bhatia, Sunil. *American Karma: Race, Culture, and Identity in the Indian Diaspora.* New York: New York University Press, 2007.

Bhatt, Amy, and Nalini Iyer. *Roots and Reflections: South Asians in the Pacific Northwest.* Seattle: University of Washington Press, 2013.

Bodnar, John E. *The Transplanted: A History of Immigrants in Urban America.* Bloomington: Indiana University Press, 1985.

Boles, John B. *A University So Conceived: A Brief History of Rice University.* Houston: Rice University, 2006.

Bonilla-Silva, Eduardo. *Racism without Racists: Color-Blind Racism and the Persistence of Racial Inequality in the United States.* Lanham, Md.: Rowman and Littlefield, 2003.

———. *White Supremacy and Racism in the Post–Civil Rights Era.* Boulder, Colo.: Lynne Rienner, 2001.

Borstelmann, Thomas. *The Cold War and the Color Line.* Cambridge, Mass.: Harvard University Press, 2009.

Bose, Sugata, and Ayesha Jalal. *Modern South Asia: History, Culture, and Political Economy.* New York: Routledge, 1998.

Bose, Sugata, and Kris Manjapra, eds. *Cosmopolitan Thought Zones: South Asia and the Global Circulation of Ideas.* Basingstoke, U.K.: Palgrave Macmillan, 2010.

Bourdieu, Pierre. *Distinction: A Social Critique of the Judgement of Taste.* Cambridge, Mass.: Harvard University Press, 1984.

Brah, Avtar. *Cartographies of Diaspora: Contesting Identities.* London: Routledge, 1996.

Brands, H. W. *India and the United States: The Cold Peace.* Boston: Twayne, 1990.

Brass, Paul R. *The Politics of India since Independence.* Cambridge: Cambridge University Press, 1994.

———. *Radical Politics in South Asia.* Cambridge, Mass.: MIT Press, 1973.

Brettell, Caroline, and Deborah Reed-Danahay. *Civic Engagements: The Citizenship Practices of Indian and Vietnamese Immigrants.* Stanford, Calif.: Stanford University Press, 2011.

Brooks, Charlotte. *Alien Neighbors, Foreign Friends: Asian Americans, Housing, and the Transformation of Urban California.* Chicago: University of Chicago Press, 2009.

Brown, Francis J., and Joseph Slabey Rouček, eds. *One America: The History, Contributions, and Present Problems of Our Racial and National Minorities.* New York: Prentice-Hall, 1952.

Brown, Judith M. *Modern India: The Origins of an Asian Democracy.* Oxford: Oxford University Press, 1985.

Bryce, Robert. *Pipe Dreams: Greed, Ego, and the Death of Enron.* New York: Public Affairs, 2002.

Bu, Liping. *Making the World Like Us: Education, Cultural Expansion, and the American Century.* Westport, Conn.: Greenwood, 2003.

Bullard, Robert D. *The Black Metropolis in the Twenty-First Century: Race, Power, and Politics of Place.* New York: Rowman and Littlefield, 2007.

———. "Housing Problems and Prospects for Blacks in Houston." *Review of Black Political Economy* 19, no. 3–4 (March 1, 1991): 175–94.

———. *Invisible Houston: The Black Experience in Boom and Bust.* College Station: Texas A&M University Press, 1987.

———, ed. *In Search of the New South: The Black Urban Experience in the 1970s and 1980s.* Tuscaloosa: University of Alabama Press, 1989.

Burke, S. M., and Lawrence Ziring. *Pakistan's Foreign Policy: An Historical Analysis.* Karachi: Oxford University Press, 1990.

Cantrell, Gregg, and Elizabeth Hayes Turner, eds. *Lone Star Pasts: Memory and History in Texas*. College Station: Texas A&M University Press, 2006.

Caram, Dorothy F., Anthony Gary Dworkin, Néstor Rodriguez, and Houston Hispanic Forum. *Hispanics in Houston and Harris County, 1519–1986: A Sesquicentennial Celebration*. Houston: Houston Hispanic Forum, 1989.

Carleton, Don E. *Red Scare! Right-Wing Hysteria, Fifties Fanaticism, and Their Legacy in Texas*. Austin: Texas Monthly Press, 1985.

Certeau, Michel de. *The Practice of Everyday Life*. Berkeley: University of California Press, 1984.

Chakrabarty, Bidyut. *Communism in India: Events, Processes and Ideologies*. New York: Oxford University Press, 2014.

———. *Left Radicalism in India*. New York: Routledge, 2014.

Chan, Sucheng. *Asian Americans: An Interpretive History*. Boston: Twayne, 1991.

Chandrasekhar, S., ed. *From India to America: A Brief History of Immigration*. La Jolla, Calif.: Population Review, 1982.

Chaplin, Joyce E. *Subject Matter: Technology, the Body, and Science on the Anglo-American Frontier, 1500–1676*. Cambridge, Mass.: Harvard University Press, 2001.

Chatterjee, Partha. *The Politics of the Governed: Reflections on Popular Politics in Most of the World*. New York: Columbia University Press, 2004.

Chaudhuri, Rudra. *Forged in Crisis: India and the United States since 1947*. London: Hurst, 2014.

Chin, Gabriel J. "The Civil Rights Revolution Comes to Immigration Law: A New Look at the Immigration and Nationality Act of 1965." *North Carolina Law Review* 75 (1996): 273–46.

Chou, Rosalind, and Joe R. Feagin. *The Myth of the Model Minority: Asian Americans Facing Racism*. Boulder, Colo.: Paradigm, 2008.

Chung, Angie Y. *Saving Face: The Emotional Costs of the Asian Immigrant Family Myth*. New Brunswick, N.J.: Rutgers University Press, 2016.

City of Sugar Land. *Sugar Land*. Charleston, S.C.: Arcadia, 2010.

Clarke, Colin, Ceri Peach, and Steven Vertovec, eds. *South Asians Overseas: Migration and Ethnicity*. Cambridge: Cambridge University Press, 1990.

Codell, Julie F. *Imperial Co-Histories: National Identities and the British and Colonial Press*. Madison, N.J.: Fairleigh Dickinson University Press, 2003.

Cohen, Benjamin B. *Kingship and Colonialism in India's Deccan, 1850–1948*. New York: Palgrave Macmillan, 2007.

Coontz, Stephanie. *The Way We Never Were: American Families and the Nostalgia Trap*. New York: Basic Books, 1992.

Cull, Nicholas J. *The Cold War and the United States Information Agency: American Propaganda and Public Diplomacy, 1945–1989*. Cambridge: Cambridge University Press, 2009.

Curtis, Edward E. *Encyclopedia of Muslim-American History*. New York: Infobase, 2010.

Dalby, Andrew. *Dictionary of Languages: The Definitive Reference to More Than 400 Languages*. New York: Columbia University Press, 1998.

Danico, Mary Yu, ed. *Asian American Society: An Encyclopedia*. Los Angeles: SAGE, 2014.

Daniels, Roger. *Coming to America: A History of Immigration and Ethnicity in American Life*. New York: HarperCollins, 1990.

Das, Ashidhara. *Desi Dreams: Indian Immigrant Women Build Lives across Two Worlds*. Delhi: Primus Books, 2012.

Das, Sudipta. "Loss or Gain? A Saga of Asian Indian Immigration and Experiences in America's Multi-Ethnic Mosaic." *Race, Gender and Class* 9, no. 2 (2002): 131–55.

Davidson, Naomi. *Only Muslim: Embodying Islam in Twentieth-Century France*. Ithaca, N.Y.: Cornell University Press, 2012.

Davis, John L. *Houston, a Historical Portrait*. Austin: Encino Press, 1983.

De León, Arnoldo. *Ethnicity in the Sunbelt: Mexican Americans in Houston*. College Station: Texas A&M University Press, 2001.

Delgado, Richard, and Jean Stefancic, eds. *Critical White Studies: Looking behind the Mirror*. Philadelphia: Temple University Press, 1997.

Dhingra, Pawan. *Life behind the Lobby: Indian American Motel Owners and the American Dream*. Stanford, Calif.: Stanford University Press, 2012.

———. *Managing Multicultural Lives: Asian American Professionals and the Challenge of Multiple Identities*. Stanford, Calif.: Stanford University Press, 2007.

Diner, Hasia R. *The Jews of the United States, 1654 to 2000*. Berkeley: University of California Press, 2006.

Dinnerstein, Leonard, and David M. Reimers. *Ethnic Americans: A History of Immigration and Assimilation*. New York: New York University Press, 1977.

Diouf, Sylviane A. *Servants of Allah: African Muslims Enslaved in the Americas*, 15th anniversary ed. New York: New York University Press, 2013.

Diwan, Kristin Smith, and Fareed Mohamedi. "The Gulf Comes Down to Earth." *Middle East Report* no. 252 (2009): 6–15.

Driver, Edwin, and Aloo Driver. *Social Class in Urban India*. Leiden: E. J. Brill, 1987.

Du Bois, W. E. B. *Black Reconstruction: An Essay toward a History of the Part Which Black Folk Played in the Attempt to Reconstruct Democracy in America, 1860–1880*. New York: Harcourt, Brace, 1935.

Dudziak, Mary L. *Cold War Civil Rights: Race and the Image of American Democracy*. Princeton, N.J.: Princeton University Press, 2002.

Dyer, Richard. *White*. New York: Routledge, 1997.

Ebaugh, Helen Rose Fuchs, and Janet Saltzman Chafetz. *Religion and the New Immigrants: Continuities and Adaptations in Immigrant Congregations*. Walnut Creek, Calif.: AltaMira, 2000.

Edgar, Andrew, and Peter R. Sedgwick. *Cultural Theory: The Key Concepts*. New York: Routledge, 2002.

Edwards, Laura F. "Southern History as U.S. History." *Journal of Southern History* 75, no. 3 (2009): 533–64.

Emerson, Michael O., Karen J. Chai, and George Yancey. "Does Race Matter in Residential Segregation? Exploring the Preferences of White Americans." *American Sociological Review* 66, no. 6 (December 2001): 922–35.

Esparza, Jesus Jesse. "La Colonia Mexicana: A History of Mexican Americans in Houston." *Houston History* 9, no. 1 (Fall 2011): 2–8.

Espiritu, Yen. *Asian American Panethnicity: Bridging Institutions and Identities.* Philadelphia: Temple University Press, 2011.

Essed, Philomena. *Everyday Racism: Reports from Women of Two Cultures.* Claremont, Calif.: Hunter House, 1990.

Ewing, Katherine Pratt. *Being and Belonging: Muslims in the United States since 9/11.* New York: Russell Sage Foundation, 2008.

Fairbanks, Robert B., and Kathleen Underwood, eds. *Essays on Sunbelt Cities and Recent Urban America.* College Station: Texas A&M University Press, 1990.

Falcone, Jessica. "Putting the 'Fun' in Fundamentalism: Religious Nationalism and the Split Self at Hindutva Summer Camps in the United States." *Ethos* 40, no. 2 (June 1, 2012): 164–95.

Falloure, David H. *Sheer Will: The Story of the Port of Houston and the Houston Ship Channel.* San Bernadino, Calif.: Published by the author, 2014.

Fanon, Frantz. *The Wretched of the Earth.* New York: Grove Press 1963.

Farooq, Mavra. "Pakistani-Chinese Relations: An Historical Analysis of the Role of China in the Indo-Pakistani War of 1971." *Pakistaniaat: A Journal of Pakistan Studies* 2, no. 3 (October 18, 2010): 76–91.

Farooqi, Mehr Afshan. "The 'Hindi' of the 'Urdu.'" *Economic and Political Weekly,* March 1, 2008, 18–20.

Feagin, Joe R. *Free Enterprise City: Houston in Political-Economic Perspective.* New Brunswick, N.J.: Rutgers University Press, 1988.

———. "The Global Context of Metropolitan Growth: Houston and the Oil Industry." *American Journal of Sociology* 90, no. 6 (May 1985): 1218–19.

———. *The New Urban Paradigm: Critical Perspectives on the City.* New York: Rowman and Littlefield, 1998.

———. *Racist America: Roots, Current Realities, and Future Reparations.* New York: Routledge, 2000.

Fenton, John Y. *Transplanting Religious Traditions: Asian Indians in America.* Westport, Conn.: Greenwood, 1988.

Fernandes, Leela. *India's New Middle Class: Democratic Politics in an Era of Economic Reform.* Minneapolis: University of Minnesota Press, 2006.

Fields, Barbara. "Slavery, Race, and Ideology in the United States of America." *New Left Review* 181 (May–June 1990): 95–118.

Fisher, Maxine P. "Creating Ethnic Identity: Asian Indians in the New York City Area." *Urban Anthropology* 7, no. 3 (1978): 271–85.

Fisher, Michael H., Shompa Lahiri, and Shinder S. Thandi. *A South-Asian History of Britain: Four Centuries of Peoples from the Indian Sub-Continent.* Westport, Conn.: Greenwood World, 2007.

Fisher, Robert. "Urban Policy in Houston, Texas," *Urban Studies* 26, no. 1 (1989): 144–54.

FitzGerald, David, and David Cook-Martín. *Culling the Masses: The Democratic Origins of Racist Immigration Policy.* Cambridge, Mass.: Harvard University Press, 2014.

Forsyth, Ann. *Reforming Suburbia: The Planned Communities of Irvine, Columbia, and the Woodlands*. Berkeley: University of California Press, 2005.

Fortney, Judith A. "International Migration of Professionals." *Population Studies* 24, no. 2 (July 1970): 217–32.

Fuermann, George M. "Houston, 1880–1910." *Southwestern Historical Quarterly* 71, no. 2 (1967): 226–46.

Gabaccia, Donna R. *From Sicily to Elizabeth Street: Housing and Social Change among Italian Immigrants, 1880–1930*. Albany: SUNY Press, 2010.

Gaddis, John Lewis. *The Cold War: A New History*. New York: Penguin, 2006.

———. *The United States and the Origins of the Cold War, 1941–1947*. New York: Columbia University Press, 2000.

Galvani, John. "Introduction to Pakistan." *MERIP Reports* 16 (April 1973): 3–5.

Ganapathy-Coleman, Hemalatha. "Raising 'Authentic' Indian Children in the United States: Dynamism in the Ethnotheories of Immigrant Hindu Parents." *Ethos* 41, no. 4 (2013): 360–86.

Ganguly, Sumit. *Conflict Unending: India-Pakistan Tensions since 1947*. New York: Columbia University Press, 2002.

———. *Engaging the World: Indian Foreign Policy since 1947*. New Delhi: Oxford University Press, 2016.

Gant, George F. "The Ford Foundation and Pakistan." *ANNALS of the American Academy of Political and Social Science* 323, no. 1 (May 1959): 150–59.

Garcia, James E. "Hostile Words in Texas: Campus Rallies against University of Texas Law Professor." *Diverse: Issues in Higher Education*, July 12, 2007.

Garner, Steve. *Whiteness: An Introduction*. New York: Routledge, 2007.

Geertz, Clifford. *The Interpretation of Cultures: Selected Essays*. New York: Basic Books, 1973.

Geiger, Andrea A. E. *Subverting Exclusion: Transpacific Encounters with Race, Caste, and Borders, 1885–1928*. New Haven, Conn.: Yale University Press, 2011.

George, Rosemary Marangoly. "'From Expatriate Aristocrat to Immigrant Nobody': South Asian Racial Strategies in the Southern Californian Context." *Diaspora: A Journal of Transnational Studies* 6, no. 1 (1997): 31–60.

George, Sheba Mariam. *When Women Come First: Gender and Class in Transnational Migration*. Berkeley: University of California Press, 2005.

Gerber, David A. *American Immigration: A Very Short Introduction*. Oxford: Oxford University Press, 2011.

Ghaswala, S. K. "Using What's Available." *Science News* 96, no. 14 (October 4, 1969): 314.

Gienow-Hecht, Jessica C. E., and Frank Schumacher, eds. *Culture and International History*. Berghahn Books, 2004.

Gilmer, Robert W. "Oil Prices and Manufacturing Growth: Their Contribution to Houston's Economic Recovery." *Economic Review* (Federal Reserve Bank of Dallas), March 1990.

Glasrud, Bruce A. "Asians in Texas: An Overview, 1870–1990." *East Texas Historical Journal* 39, no. 2 (2001): 10–22.

Gmelch, George. "Return Migration." *Annual Review of Anthropology* 9 (1980): 135–59.

Godfrey, Martin. "Migration of Professionals from Commonwealth Developing Countries." *Journal of the Royal Society of Arts* 125, no. 5254 (1977): 642–53.

Gordon, Peter, Harry W. Richardson, and Soojung Kim. "Where Americans Live, Work and Do Business: Thirty-Five Year Trends." Paper presented at the 47th Annual Western Regional Science Associations meeting, Kona, Hawaii, February 2008.

Gould, Harold A. *Sikhs, Swamis, Students and Spies: The India Lobby in the United States, 1900–1946.* Thousand Oaks, Calif.: SAGE, 2006.

Graber, Doris A. *Crime News and the Public.* New York: Praeger, 1980.

Graham, Sarah Ellen. *Culture and Propaganda: The Progressive Origins of American Public Diplomacy, 1936–1953.* Burlington, Vt.: Routledge, 2015.

Greene, Casey. "Guardians against Change: The Ku Klux Klan in Houston and Harris County, 1920–1925." *Houston Review* 10, no. 1 (2008): 2–5.

Guha, Ramachandra. *India after Gandhi: The History of the World's Largest Democracy.* New York: Harper Perennial, 2008.

Gupta, Dipankar. *Interrogating Caste: Understanding Hierarchy and Difference in Indian Society.* New Delhi: Penguin Books India, 2000.

Gutiérrez, Ramón A., and Tomás Almaguer, eds. *The New Latino Studies Reader: A Twenty-First-Century Perspective.* Oakland: University of California Press, 2016.

Hall, Stuart. "Ethnicity: Identity and Difference." *Radical America* 23, no. 4 (1991): 9–20.

Haney-Lopez, Ian. *White by Law: The Legal Construction of Race.* New York: New York University Press, 2006.

Harpalani, Vinay. "Desicrit: Theorizing the Racial Ambiguity of South Asian Americans." *New York University Annual Survey of American Law* 69 (2013): 77–184.

Hashmi, Sultan S., and Mehboob Sultan. "Population Trends and Rates of Population Growth in Pakistan: Assessment of Preliminary Results of the 1998 Census." *Pakistan Development Review* 37, no. 4 (1998): 495–506.

Hayden, Dolores. *Redesigning the American Dream: The Future of Housing, Work, and Family Life.* New York: W. W. Norton, 2002.

Helweg, Arthur Wesley. *Strangers in a Not-So-Strange Land: Indian American Immigrants in the Global Age.* Belmont, Calif.: Wadsworth, 2004.

Helweg, Arthur Wesley, and Usha M. Helweg. *An Immigrant Success Story: East Indians in America.* Philadelphia: University of Pennsylvania Press, 1990.

Herskowitz, Mickey. *Sharpstown Revisited: Frank Sharp and a Tale of Dirty Politics in Texas.* Austin: Eakin Press, 1994.

Hess, Gary R. "The Forgotten Asian Americans: The East Indian Community in the United States." *Pacific Historical Review* 43, no. 4 (1974): 576–96.

Hilliker, J. F. "Lord William Bentinck's Resolution of 1835 on Indian Education: A Rejected Draft." *Journal of the Royal Asiatic Society of Great Britain and Ireland* 113, no. 1 (1981): 40–45.

Hing, Bill Ong. *Defining America through Immigration Policy.* Philadelphia: Temple University Press, 2003.

———. *Making and Remaking Asian America through Immigration Policy, 1850–1990.* Stanford, Calif.: Stanford University Press, 1993.

Hinnershitz, Stephanie. *A Different Shade of Justice: Asian American Civil Rights in the South*. Chapel Hill: University of North Carolina Press, 2017.

hooks, bell. *Black Looks: Race and Representation*. Boston: South End Press, 1992.

Horne, Gerald. *The End of Empires: African Americans and India*. Philadelphia: Temple University Press, 2008.

Hossain, Moazzem, Iyanatul Islam, and Reza Kibria. *South Asian Economic Development: Transformation, Opportunities and Challenges*. New York: Routledge, 1999.

Hsu, Madeline Y. *Dreaming of Gold, Dreaming of Home: Transnationalism and Migration between the United States and South China, 1882–1943*. Stanford, Calif.: Stanford University Press, 2000.

———. *The Good Immigrants: How the Yellow Peril Became the Model Minority*. Princeton, N.J.: Princeton University Press, 2015.

Hsu, Madeline Y., and Ellen D. Wu. "'Smoke and Mirrors': Conditional Inclusion, Model Minorities, and the Pre-1965 Dismantling of Asian Exclusion." *Journal of American Ethnic History* 34, no. 4 (2015): 43–65.

Hurley, Marvin. *Decisive Years for Houston*. Houston: Houston Magazine, 1966.

Iceland, John. *Where We Live Now: Immigration and Race in the United States*. Berkeley: University of California Press, 2009.

Jackson, Kenneth T. *Crabgrass Frontier: The Suburbanization of the United States*. New York: Oxford University Press, 1985.

Jaffrelot, Christophe. *The Pakistan Paradox: Instability and Resilience*. New York: Oxford University Press, 2015.

Jalal, Ayesha. *Democracy and Authoritarianism in South Asia: A Comparative and Historical Perspective*. Cambridge: Cambridge University Press, 1995.

———. *The Sole Spokesman: Jinnah, the Muslim League and the Demand for Pakistan*. Cambridge: Cambridge University Press, 1994.

———. *The State of Martial Rule: The Origins of Pakistan's Political Economy of Defence*. Cambridge: Cambridge University Press, 1990.

———. *The Struggle for Pakistan: A Muslim Homeland and Global Politics*. Cambridge, Mass.: Harvard University Press, 2014.

James, Roberta. "Halal Pizza: Food and Culture in a Busy World." *Australian Journal of Anthropology* 15, no. 1 (April 2004): 1–11.

Jensen, Joan M. "Apartheid: Pacific Coast Style." *Pacific Historical Review* 38, no. 3 (1969): 335–40.

———. *Passage from India: Asian Indian Immigrants in North America*. New Haven, Conn.: Yale University Press, 1988.

Johnson, Dale L., ed. *Middle Classes in Dependent Countries*. Beverly Hills, Calif.: SAGE, 1985.

Johnston, Marguerite. *Houston: The Unknown City, 1836–1946*. College Station: Texas A&M University Press, 2011.

Joseph, P. T. *The Amiable American*. Trivandrum, India: St. Joseph's Press, 1963.

Joshi, Khyati Y., and Jigna Desai, eds. *Asian Americans in Dixie: Race and Migration in the South*. Urbana: University of Illinois Press, 2013.

Joshi, Sanjay. *Fractured Modernity: Making of a Middle Class in Colonial North India*. New Delhi: Oxford University Press, 2001.

———, ed. *The Middle Class in Colonial India*. New Delhi: Oxford University Press, 2010.

Jung, Moon-Ho. *Coolies and Cane: Race, Labor, and Sugar in the Age of Emancipation*. Baltimore: Johns Hopkins University Press, 2006.

———. "Seditious Subjects, Race, State Violence, and the U.S. Empire." *Journal of Asian American Studies* 14, no. 2 (June 2011): 221–47.

Kao, Grace. "Asian Americans as Model Minorities? A Look at Their Academic Performance." *American Journal of Education* 103, no. 2 (February 1995): 121–59.

Kaplan, Barry J. "Race, Income, and Ethnicity: Residential Change in a Houston Community, 1920–70." *Houston Review* 3 (Winter 1981): 178–202.

Karam, Nicolette. *The 9/11 Backlash: A Decade of U.S. Hate Crimes Targeting the Innocent*. Berkeley, Calif.: Beatitude Press, 2012.

Karski, Jan. *Story of a Secret State: My Report to the World*. Washington, D.C.: Georgetown University Press, 1944.

Kazin, Michael, and Joseph Anthony McCartin, eds. *Americanism: New Perspectives on the History of an Ideal*. Chapel Hill: University of North Carolina Press, 2006.

Kāẓmī, Muḥammad Raẓā. *A Concise History of Pakistan*. Karachi: Oxford University Press, 2012.

Kean, Melissa. *Desegregating Private Higher Education in the South: Duke, Emory, Rice, Tulane, and Vanderbilt*. Baton Rouge: Louisiana State University Press, 2008.

Keely, Charles B. "Immigration Composition and Population Policy." *Science* 185, no. 4151 (1974): 587–93.

Kellar, William Henry. *Make Haste Slowly: Moderates, Conservatives, and School Desegregation in Houston*. College Station: Texas A&M University Press, 1999.

Khan, Liaquat Ali. *Pakistan, the Heart of Asia; Speeches in the United States and Canada, May and June 1950*. Cambridge, Mass.: Harvard University Press, 1951.

Khan, Mohammad Ayub. *Friends Not Masters: A Political Autobiography*. New York: Oxford University Press, 1967.

Khan, Sagheer Ahmad. *Governance in Pakistan: Hybridism, Political Instability, and Violence*. Karachi: Oxford University Press, 2016.

Khan, Yasmin. *The Great Partition: The Making of India and Pakistan*. New Haven, Conn.: Yale University Press, 2007.

Khandelwal, Madhulika S. *Becoming American, Being Indian: An Immigrant Community in New York City*. Ithaca, N.Y.: Cornell University Press, 2002.

Kibbee, Robert J. "Higher Education in Pakistan: Problems That Beset the Student Community." *Journal of Higher Education* 33, no. 4 (April 1962): 179–89.

Kibria, Nazli. "The Contested Meanings of 'Asian American': Racial Dilemmas in the Contemporary US." *Ethnic and Racial Studies* 21, no. 5 (January 1, 1998): 939–958.

———. "Diaspora Diversity: Bangladeshi Muslims in Britain and the United States." *Diaspora: A Journal of Transnational Studies* 18, no. 1/2 (Spring/Summer 2009): 138–58.

Kim, Claire Jean. "The Racial Triangulation of Asian Americans." *Politics and Society* 27, no. 1 (March 1, 1999): 105–38.

Kizilbash, Mehdi. "The Employment of Returning U.S. Educated Indians." *Comparative Education Review* 8, no. 3 (December 1964): 320–26.

Kluger, Richard. *Simple Justice: The History of* Brown v. Board of Education *and Black America's Struggle for Equality.* New York: Alfred A. Knopf, 1975.

Koshy, Susan. "Category Crisis: South Asian Americans and Questions of Race and Ethnicity." *Diaspora: A Journal of Transnational Studies* 7, no. 3 (1998): 285–320.

Kramer, Paul A. "Is the World Our Campus? International Students and U.S. Global Power in the Long Twentieth Century." *Diplomatic History* 33, no. 5 (November 1, 2009): 775–806.

Kraut, Alan M. *The Huddled Masses: The Immigrant in American Society, 1880–1921.* Arlington Heights, Ill.: Harlan Davidson, 1982.

Kreneck, Thomas H. *Del Pueblo: A History of Houston's Hispanic Community.* College Station: Texas A&M University Press, 2012.

———. *Mexican American Odyssey: Felix Tijerina, Entrepreneur and Civic Leader, 1905–1965.* College Station: Texas A&M University Press, 2001.

Krenn, Michael L. *The Color of Empire: Race and American Foreign Relations.* Issues in the History of American Foreign Relations. Washington, D.C.: Potomac Books, 2006.

Krueger, Anne O. *Economic Policies at Cross-Purposes: The United States and Developing Countries.* Washington, D.C.: Brookings Institution, 1993.

Kruse, Kevin M. *White Flight: Atlanta and the Making of Modern Conservatism.* Princeton, N.J.: Princeton University Press, 2005.

Kruse, Kevin M., and Thomas J. Sugrue, eds. *The New Suburban History.* Chicago: University of Chicago Press, 2006.

Kumar, Amitava. *Bombay—London—New York.* New York: Routledge, 2013.

———. *A Foreigner Carrying in the Crook of His Arm a Tiny Bomb.* Durham, N.C.: Duke University Press, 2010.

Kurashige, Lon. *Two Faces of Exclusion: The Untold History of Anti-Asian Racism in the United States.* Chapel Hill: University of North Carolina Press, 2016.

Kurien, Prema. *A Place at the Multicultural Table: The Development of an American Hinduism.* New Brunswick, N.J.: Rutgers University Press, 2007.

———. "Religion, Ethnicity and Politics: Hindu and Muslim Indian Immigrants in the United States." *Ethnic and Racial Studies* 24, no. 2 (January 1, 2001): 263–93.

Kusmer, Kenneth L., and Joe W. Trotter, eds. *African American Urban History since World War II.* Chicago: University of Chicago Press, 2009.

Kux, Dennis. *India and the United States: Estranged Democracies, 1941–1991.* Washington, D.C.: National Defense University Press, 1992.

———. *The United States and Pakistan, 1947–2000: Disenchanted Allies.* Washington, D.C.: Woodrow Wilson Center Press, 2001.

Lake, Marilyn, and Henry Reynolds. *Drawing the Global Colour Line: White Men's Countries and the International Challenge of Racial Equality.* Cambridge: Cambridge University Press, 2008.

Lall, Marie. "Educate to Hate: The Use of Education in the Creation of Antagonistic National Identities in India and Pakistan." *Compare: A Journal of Comparative Education* 38, no. 1 (January 2008): 103–19.

Lambert, Richard D., and Marvin Bressler. *Indian Students on an American Campus.* Minneapolis: University of Minnesota Press, 1956.

Lassiter, Matthew D. *The Silent Majority: Suburban Politics in the Sunbelt South.* Princeton, N.J.: Princeton University Press, 2006.

Layton, Azza Salama. *International Politics and Civil Rights Policies in the United States, 1941–1960.* Cambridge: Cambridge University Press, 2000.

Leach, Edmund, and S. N. Mukherjee, eds. *Elites in South Asia.* Cambridge: Cambridge University Press, 1970.

Lebovic, Sam. "From War Junk to Educational Exchange: The World War II Origins of the Fulbright Program and the Foundations of American Cultural Globalism, 1945–1950." *Diplomatic History* 37, no. 2 (April 2013): 280–312.

Lee, Erika, and Judy Yung. *Angel Island: Immigrant Gateway to America.* Oxford: Oxford University Press, 2010.

Lee, Jennifer, and Min Zhou, eds. *Asian American Youth: Culture, Identity and Ethnicity.* New York: Routledge, 2004.

———. *The Asian American Achievement Paradox.* New York: Russell Sage Foundation, 2015.

Leffler, Melvyn P. "The American Conception of National Security and the Beginnings of the Cold War, 1945–48." *American Historical Review* 89, no. 2 (1984): 346–81.

———. *The Specter of Communism: The United States and the Origins of the Cold War, 1917–1953.* New York: Hill and Wang, 1994.

Leffler, Melvyn P., and David S. Painter, eds. *Origins of the Cold War: An International History.* New York: Routledge, 1994.

Leonard, Karen Isaksen. *Making Ethnic Choices: California's Punjabi Mexican Americans.* Philadelphia: Temple University Press, 1992.

Lessinger, Johanna. *From the Ganges to the Hudson: Indian Immigrants in New York City.* Boston: Allyn and Bacon, 1995.

Lewis, Valerie A., Michael O. Emerson, and Stephen L. Klineberg. "Who We'll Live With: Neighborhood Racial Composition Preferences of Whites, Blacks and Latinos." *Social Forces* 89, no. 4 (June 2011): 1385–1407.

Li, Wei, and Emily Skop. "Diaspora in the United States: Chinese and Indians Compared." *Journal of Chinese Overseas* 6, no. 2 (September 2010): 286–310.

Lieven, Anatol. *Pakistan: A Hard Country.* New York: Public Affairs, 2011.

Lin, Wan-Ying, Hayeon Song, and Sandra Ball-Rokeach. "Localizing the Global: Exploring the Transnational Ties That Bind in New Immigrant Communities." *Journal of Communication* 60, no. 2 (June 2010): 205–29.

Ling, Huping. "A History of Chinese Female Students in the United States, 1880s–1990s." *Journal of American Ethnic History* 16, no. 3 (1997): 81–109.

Lipsitz, George. *How Racism Takes Place.* Philadelphia: Temple University Press, 2011.

———. *The Possessive Investment in Whiteness: How White People Profit from Identity Politics.* Philadelphia: Temple University Press, 2009.

Liu, Lisong. *Chinese Student Migration and Selective Citizenship: Mobility, Community and Identity between China and the United States.* New York: Routledge, 2015.

Lockwood, David. *The Indian Bourgeoisie: A Political History of the Indian Capitalist Class in the Early Twentieth Century.* London: I. B. Tauris, 2012.

Long, Roger D. *A History of Pakistan.* Karachi: Oxford University Press, 2015.

López, A. Ricardo, and Barbara Weinstein, eds. *The Making of the Middle Class: Toward a Transnational History.* Durham, N.C.: Duke University Press Books, 2012.

Lopez, David, and Yen Le Espiritu. "Panethnicity in the United States: A Theoretical Framework." *Ethnic and Racial Studies* 13, no. 2 (April 1, 1990): 198–224.

López, Ian Haney. *White by Law: The Legal Construction of Race,* 10th anniversary ed. New York: New York University Press, 2006.

Lowe, Lisa. "Heterogeneity, Hybridity, Multiplicity: Marking Asian American Differences." *Diaspora: A Journal of Transnational Studies* 1, no. 1 (1991): 24–44.

Lux, Donald. "Technical Education in India." *Comparative Education Review* 7, no. 3 (February 1964): 301–6.

Maira, Sunaina. *The 9/11 Generation: Youth, Rights, and Solidarity in the War on Terror.* Philadelphia: Temple University Press, 2016.

———. *Desis in the House: Indian American Youth Culture in New York City.* Philadelphia: Temple University Press, 2002.

McClain, Charles. *Asian Indians, Filipinos, Other Asian Communities, and the Law.* New York: Routledge, 1994.

McComb, David G. *Houston, the Bayou City.* Austin: University of Texas, 1969.

McDonald, John F. *Postwar Urban America: Demography, Economics, and Social Policies.* New York: Routledge, 2015.

McGarr, Paul M. *The Cold War in South Asia: Britain, the United States and the Indian Subcontinent, 1945–1965.* Cambridge: Cambridge University Press, 2013.

———. "'Quiet Americans in India': The CIA and the Politics of Intelligence in Cold War South Asia." *Diplomatic History* 38, no. 5 (November 1, 2014): 1046–82.

McIntyre, Alice. *Making Meaning of Whiteness: Exploring Racial Identity with White Teachers.* Albany: SUNY Press, 1997.

McMahon, Robert J., ed. *The Cold War in the Third World.* New York: Oxford University Press, 2013.

———. *The Cold War on the Periphery: The United States, India, and Pakistan, 1947–1965.* New York: Columbia University, 1994.

Melendy, H. Brett. *Asians in America.* New York: Hippocrene Books, 1981.

Melosi, Martin V., and Joseph A. Pratt, eds. *Energy Metropolis: An Environmental History of Houston and the Gulf Coast.* Pittsburgh, Pa.: University of Pittsburgh Press, 2007.

Metcalf, Barbara D. "Urdu in India the 21st Century: A Historian's Perspective." *Social Scientist* 31, no. 5/6 (2003): 29–37.

Metcalf, Barbara D., and Thomas R. Metcalf. *A Concise History of Modern India.* Cambridge: Cambridge University Press, 2006.

Meyer, Leopold L. *The Days of My Years: Autobiographical Reflections of Leopold L. Meyer.* Houston: Universal Printers, 1975.

Miller, Char, and Heywood T. Sanders, eds. *Urban Texas: Politics and Development.* College Station: Texas A&M University Press, 1990.

Mishra, Sangay K. *Desis Divided: The Political Lives of South Asian Americans.* Minneapolis: University of Minnesota Press, 2017.

Mobasher, Mohsen M., and Mahmoud Sadri, eds. *Migration, Globalization, and Ethnic Relations: An Interdisciplinary Approach.* Upper Saddle River, N.J.: Pearson Prentice Hall, 2004.

Molina, Natalia. *How Race Is Made in America: Immigration, Citizenship, and the Historical Power of Racial Scripts*. Berkeley: University of California Press, 2014.

Mollenkopf, John H. *The Contested City*. Princeton, N.J.: Princeton University Press, 1983.

Mukerji, S. N. *History of Education in India*, 5th ed. Baroda, India: Acharya Book Depot, 1966.

Myrdal, Gunnar. *American Dilemma: The Negro Problem and Modern Democracy*. New York: Harper and Brothers, 1944.

Nagel, Joane. "Constructing Ethnicity: Creating and Recreating Ethnic Identity and Culture." *Social Problems* 41, no. 1 (February 1, 1994): 152–76.

Neumann, Tracy. *Remaking the Rust Belt: The Postindustrial Transformation of North America*. Philadelphia: University of Pennsylvania Press, 2016.

Ng, Franklin, ed. *Adaptation, Acculturation, and Transnational Ties among Asian Americans*. New York: Garland, 1998.

Nickerson, Michelle, and Darren Dochuk, eds. *Sunbelt Rising: The Politics of Space, Place, and Region*. Philadelphia: University of Pennsylvania Press, 2011.

Noman, Omar. *The Political Economy of Pakistan, 1947–85*. New York: Kegan Paul International, 1988.

Obeng, Pashington. *Shaping Membership, Defining Nation: The Cultural Politics of African Indians in South Asia*. Lanham, Md.: Lexington Books, 2007.

Oh, Tai K. "Estimating the Migration of U.S.-Educated Manpower from Asia to the United States." *Social and Economic Studies* 22, no. 3 (1973): 335–57.

Okamoto, Dina G. "Toward a Theory of Panethnicity: Explaining Asian American Collective Action." *American Sociological Review* 68, no. 6 (2003): 811–42.

Okihiro, Gary Y. *Margins and Mainstreams: Asians in American History and Culture*. Seattle: University of Washington Press, 1994.

Oliver, Melvin L., and Thomas M. Shapiro. *Black Wealth/White Wealth: A New Perspective on Racial Inequality*. New York: Routledge, 1995.

Omi, Michael, and Howard Winant. *Racial Formation in the United States: From the 1960s to the 1980s*. New York: Routledge and Kegan Paul, 1986.

Ong, Paul M., Lucie Cheng, and Leslie Evans. "Migration of Highly Educated Asians and Global Dynamics." *Asian and Pacific Migration Journal* 1, no. 3–4 (September 1992): 543–67.

Opitz, Donald L., Staffan Bergwik, and Brigitte Van Tiggelen, eds. *Domesticity in the Making of Modern Science*. New York: Palgrave Macmillan, 2016.

Orfield, Gary, and Chungmei Lee. *Why Segregation Matters: Poverty and Educational Inequality*. Cambridge, Mass.: Civil Rights Project at Harvard University: January 2005.

Osgood, Kenneth. *Total Cold War: Eisenhower's Secret Propaganda Battle at Home and Abroad*. Lawrence: University Press of Kansas, 2006.

Pandey, Gyanendra. *A History of Prejudice: Race, Caste, and Difference in India and the United States*. Cambridge: Cambridge University Press, 2013.

———. *Remembering Partition: Violence, Nationalism and History in India*. Cambridge: Cambridge University Press, 2001.

Parker, Jason C. *Hearts, Minds, Voices: U.S. Cold War Public Diplomacy and the Formation of the Third World*. New York: Oxford University Press, 2016.

Patel, Shaista. "Complicating the Tale of 'Two Indians': Mapping 'South Asian' Complicity in White Settler Colonialism along the Axis of Caste and Anti-Blackness." *Theory and Event* 19, no. 4 (2016).

Patterson, Orlando. *The Ordeal of Integration: Progress and Resentment in America's "Racial" Crisis.* Washington, D.C.: Civitas/Counterpoint, 1997.

Paul, Santosh. *The Maoist Movement in India: Perspectives and Counterperspectives.* New York: Routledge, 2013.

Peach, Ceri. "South Asian Migration and Settlement in Great Britain, 1951–2001." *Contemporary South Asia* 15, no. 2 (June 2006): 133–46.

Pecoud, Antoine. "Thinking and Rethinking Ethnic Economies." *Diaspora: A Journal of Transnational Studies* 9, no. 3 (Winter 2000): 439–62.

Pegoda, Andrew Joseph. "The University of Houston and Texas Southern University: Perpetuating 'Separate but Equal' in the Face of Brown v. Board of Education." *Houston History* 8, no. 1 (Fall 2010): 19–23.

Peshkin, Alan. "Education, the Muslim Elite, and the Creation of Pakistan." *Comparative Education Review* 6, no. 2 (October 1962): 152–59.

Phelps, Wesley G. *A People's War on Poverty: Urban Politics and Grassroots Activists in Houston.* Athens: University of Georgia Press, 2014.

Platt, Harold L. *City Building in the New South: The Growth of Public Services in Houston, Texas, 1830–1910.* Philadelphia: Temple University Press, 1983.

Plummer, Brenda Gayle. *Rising Wind: Black Americans and U.S. Foreign Affairs, 1935–1960.* Chapel Hill: University of North Carolina Press, 1996.

Poe, Tracy N. "The Labour and Leisure of Food Production as a Mode of Ethnic Identity Building among Italians in Chicago, 1890–1940." *Rethinking History* 5, no. 1 (March 2001): 131–48.

Portes, Alejandro. "The Rise of Ethnicity: Determinants of Ethnic Perceptions among Cuban Exiles in Miami." *American Sociological Review* 49, no. 3 (1984): 383–97.

Potts, Charles S. *Railroad Transportation in Texas.* Austin: University of Texas, 1909.

Prakash, Gyan. *Another Reason: Science and the Imagination of Modern India.* Princeton, N.J.: Princeton University Press, 1999.

———. *Mumbai Fables.* Princeton, N.J.: Princeton University Press, 2010.

Prashad, Vijay. *The Karma of Brown Folk.* Minneapolis: University of Minnesota Press, 2000.

Pratt, Joseph A. "Coming to Houston: 170 Years of Migration." *Houston Review of History and Culture* 3, no. 1 (Fall 2005): 4–9.

Prevots, Naima. *Dance for Export: Cultural Diplomacy and the Cold War.* Middletown, Conn.: Wesleyan University Press, 2012.

Pruitt, Bernadette. *The Other Great Migration: The Movement of Rural African Americans to Houston, 1900–1941.* College Station: Texas A&M University Press, 2013.

Purkayastha, Bandana. *Negotiating Ethnicity: Second-Generation South Asian Americans Traverse a Transnational World.* New Brunswick, N.J.: Rutgers University Press, 2005.

Quraishi, Uzma. "Racial Calculations: Indian and Pakistani Immigrants in Houston, 1960–1980." *Journal of American Ethnic History* 38, no. 4 (Summer 2019): 55–76.

Raghavan, Srinath. *War and Peace in Modern India.* Basingstoke, U.K.: Palgrave Macmillan, 2010.

Rahman, Shafiqur. *The Bangladeshi Diaspora in the United States after 9/11: From Obscurity to High Visibility.* El Paso, Tex.: LFB Scholarly Publishing, 2011.

Rakove, Robert B. *Kennedy, Johnson, and the Nonaligned World.* New York: Cambridge University Press, 2013.

Raman, Venkata. *A Hindu in America.* Bangalore: Raman Publications, 1969.

Ramdin, Ron. *Reimaging Britain: 500 Years of Black and Asian History.* London: Pluto Press, 1999.

Rana, Junaid Akram. *Terrifying Muslims: Race and Labor in the South Asian Diaspora.* Durham, N.C.: Duke University Press, 2011.

Rangaswamy, Padma. *Namasté America: Indian Immigrants in an American Metropolis.* University Park: Pennsylvania State University Press, 2008.

Reddy, Sujani K. *Nursing and Empire: Gendered Labor and Migration from India to the United States.* Chapel Hill: University of North Carolina Press, 2015.

Reimers, David M. *Other Immigrants: The Global Origins of the American People.* New York: New York University Press, 2005.

———. "An Unintended Reform: The 1965 Immigration Act and Third World Immigration to the United States." *Journal of American Ethnic History* 3, no. 1 (1983): 9–28.

Rhoads, Edward J. M. "The Chinese in Texas." *Southwestern Historical Quarterly* 81, no. 1 (1977): 1–36.

Richardson, John G. *Handbook of Theory and Research for the Sociology of Education.* New York: Greenwood, 1986.

Ritterband, Paul. "Law, Policy, and Behavior: Educational Exchange Policy and Student Migration." *American Journal of Sociology* 76, no. 1 (1970): 71–82.

Roediger, David R. *The Wages of Whiteness: Race and the Making of the American Working Class.* New York: Verso, 1991.

Rogers, Susan. "Superneighborhood 27: A Brief History of Change." *Places Journal* 17, no. 2 (April 15, 2005): 36–41.

Rosales, Francisco A., and Barry J. Kaplan, eds. *Houston: A Twentieth Century Urban Frontier.* Port Washington, N.Y.: Associated Faculty Press, 1983.

Rosenberg, Samuel. *American Economic Development since 1945: Growth, Decline, and Rejuvenation.* New York: Palgrave Macmillan, 2003.

Rothstein, Richard. *Class and Schools.* Washington, D.C.: Economic Policy Institute, 2004.

Rotter, Andrew Jon. *Comrades at Odds: The United States and India, 1947–1964.* Ithaca, N.Y.: Cornell University Press, 2000.

Roy, Modhumita. "The Englishing of India: Class Formation and Social Privilege." *Social Scientist* 21, no. 5/6 (May–June 1993): 36–62.

Roy, Tirthankar. *India in the World Economy: From Antiquity to the Present.* New York: Cambridge University Press, 2012.

Rudrappa, Sharmila. *Ethnic Routes to Becoming American: Indian Immigrants and the Cultures of Citizenship.* New Brunswick, N.J.: Rutgers University Press, 2004.

Rutherford, Jonathan, ed. *Identity: Community, Culture, Difference.* London: Lawrence and Wishart, 1998.

Saito, Leland T. *Race and Politics: Asian Americans, Latinos, and Whites in a Los Angeles Suburb.* Urbana: University of Illinois Press, 1998.

Salam, Abdus. "Pakistan: The Case for Technological Development." *Bulletin of the Atomic Scientists*, March 1964.

San Miguel, Guadalupe. *Brown, Not White: School Integration and the Chicano Movement in Houston.* College Station: Texas A&M University Press, 2001.

———. *"Let All of Them Take Heed": Mexican Americans and the Campaign for Educational Equality in Texas, 1910–1981.* Austin: University of Texas Press, 1987.

Sassen, Saskia. *Globalization and Its Discontents.* New York: New Press, 1998.

Sathasivam, Kanishkan. *Uneasy Neighbors: India, Pakistan and US Foreign Policy.* Burlington, Vt.: Ashgate, 2005.

Sattar, Abdul. *Pakistan's Foreign Policy, 1947–2012: A Concise History.* Karachi: Oxford University Press, 2013.

Saxenian, Anna Lee. *The New Argonauts: Regional Advantage in a Global Economy.* Cambridge, Mass.: Harvard University Press, 2006.

Schiller, Nina Glick, Linda Basch, and Cristina Szanton Blanc. "From Immigrant to Transmigrant: Theorizing Transnational Migration." *Anthropological Quarterly* 68, no. 1 (1995): 48–63.

Schreuder, Deryck M., ed. *Universities for a New World: Making a Global Network in International Higher Education, 1913–2013.* Thousand Oaks, Calif.: SAGE, 2013.

Schulman, Bruce J. *From Cotton Belt to Sunbelt: Federal Policy, Economic Development, and the Transformation of the South, 1938–1980.* Durham, N.C.: Duke University Press, 1994.

Schulman, Bruce J., and Julian E. Zelizer, eds. *Rightward Bound: Making America Conservative in the 1970s.* Cambridge, Mass.: Harvard University Press, 2008.

Schwandt, Thomas A. *The SAGE Dictionary of Qualitative Inquiry.* Thousand Oaks, Calif.: SAGE, 2014.

Shabazz, Amilcar. *Advancing Democracy: African Americans and the Struggle for Access and Equity in Higher Education in Texas.* Chapel Hill: University of North Carolina Press, 2004.

Shaffer, Robert. "J. J. Singh and the India League of America, 1945–1959: Pressing at the Margins of the Cold War Consensus." *Journal of American Ethnic History* 31, no. 2 (2012): 68–103.

Shah, Nayan. *Stranger Intimacy: Contesting Race, Sexuality and the Law in the North American West.* Berkeley: University of California Press, 2012.

Shankar, Lavina Dhingra, and Rajini Srikanth, eds. *A Part, Yet Apart: South Asians in Asian America.* Philadelphia: Temple University Press, 1998.

Shankar, Shalini. *Desi Land: Teen Culture, Class, and Success in Silicon Valley.* Durham, N.C.: Duke University Press, 2008.

Sharma, Nitasha Tamar. *Hip Hop Desis: South Asian Americans, Blackness, and a Global Race Consciousness.* Durham, N.C.: Duke University Press, 2010.

Shelton, Beth Anne, et al. *Houston: Growth and Decline in a Sunbelt Boomtown.* Philadelphia: Temple University Press, 1989.

Shelton, Kyle. *Power Moves: Transportation, Politics, and Development in Houston.* Austin: University of Texas Press, 2017.

Short, John Rennie. *Urban Theory: A Critical Assessment.* New York: Palgrave Macmillan, 2006.

Shukla, Sandhya. *India Abroad: Diasporic Cultures of Postwar America and England.* Princeton, N.J.: Princeton University Press, 2003.

Sikkink, David, and Michael O. Emerson. "School Choice and Racial Segregation in US Schools: The Role of Parents' Education." *Ethnic and Racial Studies* 31, no. 2 (February 2008): 267–93.

Sinha, Mrinalini. *Specters of Mother India: The Global Restructuring of an Empire.* Durham: Duke University Press, 2006.

Sircar, Arpana. *Work Roles, Gender Roles, and Asian Indian Immigrant Women in the United States.* Lewiston, N.Y.: Edwin Mellen Press, 2000.

Sisson, Richard, and Leo E. Rose. *War and Secession: Pakistan, India, and the Creation of Bangladesh.* Berkeley: University of California Press, 1990.

Skop, Emily. *The Immigration and Settlement of Asian Indians in Phoenix, Arizona, 1965–2011: Ethnic Pride vs. Racial Discrimination in the Suburbs.* Lewiston, N.Y.: Edwin Mellen Press, 2012.

Slate, Nico. *Colored Cosmopolitanism: The Shared Struggle for Freedom in the United States and India.* Cambridge, Mass.: Harvard University Press, 2012.

Smith, Jane I. *Islam in America.* New York: Columbia University Press, 2010.

Smith, Michael P., ed. *After Modernism: Global Restructuring and the Changing Boundaries of City Life.* Vol. 4. New Brunswick, N.J.: Transaction, 1992.

Sohi, Seema. *Echoes of Mutiny: Race, Surveillance, and Indian Anticolonialism in North America.* New York: Oxford University Press, 2014.

Spickard, Paul R. *Race in Mind: Critical Essays.* Notre Dame, Ind.: University of Notre Dame Press, 2015.

Sreekumar, Sharmila. *Scripting Lives: Narratives of "Dominant Women" in Kerala.* New Delhi: Orient BlackSwan, 2009.

Steptoe, Tyina L. *Houston Bound: Culture and Color in a Jim Crow City.* Oakland: University of California Press, 2016.

Sutherland, Gail Hinich. "The Wedding Pavilion: Performing, Recreating, and Re-gendering Hindu Identity in Houston." *International Journal of Hindu Studies* 7, no. 1–3 (February 2003): 117–46.

Swidler, Ann. "Culture in Action: Symbols and Strategies." *American Sociological Review* 51, no. 2 (April 1986): 273–86.

Syamroy, Bedprakas. *India's Journey towards Sustainable Population.* Cham, Switzerland: Springer, 2017.

Tahir-Kheli, Shirin R. *India, Pakistan, and the United States: Breaking with the Past.* New York: Council on Foreign Relations, 1997.

Takaki, Ronald T. *A Different Mirror: A History of Multicultural America.* Boston: Little, Brown, 1993.

———. *Strangers from a Different Shore: A History of Asian Americans.* Boston: Little, Brown, 1989.

Talbot, Ian. *Pakistan: A Modern History.* London: C. Hurst, 1998.

———. *Provincial Politics and the Pakistan Movement: The Growth of the Muslim League in North-West and North-East India, 1937–47.* Karachi: Oxford University Press, 1988.

Talbott, Strobe. *Engaging India: Diplomacy, Democracy, and the Bomb.* Washington, D.C.: Brookings Institution Press, 2010.

Tatum, Beverly Daniel. *Why Are All the Black Kids Sitting Together in the Cafeteria?* New York: Basic Books, 2003.

Tchen, John Kuo Wei, and Dylan Yeats. *Yellow Peril! An Archive of Anti-Asian Fear.* New York: Verso, 2014.

Thorat, Sukhadeo, and Umakant, eds. *Caste, Race, and Discrimination: Discourses in International Context.* Jaipur: Rawat Publications, 2004.

Tomlinson, B. R. *The Economy of Modern India, 1860–1970.* Cambridge: Cambridge University Press, 1993.

Tournès, Ludovic, and Giles Scott-Smith, eds. *Global Exchanges: Scholarships and Transnational Circulations in the Modern World.* New York: Berghahn Books, 2017.

Tragen, Irving G. "Statutory Prohibitions against Interracial Marriage." *California Law Review* 32 (1944): 269–80.

Treviño, Roberto R. *The Church in the Barrio: Mexican American Ethno-Catholicism in Houston.* Chapel Hill: University of North Carolina Press, 2006.

Tuan, Mia. *Forever Foreigners or Honorary Whites? The Asian Ethnic Experience Today.* New Brunswick, N.J.: Rutgers University Press, 1999.

Unfried, Berthold, ed. *Practices of International Solidarity and International Development.* Vienna: ITH, 2012.

Unger, Corinna R. "Towards Global Equilibrium: American Foundations and Indian Modernization, 1950s to 1970s." *Journal of Global History* 6, no. 1 (2011): 121–42.

Venkataramani, M. S. *Undercurrents in American Foreign Relations: Four Studies [by] M. S. Venkataramani.* New York: Asia Pub. House, 1965.

Visram, Rozina. *Asians in Britain: 400 Years of History.* Sterling, Va.: Pluto Press, 2002.

Von der Mehden, Fred R. *The Ethnic Groups of Houston.* Houston: Rice University Studies, 1984.

Von Eschen, Penny M. *Satchmo Blows Up the World: Jazz Ambassadors Play the Cold War.* Cambridge, Mass.: Harvard University Press, 2004.

Wallerstein, Immanuel M. *The Modern World-System: Capitalist Agriculture and the Origins of the European World-Economy in the Sixteenth Century.* New York: Academic Press, 1974.

Watson, Dwight. *Race and the Houston Police Department, 1930–1990: A Change Did Come.* College Station: Texas A&M University Press, 2005.

Wells, Wyatt C. *American Capitalism, 1945–2000: Continuity and Change from Mass Production to the Information Society.* Chicago: Ivan R. Dee, 2003.

Westad, Odd Arne. *The Cold War: A World History.* New York: Basic Books, 2017.

———. *The Global Cold War: Third World Interventions and the Making of Our Times.* Cambridge: Cambridge University Press, 2007.

Whitley, DeAndre K., and Keith E. Noel. *Pakistan: U.S. Relations and Foreign Assistance.* New York: Nova Science, 2012.

Wiebe, Robert H. *Who We Are: A History of Popular Nationalism.* Princeton, N.J.: Princeton University Press, 2012.

Wieck, Randolph. *Ignorance Abroad: American Educational and Cultural Foreign Policy and the Office of Assistant Secretary of State.* New York: Praeger, 1992.

Wiese, Andrew. *Places of Their Own: African American Suburbanization in the Twentieth Century*. Chicago: University of Chicago Press, 2004.

Williams, Daniel. *God's Own Party: The Making of the Christian Right*. New York: Oxford University Press, 2010.

Williams, Raymond Brady. *Religions of Immigrants from India and Pakistan: New Threads in the American Tapestry*. Cambridge: Cambridge University Press, 1988.

Williamson, Lola. *Transcendent in America: Hindu-Inspired Meditation Movements as New Religion*. New York: New York University Press, 2010.

Wilson, Ezell. "Third Ward, Steeped in Tradition of Self-reliance and Achievement." *Houston History* 8, no. 2 (Spring 2011): 31–35.

Wilson, William J. *The Declining Significance of Race: Blacks and Changing American Institutions*. Chicago: University of Chicago Press, 1978.

Wolf, Elinor K. "Anatomy of the Problem: Who Should Come?" *Annals of the American Academy of Political and Social Science* 335, no. 1 (May 1, 1961): 153–65.

Wong, Morrison G., and Charles Hirschman. "The New Asian Immigrants." In *Culture, Ethnicity, and Identity: Current Issues in Research*, edited by William C. McCready, 381–403. New York: Academic Press, 1983.

Wu, Ellen D. *The Color of Success: Asian Americans and the Origins of the Model Minority*. Princeton, N.J.: Princeton University Press, 2013.

Wulf, Andrew James. *U.S. International Exhibitions during the Cold War: Winning Hearts and Minds through Cultural Diplomacy*. Lanham, Md.: Rowman and Littlefield, 2015.

Xenos, Peter, et al. *Asian Indians in the United States: A 1980 Census Profile*. Papers of the East-West Population Institute, No. 111. Honolulu, Hawaii: East-West Center, 1989.

Xu, Jun, and Jennifer C. Lee. "The Marginalized 'Model' Minority: An Empirical Examination of the Racial Triangulation of Asian Americans," *Social Forces* 91, no. 4 (June 2013): 1363–97.

Yancy, George. *Black Bodies, White Gazes: The Continuing Significance of Race*. Lanham, Md.: Rowman and Littlefield, 2008.

Zaidi, Z. H., and National Archives of Pakistan. *Quaid-I-Azam Mohammad Ali Jinnah Papers*. Islamabad: Quaid-I-Azam Papers Project, National Archives of Pakistan, 1993.

Zhou, Min, and J. V. Gatewood, eds. *Contemporary Asian America: A Multidisciplinary Reader*. 2nd ed. New York: New York University Press, 2007.

Ziring, Lawrence. *Pakistan: At the Crosscurrent of History*. Oxford: Oneworld, 2003.

INDEX